Superpower Rivalry
in the
Indian Ocean

SUPERPOWER RIVALRY
IN THE
INDIAN OCEAN
INDIAN AND AMERICAN PERSPECTIVES

Edited by
SELIG S. HARRISON
Carnegie Endowment for International Peace
K. SUBRAHMANYAM
Institute of Defense Studies and Analyses, New Delhi

New York   Oxford
OXFORD UNIVERSITY PRESS

1989

Tallahassee, Florida

Oxford University Press

Oxford   New York   Toronto
Delhi   Bombay   Calcutta   Madras   Karachi
Petaling Jaya   Singapore   Hong Kong   Tokyo
Nairobi   Dar es Salaam   Cape Town
Melbourne   Auckland
and associated companies in
Berlin   Ibadan

Library of Congress Cataloging-in-Publication Data
Superpower rivalry in the Indian Ocean : Indian and American
perspectives / [edited by] Selig S. Harrison [and] K. Subrahmanyam.
p.   cm. Includes index. ISBN 0-19-505497-0
1. Indian Ocean Region—Politics and government.   2. Indian Ocean
Region—Strategic aspects.   3. Indian Ocean Region—Economic
conditions.   I. Harrison, Selig S.   II. Subrahmanyam, K.
DS341.S94 1989   320.9182'4—dc19   88–1480   CIP

2 4 6 8 9 7 5 3 1

Printed in the United States of America
on acid-free paper

Preface

Against a background of continuing Soviet-American rivalry in the Indian Ocean/Persian Gulf region, six American and six Indian experts met in New Delhi from November 25 to December 1, 1984, for an intensive effort to bridge growing Indo-American differences over regional military, political, economic, and arms control issues. Sponsored by the Carnegie Endowment for International Peace and the Institute of Defense Studies and Analyses, New Delhi, with the support of the Ford Foundation, the Indo-American Task Force on the Indian Ocean adopted ten policy recommendations on June 7, 1985, on the eve of Prime Minister Rajiv Gandhi's United States visit (Appendix A). Addressing the superpowers, the task force outlined guidelines for a renewed and broadened Soviet-American arms control dialogue relating to the Indian Ocean/Persian Gulf region, including negotiations on naval limitations, an Afghanistan settlement, and mutual restraint in Iran and Pakistan. At the same time, the task force proposed confidence-building measures by Washington and New Delhi to manage the tensions resulting from the continued U.S. naval presence in the region and an expanding Indian naval role.

The essays in this book originated as working papers for the task force prepared by six of its members and have subsequently been updated and revised by the authors. The other American members of the group were Gary Sick, former National Security Council specialist on the Indian Ocean and the Persian Gulf and author of *All Fall Down: America's Tragic Encounter with Iran;* George W. Shepherd, Jr., Professor of International Relations at the University of Denver and a specialist in the foreign policies of East African states; and W. Howard Wriggins, Professor of Government at Columbia University and former U.S. Ambassador to Sri Lanka. The other Indian members were V. S. Mani, Professor of Law at Jawaharlal Nehru University and specialist in the Law of the Sea; K. R. Singh, Professor of West Asian and African studies at Jawaharlal Nehru University and author of *The Persian Gulf: Arms and Arms Control;* and M. A. Vellodi, former Secretary of the Ministry of External Affairs, Government of India, and Indian representative on the United Nations' Ad Hoc Committee on the Indian Ocean.

A report on the work of the task force containing selections from its tape-recorded discussions, *India, the United States and the Indian Ocean,* was published in 1985 by the Endowment and the Institute.

Washington, D.C.   S. S. H.
New Delhi   K. S.
October 1988

Contents

Contributors

WALTER K. ANDERSEN prepared his contribution while on leave from his position as Political Analyst for India, Sri Lanka, and the Indian Ocean in the Bureau of Intelligence and Research, U.S. Department of State. He has written extensively on South Asian and Indian Ocean politics and security issues, including *The Brotherhood in Saffron* (Westview, 1987).

VICE-ADMIRAL M. P. AWATI retired in 1983 as Flag Officer and Commander-in-Chief, Western Command, Indian Navy, and formerly served as Commander of the Eastern Command. He is now President of the Tolani Shipping Company in Bombay.

JOEL LARUS, Professor of Politics at New York University, has contributed studies on the international legal controversy surrounding the U.S. naval base at Diego Garcia to *Strategic Review, Round Table, The Proceedings of the U.S. Naval Institute,* and other journals. His three books include *Nuclear Weapons Safety and the Common Defense* (Ohio University Press, 1967).

C. RAJA MOHAN, a Research Associate at the Institute of Defense Studies and Analyses, New Delhi, specializes in the economic resources of the seabed. His studies of nuclear issues have appeared in *Nuclear Myths and Realities* (ABC Publishers, 1981) and *Proliferation and International Security* (I.D.S.A.).

K. SUBRAHMANYAM is former director of the Institute of Defense Studies and Analyses, New Delhi. He has served as Secretary, Department of Defense Production, Government of India, and as Chairman of the Joint Intelligence Committee in the Cabinet Secretariat. His studies on strategic issues include *Indian Security Perspectives* (ABC Publishers, 1982) and *The Second Cold War* (ed., ABC Publishers, 1983).

SELIG S. HARRISON is a Senior Associate of the Carnegie Endowment for International Peace. He has served as South Asian Bureau Chief of *The Washington Post* and Senior Fellow in Charge of Asian Studies at the Brookings Institution. His four books on Asian affairs include *India: The Most Dangerous Decades* (Princeton University Press, 1960) and *The Widening Gulf: Asian Nationalism and American Policy* (The Free Press, 1978).

Superpower Rivalry
in the
Indian Ocean

Introduction

SELIG S. HARRISON
K. SUBRAHMANYAM

Fears of a global nuclear war often obscure recognition of the dangerous military tensions between the United States and the Soviet Union in critical regions of the world where their interests conflict. This book focuses on one of the most explosive theaters of the superpower rivalry: the vast region embracing the Indian Ocean, the Persian Gulf, and 42 littoral states. One-third of the world's population lives in this politically turbulent area. Three American and three Indian authors, reflecting differing perspectives and areas of expertise, explore the principal factors that have led to the superpower confrontation; the impact of American, Soviet, and other extra-regional military forces on the littoral states; the emergence of indigenous military powers, especially India; the regional economic environment; and possible avenues toward regional arms control. The unifying theme running through these essays is a central emphasis on Indo-American relations and on the importance of Indian Ocean issues as basic sources of tension between the two countries.

Both American and Indian authors share a common concern that endemic instability in the Indian Ocean/Persian Gulf region, arising from interacting regional and extra-regional factors, could draw the superpowers into a direct confrontation. Among the more sensitive focal points of such instability are the civil war in Afghanistan and its spillover in the Afghanistan-Pakistan borderlands; the Indo-Pakistan nuclear arms race; ethnic tensions in Sri Lanka; Iran-Iraq tensions; and uncertainty surrounding the political future of Iran.

The danger of a superpower confrontation is underlined by the continuing superpower military presence in the region. The American naval presence in early 1987 consisted of 12 regularly deployed combat vessels, including a car-

rier battle group; two support vessels; a tanker fleet on contract; and intermittent attack submarine patrols. The Soviet Union maintained seven regularly deployed combat vessels, including two attack submarines, and 17
auxiliary support vessels. Although the United States has achieved naval
superiority, the Soviet Union will increasingly be able to challenge American
dominance as its ambitious naval construction program gains momentum. In
addition to its projected Forrestal-class aircraft carrier, the first Soviet vessel
to carry fixed-wing aircraft, Moscow is building an improved version of its
28,000-ton, nuclear-powered Kirov guided-missile cruiser.

In measuring the extent of the superpower presence in the region, it has
been necessary to take into account not only blue-water naval forces but also
the growth of rapid deployment forces, Soviet land-based forces in the Transcaucasus, a Soviet force of some 115,000 men in Afghanistan from 1980 to
1988, and the full range of American and Soviet infrastructural support facilities. The United States is developing the most elaborate network of such support facilities in conjunction with the Central Command and its Rapid Deployment Joint Task Force. With responsibility for 19 countries, the Central
Command can call on forces totaling 300,000 men in time of crisis. To support its rapid deployment forces, the United States maintains bases and access
facilities at Diego Garcia, Oman, Somalia, and Kenya. The American navy
maintains 17 mammoth "roll-on, roll-off" container ships at its Diego Garcia
base, loaded with enough tanks, rocket launchers, and amphibious armored
personnel carriers to enable 12,500 U.S. marines to fight for 30 days without
resupply. Moscow maintains more limited facilities at Dahlak Island off Ethiopia, Socotra, and Aden and has intermittently probed for new facilities elsewhere. The Soviet Union also maintains several companies of naval infantry
in its Indian Ocean forces.

Looking ahead to emerging changes in military technology, the introduction of sea-launched cruise missiles by both the American and Soviet navies
is likely to arouse profound anxieties among the littoral states, given the difficulty of distinguishing between conventional and nuclear cruise missile
deployments. Other forms of new and destabilizing military activity in the
Indian Ocean/Persian Gulf region by the superpowers could well develop in
the event of a failure of global arms control efforts, especially the collapse of
the Anti-Ballistic Missile (ABM) Treaty. The northern Arabian sea, in particular, could acquire special sensitivity in the context of American anti-
satellite and other interception systems related to the Strategic Defense Initiative and Soviet counter measures. For the Soviet Union, too, Indian Ocean
deployments are increasingly linked to the use of outer space for military purposes.

Walter K. Andersen and Vice-Admiral M. P. Awati present comprehensive analyses of the military environment in the Indian Ocean/Persian Gulf
region from contrasting American and Indian perspectives.

Andersen argues that the stereotype of a Soviet-American naval "rivalry"
is misleading. He writes that the American decision in 1979 "to build up a
powerful fleet continuously present in the northwest quadrant of the Indian

Ocean . . . had relatively little to do initially with the Soviet naval presence, which was relatively modest and no real challenge. Rather, the threat came from the Soviet capability to threaten the states of Southwest Asia from the land. The United States could not possibly match this, but it could develop a sea-based deterrent to a possible attack." Emphasizing American concern over access to petroleum supplies, Andersen points to the 1973 Arab oil embargo, the Soviet occupation of Afghanistan, in 1979, and the Iranian revolution as events that triggered the American buildup in the region. Above all, he stresses the growth in Soviet air and ground forces based in the southern military districts of the Soviet Union. As for the Soviet naval presence, he seeks to show that Moscow has deployed naval power in the Indian Ocean water-spread primarily for diplomatic and political purposes. He discounts several of the motivations most often cited to explain Soviet naval activity in the region, such as the desire to outflank China and to prepare for the disruption of Western oil supply lines in time of crisis. Moscow is concerned that the United States might target nuclear missiles at the Soviet Union from submarines operating in the Indian Ocean, but its naval forces in the region are not dedicated primarily to anti-submarine warfare. In any case, Andersen contends, the United States does not regularly deploy nuclear submarines in the Indian Ocean, and the new American Trident D-5 nuclear missile submarine will be able to reach the Soviet Union from behind a protective screen near the continental United States, making it unnecessary to launch missiles from the Indian Ocean.

Admiral Awati offers a sharply divergent analysis, contending that "the Indian Ocean provides the United States with an ideal spot for the deployment of sea-based missiles aimed at the U.S.S.R." During the Reagan Administration in particular, he maintains, Defense Secretary Caspar Weinberger has explicitly articulated a strategy even more ambitious than the Dulles doctrine of containment, in which the Soviet landmass "is to be hemmed in from all sides—across the Arctic ice cap, from the West, from China, Japan, the Pacific and from the Indian Ocean." Soviet deployments in the Indian Ocean are essentially defensive, he maintains, focused not only on the American presence but also on the potential threat posed by China, especially in the northern Indian Ocean.

While focusing on the origins and character of the superpower naval confrontation, Admiral Awati provides a detailed critique of the problems confronting the Indian navy in its significant expansion program. Already, he notes, it has surpassed other littoral navies in the region, acquiring capabilities for modest naval operations in the northern Arabian Sea and the northern Indian Ocean as well as a growing reach to the western Indian Ocean. In 1987, the Indian navy had one aircraft carrier and another on order; three Soviet missile destroyers; 9 Soviet submarines; 24 frigates of mixed size and origin, including 8 made in India; one maritime reconnaissance aircraft squadron; and enough replenishment ships, support tankers, and repair ships to support a small task force. Six more Soviet missile destroyers, 2 Soviet missile cruisers, and 6 West German submarines were on order. Awati speculates that the Navy will double its frigate force by 1995 and points to its new naval bases at Karwar, north of Bombay, and in the Andaman islands as symbols of an expanding naval role.

As the three principal missions of the Indian navy, Awati cites safeguarding Indian coastal waters, protecting the flow of trade in wartime, and combatting potential adversaries, notably Pakistan. But he also lists a fourth significant mission: "To be in a position to assist island republics of the Indian Ocean—notably Mauritius, the Seychelles, and possibly Sri Lanka in the future—in case they seek Indian assistance, particularly against threats of subversion." To deal with the growing responsibilities that he anticipates, he proposes a new "peninsular command structure" encompassing the three existing naval commands and calls for an end to the inter-service rivalry that has so far blocked the establishment of an amphibious Indian Marine Force.

For the foreseeable future, Awati believes, India's principal naval adversary will be Pakistan, which he describes as a "proxy" of the United States. In dealing with Pakistan alone, the Indian navy would seek to bring an "overwhelming concentration of force" to bear, as it did in its 1971 operations against Karachi harbor. But "when dealing with superpowers, the Indian navy would quite rightly adopt different tactics—tactics that will perhaps persuade the superpower to leave well enough alone for two very good reasons. One reason is the Indian navy's demonstrable capability to inflict unacceptable damage if the superpower pursued a course of action considered by India to be inimical to its interests. Another is that the other superpower would in all probability intervene on India's side and thus raise the stakes." The Soviet navy does not have exclusive rights to access to Indian facilities, he observes, "but in the event of an international conflict, it would most probably invoke the 1971 bilateral treaty with India under which it could obtain such rights, always provided that this was also in India's own interests."

Selig S. Harrison examines the interplay of American, Soviet, and Indian interests in the Indian Ocean, focusing initially on the western Indian Ocean island states of Mauritius, the Seychelles, and Madagascar. After analyzing the Soviet-American competition for bases and facilities in the context of local political factors in these states, he assesses Indian efforts to project economic, political, and military power in the western Indian Ocean. In contrast to the eastern Indian Ocean, where the Indian navy is building a "defensive bastion" against Chinese and other maritime pressures, the western Indian Ocean, in his view, offers a more favorable opening for the relatively unimpeded development of enhanced Indian influence.

Against the background of India's emerging power, Harrison sees a potential threat to American security interests in the Indian Ocean if the United States continues to pursue what he sees as a self-defeating "tilt" toward Pakistan in its South Asia policy. "So far," he declares, "New Delhi has carefully stopped short of de facto military collaboration with Moscow, but it would be unwise to assume that such restraint will continue to govern Indian policy regardless of the nature of U.S. policies toward Pakistan. . . . Multiplying American weapons aid to Islamabad could lead over time to a variety of punitive, anti-American moves in the Indian Ocean designed to limit the American military presence or to constrain and harass American forces in their use of existing facilities, including Diego Garcia." By the same token, if the United States were to give "greater recognition to Indian regional primacy," New Delhi would adapt to the American presence. Harrison proposes a trade-off with India designed to produce a benign Indian posture concerning American access to the Indian Ocean. He urges the United States to recast its military aid policies toward Pakistan and to redefine its commitments to Islamabad under the 1959 U.S.-Pakistan security agreement, limiting American combat intervention in South Asia solely to cases involving aggression by Soviet or Afghan Communist forces. In his view, such a redefinition of the 1959 agreement has been necessitated by the regular deployment of an American carrier battle group in the northern Arabian Sea. While the United States views this deployment as a deterrent to Soviet aggression in the Gulf, many Indians fear that American forces stationed so close to South Asia might be used to help Pakistan in the event of another Indo-Pakistan war. In return for a more detached American posture toward South Asia, he believes, India "should be prepared to make a tacit, pragmatic accommodation with U.S. use of the Diego Garcia base for purposes relating to U.S. global military communications and the deployment of U.S. forces in the Persian Gulf and Southwest Asia, except for contingencies involving India and Pakistan alone."

Surveying public opinion in a wide spectrum of littoral states, Harrison finds widespread anxiety concerning the superpower military presence. However, in place of the fully demilitarized Indian Ocean Zone of Peace originally envisaged, the littoral states are now seeking to stabilize the Soviet-American rivalry through arms control initiatives, centering on a resumption of the regional arms limitation negotiations conducted by Washington and Moscow during 1977 and 1978. Harrison spells out the achievements of the 1977–78 dialogue, the specific issues that were unresolved when the talks were broken off by the United States, and the possible guidelines for a renewed regional arms control effort. He emphasizes the changes in the regional environment that would condition such an effort, exploring the problems likely to follow the Afghan peace settlement. The Soviet withdrawal from Afghanistan offers an opportunity for the first steps toward a larger regional arms control dialogue, he concludes, linking concessions formally barring Soviet bases in Afghanistan with a U.S. quid pro quo concerning one or more of its bases in the Gulf and the Indian Ocean. Harrison advances proposals for Soviet-American mutual restraint agreements in Iran and Pakistan as well as for arms control trade-offs incorporating some elements of the draft agreement already negotiated in the 1977–78 dialogue, together with new land-sea trade-offs necessitated by the buildup of regional military bases and deployments during the past decade.

In his wide-ranging historical assessment of arms control efforts, K. Subrahmanyam reflects changing Indian attitudes toward the Zone of Peace concept. While India supported the original version of the concept presented to the United Nations in 1971, New Delhi now has "serious reservations about the subsequent interpretations of, additions to, distortions of, and overlays to the resolution." In its initial form, he points out, the Zone of Peace proposal, inspired by the Antarctic and the Tlatelelco treaties, was designed to prevent the introduction of extra-regional nuclear forces into the Indian Ocean, where they were not yet present. "It was a measure to halt the spatial proliferation of nuclear weapons," he writes. But efforts were subsequently made to alter the original proposal by enlarging the concept of the projected zone to embrace not only the waterspread but also littoral and hinterland states and by extending the idea of Indian Ocean denuclearization to the littoral states. When many of the littoral states became increasingly dependent on affluent Western nations for economic assistance following the oil price hike of 1973, extra-regional nuclear powers were able to exploit differences among the littoral states, inducing some of them to support such alterations and to sign the Nuclear Non-Proliferation Treaty. India, by contrast, "had a far more realistic view about the game of 'non-proliferation' and therefore refused to accept a regime . . . which violates the basic international norm that all nations of the world are equally entitled to the same categories of weapons of offense and defense. Nor was India taken in by the concept of a nuclear-weapon-free zone, which legitimized nuclear weapons in the hands of a few powers."

Subrahmanyam sees little prospect for progress toward regional arms control because the United States opposes arms control proposals " 'not invented here.' " In the case of the Indian Ocean, the United States is "not willing to forgo the current asymmetric strategic advantages that the Indian Ocean provides as a strategic deployment area vis-à-vis the Soviet Union." But he warns that there will be "greater balance" when Soviet aircraft carriers are able to operate not only in the Indian Ocean but also "in the ocean space south of the United States, and the Soviet Union gets increased access to port facilities in Latin America." Although the present asymmetry will not change until "the mid-1990s," the United States is making a mistake, his argument runs, by seeking to balance Soviet superiority on land with a naval presence in the Indian Ocean. This will only lead to counter-deployments of submarines armed with surface skimmer missiles and cruise missiles, as well as carriers, and "may necessitate the Soviets securing further infrastructure support for such deployment in addition to what it now has at Aden and Dahlak." The United States could best serve its interests, he declares, by pursuing regional arms control negotiations that could be linked to larger arms control trade-offs.

Rejecting the characteristic American view that Moscow triggered the superpower military buildup in the region with its intervention in Afghanistan, Subrahmanyam recalls that the Rapid Deployment Force (RDF) was first envisaged in a Presidential directive in August 1977 not as a response to events in Afghanistan but possibly in anticipation of them. He emphasizes the broad pattern of interaction between American and Soviet moves during the mid-1970s that led up to the Soviet intervention. Thus, Moscow's decision to intervene may have been triggered by the prospect of the RDF, the rupture of the Indian Ocean arms control negotiations in 1978, the stationing of the U.S. carrier battle group in the Arabian Sea in 1979, American strategic overtures to China, and, finally, fears of American intervention in Iran during the hostage crisis. In American eyes, he adds, Soviet moves in Ethiopia, the 1978 coup in South Yemen, and increasing Soviet arms flows into Iraq must have been seen as posing threats to Saudi Arabia and the Gulf oil fields. But these events can be traced, in turn, to earlier efforts by pro-American Egyptian, Iranian, and Saudi leaders to wean Soviet-oriented Somalia, South Yemen, and Afghanistan away from their Moscow connection.

Joel Larus and C. Raja Mohan approach their analyses of the economic environment in the Indian Ocean from radically differing perspectives, but both show that Indian and American economic interests need not come into conflict.

Larus examines the potential for the development of fishing, seabed petroleum, and seabed mining resources, focusing most sharply on seabed mining opportunities resulting from the discovery of polymetallic manganese and sulfide nodules in the Indian and other oceans. Reviewing the differences between India and the United States concerning the seabed mining provisions of the Law of the Sea Treaty, he devotes special attention to a little-remembered 1970 proposal by the Nixon Administration concerning seabed mining. In contrast to the Treaty's plan for an international seabed mining authority, superseding sovereign national control over seabed mining ventures, the Nixon plan envisaged trusteeship zones under the control of coastal states as managing trustees. Private companies would have operated not under the control of an international authority, as in the Treaty, but under concessions from the coastal states. However, Larus emphasizes, the underlying Treaty concept that the oceans constitute the "common heritage of mankind" was recognized in the Nixon plan, which provided for the allocation of a designated portion of the funds accruing from mining activity to Third World states. At various times, the Nixon plan set this portion at 66 percent, 50 percent, and finally 33 percent.

Larus suggests that the 1970 American proposal offers a way out of the seabed mining impasse that has resulted from the American refusal to sign the Treaty. Half of all funds earned by nationally licensed seabed mining enterprises would go to a fund administered by Third World states for Third World development. The 1970 plan is an "economically realistic way to exploit the resources of the common space for the developing nations," he says, in contrast to Treaty provisions giving what he sees as punitive taxation, royalty, and technological transfer powers to the projected international authority. In this connection, Larus objects to India's support for the Treaty's seabed mining provisions. Citing Indian expenditures of more than $100 million to date in developing its own seabed mining program, and the probable outlay of $1.5 billion to bring each of its Indian Ocean mining sites into operation, he urges New Delhi to shed its Third World self-image, divorcing itself from the projected international authority in favor of a more profitable, nationalistic policy. "Every developing state in the world, except India, can someday expect to realize—cost free—material benefits from the authority's mining operations, operations that will be based on the initiative, creativity, and venture capital of leading industrial nations of the West *and India*. India will never be in this category because its financial/personnel commitment to a national seabed mining operation in no way resembles the policy of any other Third World state."

Raja Mohan, expressing support for the Law of the Sea Treaty, sees "valid reasons" for India to continue with its seabed mining efforts. He views with alarm the successful American effort to promote a boycott of the Treaty by Japan and West European nations and a concomitant agreement by these nations not to violate each other's seabed claims. "The battle for the seabed is taking a dangerous turn," he warns, "and an ugly situation could develop if two treaty systems—one under the auspices of the United Nations and the other with U.S. protection—begin to operate and squabble over mining rights." For the immediate future, he foresees uncertainty over seabed mining due to the high investments involved and depressed metal markets. But the long-term prospect is more hopeful and warrants a continued Indian investment in seabed development under the terms of the Law of the Sea Treaty.

Apart from his discussion of seabed mining, offshore petroleum prospects, fishery development, and opportunities for exploiting recent technological advances in ocean sciences and engineering, Raja Mohan devotes his essay primarily to putting the resource potential of the Indian Ocean/Persian Gulf region into perspective. He seeks to destroy the central argument generally made to justify the projection of American naval power into the region: that the United States has a "dangerous dependence" on regional resources and that its access to these resources is threatened by possible Soviet aggression and regional instability. Ridiculing Western "overdramatization" of the oil price increases in the early 1970s, he maintains that the importance of Gulf oil is declining in the wake of falling world energy consumption, energy conservation in the West, growing non-OPEC production, and greater reliance on non-petroleum sources of energy. He cites the experience of the Iran-Iraq war to disprove the argument that local conflicts may lead to a cutoff of oil supplies from the region. "Even if there is a dramatic and radical change in the nature of the power elites of the local states," he writes, "it is unlikely that oil would be cut off, given the dependence of these states on a single commodity for economic survival." As for the fears of a Soviet threat to Gulf oil, he criticizes what he sees as an "obsession" with no demonstrated foundation in reality. American specialists have fluctuated erratically, he observes, between one extreme in which Moscow is depicted as seeking to lure the NATO allies into energy dependence with their surplus oil and another extreme in which an oil-short Soviet Union is depicted as bent on grabbing Gulf oil. Such arguments cannot mask the "real motivations" behind the American military presence, namely, the desire to maintain local allies and block changes in local power elites in order to extend American political and military influence.

In an extensive analysis of "the mythology of strategic minerals," Raja Mohan challenges the conventional wisdom that the United States is dependent on the non-petroleum mineral resources of the Indian Ocean/Persian Gulf region. He seeks to demonstrate the declining importance of metals as a result of structural changes in Western economies, including competition from plastics, composites, optical fibers, and ceramics. He alleges that domestic U.S. mining interests have raised the bogey of dependence to protect their own markets and profits. Recycling, substitution, conservation, and improved materials management have diminished American dependence on imported minerals, and the American share of direct investment in mining and smelting in developing countries has dropped from 60 percent in 1950 to 42 percent in 1968 and 32 percent in 1978.

The essays in this book constitute a powerful reminder that the world's two largest democracies have sharply divergent worldviews. Yet American and Indian authors alike have noted the convergence of interests between the two countries on a variety of basic issues, especially maintaining freedom of the seas, the security of shipping traffic, and access to the petroleum supplies of the Gulf. More important, as the changes now taking place in the Soviet Union suggest, the possibility of a gradual Soviet-American accommodation cannot be ruled out, both at the global level and in such arenas of regional confrontation as the Indian Ocean and the Gulf. Should such an accommodation occur, many of the proposals in these pages for arms limitations, political settlements, and economic development might well acquire a new relevance.

1

Emerging Security Issues in the Indian Ocean: An American Perspective

WALTER K. ANDERSEN

The Indian Ocean assumed renewed importance in the mid-1980s with the escalation of the attacks on shipping in the Persian Gulf by Iran and Iraq. The naval commitment of the United States to the northwest quadrant of the Indian Ocean reached levels of the late 1970s, and American determination to assure the flow of oil was symbolized by the American decision to reflag Kuwaiti tankers and to provide military escorts. This enhanced U.S. activity underscored the continued importance of U.S. military facilities in the Philippines, as well as the uncertain positions of these facilities in the context of recent political developments there. In this fluid situation, the Soviet Union, under the leadership of Mikhail Gorbachev, has sought to enhance its own influence, and Gorbachev's resuscitation of a Soviet-proposed Asian Collective Security scheme demonstrates a renewed Soviet commitment to play a more influential role in Asian affairs.

During the early 1970s, the Indian Ocean first became identified as a distinct area attracting international attention as well as a source of international conflict. A fundamental cause for this interest, by the superpowers in any event, was (and is) the state of inter- and intra-state instability endemic to the subregions bordering on the Indian Ocean. The Iran-Iraq war underscored the continuing tensions in the area. The Soviet Union views this instability as an opportunity for enhanced political influence; simultaneously it is perceived as threatening the economic and strategic interests of the United States. The Western countries see a possible threat to their access to critical regional natural resources as well as to freedom of commercial sea lanes. They are also concerned about the possibility of an alliance between some of the littoral states (or anti-Western elements in some states) and the Soviet Union. That the Soviet Union has similar concerns has been indicated by its fears of an unfriendly regime in Afghanistan when Soviet forces withdraw. In addition, the development of submarine-launched ballistic missiles by the United States led Moscow to consider a possible strategic threat from the south.

In reaction to instability along the Indian Ocean littoral, both superpowers in the early 1970s deployed naval forces on a regular basis to the Indian Ocean. But until the late 1970s the United States did not consider its interests sufficiently threatened to commit carrier task forces permanently to the Indian Ocean, which would have given it naval supremacy there. As a result, the Soviet Union was able to establish itself as the largest continuous naval presence in the Indian Ocean through most of the 1970s.

The U.S. perception of the strategic importance of the Indian Ocean changed dramatically in the late 1970s. This change in perception was brought about by the fall of the Shah, which shattered the Nixon Doctrine's assumption that powerful subregional states could protect U.S. interests, and by the Soviet occupation of Afghanistan, which brought home to the West the realization that the Soviet Union was the most powerful Indian Ocean hinterland state and that Moscow was prepared to use force against its southern neighbors to protect its perceived interests. In response, the United States established naval supremacy in the Indian Ocean (see Table 1.1) and initiated efforts to upgrade its lift capacity to enable Washington to react quickly to a crisis threatening access to the oil resources of the region. This capability is principally intended to serve as a deterrent against Soviet land-based military moves that would threaten the oil-producing areas of Southwest Asia. U.S. policy in the Indian Ocean is driven by a forward strategy while the Soviet Union's strategy is grounded on the fact that it is a land power with potential enemies on its borders and with no need to cross water for defense.

Barring some significant U.S.-Soviet disarmament agreement addressing U.S. fears regarding Soviet moves, Washington will probably continue to adhere to its policy of maintaining a deterrence credibility in the Southwest Asian region, which, among other things, involves maintaining naval supremacy. Strategists in the United States and elsewhere have argued about how much and what kind of military force is needed to deter the Soviet Union, but in the United States at least few disagree about the necessity of a U.S. deterrent force in the Indian Ocean. Since the advent of Mikhail Gorbachev, the Soviet Union has taken steps that could reduce U.S. concerns, such as the 1988 Soviet agreement at Geneva to withdraw troops from Afghanistan. However, as noted earlier, the threat to access to raw materials does not come only from Moscow.

The U.S. decision in 1987 to reflag and escort Kuwaiti tankers in the Persian Gulf—at the request of Kuwait and with the general backing of other Arab Gulf states—aroused concerns within the United States and elsewhere that America might become directly involved in the Iran-Iraq conflict. In addition to warning of the potential for the large-scale loss of American lives, critics pointed out that such involvement might strengthen hard-line elements in Tehran, enhancing Soviet influence and postponing progress toward the long-range goal of better U.S.-Iranian relations. While the U.S. protective role was not formally challenged, the loss of American lives in the *Stark* incident and of both American and Iranian lives in the *Vincennes* tragedy stimulated sharp U.S. political debate before the mid-1988 Iran-Iraq cease fire. But even this debate did not significantly undermine American support for a deterrent force in the Indian Ocean.

The Soviet Union, the proximate superpower, is likely to continue seeking ways to make the Gulf area safer for Soviet security, an objective that potentially threatens the Western interest in access to the vital oil reserves of the region. As long as the Soviet Union remains committed to a policy of undermining Western interests in the area, the United States and its allies will have a compelling reason to maintain the means of responding effectively. A similarly compelling reason for maintaining Western military forces in the area is the threat of regional instability to continued Western access to the still vital oil reserves.

Littoral states for their part have also upgraded their naval capabilities (as well as their military capabilities in general) during the 1970s in reaction to unresolved regional problems and, in a few cases, to potential threats posed by the presence of the superpowers in the Indian Ocean. (See Table 1.2 for the generally upward trends in military expenditures.) The littoral states, however, have been unable collectively to oppose outside intrusion, in large part because of antagonisms among them. The Iran-Iraq war is only the most recent example of differences regarding the presence of outside military forces. Indeed, many littoral states have welcomed outside military assistance and a nearby presence of one or the other superpower as assets against perceived domestic or subregional foes. The present state of relations between the two superpowers makes it unlikely that either would pay much heed to efforts at excluding them from the Indian Ocean area. At the same time, the growing stockpiles of missiles in the navies of littoral states have increased the potential costs of "gunboat diplomacy" by either the superpowers or others. Such a capability on the part of littoral states has increased the danger to the sea lanes, as the Iraqis and Iranians demonstrated in the mid-1980s "tanker war" (see Table 1.7).

The developing political polarization (i.e., between those with military links to the Soviet Union and those with ties to the West) among Indian Ocean littoral states will only partly be resolved by international politics. More important determinants of future trends are likely to be the contributions that individual countries and subregions make to their own economic and social development and an effort to resolve long-standing subregional animosities among neighboring states.

Origins of External Interest in the Indian Ocean

The United States and the Soviet Union initially deployed naval forces to the Indian Ocean for reasons that had very little to do with U.S.-Soviet rivalry in the Indian Ocean itself. Nor did either superpower move to fill a vacuum left by the British withdrawal in the late 1960s and early 1970s. Indeed, the Indian Ocean was a very low-priority concern to both nations until the early 1970s, and the Atlantic and Pacific ocean areas are still far more important to both than the Indian Ocean. At least initially, Soviet concerns were focused primarily on enhancing its political influence among littoral states. The United States for its part wanted to signal its interest in assuring a flow of oil from the unstable Southwest Asian region. Both goals remain important objectives to the superpowers.

The British Withdraw

For almost 200 years the British exercised predominant military power in the Indian Ocean by establishing bases at key choke points and along critical sea lanes. In the 1960s, however, the costs of maintaining military facilities became a major issue in domestic British politics, and significant elements in both the Labor and Conservative parties advocated a reduction of forces there.[1] The White Paper on Defence (Command Papers 2901 and 2902) released on February 22, 1966, virtually ruled out unilateral British activities in the Indian Ocean; and Prime Minister Harold Wilson in early 1968 announced his government's intention to cut drastically the British presence east of Suez by the end of 1971, a statement that alarmed some littoral states, especially the smaller ones that felt threatened by larger neighbors. For example, the ruler of Abu Dhabi unsuccessfully floated a proposal that the Persian Gulf sheikhdoms pay for the costs of a British naval presence in the Persian Gulf.[2] On the other side of the Indian Ocean, Singapore and Malaysia were equally disturbed and pushed successfully for a multilateral defense agreement—the Five Power Defence Agreement (FPDA; comprising Singapore, Malaysia, the United Kingdom, Australia, and New Zealand). These five powers agreed to consult together regarding any unilateral or joint action against a threat or act of aggression against Malaysia and Singapore.[3]

Still another British White Paper was issued in March 1971 spelling out the process of shutting down the remaining British facilities (e.g., a naval communications center on Mauritius, an airfield on Gan in the Maldives, and the Masirah airfield in Oman) and granting independence to the remnants of Empire (e.g., the Seychelles in 1976), with the prominent exception of the British Indian Ocean Territory, which includes the atoll of Diego Garcia on which the United States now maintains a base.

These actions left France, the other European power with a traditional association in the Indian Ocean and a naval presence there, the most powerful outside naval power in the interim before the superpowers began to expand their presences. Nonetheless, France also voluntarily reduced its ground forces in the area and was obligated to shut down military bases, including its large-scale naval facility at Diego Suarez (in the Malagasy Republic). The French shifted their naval operations to La Réunion, an island 560 miles to the east of the Malagasy Republic (and whose population has voted for the status of an overseas French department) and to Mayotte. These facilities enable France to retain a commanding presence on the sea route from the Cape of Good Hope. Farther north, the French retained access to air and naval facilities at Djibouti, providing it an important presence at the choke point of the Red Sea.

The Superpowers Enter: The Soviet Union

As far as the United States and the Soviet Union were concerned, the Indian Ocean remained a very low-priority concern until the early 1970s, though they both had maintained modest naval presences to underscore the fact that they did have interests in the region. The first Soviet ship (other than merchant ships) to enter the Indian Ocean was an oceanographic research ship in 1957, followed by yearly visits of research ships after that, possibly signaling Soviet intent to conduct submarine and anti-submarine operations in the Indian Ocean. In 1965, a single Soviet warship made a port visit to the Indian Ocean, a symbolic advance guard for the Soviet Navy's forward deployment strategy, successfully advocated by Admiral Sergey Gorshkov. In addition, the Soviet Union in the 1960s supplied arms at very competitive prices to a number of states around the Indian Ocean, and it sought naval basing rights from some of the recipients.

The Soviet decision to deploy ships regularly to the Indian Ocean in the late 1960s probably had very little to do with the British decision to withdraw east of Suez. The Soviet bureaucracy had undoubtedly considered this step long before the British announcement. One compelling factor might have been the U.S. option to deploy SSBNs to the Indian Ocean. The Kremlin undoubtedly had searched for signs of such a deployment and may have concluded that the United States might be on the verge of doing so. Between 1962 and 1966, the United States and Great Britain agreed on the joint development of a communications facility on Diego Garcia. While these talks were going on in 1963, the United States and Australia agreed to develop still another communications facility on the North West Cape in Western Australia.

With the introduction, in 1964, of the long-range Polaris A-3 ballistic missiles and, in 1971, of the Poseidon C-3 (both with a range of 2500 nautical miles) into the U.S. arsenal, the Arabian Sea became a plausible deployment option for the United States. The Trident C-3 (SLBM range 4230 miles) and the imminent development of the Trident II (D-5) missiles (range 6000-plus natuical miles) both increase the target area within the Soviet

Union and the accuracy of the missile, as well as expanding the ocean area to be searched by the Soviet Union.[4]

But the Soviet SLBM concern is highly speculative and the United States has officially denied such deployment to the Indian Ocean. (The Soviet Union tacitly admitted non-deployment in the 1977–78 Naval Arms Limitation Talks when it agreed in principle to a freeze. The Soviets had entered the talks largely to *forestall* such a deployment.) The closest operating base capable of supporting a U.S. SSBN is Guam in the western Pacific Ocean and Rota in Spain, both such a great distance from the Indian Ocean that transit times would significantly reduce the on-station time for each submarine. The newest Trident SLBM, the D-4, theoretically removes this constraint, but it will also enable the U.S. SLBM force to strike at the Soviet Union from behind a protective screen closer to the continental United States.

Nonethless, from the Soviet point of view, it can be assumed that the United States retains the Indian Ocean deployment option. Besides the technical advantages noted above, the specific bathythermal conditions of the Indian Ocean, which has steep temperature gradients and a high salt content (thus reducing the range and reliability of low-frequency sonar equipment), might be viewed as an incentive to deploy, as would be the advantage of complicating Soviet ABM defenses and thinning out Soviet ASW deployment patterns. It is likely that the Soviets calculated that such a potential SLBM threat, even if only potential, would have to be countered with a significant naval presence possessing an ASW capability. There is little doubt that blocking an SLBM deployment was the primary motive behind Moscow's decision to join the U.S.-proposed 1977–78 Naval Arms Limitation Talks.[5] Former Foreign Minister Andrei Gromyko recently reasserted the Soviet Union's continued concern over SLBMs in the Indian Ocean in 1984 as part of his response to a query by UN Secretary General Perez de Cuellar regarding limiting naval activities and naval armaments. Gromyko responded *inter alia* that "The Soviet Union has actively pressed for elaboration of measures to contain the naval armaments race both on a bilateral basis, in particular within the framework of Soviet-American talks on limiting and subsequently reducing military activities in the Indian Ocean and in the context of . . . *reducing strategic armaments*" (emphasis added).[6]

However, the primary Soviet naval mission has probably never been directed against a potential U.S. strategic deployment to the Indian Ocean, a conclusion reached early on by U.S. official analysts. William E. Colby, then director of the CIA, testified before a congressional committee in 1974 that "the activities of Soviet naval units there [in the Indian Ocean] have not indicated an anti-Polaris mission."[7] He probably meant to say that the Soviet deployment was not *primarily* ASW, for a separate study indicates that at least 20 percent of the Soviet ships present in the Indian Ocean in 1974–75 had an ASW capability.[8] Indeed, in those same hearings Colby speculated that the Soviet Union probably would enhance its capabilities for land-based air reconnaissance and anti-submarine warfare (both of which were done later).

Still another reason for the Soviet deployment that may have been linked to the potential SSBN threat—and one mentioned in the Colby testimony—is that the Soviets might create a force that could pose a counter-threat to Western oil routes if Moscow concluded that SSBNs had become a major security threat to the Soviet Union. However, Colby revealed that the lack of a significant submarine capability at that time suggested that interdiction was not a major Soviet objective (and probably still is not, considering the modest Soviet submarine deployment to the Indian Ocean). Any serious Soviet effort at interdiction would probably lead to a general war, and the Soviet ships would then be quickly eliminated. Consequently, any long-range interdiction option would have to depend on land-based aircraft operating from the southern reaches of the Soviet Union (or from air bases in Afghanistan).

The Soviets undoubtedly would have deployed ships to the Indian Ocean even had there not been a U.S. SLBM option. Having achieved nuclear parity with the United States, the Soviet Union was no longer willing to play the role of supporting cast member and acquiesce in what it perceived to be an illegitimate Western monopoly of influence in an adjacent area. For example, Foreign Minister Gromyko, at the 24th Party Congress in 1971, declared that thereafter no matter affecting the Soviet Union could be settled without its participation.[9] Warships would strongly signal that interest.

Still another reason for deployment—and one strongly advocated by Admiral Sergei Gorshkov—may have been a decision to use the navy to gain influence among political elites who had just taken power from colonial masters or who were embroiled in national liberation struggles. Soviet commentaries of the time (and to a certain extent even now) expressed confidence that such elites would look to the "sacred center" of the socialist faith for guidance.

The sharp deterioration of Sino-Soviet relations in the 1960s provided another compelling reason to dispatch warships to the Indian Ocean. The People's Republic of China had scored some signal successes in enhancing its influence among littoral states, especially in east Africa and Soviet warships would be one means of convincing political elites that the Kremlin had more to offer to keep them in power than did the People's Republic.

Some analysts have speculated that there were important economic reasons for projecting Soviet seapower—protecting shipping routes to the Indian Ocean states, and the routes between the eastern and western ports of the Soviet Union, as well as the expanding Soviet fishing fleet in the Indian Ocean. In my view, these were (and are) a much lower order of concern. A very small percentage of Soviet trade transits the Indian Ocean, and the Soviet Union, unlike the West, is not heavily dependent on the oil and mineral resources from the Indian Ocean littoral states. Nonetheless, the Indian Ocean transit route is likely to become more important as the eastern reaches of the Soviet Union are developed. In addition, the rail and road links to the Pacific coastal ports might be endangered in a future crisis with China.

A number of instruments were used to enhance Soviet influence and power, but this paper will focus only on the military. Already in the early

1960s, the Soviet navy under the leadership of Admiral Sergei Gorshkov had apparently convinced the Kremlin leadership that advances in nuclear weapons technology required an expansion of the defensive perimeter of the Soviet Union. In order to achieve this, sea power was essential, in particular warships equipped with anti-submarine and anti-carrier capabilities. The scale of Soviet out-of-area operations increased between 1964 and 1974 by a multiple of 12—expanding from 4000 ship days per year to 46,000.[10] ASW missions clearly governed the outward deployment in the Atlantic, the Pacific, and the Mediterranean. The deployments to the Indian Ocean, however, were apparently governed more by considerations regarding the diplomacy of sea power, another topic much talked about by Gorshkov.

In March 1968, Moscow dispatched three warships to the Indian Ocean on a flag-showing mission to a number of ports; these ships returned to the Pacific fleet in July of that year. This was followed by still another series of flag-showing visits in November to ports in East Africa, the Red Sea, and the Persian Gulf. From the spring of 1969 onward, the Soviet Union has maintained a continuous naval presence, drawn primarily from its Pacific fleet. In one of the first systematic studies of the Soviet navy in the Indian Ocean, Geoffrey Jukes concluded that the Soviet Union's modest naval presence in the early 1970s was not on a sufficient scale to have a far-reaching naval objective. Rather, he concluded that its purposes appeared to be political, and area familiarization linked to an anti-carrier and anti-Polaris role.[11]

The first apparent example in the Indian Ocean of the Soviet's employment of naval forces for political purposes[12] occurred in 1968, when Soviet ships visited Aden, just after the revolt against the government of President Quhtan as-Shaabi. While this visit had surely been planned earlier, Moscow's decision to go ahead with the visit gave the Soviet Union the chance to display military support of the as-Shaabi regime and thereby increase the prospect of strengthened relations with South Yemen. Soon after, the Soviets began a series of visits to Somalian ports to underscore its friendship with the new regime of President Mohammed Siad Barre, who had seized power in October 1969. In late 1971, Soviet ships trailed three days behind the U.S.S. *Enterprise* task force during the Indo-Pakistani war. However, by suggesting a readiness to intervene on India's side in the event of action by the *Enterprise* in support of Pakistan, Moscow gained an enormous public relations coup in India at little real risk to itself.

Soviet ships in the spring of 1973 demonstrated support to Iraq in its border dispute with Kuwait. A four-ship Soviet naval squadron and the Soviet naval Commander-in-Chief visited Iraq, presumably to commemorate a treaty of friendship and cooperation between the Soviet Union and Iraq signed the previous year. Admiral Gorshkov's inclusion in the visit was not announced until just days before his arrival, and the Soviet warships arrived without prior announcement. In 1977, after being ordered out of Somalia, the Soviet Union mounted a massive airlift of supplies to Ethiopia. Equipment was flown to either Addis Ababa or Aden, then transhipped by sea to Ethiopia. Cuban proxies, numbering about 16,000–17,000, were also dispatched on

Soviet transports, to assist in the fighting first against Somalia and then against Marxist insurgents in Eritrea. In 1979, the aircraft carrier *Minsk* task group, en route through the Indian Ocean to the Pacific fleet, spent several days at Maputo, underscoring Soviet support for Mozambique vis-à-vis Rhodesia and South Africa.

This display of friendship for sitting regimes in need of assistance helped Moscow gain access to military installations in Somalia, Ethiopia, South Yemen, and Iraq. (The Soviets tried, and failed, to gain such facilities in India, Pakistan, and Indonesia). In the case of Somalia, the Soviets were given permission to use shore facilities; and Soviet naval aircraft were based in Somalia. In 1978, one year after losing its military position in Somalia as a result of Soviet support to Ethiopia during the ongoing Ethiopian-Somalian conflict, Soviet Il-38 reconnaissance aircraft began to make flights from South Yemen. The Soviet Union had initiated such flights even earlier out of Somalia, suggesting that the Kremlin intended to develop an operational naval capacity resembling the pattern of the Soviet naval buildup in the Mediterranean during the mid-1960s. The Soviets were to receive access rights (now virtually unrestricted) to the Dahlak Archipelago in Ethiopia. To sum up, the Soviet strategy amounts to what the French strategists refer to as "nibbling" tactics against the United States. For example, the Soviet naval presence in the Horn in the late 1970s, combined with the impression then of an uncertain U.S. administration, caused Saudi Arabia, a key country for American interests, to reexamine its policy options, including its relations with the Soviet Union.

The Superpowers Enter: The United States

The United States has maintained a three-ship force (the MIDEASTFOR) consisting of a flagship and two destroyers, located at Bahrain in the Persian Gulf, since 1949.[13] The United States also maintained a SAC recovery base at Dharan from 1951 until the early 1960s, when it was terminated at Saudi request. Bilateral defense agreements were negotiated with Iran and Pakistan in 1950 and 1954, respectively, which interlocked with the Baghdad Pact of 1955 (CENTO after 1958). Finally, after the 1962 Chinese incursion into India, a substantial U.S. military aid program was initiated at Indian request, and this survived until the Indo-Pakistani war in late 1965.

After years of relative disinterest, U.S. concerns regarding the Indian Ocean took on new importance with the deterioration of U.S.-Soviet relations during the early 1960s and the growing U.S. military involvement in Southeast Asia. In 1960, the carrier U.S.S. *Bonhomme Richard* visited the Indian Ocean. Gary Sick, in his thorough discussion of the developing U.S. Indian Ocean policy, points out that the American naval establishment at the time was beginning to look for a facility in the area that was strategically located as well as relatively immune from nationalist pressures.[14]

India was to play a major role in the decision to establish such a facility. The United States dispatched the U.S.S. *Enterprise* to the Bay of Bengal in the wake of the 1962 Sino-Indian war to help provide air cover to Calcutta if that became necessary.[15] This experience of Chinese aggression against India convinced many in the State Department that the United States needed military muscle to back diplomatic initiatives in southern Asia. Even though the White House and the Department of Defense were still skeptical of such a need, the State Department view prevailed. Talks with Great Britain were initiated in 1963 and a U.S. survey was carried out in 1964 (and again in 1967) to locate site(s) suitable for U.S. needs in the Indian Ocean.

In 1963, the U.S.S. *Essex* and a naval task force participated in the first annual MIDLINK exercises with CENTO partners. In 1964, President Johnson sent a carrier force unassociated with MIDLINK to the Indian Ocean to underscore U.S. interest in the Indian Ocean.

Great Britain detached several islands in the Chagos Archipelago to create the British Indian Ocean Territory (BIOT)—which included Diego Garcia. The United States in turn canceled some $414 million in research and development costs for the Polaris missile system, which had been part of the British obligation toward costs associated with this missile.[16] The agreement in 1966 regarding Diego Garcia envisaged an austere communications facility. It stipulated that administrative authorities (i.e., the U.S. navy and the Royal Navy) of each side were to bear the costs of its respective installations. The initial period covered by the agreement was 50 years, with a provision for a 20-year extension.

The British decision to withdraw its forces east of Suez had a much greater impact on the U.S. view of its interests in the Indian Ocean than on that of the Soviet Union. The British decision was taken at a time when U.S. forces were already stretched thin because of the involvement in Vietnam and when domestic opposition to overseas U.S. commitments was growing. The Nixon Doctrine, announced in 1969, was an effort at minimizing U.S. military commitments in Asia (outside of Vietnam) and maximizing reliance on major sub-regional powers to maintain stability in their own area.[17] In line with this, the United States significantly stepped up its technological and military assistance programs to Iran and Saudi Arabia. Washington also increased its diplomatic presence in littoral states. Underlying these moves were certain assumptions: U.S. interests in the Indian Ocean were secondary to interests in Europe and East Asia, and regional developments were not significantly susceptible to U.S. military pressure.

In one of the first series of congressional hearings on the Indian Ocean, in 1971, Ronald I. Spiers, then Director of the Bureau of Politico-Military Affairs in the Department of State, listed *inter alia* major U.S. interests in the Indian Ocean: concern for the growing Soviet influence around the choke point to the Red Sea; regional instability that might adversely affect Western access to Persian Gulf oil; and the continued right of free passage for U.S. commercial and military traffic. He noted that "It is to our interest that countries of the area not pass under the control of forces hostile to us. Specifically, we would be concerned if Chinese or Soviet influence in the area extended to control of the water areas of significant parts of the littoral. *We do not en-*

visage an immediate threat of this nature, however" (emphasis added).[18] Robert J. Pranger, Deputy Assistant Secretary of Defense (International Security Affairs), testifying along with Spiers, added that the United States was apprehensive about the reduced time that it would take for the Soviet Union to augment its military presence in the Indian Ocean once the Suez Canal was reopened.[19]

In his testimony, Spiers noted that Congress had appropriated $5.4 million in the FY 1971 Military Construction Bill to establish a communications facility on Diego Garcia. He pointed out that such facilities were not merely a response to increased Soviet naval activity in the Indian Ocean, but were also needed to fill a communications gap then existing in the south, central, and northeast portions of the Indian Ocean that could not be covered by existing U.S. naval communications facilities. In response to questioning, he stated that the United States planned to construct on Diego Garcia a small logistical petroleum storage facility to meet the needs of the communications unit, an 8000-foot runway capable of handling C-130 and C-140 transport aircraft, and a turnaround basin in the channel of the atoll.[20]

The record indicates that U.S. officials had no serious plans for Diego Garcia beyond that of a very modest communications facility. The administration still considered the Indian Ocean and its littoral marginal to core U.S. security interests, a view that did not change until the 1973 Arab-Israeli war and the 1973–74 oil embargo. For example, Joseph Sisco, Undersecretary of the State Department, told a congressional committee in May 1973 that U.S. interests in the area were "marginal," that "the Nixon Doctrine is quite applicable—namely, we ourselves don't want to become involved [in the area]."[21]

This complacent view was soon to change markedly. About one year after Sisco's remarks, Rear Admiral Charles D. Grojean, Director of Politico-Military Policy Division, Office of the Chief of Naval Operations, requested substantial additional funds from a congressional committee to transform Diego Garcia into a support facility for the growing number of U.S. ships in the Indian Ocean. He stated that such a support facility was needed "if we wish to have the capability to move or maintain our ships in the area without degrading our posture in the Western Pacific."[22] The number of U.S. ship days in the Indian Ocean increased from 1246 in 1970 to 2154 in 1973. (The comparable Soviet increase was from 4930 ship days to 9000.)[23] In response to the uncertainty aroused by the 1973 Arab-Israeli war, the United States instituted periodic deployments from the Pacific Fleet (usually three per year), with every other deployment to include an aircraft carrier. In March 1975, President Ford declared that facilities on Diego Garcia were "essential to the national interests of the United States,"[24] the first high-level statement to indicate that the "essential interests" of the United States were involved. The Arab-Israeli war, as noted earlier, convinced many Americans that the United States needed a facility of its own in case of another Middle East conflict, since NATO allies and others had refused to permit refuelings or overflights during that conflict.

Admiral Thomas H. Moorer, Chairman of the Joint Chiefs of Staff, spelled out what the Department of Defense was seeking: dredging of the lagoon of the atoll so that it could handle a tender, increasing the POL capacity by 480,000 barrels (capable of supporting a carrier force for up to 60 days), and increasing the runway from 8000 to 12,000 feet to accommodate heavy-cargo aircraft.[25] However, Congress pressured the administration to delay any new construction until it had pursued all possible avenues that might lead to a naval arms limitation agreement in the Indian Ocean and to report back the administration's findings. (The Ford Administration did report back to Congress in April 1976 that such talks would pose several technical problems, but that these problems were not sufficient to negate talks, a formulation that clearly indicated a major internal debate over the question.)

Perhaps no littoral country reacted more negatively than India to the news of the U.S./British decision to establish a communications facility on Diego Garcia and to the debate over the planned expansion of the facility in the mid-1970s. India's strong backing of the Lusaka Non-Aligned Summit proposal for a Zone of Peace, according to one Indian analyst, was influenced by the establishment of the facility.[26] Prime Minister Indira Gandhi stated that "Military bases of outside powers would create tensions and great power rivalry."[27] Y. B. Chavan, Minister of External Affairs, told Parliament on March 18, 1976, that the facilities on Diego Garcia might possess a nuclear capability.[28] Behind many of the comments of Indian leaders was the assumption that the proximity of Diego Garcia to India (1200 miles from the tip of southern India) would give the United States the means to assert pressure against India, perhaps analagous to the *Enterprise* incident in 1971.

The opinion of other littoral states varied (at least privately), usually depending on whether the presence of the United States was perceived as necessary to neutralize any perceived danger from the Soviet Union or from a potentially unfriendly neighbor. Guy Pauker points out that in Indonesian military circles during the mid-1970s there was considerable support for the United States at least to match the Soviet naval presence in the Indian Ocean. He reported at the time that "Some Indonesian strategists go even further . . . and consider it entirely possible that if Great Britain withdrew completely from the Indian Ocean and the United States made no efforts to fill at least partially the vacuum, then India might agree with the Soviet Union on a division of the Indian Ocean area into spheres of influence. According to this thesis, India would seek a dominant role in Southeast Asia and perhaps East African waters, leaving control of the high seas to the Soviets."[29]

The debate in (and out of) Congress in the mid-1970s reveals a lack of consensus over what U.S. interests were in the Indian Ocean and over whether the Soviets posed a threat to those interests. One leading critic of an expanded U.S. naval presence in the Indian Ocean pointed out at the time that the Soviet Union had "a number of weaknesses and vulnerabilities that have particular significance in the Indian Ocean."[30] Among the "weaknesses" noted were the lack of fixed-wing aircraft to provide protection for naval forces and the lack of aircraft for reconnaissance, Western control over most of the egress and ingress points (making wartime reinforcement to the Indian Ocean almost impossible), and the lack of reliable and secure shore-based facilities. However, as others have pointed out, such arguments overlook the political uses to which the Soviets could put their navy to gain advantages vis-à-vis the United States, inasmuch as the deployment of Soviet warships to distant waters strengthens Moscow's image as a great power and thus elicits the appreciation of nations wanting to use a close relationship with the Soviet Union to support their own foreign policies. The bottom line to these countering arguments favoring an enhanced U.S. deployment is that the Soviet Union would be encouraged to step up its activities to weaken the position of the West (and its regional friends) unless the United States were present to induce caution on the part of the Kremlin and its friends.

Developing Interests of Other Powers

The Soviet Union and the United States are not the only external navies in the Indian Ocean. The French maintain a significant permanent fleet and Great Britain deploys intermittently, though it does not, like France, possess onshore military facilities. The Falklands/Malvinas fighting forced Great Britain to reconsider naval power projection beyond the NATO area, though most of the debate has centered on Atlantic sea lanes and possessions. The French for their part have developed a strategic doctrine justifying a naval presence in the Indian Ocean (and elsewhere), attributed by its analysts largely to General André Beaufré.[31]

French navy spokesmen, following Beaufré, distinguish between two strategies open to France's enemies: "direct strategy" and "indirect strategy."[32] The former is most likely to be carried out in Europe but is deterred by France's nuclear capability. Consequently, an enemy is likely to try the piecemeal approach to weaken the country by nibbling away at French interests outside of Europe. France, as its strategists point out, depends on imported raw material, much of it from the Indian Ocean area. In addition, France has declared a 200-nautical-mile economic zone around its numerous island possessions in the Indian and Pacific oceans. (The cumulative economic zone area around all its island possessions totals about 4 million square miles.) France has already begun to explore for oil off the Indian Ocean island of Kerguelen, and there are beds of mineral-rich nodules close to its possessions in both the Indian and Pacific oceans. These assets are tempting prizes in the worldwide competition for resources, and their denial to France would affect it adversely. In addition to a threat from the Soviet Union, French naval analysts point out that France's overseas possessions are endangered by the proliferation of arms among Third World states, who either on their own or as proxies of an adversary (read the Soviet Union) might challenge France.

In response to possible "nibbling" tactics, the French have adopted a doctrine akin to flexible response, aimed at deterring an adversary by convincing it that France can inflict severe pain if attacked. The French would incrementally increase the level of violence employed to convince an aggressor that further action is not worth the effort.

In terms of recent deployments, during most of 1983 the French maintained a single task group in the Indian Ocean.[33] It has established a pattern recently of deploying six to eight combatants and three or four ships to the Indian Ocean. This force usually consists of two submarines, a destroyer, and four frigates. The French Indian Ocean Squadron is headed by the replenishment oiler *La Charente,* converted with flagstaff facilities. In response to the shipping war in the Persian Gulf, France dispatched an aircraft carrier to the Indian Ocean, as well as mine sweepers and escort patrols to keep open shipping lanes in the Gulf. The French maintain a permanent base for their Indian Ocean Squadron at Mayotte, astride the entrance to the Mozambique Channel. There are also French port facilities at Djibouti and La Réunion, where joint service operations are coordinated through the Indian Ocean.

In addition, the French have cooperated in a low-key fashion with the U.S. navy. According to one U.S. naval analyst, the French have facilitated arrangements for fuel and logistics "on many occasions." Moreover, he notes that the French have relayed to the United States communications traffic of common interest.[34] Such cooperation has increased since the outbreak of the "tanker war" in 1987.

The only other external power with both a significant strategic reason to deploy to the Indian Ocean and a developing capability to do so is China. The Soviet Union continues to be perceived by China as its major security threat,[35] and China presently possesses a strategic capacity to hit targets in the Asian part of the Soviet Union from its launching sites in northwestern China, but this capability is vulnerable to a Soviet preemptive counter-force strike with SS-20s deployed in the Soviet Union. Such a strike would leave China exposed without a second-strike capability.

The risk of an SS-20 attack on China has led Beijing to follow the example of the four other nuclear powers and establish a submarine-based ballistic missile force. The Chinese have in fact moved to develop an SLBM capability. A significant step in that direction was taken with the successful test-firing of China's first sea-launched missile in October 1982, designated to be the CSS-NX-4, a variant of the T3 IRBM with a range of about 1500 miles.[36] This SLBM was reportedly test-fired from an underwater platform and is believed to be a two-stage solid-propellant missile that is comparable in size and capability to the early U.S. Polaris system. In addition, China's first SSBN—the Xia-class—is reported to be on trial.[37] One analyst reports that China will have 12 Xia-class submarines by 1992.[38] When the Chinese SLBMs become fully operational and are deployed abroad, there will be a need for them to cruise into deeper ocean water to escape detection by Soviet ASW capabilities. One possible choice is the Indian Ocean. An Indian Ocean deployment would enable China to target the European heartland of the Soviet Union.

China, under Deng Ziaoping's leadership, has been moving beyond a coast guard role for its navy and toward a limited blue-water naval capability that conceivably could be used as a protective surface fleet for its SSBNs. Over the last few years the navy has acquired new guided-missile destroyers as well as some experience in operating at a long distance from home ports; China has also incorporated additional 15,000-ton oceangoing supply ships and has mastered the technique of resupply by sea.[39]

Nonetheless, the Chinese navy is still largely composed of small coastal defense craft with poor deep-seagoing capabilities.[40] Furthermore, Chinese ships are generally based on Soviet designs dating from the 1940s and 1950s. Chinese destroyers and frigates are highly vulnerable to enemy submarines and aircraft because they lack modern sensors and weapons. They have little in the way of early warning (EW) or electronic countermeasures (ECM) and, apparently, have yet to deploy an operational SAM system. As a result, Chinese surface ships are not likely to operate beyond land-based cover during a crisis.

In addition, the Peoples Liberation Army naval air force is composed largely of obsolete aircraft and dated technology. China's lack of sophisticated airborne sensors and seaborne helicopters would make it difficult for the Chinese to detect and then destroy Soviet submarines in wartime. China will probably not be in a position to deploy to the Indian Ocean until the 1990s or—more likely—even beyond. This is partly due to budgetary constraints. The Director of U.S. Naval Intelligence informed a congressional committee in 1983 that "China will remain principally a regional power for the rest of the century."[41] Major reasons for the slow pace in the development of a Chinese capability to project power is the low priority accorded the military in the Four Modernizations program and the high cost of sophisticated technology. According to one analyst, the Chinese navy is likely to remain in an inferior position to the army and air force in the bargaining for funds.[42]

Perhaps an even more fundamental reason reducing the chances for a deployment to the Indian Ocean is the need for the Chinese to use their assets to counter the growing Soviet naval forces under the command of its Pacific Ocean fleet. This fleet is the largest of the Soviet Union's four fleets and more powerful than the entire Chinese navy.[43]

Soviet naval forces in the Pacific have grown steadily from the mid-1960s, from about 50 principal surface combatants to almost 90 today. The addition to the fleet of such vessels as Kiev-class carriers, Kara-class missile cruisers, and Krivak-class missile destroyers also signifies a significant qualitative increase in Soviet naval capabilities in the Pacific. This quantitative and qualitative improvement can also be seen in sub-surface capabilities in the addition to the fleet of nuclear-powered submarines like the Delhi III–class SSBN, Victor III–class SSN, and the new class of diesel-electric Kilo conventional attack submarines. The jump in Soviet warship strength in the region has been matched by an increase in the striking power of Soviet naval aviation. Since the mid-1960s the number of Soviet naval aircraft has increased over 50 percent to a current force of about 440 aircraft. Some 30 naval long-range BACKFIRE B aircraft—deployed to the Far East since 1980 and adding to air force BACKFIRE in the area—can strike anywhere in China and in much of the Pacific as well. Moreover, an 8000-man naval infantry division based near Vladivostok constitutes the largest contingent of naval infantry in the Soviet navy.

Japan, it might be argued, also has a compelling reason to project naval force to defend critical Indian Ocean sea lanes linking it to Persian Gulf oil and to trading partners in Asia, Africa, and Europe. Almost one-half of Japan's oil imports in 1986 came from the Persian Gulf, and a reduction in supplies would force Tokyo to look elsewhere, forcing up the price of oil. However, the probability of Japanese naval deployments beyond the 1000-mile radius now being talked about is low, given the political constraints within Japan, the restrictions imposed by Article 9 of the Japanese Constitution, and the sure adverse reaction of several Indian Ocean littoral states (e.g., Indonesia) to any semblance of a resurgent Japanese military capability that reaches into the South China Sea and beyond. Indeed, it may be some time before the Japanese even have the capability to protect the area within the 1000-mile radius (measured from Tokyo). However, a Japanese capability of sea control in this area could affect Indian Ocean deployments in that more U.S. ships presently stationed in Japan could be moved into the Indian Ocean without degrading the defense posture in East Asia.

Japan has the technological capacity to develop an SSBN and could, if it made a determined effort, probably develop an SLBM, although such a prospect is farfetched under present circumstances. Were Japan, for some reason, to develop an atomic capability (unlikely as long as the United States maintains a credible commitment to its defense), the likely route would be SLBMs. Unlike the United States, the Soviet Union, and China, Japan could not afford to have a land-based deterrent since it does not have sufficient landmass to guarantee an assured second-strike capability with land-based missiles. Even if it were to move along the nuclear weapons route, the chances of a Japanese deployment in the Indian Ocean seems remote given the virtually guaranteed opposition of the Southwest Asian states and China to a militarily revived Japan. The Soviet Union has also become increasingly outspoken in its opposition to a stronger Japanese military.

Southwest Asia and American Strategy in the Indian Ocean

In 1979, the United States made a decision to build up a powerful fleet continuously present in the northwest quadrant of the Indian Ocean. As noted below, this decision apparently had little to do initially with the Soviet naval presence, which was relatively modest and no real challenge. Rather, the threat came from the Soviet capability to threaten the states of Southwest Asia from the land. The United States could not possibly match this, but it could develop a sea-based deterrent to a possible attack. What led the United States to revise the previous low-priority role accorded the Indian Ocean?

The key issue for the United States was (and is) access to oil. Events in the 1970s and early 1980s (e.g., the 1973 oil embargo, the 1979 Soviet invasion of Afghanistan, the 1980 outbreak of fighting between Iraq and Iran, the escalation of the "tanker war" in 1987, etc.) underscored the dependence of the West on Persian Gulf oil and aroused apprehensions that this flow could be shut off by efforts of the Soviet Union or by radical internal political developments in the region.[44] These events convinced many Americans that the United States could not rely on others to help protect its interests in the area, and that therefore the United States had to deploy military forces to the Indian Ocean. The United States was jolted when NATO allies refused to permit overflights to resupply Israel in the 1973 war. In addition, the collapse of the Shah demolished the Nixon Doctrine's hope that powerful regional states, by maintaining stability within their regions, would reduce the potential need for U.S. military deployments to Asia. The Soviet occupation of Afghanistan, the first use since World War II of Soviet ground forces outside the Warsaw Treaty Organization states, brought the Indian Ocean to the forefront as the third area of U.S. strategic concern.

The United States' commitment to the Gulf was asserted in the so-called Carter Doctrine, enunciated first during the former president's State of the Union Address in January 1980. In the wake of the Soviet occupation of Afghanistan, Carter warned the Kremlin that the United States would resist, with force if necessary, any attack on the area.[45] President Reagan subsequently affirmed this doctrine, adding two new features to it: He placed the Persian Gulf issue within the context of global U.S.-Soviet confrontation and he pledged U.S. commitment to the security of friendly states. Regarding the second feature, the President noted at the time of congressional debate over the sale of Airborne Warning and Control Systems (AWACs) to Saudi Arabia that the United States would not permit Saudi Arabia to become another Iran. In line with this, the U.S. administration, in its presentation to Congress, unilaterally made a general policy commitment to the security and integrity of Israel and other friendly states in the area.[46]

The groundwork for the present U.S. Indian Ocean policy was essentially put together during the last several months of the Carter Administration. Secretary of Defense Harold Brown stated in his final written budget report to the Congress in early 1980 that "The Soviet invasion of Afghanistan, its foothold in South Yemen and the Horn of Africa and the Soviet naval presence in the Red Sea only make a volatile situation potentially more explosive."[47] He concluded his introductory remarks with the comment that "The United States may well be at . . . a turning point today. We face a decision that we have been deferring for too long; we can defer it no longer. We must decide now whether we intend to remain the strongest nation in the world. The alternative is to let ourselves slip into inferiority, into a position of weakness in a harsh world where principles unsupported by power are victimized and to become a nation with more of a past than a future."[48] The FY 1981 Budget Authority (BA) that he submitted was 5.4 percent higher than the previous year's request.

Secretary Brown listed a number of steps already taken to meet the perceived threats to the oil-producing areas of the Middle East. The United States had increased the number of surface combatants under the control of the commander of the MIDEASTFOR from three to five ships and the number of naval battle force deployments into the Indian Ocean from three to four annually.[49] "We will need," he added, "to enlarge our presence further."[50]

Most of those added measures had to do with providing the United States a more mobile deployment force for use in a crisis threatening access to Persian Gulf oil. The origins of the concept of a rapidly deployable force[51] for use outside the NATO area can be traced to a 1977 order of President Carter to the Department of Defense to establish such forces. In July 1979, Secretary Brown stated that the United States was seriously considering an increase in its security presence in the Indian Ocean/Persian Gulf region and declared that the "United States would commit our forces [there] if we judged our vital interests were involved."[52] In August 1979, the Joint Chiefs of Staff began to take steps on the five-year program of the Department of Defense, a process accelerated after the seizure of the American hostages in Iran in November 1979. In early October 1979, President Carter announced the formation of a rapid deployment force and later in the month specific guidance was given the services regarding the establishment of a command structure. On January 4, 1980, administration officials stated that the government had decided to maintain a permanent naval presence in the Indian Ocean as a result of the Afghanistan and Iranian crises. On January 9, it was announced that the United States would seek military facilities in the region. The Carter Administration informed Great Britain on January 12 of its intention to enlarge the facilities on Diego Garcia.

Secretary Brown, in his last *Annual Report* to the Congress, noted that the United States had already established a Joint Task Force "to plan, train, and exercise as well as prepare selected units of the Rapid Deployment Joint Task Force for deployment," that he had selected a Marine Corps lieutenant general to command the new task force (known by its acronym as RDJTF) and had designated specific units as components of it. In addition, he stated that the United States planned to fund the first 2 of 14 maritime prepositioning ships to be acquired over a five-year period, as well as the equipment for three marine brigades to be placed abroad these ships, and to develop and produce a C-X aircraft able to hold outsized cargo.[53]

Indeed, by the end of 1980 the Pentagon had already deployed seven prepositioned ships to the Indian Ocean at Diego Garcia, increased the carrier battle group presence in the Arabian Sea from one to two, made available 300 jet transports and 500 turboprop transports for airlift, and had submitted for congressional review the purchase of eight roll-on/roll-off freight and troop carriers that could reach Suez from the East Coast of the United States within 11–12 days.[54] On the diplomatic front, the United States very quickly worked out access agreements with Oman (April 9, 1980), Kenya (June 27, 1980), and Somalia (August 22, 1980).

The RDJTF came into existence formally on March 1, 1980, as part of the Readiness Command located at MacDill Air Force Base; it was established as a separate unified command—the U.S. Central Command (USCENTCOM) —on January 1, 1983. It is responsible for the region surrounding the Persian Gulf and the Red Sea, as well as states on either side of this region. Within its geographic purview are:

Northern Tier
Afghanistan
Iran
Pakistan

Arab States

Bahrain	Oman
Iraq	Qatar
Jordan	Saudi Arabia
Kuwait	South Yemen
North Yemen	United Arab Emirates

Africa

Djibouti	Kenya
Egypt	Somalia
Ethiopia	Sudan

Congressional testimony suggests that USCENTCOM's geographic area of responsibility (which of course does *not* include India) was determined by a judgment of that area that a crisis induced by a Soviet security threat to U.S. interests in Southwest Asia might require a deployment of U.S. forces to counter such Soviet pressures.[55] The presence of Soviet troops in Afghanistan was surely a major reason for including Pakistan. Dr. James R. Blaker, Assistant Secretary of Defense for Policy Analysis, stated in congressional testimony that USCENTCOM, like the other unified commands in the Pacific or Europe, "has operational command of the U.S. ground, air and naval forces in its geographic area of responsibility."[56] CINCPAC maintains its unified command within the Indian Ocean itself, though USCENTCOM has responsibility for the Red Sea and the Persian Gulf. It also has responsibility for managing security assistance to the countries within its geographic purview.

Committed to the Central Command are:

Army
   1 Airborne Division
   1 Airmobile/Air Assault Division
   1 Mechanized Infantry Division
   1 Light Infantry Division
   1 Air Cavalry Brigade

Air Force
   7 Tactical Fighter Wings**
   2 Strategic Bomber Squadrons***

Navy
   3 Carrier Battle Groups

1 Surface Action Group
5 Maritime Patrol Air Squadrons

Marine Corps
1⅓ Marine Amphibious Forces*

* A marine amphibious force typically consists of a reinforced marine division and a marine aircraft wing (containing roughly three times as many tactical fighter/attack aircraft as an air force TFW).

** Includes support forces, does not include 3½ TFWs available as attrition fillers.

*** These bombers and associated reconnaissance, command and control, and refueling aircraft make up the air force's strategic projection force.

Source: Report of the Secretary of Defense Caspar W. Weinberger to the Congress on the FY 1985 Budget, FY 1986 Authorization Request and FY 1985–89 Defense Programs (Washington, D.C., G.P.O.: 1984), p. 212.

General Robert C. Kingston, then commanding general of USCENTCOM, informed a Senate committee in mid-1983 that a full deployment to USCENTCOM would involve nearly 300,000 personnel.[57] A substantial part of these forces, however, has a prior commitment to NATO or Korea, and in case of a far-flung crisis might not be available to Southwest Asia. Some of the troops are tied specifically to it: the 83nd Airborne Division, the 101st Air Assault Division, five tactical fighter wings and the 7th Marine Amphibious Brigade, and an air wing from the Marine Amphibious Forces.[58] An 1800-man marine amphibious unit is regularly deployed to the Indian Ocean.

Administration officials have consistently specified three threats to U.S. interests in the Persian Gulf:[59] direct Soviet intervention, regional aggression by one Gulf country against another, or other civil strife within one of the Persian Gulf countries. In the first several months after the Soviet occupation of Afghanistan, there was a tendency to focus on the first threat, though the latter two are now discussed as the more likely contingencies that would threaten U.S. interests. Indeed, the major reason for the post-1987 escalation of U.S. naval forces is the threat to shipping lanes caused by the Iran-Iraq war.

Nonetheless, the large-scale commitment to USCENTCOM is intended to serve as a deterrent to Soviet moves against the Persian Gulf states, clearly a worst-case scenario and not now an immediate threat. In the latter two cases, congressional testimony by administration spokesmen suggests that the United States hopes to reduce the dangers of threats from both the Soviet Union and an assertive Iran by providing friendly states with the means to protect themselves, by encouraging greater regional cooperation—and by using direct U.S. force only as a last resort and only when invited to do so. General Kingston told a congressional committee: "I believe in most cases it would be inappropriate for US combat power to be associated with the most likely threats." Rather, "The most likely situation that I envision is that the United States would be asked to assist a friendly nation by providing communication and in-country transportation, namely, tactical air."[60] Then Defense Deputy Secretary Frank Carlucci seconded this in separate testimony by noting that "we hope to rely on friendly states to provide military forces [to meet the latter two crises]."[61]

The arms sales and assistance from the United States to littoral states, as explained by executive officials in congressional testimony, seem to constitute a much modified version of the Nixon Doctrine—providing states the means to resist Soviet aggression and the confidence to resist Soviet blandishments. The statistics show that Saudi Arabia and Egypt, or the states within the USCENTCOM area, are by far the largest recipients of U.S. arms deliveries since 1980, again underscoring the importance that the United States attaches to these two states. (See Table 1.3 for recent U.S. military sales.)

In the event that the United States and regional states feel it necessary for the United States to respond (to any contingency) with troops, U.S. defense analysts emphasize that such a deployment in the Persian Gulf area would need substantial combat power.[62] If the contingency area is accessible, then an amphibious assault could be undertaken: naval units would have to be present to establish local sea control, land-based or carrier-based aircraft would have to be available in order to achieve local air superiority, and a secure beachhead would have to be established in order to commence resupply and to reinforce the assaulting forces.

To be effective, analysts argue, the response to a crisis in the Indian Ocean would probably have to be achieved within a matter of days by smaller, highly trained units. There was considerable skepticism on this score when the rapid deployment scheme was announced, but there is more confidence now that it can be done. After the Bright Star–82 exercises (which involved the transport of over 6000 U.S. troops to Egypt, Sudan and Oman), General Kingston noted that with advance notice (4–5 days) he could expect to get an airborne brigade "on the ground" in the Persian Gulf region within 48 hours, and an airborne division within 10–14 days.[63] One analyst[64] estimates that the United States could now dispatch within 36 hours to the scene of crisis the marines already stationed in the Indian Ocean and a 1200-man marine amphibious unit from the U.S. fleet in the Mediterranean; a paratroop battalion from the 82nd Division within 48 hours; and a full brigade from the 82nd Airborne Division within 4 days. Still other units that could be expected to arrive quickly are: a reinforced paratroop battalion (stationed in Italy) with dedicated aircraft and trained in mountain warfare, 1200 men from the 7th Marine Brigade stationed in California, the 6th Air Cavalry Attack Brigade, combined elements of the 101st Airborne Division, and the 24th Mechanized Infantry Division.

The United States has concentrated on improving its air- and sealift capabilities primarily to create a more credible deterrent against any Soviet thrust into the region. However, it could also be employed to help blunt an Iranian thrust across the Persian Gulf, though clearly the U.S. would want to avoid such a deployment, and has provided equipment and training to the Arab Gulf states to give them the means to protect their own interests. Besides the Near Term Positioning Ships (NTPS) stationed at Diego Garcia, the U.S. plans to charter 13 TAKX prepositioned self-sustaining roll-on/roll-off ships to support three marine amphibious brigades (47,000 men); four or five of these vessels will have the capability of carrying supplies and equipment for one marine brigade. The marines airlifted to meet the ships would take a 2-day supply with them on the aircraft; the ships would carry another 30 days of supply.[65] Then Defense Secretary Weinberger announced in early 1984[66] that the first TAKX force will be ready in late 1984 and the second and third in 1985 and 1986, respectively. The last one will be deployed to Diego Garcia, replacing six NTPSs, and the other two will be deployed outside the Southwest Asia area. In addition to this, a program is under way to procure and modify eight SL–7 container ships with partial roll-on/roll-off capability. These ships, capable of 33 knots, could arrive in the Persian Gulf area within 11½ days after leaving Norfolk, transiting the Suez Canal. Eight such SL–7s can carry an entire army mechanized division.

Regarding airlift capabilities, in January 1983 the United States announced an airlift program calling for procurement of five C-5Bs (to move assembled heavy equipment) and 44 KC-10 aircraft (which can operate as a transport aircraft or a tanker—or both simultaneously). In late 1983, the administration began a long-proposed program to enhance the capabilities of the Civil Reserve Air Fleet (CRAF) by adding cargo-convertible features to existing wide-body passenger aircraft. The U.S. Defense Department estimates that by 1990 the United States will expand its inter-theater airlift capability by about 75 percent and more than double its ability to move outsized equipment by air.

The major objective of USCENTCOM, according to administration spokesmen, is to serve as a deterrent—especially against Soviet action—and decisions about its size, combat equipment, and mobility are influenced by its expected impact on the international behavior of other states and groups. Hence the emphasis on lift capacity, prepositioning, and demonstrated capability of moving troops (through regularly scheduled exercises) to crisis areas to demonstrate to others that the United States could, if needed, move quickly to meet one of the three contingencies noted above. There is little disagreement that, from a military strategic standpoint (though not necessarily from a political one), the deterrence objectives of USCENTCOM would be better served by a permanent military presence closer than Diego Garcia to the Persian Gulf. The countries of the region are presently reluctant to grant the United States the right to station permanently troops on their soil. However, their desire for U.S. naval protection of sea lanes has led to enhanced cooperation.

Arrangements for access (in a crisis) and prepositioning agreements[67] have been worked out with Oman, Kenya, and Somalia. In Oman, the United States has expanded the runways at Masirah to handle heavy transports and fighter bombers, and construction is now underway for facilities to store water, fuel, and ammunition. The runway can handle C-141s, C-130s, and P-3s. The United States can also use the air base at Thamrit (in Dofar province) and port and naval facilities at Salalah near the South Yemeni border. Egypt has offered access to the base at Ras Banas located on the Red Sea, where the Egyptian government is upgrading the airfield and port facilities, though U.S. funding for Ras Banas has been delayed. There are also small construction projects in Kenya and Somalia. Kenya has permitted the United States the right to use airfield and port facilities at Mombasa, and Somalia, its seaports and airfields at Mogadishu and Berbera. In addition, Bahrain, site of the original U.S. naval facilities in the Persian Gulf region, signed an agreement in 1977 that provided the United States with essentially the same access rights as before.

Saudi Arabia, while not concluding an access agreement with the United States, has spent large sums on its own for port and air facilities that might be used by the United States in a crisis situation if Jidda so permits. The advantage of the Saudi air and naval base at Dharan (as well as the airfield at Ras Banas) is that both are convenient staging areas for air operations in the Gulf. In addition, Dharan and Ras Banas (800 miles and 1200 miles from northern Iran, respectively) would be well within B-52 range (5000 miles) of a potential Southwest Asia conflict involving Soviet intervention in Iran. Finally, the 1982 U.S. basing agreement with Turkey, according to some reports, gives the U.S. authority to build NATO air bases at Konya, Van, and Kars in eastern Turkey.[68] Even though these facilities are designated exclusively for NATO use, a Soviet attack into Iran along Turkey's eastern borders might be construed as a threat to NATO requiring action to stem the Soviet advance.

In addition to these arrangements, facilities on Diego Garcia have been expanded considerably. Since 1979, the United States has spent hundreds of millions of dollars for additional construction, as well as maintaining 18 NTPSs there to support a 12,000-man marine amphibious brigade for two weeks of combat. Its protected harbor can shelter a carrier task group, and its extended runways can handle B-52s. But Diego Garcia, 1400 miles from the Persian Gulf, is not an ideal staging area and remains an "austere" facility in comparison to U.S. facilities on Guam and in the Philippines. While Diego Garcia does enable the United States to deploy naval forces and reconnaissance aircraft to the Indian Ocean with greater dispatch and to maintain equipment for rapid insertion of a limited number of combat troops, it does not provide the capability of sustaining a major operation for any length of time.

The escalation of the Gulf "tanker war," resulting in over a hundred attacks on shipping in 1986, led Kuwait, a prime target of Iranian attacks, to ask the United States and the Soviet Union in late 1986 to protect its tanker fleet. Following a swift Soviet agreement either to lease or reflag Kuwaiti tankers (or both), the United States responded that it would reflag all the tankers Kuwait wanted reflagged, which is probably what Kuwait wanted in the beginning since it almost immediately responded positively to the American offer.[69]

The reactive U.S. move was probably governed by an American desire to prevent Moscow from becoming responsible for protecting Western interest in access to Persian Gulf oil and to prevent the Soviets from developing closer cooperative arrangements with the Gulf states. The United States provides naval escorts to the reflagged tankers and the growing alarm of the Arab Gulf states toward Iranian aggressiveness has led most of them to sanction port visits by U.S. ships. Oman allows P-3 patrol planes operating out of Diego Garcia to use its facilities. The Saudis have agreed to use their American-made AWACS to maintain patrol over the southern half of the Gulf.[70] The Saudis also have reportedly allowed two of their four minesweepers to help clear Kuwaiti waters as part of a joint operation with the United States and Kuwait. The UAE has agreed to allow Saudi AWACS to overfly its territory. Kuwait in mid-1987 reportedly agreed to allow landing rights to U.S. aircraft involved in the reflagging operations and to supply free fuel to U.S. ships participating in the escort operation.[71]

While there is considerably more cooperation with Washington on the part of the Arab Gulf states, they are far from granting base rights to the United States. Indeed, the increased U.S. involvement with the security of the Arab Gulf states has set off a debate in the U.S. about the appropriate levels of American involvement. Perhaps the arguments against the U.S. reflagging operation specifically and close security cooperation with the Arab Gulf states generally were most succinctly summarized by Robert E. Hunter in testimony before the Senate Foreign Relations Committee.[72] He argued that the United States would now be perceived by Iran, the "strategic prize" in the Gulf, as a belligerent and thus invite a confrontation that would drive Iran closer to the Soviet Union. Such a development would undermine a major strategic American objective in the Gulf. Still others criticize the administration for not resorting to the War Powers Act when deciding to reflag and escort the Kuwaiti tankers. Since the initial furor, the criticism has died down, in part because the Iranians have not threatened the U.S. ships and in part because of a recognition that access to Persian Gulf oil is critically important to Western interests.

The "tanker war" has resulted in a considerable expansion of Western deployments to the area, including that of the United States. The Soviet's naval contingent, in contrast, has remained rather stable, perhaps reflecting Moscow's recognition that the buildup is not directed against it. However, the Soviet Union has deployed naval warships to the Persian Gulf for the first time, and their task is primarily to escort Soviet-flagged ships. The American decision to increase its deployments brought U.S. strength approximately to the 1982 level, when the United States cut the number of carrier battle groups from two to one.

In April 1986, U.S. naval ships were ordered to remain for a longer time in the Persian Gulf, and the deployment of the carrier *Kitty Hawk* was extended.[73] Then Secretary of Defense Weinberger ordered the battle group to begin spending its full deployment closer to the Strait of Hormuz.[74] Within a week of the May 11, 1987, reflagging announcement, the Iraqis inadvertently attacked the U.S.S. *Stark,* which caused Washington to rethink the potential threat to the more heavily engaged fleet. On May 21, the decision was made to increase the MIDEASTFOR from six to nine ships.[75] At the end of June, a battleship group was ordered to join the carrier battle group already in the

Arabian Sea.[76] After the reflagged *Bridgeton* tanker struck a mine off Farsi island in July, minesweepers and RH-5B Sea Stallion helicopters were transferred from Diego Garcia to the Persian Gulf.

Other Rapid Deployment Forces

The United States is not the only country developing a rapid deployment force for potential use in the Indian Ocean region (and elsewhere). France and Great Britain, as well as several Persian Gulf states collectively, are in the process of doing so.

All these countries are sensitive to the potential for Soviet thrusts into Southwest Asia, and, according to the prescription of one school of strategists, they might decide that a quick insertion of troops in an imminent crisis area may be enough to dissuade the Soviet Union from intervening in a crisis. They also have an interest in preserving access to Persian Gulf oil. The rapid deployment forces of France and Great Britain are closely tied to employment in Europe, and the Gulf Cooperation Council forces could be used against neighboring hostile powers. In future crises, particularly any involving the Soviet Union, the various governments mentioned here may decide that the military objective can best be achieved through joint efforts.

France already has a sizeable rapid reaction force, and the new Force d'Action Rapide (FAR) is planned to number 47,000 and be considerably better equipped and organized for independent deployment, as is the case of USCENTCOM.[77] When fully established, FAR will include an air mobile division, a light infantry division, a parachute division, a marine infantry division, an Alpine division, and a logistics brigade. Except for the light armored brigade, all the others are existing divisions. France has already stationed about 5000 rapidly deployable troops in Djibouti.

The British, after a vigorous debate concerning the size and functions of their deployment force, decided to develop a lean force of only 5000.[78] They announced plans to purchase about six additional C-130 cargo planes from the United States to give this force a greater mobility in a crisis.

The French and the British now maintain the largest non-littoral navies in the Indian Ocean, after that of the United States and the Soviet Union, though the French have surpassed that of the Soviets in fire power and both navies have more modern ships in the Indian Ocean than the Soviet Union.[79] The British had maintained what it refers to as an "armilla" of two combatants and one auxiliary in the Gulf since October 1980. In 1987, the English reportedly expanded this to three combatants, four minesweepers, and two auxiliaries, the additional ships needed to escort British-flagged vessels. In mid-1987, the French dispatched the aircraft carrier *Clemenceau,* two combatants, and an auxiliary to the Gulf of Oman as part of the preparations for French military escort of its own commercial vessels. The Indian Ocean is one of the French naval commands (ALIndian) and it normally includes a fleet tanker, headquarters of ALIndian, five escort ships, one patrol craft, two depot and repair ships, and one landing ship. France is the only country that has so far announced a policy of assisting any ship threatened by the Iranians.

In addition to the French and the British, other NATO allies have deployed ships to the Persian Gulf area. The Dutch and the Belgians announced their intention to send minesweepers in early October, 1987. Italy reportedly conducted its first escorted convoy of Italian-flagged ships into the gulf in late 1987. West Germany, whose constitution forbids the use of its armed forces outside the NATO area, announced that its ships would fill gaps in NATO areas brought on by the Persian Gulf deployments of its allies. It is reasonable to assume that considerable logistical cooperation and intelligence sharing exists between these NATO allies.

Missions of the Soviet Navy in the Indian Ocean

As already mentioned, the initial reasons for a Soviet deployment to the Indian Ocean in the late 1960s seemed governed largely by political motives and, to a lesser degree, by concerns regarding a U.S. SLBM deployment. Nonetheless, there are many analysts who argue that another major reason for the forward deployment of the Soviet fleet is sea denial—guerrilla warfare on the sea.[80] Retired U.S. Admiral Robert J. Hanks, one of the leading proponents of this view, argues that a "half dozen Soviet submarines deployed along oil transit lanes in the Indian Ocean and South Atlantic Ocean . . . could demand an immense U.S. or allied effort to counter, in order to ensure the survival of enough tankers to keep adequate supplies of petroleum available."[81] He claims, in addition, that the Soviet establishment of bases at or near key choke points (e.g., Soviet facilities in Ethiopia and South Yemen close to the Bab el-Mandeb and at Cam Ranh Bay astride trade routes to the Strait of Malacca) significantly increases the naval forces required by the United States to retain sea control.[82] Much of the U.S. Department of Defense testimony before congressional committees suggests considerable support for this view, and it is at least one of the arguments for a 600-ship U.S. navy, including increasing the number of aircraft carriers from 13 to 15.

Still another argument regarding Soviet deployment is that the Kremlin, in response to the possibility of a two-front threat, has deployed forward to outflank both China and NATO from the sea.[83] One advocate of this view argues that "By enveloping Europe on both its wet flanks, the Soviet position would coalesce with that in the Indian Ocean into a strategic combination which surrounds the Arabian Peninsula, extends into the Persian Gulf and stretches to the coast of India."[84]

However, the relatively modest Soviet naval deployments to the Indian Ocean do suggest more limited goals of ASW activity and naval diplomacy.[85] The deployment level established in the early 1970s and the types of ships involved have remained relatively constant with periodic surges that usually accompanied a crises-induced dispatch of additional U.S. warships to the Indian Ocean. In March 1974, the Soviets, according to one report,[86] had one cruiser, seven other combatants (destroyers and destroyer escorts), one amphibious ship, and 17 support ships. Ten years later, during 1983–84, there were on the average about two to three submarines, eight surface combatants, two amphibious ships, and 12 support ships.[87] The relatively small number of surface combatants since 1974 (about ten on an average in any given year) and submarines (two on the average for the same period) suggests that sea denial and interdiction are not major missions. The Soviets have not responded to the Western buildup in the wake of the 1986–87 shipping war in the Gulf, probably to avoid undermining ties with Iran and to be able to portray themselves as a potential nonthreatening mediator. In addition, the Soviet Union's economic interests are only marginally affected by the shipping war, while the West has a major stake in keeping the sea lanes open.

The figures on Soviet deployments noted above do not include the relatively recent year-round deployment of the Soviet navy to the South China Sea, where currently between 16 and 22 ships operate out of Cam Ranh Bay in Vietnam. This deployment involves on the average 2–4 submarines, 4–6 surface ships, 10–12 support ships, as well as TU-95 BEAR and TU-16 BADGER reconnaissance and strike aircraft.[88]

The Soviet Union has maintained a continuous presence in the South China Sea since January 1979, and it was significantly expanded after the February 1979 Sino-Vietnamese fighting. One defense analyst, scrutinizing deployments there, concludes that the Soviet deployment in the South China Sea has an ASW emphasis directed largely against the PRC.[89]

Acquiring facilities became an important objective after the Soviet Union decided to deploy regularly to the Indian Ocean, and it has made a concerted effort to acquire bases and facilities there. Its first overtures were to India and Pakistan in the late 1960s, but these were unsuccessful. However, Moscow was to be more successful later in countries that were in need of Soviet security assistance against either domestic or external foes.

The first successful Soviet foothold was Somalia.[90] Before President Barre terminated access rights to the Soviet Union in November 1977, the Soviet navy used Berbera as a supply base (denied at the time by both sides, but obvious after the Soviets were ejected). The Soviets added barracks, a repair barge, and a floating drydock that permitted repairs and overhauling of naval ships as large as guided-missile destroyers. The Soviet Union also constructed POL facilities and expanded the airfield near Berbera to over 12,000 feet in length, enabling it to handle all types of Soviet aircraft, including the TU-BEAR D long-range reconnaissance aircraft and the Il-38 MAY. In addition, there was a missile-handling and storage facility and a communications station used for command and control of the Indian Ocean Squadron.

In South Yemen, the Soviet Union now has access to port facilities at Aden and the use of Aden International and Al Anad airfields.[91] A large structure is now under construction in the mountains behind Aden by the Russians. According to one source, it is intended to house communications and command facilities for Soviet naval forces throughout the Indian Ocean.[92] In Ethiopia, there is a Soviet-constructed naval facility on Dahlak Island, consisting of storage buildings, a floating drydock, floating piers, and navigational facilities. The Soviet Union reportedly has unrestricted use of this Ethiopian site, making it for all intents a base in the classical sense of that word. The Soviet Union also stages reconnaissance flights from an airfield at Asmara. In Vietnam, the Soviets use airfield and port facilities at Da Nang and Cam Ranh Bay, which includes a floating drydock. They also maintain "anchorages" at scattered locations in the Indian Ocean. Finally, Moscow has access to several airfields in Afghanistan, which Moscow could use (though apparently does not do so now) for reconnaissance and ASW activities in the Indian Ocean.

Between 1968 and 1980, the Soviet Union routinely maintained a more impressive standing capability in the Indian Ocean than did the U.S. MIDEASTFOR, which normally consisted of a minor combatant flagship and two destroyers. However, the Soviets have never been able to match the U.S. navy's ability to respond quickly to crisis in the region.[93] The United States has been able to move attack carrier task groups from both the Mediterranean and Pacific Fleets and thus establish strategic and naval superiority. For example, during the 1971 Indo-Pakistani war, Task Group 74, built around the U.S.S. *Enterprise,* reached the Andaman Sea on December 14, 1971, three days earlier than the first of two Soviet groups dispatched. A similar situation developed two years later in the Arabian Sea during the Arab-Israeli war and again in late 1979, when the U.S. Embassy in Tehran was seized. Much of the Soviet problem on this score can probably be traced to the uncertainty over the availability of the Suez Canal during a crisis, forcing the Kremlin to draw on the distant Pacific fleet rather than on warships in the Mediterranean or the Black Sea. The deployment to the South China Sea alleviates the time factor somewhat, though this strategy is undoubtedly tied to a China mission, and increasing regional responsibilities of the Soviet Pacific fleet make the Indian Ocean an increasing burden to the Soviet Union—but one it clearly seems willing to bear. The deployment of the first Soviet aircraft carriers, expected in the 1990s, will, however, give the Soviet Union a significantly enhanced capability to "show the flag" and to engage in power projection missions. However, geography (at egress points, the Soviet navy can be bottled up) and greater U.S. firepower make it unlikely that Moscow would want to put its small number of aircraft carriers in such an exposed position during any crisis.

The most significant Soviet challenge to U.S. interests in Southwest Asia does not come from its naval presence in the Indian Ocean, but rather from the Soviet air and ground forces located in the southern military districts of the Soviet Union itself and the potential use of airfields in Afghanistan, the closest of which (Shindad) is located only 350 miles from the Strait of Hormuz. The United States cannot match such land-based power. It is this asymmetry of land forces that has led the United States to establish maritime supremacy in the Indian Ocean vis-à-vis the Soviet Union and to establish a rapid deployment force and USCENTCOM. This factor has also influenced the American (and others') approach to the Indian deliberations—that is, U.S. interests would be adversely affected unless the larger question of Soviet hinterland forces were brought into the discussions.

In this regard, the Soviet willingness to use troops in Afghanistan, which sent shock waves through Western capitals, and the uncertain situation in Iran (whose domestic stability might be severely strained in the wake of Ayatollah Khomeini's death) forced American strategists to reevaluate the probabilities for Soviet intervention in Southwest Asia, either overtly or covertly. With its strong military potential along the frontiers of coastal states of the northwestern reaches of the Indian Ocean, and only a few hours' flying time from the Persian Gulf and the Arabian Sea, the Soviet Union was suddenly perceived as the most powerful Indian Ocean hinterland state.

Stationed in the southern military districts of the Soviet Union[94] and facing Southwest Asia are 29 divisions, more than 800 tactical aircraft, and 400 helicopters, not counting the forces that have been in Afghanistan. While the units there (excluding, of course, any troops in Afghanistan) are now at a relatively low level of readiness, they are receiving more modern tanks, armored personnel carriers, and other replacements for outdated equipment. Several air defense regiments equipped with older aircraft have been replaced by ground attack aircraft and airfields have been modified to handle them. The deep-penetration FENCER (radius 1100 miles) is deployed in the southern Soviet Union and could attack targets throughout Southwest Asia, and other tactical aircraft could extend the range into the Arabian Sea by using airfields in Afghanistan. In addition, such long-range strike aircraft as the BACKFIRE (unrefueled combat radius of 550 kilometers), the TU-95 BEAR (unrefueled combat radius of 8300 kilometers), and the soon-to-be-commissioned BLACKJACK (unrefueled combat radius of 4500 miles) pose a serious threat to U.S. naval forces in the Arabian Sea and beyond.

Consequently, maintaining maritime supremacy and a credible rapid deployment force is the essential ingredient of the U.S. trip-wire strategy in Southwest Asia—getting forces quickly to the scene and placing the escalation burden on the Kremlin. Some defense analysts argue that it is not now necessary for the United States to station troops on a permanent status in forward positions (and thus avoid the adverse political fallout from such deployment),[95] since the United States is likely to have sufficient warning time to respond to Soviet action, were it to make the political decision to do so. More than 60 percent of the Soviet troops in the Caucasus, Transcaucasus, and Turkestan are in a Category III level of readiness, and it would take some time to call up reservists and to prepare and equip them for intervention. The Soviet Indian Ocean Squadron as now constituted has a limited offensive capability. It would need to be reinforced extensively from the Pacific and/or Northern fleets in order credibly to challenge the U.S. carrier task forces. Such reinforcement would take 18 days to a month. The availability of U.S. lift capability is thus the key to deterring an actual Soviet attack. In addition, a 600-ship fleet with 15 carriers, the current administration's goal, would enable the United States to deploy attack carrier groups to the Indian Ocean without at the same time degrading resources in other potential combat theaters, thus permitting the United States to establish naval superiority necessary for keeping the sea and air lanes open for troop reinforcements from the United States and elsewhere. Past Soviet behavior suggests that when faced with the prospect of a resolute U.S. response, Moscow has drawn back from taking aggressive action.

The recent buildup of U.S. forces in and around the Persian Gulf has not resulted in a reactive Soviet buildup in the area, a marked departure from previous Soviet behavior.[96] This is perhaps a product of General Secretary Gorbachev's more prudent policies, but more likely it reflects a Soviet recognition that the recent buildup is not threatening to Soviet interests. Indeed, the Soviets have reacted angrily to several Iranian attacks on their shipping in the Persian Gulf and have since 1986 escorted Soviet-flagged vessels carrying war material to Iraq. By late 1987, Soviet officials claimed that there were six Soviet frigates, three minesweepers, and a small intelligence-gathering ship in the immediate vicinity of the Persian Gulf.[97]

Expansion of Littoral Navies

In the past decade or so, many Indian Ocean states have significantly upgraded and expended their naval forces, though few (with the possible exceptions of India and—in a more limited sense—Australia, the two largest littoral state navies, respectively) possess a projective capability. These two states, unlike most other littoral states (with the exception of South Africa), have the trained personnel, indigenous manufacturing capability, and continuous political support of the navy to permit the development of a blue-water capability.

A particular favorite of littoral navies has been the fast patrol boat. There are several reasons for this interest in small warships. The increasing importance of offshore oil, gas, and mineral resources has led many littoral states to extend their sovereignty over large areas of the ocean, and small warships can be used to enforce these claims. Recent technological developments (light, reliable, and precise anti-ship missiles) have made relatively small platforms a potent challenge to large ships and large navies that might intrude into offshore areas. Fast patrol boats armed with anti-ship missiles can deny others easy entry, and can do so relatively inexpensively.

Still another reason for the expansion of littoral navies (and military forces generally) has been the existence of regional adversaries. Almost every region around the Indian Ocean exhibits intra-regional tensions: South Africa and its black neighbors; Somalia, Sudan, and Ethiopia; Iran and Iraq; India and Pakistan; the ASEAN states; and the Indochinese states (and possible renewed Indonesian-Australian tensions). External powers, including the superpowers, have often been willing arms suppliers to one side or the other (or even both sides) in an effort to enhance their own political influence. Often, the ultimate objective of such assistance is to gain basing and overflight rights to protect and advance their own interests. Publicly, the littoral states often appear united in international forums against external naval presences; but in fact they tend to be divided between those more powerful countries that could expect to be dominant in their part of the Indian Ocean if the navies of external powers were to leave and those who could foresee domination over them by their more or less friendly neighbors. Addressing himself to the South Asian situation, R. R. Chari, a former Director of the Institute for Defence Studies and Analyses, argued in an essay that an Indian quest for a blue-water capability would alarm Indian neighbors and would "militate against proposals that the Indian Ocean be converted into a Zone of Peace."[98]

It is no secret that several littoral states have avidly sought from the superpowers (and other external powers as well) arms, proxy troops, and even a nearby naval presence to protect the government from either a domestic or regional challenge or even from the possible blandishments of an outside power. Unless regional states can put their own domestic and regional houses in order, littoral states will continue to bid for support from the outside, and the superpowers are likely to remain players in this game. Kuwait, for example, recently turned to the Soviet Union for a wide range of sophisticated weapons after the United States had turned down its requests. For the Soviet Union, this is not merely a commercial transaction. It expects to enhance its influence in the Persian Gulf area. Kuwait subsequently turned to the Soviet Union and the United States for help in protecting the shipping lanes of the Gulf from Iranian attack. Given the Arab Gulf states' fears of Iran, it is not surprising that they have not opposed the protective role provided to Kuwaiti tankers.

Along the east coast of Africa, the Republic of South Africa, the economic and military giant of sub-Saharan Africa (if not all Africa), maintains the most effective navy. Its naval training establishment and dockside technicians are by far the best in Africa, and it possesses an indigenous capability to construct sophisticated warships. However, its navy is small (about 6700 men), cut off from Western military technology, and increasingly focused on close-by protection of the republic's coastline and harbors. The present leadership seems far less concerned about seeking help from the West (or extending help to the West) than previously, reflecting perhaps a greater self-confidence about its own ability to protect itself from aggressors. Pretoria has announced that South Africa can no longer be relied upon to defend the sea lanes around the Cape of Good Hope, and that this goal, if carried out at all, must become the responsibility of the Western powers.[99] In line with this policy, the 1984 edition of *Jane's Fighting Ships*[100] notes that the only projected naval building program of South Africa is fast attack craft, which are to be armed with surface-to-surface missiles. Still another source[101] notes that the government plans to construct a number of 1500-ton corvettes to be armed with surface-to-surface, surface-to-air, and anti-submarine weapons. South Africa's confidence, regarding its neighbors at least, is well-founded. All possess minuscule navies, primarily aging patrol ships from the colonial era. Given their preoccupation with domestic instability, this is not likely to change any time soon.

The Indian Ocean island republics also possess minuscule navies. Many in the West feared that the high potential for instability in some of them, combined with some recent leftist political victories, would result in governments more favorably inclined to the Soviet Union. This has not happened in Mauritius and the Seychelles, two states of particular concern on this score. Leaders in both countries recognize that the West offers far more economically than does the Soviet Union—and economic growth is the key to some kind of stable political order. Indeed, Mauritius has effectively dropped its demands for the incorporation of Diego Garcia, and the Seychelles is now allowing NATO warships to call without requiring them to guarantee that they have no nuclear armaments on board.[102]

A massive flow of arms has poured into the Horn of Africa over the past several years, though little has been spent on naval forces. Ethiopia, for example, has only a 1500-person navy and a handful of ships. Somalia has about 600 naval personnel, and its Soviet-supplied ships—mainly patrol craft—are likely to deteriorate unless replacements and refits can be arranged. Djibouti similarly has a tiny navy, but the stationing of French Foreign Legion troops and naval units there is security insurance against outside foes.

Egypt possesses a modest naval force, about one-half the personnel size of India's. However, with 16 submarines and 4 more on order, the Egyptian navy packs a considerably more potent sub-surface threat to hostile intruders than does the Indian navy. Most of Egypt's ships operate in the Mediterranean, where one perceived threat is the growing naval capabilities of Libya (most of it supplied by the Soviet Union), which now possesses 33 anti-ship guided-missile-carrying ships and 6 submarines, with 2 more on order.[103] On the Red Sea, Egypt, like Sudan, relies on land-based air defenses to protect its shores.

The oil-rich Arab states of Southwest Asia have poured enormous amounts of money into defensive systems since the oil price hikes of the early 1970s. Saudi Arabia, the richest of them, has the largest naval program, and it is nearing completion of a U.S.-designed naval expansion program. The principal new combatants included in the program are nine PGG-1–class missile boats and four missile corvettes armed with eight Harpoon missiles each.[104] In addition, Saudi Arabia has purchased four mine sweepers, eight landing craft, and some 35 coastal patrol boats. Moreover, two small frigates and two 10,475-ton replenishment oilers were delivered in 1986.[105]

The smaller Arab Persian Gulf states have all assembled navies built around missile-armed fast patrol boats. Perhaps the best in terms of training and indigenous technical capabilities is the 2000-man Omani navy, now rapidly moving away from British tutelage and taking full command of its own resources with Omani personnel. The acquisition of 2000-ton landing ships reflects a requirement for all-weather open-ocean capabilities along Oman's long Arabian Sea coastline. Oman is undoubtedly concerned about

South Yemen's Soviet-supplied navy, which includes a Ropucha-class LST, the only foreign fleet to receive it, and four smaller Polnochny-B–class landing ships.[106]

At the other end of the Persian Gulf, Kuwait's well-designed missile-equipped coastal force has not yet been challenged by Iran, even though Kuwait continues to serve as a major port for war items destined for Iraq. In 1987, Iran shelled Kuwaiti territory, undoubtedly to warn it to reduce the level of assistance. The Kuwaiti decision to seek superpower protection of its tankers underscores Kuwait's fears of even more damaging Iranian moves.

Iraq for its part has a modest blue-water navy on order, including four frigates and six corvettes armed with surface-to-surface and surface-to-air missiles, but they and other ships on order face the daunting task of transiting through a relatively narrow sea threatened by an implacable enemy. Even if those ships were to reach home ports, they would face the danger of attack from nearby Iranian airfields. The Iranian navy, once a significant force with blue-water capabilities (including three destroyers, four frigates, and four corvettes), suffers from lack of maintenance, personnel, and spare parts for its U.S.-supplied inventory. Despite its deteriorating condition, the Iranian Navy still has some punch and conceivably could assist the air force (possessing U.S.-supplied F-4s, F-5s, and F-14s) in attacks on selective targets in the Persian Gulf in retaliation against Iraq's attack, using AM-39 Exocet-equipped Super Etendard fighter bombers supplied by France, on shipping at Kharg Island. So far, however, Iran's navy has not ventured far out of port, but its Gulf neighbors fear Iranian use of Chinese-supplied Silk-worm missiles and attacks on shipping by patrol boats and by mine-laying operations.

India is the prominent exception to the essentially coastal navies mentioned so far. India is the only littoral state, other than Australia, to possess a projection capability—in the form of two aircraft carriers, missile destroyers, and ocean submarines. Possession of two replenishment ships, five support tankers, and one repair ship[107] enables India to sustain a naval task force in more distant waters of the Indian Ocean. The Navy continues to expand; its 1985–86 budget grew by 6.5 percent to $6.4 billion.[108] Among the recent acquisitions was a second aircraft carrier from Great Britain. There are enough fleet escorts to sustain a second carrier battle group. A fourth Soviet-built destroyer arrived in mid-1987, and two more are under construction.

The Indian navy's successful effort to bottle up the Pakistani navy in 1971 gave it a mission, and thus a powerful argument vis-à-vis the other branches of the armed forces for a larger share of the military budget. Still another incentive for expanding the navy was the perceived danger posed by the entry of the U.S.S. *Enterprise* into the Bay of Bengal in 1971. This incident, according to one Indian source, taught India two lessons: that the naval resources of a powerful outside state could be used to intimidate India and that such intimidation could be rendered largely ineffective if littoral states are determined to resist.[109] Since the early 1970s, the Indian navy has embarked on a steady program of expansion. In 1969, the navy ranked third among the services in total capital construction, but by 1974 the situation had reversed itself and the navy ranked first, retaining that position in capital expenditures ever since.[110] The Indian military services have undergone a modernization of equipment, requiring extensive foreign purchases, in the past several years. In December 1982, an agreement was signed with the Soviet Union that, according to some sources, might represent its largest single naval acquisition since World War II. Reportedly,[111] this purchase involved at least 16 ships, including three Kresta II–class "cruisers,"[112] three additional Kashin-class guided-missile destroyers, three or more guided-missile corvettes, four to six Natya-class ocean escort minesweepers, and three to five Foxtrot-class submarines. India has also made substantial non-Soviet purchases as well. In late 1981, for example, New Delhi signed an agreement with Howaldtswerke of West Germany for the construction of two Type-1500 submarines and the supply of "packages" for the building of two more submarines at Mazagon Shipyard in Bombay.[113]

These acquisitions suggest a mission somewhat greater than neutralizing the Pakistan navy in a possible future conflict. Of special interest is the possession of tankers and other elements of the capability to sustain a naval task force in distant waters of the Indian Ocean. However, the navy's precise blue-water role is apparently still the subject of internal debate, according to some analysts.[114] Nonetheless, the new acquisitions will give India the capability to extend its defensive perimeter against a possible challenge on the part of a major naval power. India's submarines could theoretically begin a forward defense posture well beyond the Andaman and Nicobar Islands to the east and to the west deep into the Arabian Sea. The Port Blair naval base in the Andamans is being upgraded, and new naval facilities are being built in the Laccadive islands and on Grand Nicobar island, just 80 nautical miles from Sumatra. An aircraft carrier group or even some destroyers and frigates working in tandem with the submarines would provide a capability superior to that of any littoral state and a serious concern to the naval forces of a major power. Closer-in defense would rely on additional frigates, corvettes, and fast patrol boats, all armed with Styx surface-to-surface missiles.

At present, the navy's functions seem to be to monitor the movements of big-power navies, to protect its Exclusive Economic Zone (EEZ), and to make it prohibitively costly for any power to challenge India's sea lanes or even India itself (what is referred to in Singapore as the "poison-shrimp" approach). Protection of the EEZ is increasingly the responsibility of India's growing coast guard, thus enhancing the navy's ability to engage in blue-water operations. Protection of the EEZ is a high-priority item for India, considering the vast area in its EEZ (about 800,000 square miles) and the oil, gas, and mineral wealth in this area, as well as India's large investment in exploiting such resources.

Sea control is possible against India's neighbors, assuming no other major naval power comes to their assistance (an unlikely scenario for at least another decade), if one assumes that the most likely candidate for that role is the PRC. Effective Chinese naval intervention on Pakistan's behalf is at least a decade or more away. India's goal in 1971, driving the enemy (Pakistan) from the sea, might change if India and Pakistan acquired (and were willing to use) nuclear weapons. In such a war, a slow-moving struggle for command of the sea is likely to be rendered pointless before it got under way. There has been considerable speculation that a limited conventional war might be fought at sea by nuclear powers, but the interests at stake in such a conflict would be so vital that it is hard to conceive of a situation in which the nuclear threshold would not be crossed.

Presently, any Indian effort at sea control beyond its immediate area is possible only with the acquiescence of major powers and other sub-regional navies. The latter, increasingly being outfitted with missile patrol boats, could deny to India such sea control in nearby waters if they decided to do so.

The Indian navy's ability to project power ashore at any distance is now quite limited. India has no independent naval infantry and has in its inventory six relatively small ex-Soviet Polnochny A and C–class LCTs, one ex-British LST-3, and four Indian-constructed LCUs.[115] Closer to home, amphibious operations would prove more practical due to the availability of land-based air support and shorter logistical lines.

Pakistan's naval forces, about one-third the personnel size of India's, is charged primarily with defending the country's Arabian Sea coastline and protecting the seaports of Karachi and Gwadar. Like almost all other Indian Ocean navies, Pakistan has acquired a fleet of fast patrol boats, some with a sea-to-sea missile capability. Memory of the successful 1971 Indian blockade of Karachi provided a strong incentive to invest in such warships, and their possession by Pakistan makes any future blockade considerably more costly. In addition, the defense of Pakistani ports is augmented by the acquisition of some 12 Mirage-50 aircraft configured to launch the Exocet AM-39 air-to-surface missile.[116]

Pakistan's two Agosta-class submarines provide it with the only true open-ocean patrol capacity for anti-submarine and anti-surface warfare operations, but their limited number reduces their usefulness in any protracted conflict. The six Gearing-class destroyers purchased from the United States since 1977 also enable Pakistan to extend the perimeter of defense. However, a major weakness of these destroyers has been their lack of surface-to-surface missile capability, presumably resolved with the purchase of Harpoon SSMs from the United States.

The navies of Southeast Asia, with the exception of the Philippines, have experienced considerable development over the past decade. ASEAN navies have focused on acquiring missile craft and light frigates, both of which are potent weapons in the congested waterways of Southeast Asia. In addition, Malaysia, Indonesia, and Singapore have improved coastal defenses with the purchase of A-4 and F-5 aircraft, and several Southeast Asian states have either decided to purchase F-16s or are considering such a purchase.

There are several reasons for this naval expansion. The states of the region fear that traditional alliances no longer represent the commitment they once did. Still another reason seems to be the lingering ASEAN/Vietnamese tension. Moreover, there is a growing worry among ASEAN states regarding the increased activity of Soviet warships in contiguous waters. This is one sub-region where the states want the U.S. navy to stay close at hand. U.S. deployments to the Indian Ocean have aroused concern that the United States would permanently degrade its presence in Southeast Asia. Finally, these states share the nearly universal desire among littoral states to protect their extensive EEZ. They are all concerned that political instability in the Philippines might work against the forthcoming consideration of U.S. bases in that country. Subic Bay is the major support facility of the Seventh Fleet, and the Clark Air Force facility is the home of the Thirteenth Air Force. These facilities are important symbols to the region of a continuing U.S. presence.

Indonesia has been the only Southeast Asian state with ambitions to project power far beyond its immediate area. President Sukarno spoke repeatedly of adopting a "revolutionary posture" against the outside world and against the "encirclement" by "old established forces" of imperialism, and he was determined to get the means to back up his assertiveness.[117] Besides threatening Indonesia's immediate neighbors, Sukarno also made implicit and explicit threats against India, threats that caused New Delhi to consider more closely its own maritime defenses. Indonesia offered naval vessels to Pakistan and made some vague threats regarding the Andaman Islands.

The Soviet Union, then assiduously cultivating Sukarno, provided him the means to expand the Indonesian navy. It provided Indonesia with a $450 million loan in 1961 for military equipment at a very low rate of interest. In February 1960, during Khrushchev's visit to Indonesia, Sukarno requested Soviet help to develop the offensive capability of his armed forces.[118] One heavy cruiser, six destroyers, 12 diesel-powered submarines, seven frigates, eight coastal escorts, 12 Komar-class missile boats, and various smaller boats were purchased on favorable credit terms from the Soviet Union and were promptly delivered, together with TU-16 medium bombers armed with air-to-surface missiles, as well as MiG-21 interceptors for the Indonesian air force. The sale of this military equipment involved items that had not been granted to any other country, and hundreds of Indonesians were trained in Soviet military academies. Such assistance enabled Indonesia to assemble the largest navy among Indian Ocean littoral states—and one that caused considerable concern at the time in India, Australia and, elsewhere.

Following the overthrow of Sukarno, the Indonesian navy was allowed to stagnate (if not deteriorate) because of the severe budgetary constraints forced on the succeeding government by runaway inflation. Continued supplies from the Kremlin after the 1965 coup would have been unlikely in any case given the strongly anti-communist sentiments (both domestically and internationally) of the new regime.

The naval missions of Indonesia are now limited to patrolling the EEZ more effectively and to the defense of the home islands. These defensive efforts are almost entirely directed toward the north and east—and not west toward the Indian Ocean, though Indonesians are concerned about Indian development of military facilities on the Andaman Islands. Considering the geographic spread of the country, these are both staggering and costly tasks. The two missions overlap somewhat in the defense of the sea area around the Natuna Islands, which face the Vietnamese coast and are subject to conflicting claims between the two powers. To enhance its ability to patrol this area, Indonesia has begun conducting naval exercises in the area. To protect the approaches to the home islands, Jakarta reportedly has decided to build three forward air defense bases: one on Sumatra to defend the western approaches, another on Sulawesi to defend the center, and a third in Irian Jaya for the east.[119]

Australia is the other Indian Ocean power besides India capable of power projection. For obvious reasons, a major focus of its security concern is Southeast Asia. Australia's major trade routes pass through this area, and trade with the ASEAN states is growing rapidly. Moreover, a hostile power could stage attacks on Australia from the area. A fundamental strategic objective of Australia (and New Zealand) is to prevent any hostile power from acquiring naval and air bases in Southeast Asia, and Soviet bases in Vietnam are perceived to pose a potential threat. The deployment of the *Minsk* carrier group and an Ivan Rogov amphibious ship to the Soviet Pacific fleet add to Australia's concern.

The Soviet presence in Vietnam provides a convincing political rationale for maintaining Australian participation in the FPDA, the primary instrument for Australia and New Zealand to pursue forward defense strategies.[120] In a series of meetings in Singapore in late 1980 and early 1981, the six FPDA countries announced their intention to upgrade significantly joint military cooperation and joint naval exercises. In June 1981, the first of the projected naval exercises—"Operation Starfish 81"—took place off the coast of Malaysia and in July 1981, "Operation Platypus 81" off the coast of Brisbane.

The Soviet invasion of Afghanistan added to Australian security apprehensions. There is evidence that the previous Australian government reacted to the Vietnamese and Soviet action by seriously rethinking the country's defense strategy. Mr. Ian Sinclair, the former Minister of Defence, in an address to the Australian Defence Association on November 19, 1982, stated that "Forward defence and the maintenance of close defence associations, through [the] Defence Cooperation Program and alliance arrangements [are seen] as strategically essential."[121] This was the first official pronouncement of a "forward defence posture" since the Vietnam war. Besides the naval exercises noted above, the Fraser government deployed maritime forces to the Indian Ocean, involved Australia in biannual ANZUS air and naval maneuvers in the Indian Ocean, permitted U.S. use of Australian facilities for B-52 aircraft, constructed patrol bases at Darwin and Cairns, expanded the army reserve from 22,000 to 30,000, and decided to construct a forward airfield at Derby and to replace Australia's tactical fighter force.

At the same time, there is a significant body of opinion in both Australia and New Zealand that wants to keep ANZUS in a limited geographic area. The 1983 victory of the Australian Labor Party (followed the next year by the victory of New Zealand's Labor Party) strengthened this view at the official level. Labor Party politicians have tended to focus on an independent capacity in an effort to preserve the country's options. Mr. Bill Hayden, now the Foreign Minister, wrote before the 1983 Labor victory that "short of nuclear war, there is a reasonable possibility that in any future conflict, Australia will have to rely on its own resources to defend itself. The first responsibility of Government is to defend Australia against any encroachment on its territorial sovereignty and it is not good enough to live in hope that someone [read the United States] will do it for us."[122] This statement underscores the understanding that each ANZUS member state will respond to a threat against other members only after observing constitutional processes. The circumstances of the threat would condition the response. A direct Soviet threat would probably elicit a full military commitment, but a threat to a member state from other countries might well include a range of responses such as diplomatic action, political and economic sanctions, and military logistical support.

Nonetheless, the Labor government has in fact followed, with only minor variations, the same general policy on security matters as the preceding Fraser government. For example, the much-heralded review of the ANZUS Treaty in Washington, D.C., in July 1983 (the first comprehensive review since the formation of ANZUS), did not result in any weakening of the Treaty provisions. But, then, ANZUS has proved to be quite flexible, allowing for joint action as the need arises and also permitting each ANZUS member to act independently or in some other security relationship.

The continued commitment to ANZUS on the part of Australia and New Zealand will be conditioned by their sense of threat. On this score, New Zealand, with few apparent threats, has felt confident enough to challenge the present functioning of ANZUS by denying entry to U.S. (and other) warships that refuse to disclose whether they carry nuclear weapons. The U.S. refusal to compromise on the non-disclosure policy has resulted in problems between the United States and New Zealand. In early 1985, the Labor government of Prime Minister David Lange, elected in July 1984, denied entry to the U.S. destroyer *Buchanan* because Washington would not deviate from its standard policy of neither denying nor confirming the presence of such weapons. The United States responded to New Zealand's action by canceling its participation in ANZUS and joint U.S.-New Zealand naval maneuvers and by curtailing the sharing of intelligence information. Secretary of State George Shultz told a U.S. Senate committee on February 21, 1985, that New Zealand "had taken a walk" on ANZUS.[123] The loss of defense cooperation, including opportunities to exercise with the U.S. Navy, is forcing the New Zealand Navy into a more self-reliant posture, including the acquisition of a replenishment tanker.

The Labor Party in Australia also has a sizeable minority that favors similar restrictions on ships carrying nuclear weapons, but the majority group has refused to take any move that might undermine ANZUS. Nor has Canberra restricted the continued U.S. use of vital defense communications facilities.[124] Australia, closer to Southeast Asia and with a larger regional perspective of its interests than New Zealand, has been rather cautious in taking any steps that would undermine the viability of ANZUS. Indeed, a traditional Australian foreign policy plank has been to assure itself of the support of a major outside power.

Regarding the Indian Ocean, the Australian Labor government has signaled its intention to play a more assertive role in the Indian Ocean, reflecting both a concern for security of the Christmas and Cocos islands as well as enhancing Australian influence among littoral states.[125] This effort appears to be part of Labor's effort to limit the geographic boundaries of ANZUS to the Southwest Pacific and the Western Australian coastline. Foreign Minister Hayden spelled out a "new" Indian Ocean policy in a June 1984 speech to the Australian Institute of International Affairs in Perth. He pointed out that Australia intended to adopt a higher profile among littoral states, particularly India and the Indian Ocean island republics. He noted that Canberra would expand its cultural activities as well as provide greater assistance to littoral states. As part of its Indian Ocean policy, Australia has established a permanent diplomatic mission in Mauritius, and has instituted a regular program of naval visits to littoral states. Hayden also defended the Australian-U.S. communications base on grounds that (1) Australia protected its interests by a new agreement with the United States involving "timely judgments about the significance for our interests of the use of the [sic] facility" and (2) Australia had concluded that U.S. SLBMs (which can receive communications from such defense facilities) are a second-strike system and thus not destabilizing.[126] Only two days before Hayden's speech, Canberra announced its decision to initiate regular deployments of Australian warships to the Indian Ocean.

Despite Australian statements of intentions, its Labor government has not appropriated funds to give Australia the means to project significant power into the Indian Ocean. This is underscored by the decision to delay consideration of the purchase of an aircraft carrier to replace the *Melbourne*.

A Superpower "Rivalry"?

The United States in 1979 established continuous supremacy in the Indian Ocean because of its fears regarding access to Persian Gulf oil, and American naval supremacy is not likely to be seriously challenged by the Soviet Union over the next decade or even beyond. On the other hand, there is no way the West can challenge the Soviet position on land as the most powerful Indian Ocean hinterland state. The Soviet occupation of Afghanistan, coming in the wake of the overthrow of the Shah, elevated Southwest Asia to one of the three major security concerns of the West. Despite the withdrawal, it will take considerable confidence-building efforts to alter this perspective. Within the United States itself, there is heated debate over how much is enough to serve as a deterrent to Soviet assertiveness, but there is little debate over the critical importance of Southwest Asia. The Soviet Union, for its part, will undoubtedly continue to maintain a significant naval presence in the Indian Ocean to probe for opportunities to enhance its political influence. Regional animosities and domestic turmoil will continue to offer possibilities on this score.

A second trend that has emerged is the growing perception among littoral states of the need for greater regional cooperation, both for faster economic growth and, in some cases, for enhanced military security. The United States actively backs this trend as a stabilizing factor, while the Soviet Union has taken a much more ambiguous view, because such regional efforts, in some cases, are a reaction to the assertiveness of the Kremlin's regional allies and in part because the Soviet Union has made its major political inroads in countries that need military support against domestic or regional rivals.

Despite the large-scale Soviet military sales to India, India clearly does not fit the model of a "needy" receiver of Soviet assistance. It is too large, too powerful vis-à-vis its neighbors, and too politically integrated, in my view, to fit. Only in the worst-case scenario of a China-Pakistan-U.S. axis directed against India would New Delhi be strongly tempted to move significantly closer to Moscow, but I think such a scenario is highly unlikely. I cannot imagine a realistic scenario in which any of these three powers would see advantages in earning the enmity of a country as powerful as India.

A third trend has been the expansion of the navies of the littoral states. This will continue as littoral states seek to protect their EEZs, to protect themselves against other regional states perceived as hostile, and to ward off unwanted great-power interference.

Regarding the superpower presence in the Indian Ocean, I think much conventional discussion is off the mark.

"Superpower rivalry" is a concept often employed by analysts in Indian Ocean littoral states, including India,[127] to explain the naval deployments of the United States and the Soviet Union. The concept assumes that U.S. and Soviet motives are governed largely—if not almost exclusively—by an interaction between the two. However, there are some problems with this approach.

The Soviet naval buildup in the Indian Ocean, occurring during the height of détente, appears to have been motivated far more by its desire to enhance its political influence, to counter China, and to establish political parity with the United States in the area, rather than by strategic considerations involving the Americans. Even Soviet surges, which are generally accepted as a response to U.S. activities in the Indian Ocean, seem to have been motivated largely by political considerations. For example, the Soviet dispatch of additional warships to the Indian Ocean at the time of the deployment of the U.S.S. *Enterprise* in 1971 seems to have been intended to enhance its political influence in India (and elsewhere) rather than to challenge the United States, despite brave words that the Soviet navy would not allow American naval intervention on Pakistan's behalf. The Soviet ships were several days behind those of the United States and no real military challenge to the U.S. task force. The Soviet action on this occasion was a spectacular political success in that the Kremlin gained enormous goodwill in India, even leading some analysts in India to speculate at the time that the Soviet naval presence in the Indian Ocean was a beneficial balancer of the United States.

The Soviet Union had many other opportunities to enhance its political influence even earlier (e.g., exploiting Western ties to South Africa and Israel), but a shortage of warships probably explains why Moscow waited so long to establish a permanent naval presence in the Indian Ocean. The present, modest Soviet ASW capabilities further support the conclusion that political considerations, rather than a strategic anti-SSBN motive, governs its decision to retain a permanent naval presence in the Indian Ocean.[128]

Interpreting the term "rivalry" narrowly, the superpowers have never really been rivals on the sea in the Indian Ocean. The Soviet Union was most active politically and militarily during the 1970s, when the United States signaled a lack of interest, which may have created the impression in the Kremlin and elsewhere that Moscow could act with relative impunity in the Third World. Since 1979, the United States has reversed itself and established, at sea in any case, overwhelming superiority vis-à-vis the Soviet Union. The Soviets have not tried to match this, though they have not left the field entirely to the Americans. The Kremlin has reacted by demonstrating greater caution.

The United States, for its part, began to focus on the area around the Persian Gulf in 1973, and for reasons of a stable energy supply that were only marginally related to the Soviet Union. Even the failure of the 1977–78 Indian Ocean Naval Arms Limitation Talks had more to do with a deterioration of superpower relations on a global level than with incompatibilities within the Indian Ocean. The Soviet occupation of Afghanistan in late 1979 did cause the United States and other Western powers to regard the Soviet Union as the most powerful hinterland state, with the capacity to use its land-based air and ground forces within its borders to challenge Western interests. However, the responding buildup of a U.S. naval presence in the northwest quadrant of the Indian Ocean had very little to do with the Soviet *naval* presence in the Indian Ocean. The United States wanted a sufficient naval capability to deter a Soviet thrust across the border, especially into Iran. The Soviet navy in the Indian Ocean is not the challenge, at least not now.

It is also unlikely that either side was motivated to fill a "vacuum" presumably brought about by the British decision to withdraw from "east of Suez." The slow-moving Soviet bureaucracy had surely already spent considerable time planning its dispatch in the mid- and late-1960s, and this process undoubtedly took place before the actual British decision to withdraw. The United States did not consider any move at the time to replace the British, nor did the Americans make a responding move to the initial Soviet deployments to the Indian Ocean in the late 1960s. The Nixon Doctrine in effect assumed that the United States had no interest in the Indian Ocean worth a military deployment. As noted above, the initial planning regarding Diego Garcia had almost nothing to do with the Soviet Union, but was linked to Chinese threats against India. In any case, it was not until the late 1970s that the United States began to think seriously of Diego Garcia as anything more than a communications facility.

Still a third reason given to explain the naval buildup of the superpowers (and a notion with considerable support in India[129]) is that the Soviet Union and the United States dispatched their navies (and other forces) to intervene in the affairs of littoral states. Regarding the United States, the possibility of intervention in the Persian Gulf was discussed by some prominent officials in the wake of the 1973–74 oil crisis, including references to intervention by the secretaries of Defense and State at the time. These references understandably aroused apprehensions about what the United States would do. They are still referred to in the literature. But this option was never considered seriously in Washington. At that time, any such move would have been politically impossible, given the popular response to the Vietnam experience. In addition, any such effort would probably have been accompanied by an effort to damage the oil fields and pipeline system, which would defeat the purpose of intervention, to say nothing of the damage to larger diplomatic objectives.

Intervention "by invitation" (which usually involves exploiting opportunities rather than manipulating events), however, is the more probable scenario. Included in this are arms assistance, the supply of proxy troops, and threats to hostile neighbors of friendly littoral states. Both the United States and the Soviet Union have engaged in politico-military diplomacy to reinforce relations with friendly states as a way of building closer political relations and gaining access to military facilities. Such opportunities are likely to continue presenting themselves to both superpowers as long as sub-regional states are unable to resolve the disputes among themselves. Kuwaiti requests for protection of its tankers in the Persian Gulf is a recent example. Besides seeking to keep open the sea lanes, the American agreement to do so was surely motivated by a desire to minimize Soviet influence (after an initial rejection by the United States, Kuwait had turned to the Soviet Union) and to rebuild confidence eroded by the Iran-Contra affair.

Naval coercive diplomacy may have declining utility to major naval powers. Many observers point out the diminishing efficacy of the navy as an instrument of pressure against smaller states.[130] In the case of the Indian Ocean, an increasing number of states are equipped with advanced military technology, including missile-armed fast patrol boats, sophisticated land-based aircraft, and submarines to challenge threats to the seas off their coasts. The costs of any such venture are becoming increasingly high as such acquisitions grow. Western intervention by force presently seems conceivable only in the Persian Gulf, and even there only in a worst-case situation of a successful and sustained oil boycott and/or a blockade of a key choke point that resulted in a severe blow to the economies of the industrial West. The chances of such a sustained blockade now seem rather remote since the oil-producing states, even the most radical and anti-Western, need to sell their oil to finance their own development plans. (Iran must sell its only major product—oil—

to finance its war with Iraq.) In addition, the industrial states have extended the time frame within which they could sustain a blockade, in the unlikely event one occurred, by reducing their dependence on Persian Gulf oil through more effective conservation methods and by stockpiling oil reserves. Even though the number of attacks on Persian Gulf shipping increased in 1987, it had no effect on oil prices.

Still another factor inhibiting coercive diplomacy is the progressive enclosure of the oceans.[131] Given prevailing doctrines concerning the limits of territorial rights of archipelagoes and exclusive economic zones, perhaps one-third of what under the old three-mile limit was regarded as high seas may cease to be so in the future. Whatever resistance is expressed in some quarters to this enclosure, a new sense of maritime frontiers is developing that will make coercive naval diplomacy more difficult to carry out.

Indian apprehension regarding intervention, broadly considered, seems to be a fear that U.S. arms assistance to Pakistan will result in that country becoming a participant in a U.S. strategic consensus, which could undermine Indian security in a number of ways. According to one prominent Indian analyst,[132] Pakistani involvement in the recurrent Middle East crises (1) could "bring active cold war confrontation to the subcontinent" or (2) a Pakistani leader's misreading of "the international balance of power could lead him to misinterpret the degree of support he could count on from extra-regional powers, and venture against India."

While there is little doubt that arms assistance is intended to reduce Soviet influence in the littoral states, including Pakistan, it has not been intended to threaten India, or weaken it, or reduce its influence regionally or internationally. Moreover, U.S. official opinion clearly does not perceive the U.S.-supplied arms to Pakistan as a threat to the existing balance of power on the sub-continent. On the matter of U.S. bases, it is highly unlikely that Pakistan under present circumstances would even consider a U.S. base/facility, even were the offer to be made. Such a move would almost certainly drive India closer to the Soviet Union, something that would undermine both U.S. and Pakistani interests as well as make the Kremlin more intransigent about leaving Afghanistan. In any case, tensions in Indo-Pakistani relations appear to have relatively little to do with the superpower ties to either, and much more to do with issues arising out of the bilateral relationship. Moreover, I cannot envisage India lining up with the Soviet Union in an attack against Pakistan (or vice versa), just as I think it implausible that the United States (or China) would assist a Pakistani venture against India.

It is conceivable that Pakistan's Middle East friends might provide it military assistance in the form of arms and money during periods of tension with India. However, this would not have much effect on the sea, since they have little to offer (or could do little) that would enable Pakistan to deny India sea control. These countries possess essentially coastal navies.

The chances of an anti-Soviet China-U.S.-Pakistan axis, which might have implications for the Indian Ocean, are remote in any time frame that I think prudent to talk about (5–10 years). It is remote, I believe, not because international events could not lead to enhanced Pakistani cooperation with China, but primarily because of the probable slow rate of the Chinese blue-water naval expansion over the next decade. Whatever warships China adds to its blue-water fleet are likely to be deployed in the East and South China seas to countr the growing Soviet naval deployments there. A larger Chinese blue-water fleet might, however, enable the United States to deploy additional ships to the Indian Ocean, were that considered necessary (as would a buildup of a blue-water Japanese navy).

The expanded deployment of the superpower navies in the early 1970s appears to have been a major Indian incentive to expand the capabilities of its navy, as was the expansion of the Iranian navy during the same period. The Indian navy, while no match for the superpowers, could make it costly for either (or for any regional state) to challenge Indian maritime objectives (e.g., trade routes, protection of its EEZ). The 1971 *Enterprise* incident, frequently mentioned in the Indian literature, clearly made an impact on Indian thinking about the potential for coercive diplomacy against it, and probably was a compelling reason for its decision to create a navy that could engage in sea denial activities at considerable distances from the Indian mainland. Any establishment of foreign bases in South Asia or nearby island republics would undoubtedly be perceived in India as a security threat and thus a good reason for expanding its navy still further. In addition, India would oppose such a move on grounds that its neighbors might become more intransigent in the conduct of their diplomacy with India. This sensitivity was reflected in a side letter to the July 29 Indo–Sri Lankan accord stipulating that Sri Lanka not permit its port facilities to be used in a way "prejudicial" to Indian interests.

An expansion of the Indian navy, in my view, is not a threat to the United States. Indeed, the Director of U.S. Naval Intelligence, in testimony before a congressional committee in 1983, specifically excluded India as a threat to U.S. naval forces.[133] Rather, a case could be made that a more capable Indian navy would enhance Indian confidence about its ability to meet challenges and thus reduce the likelihood of a perceived necessity to develop closer security ties with the Soviet Union. Such an expansion, however, could well undermine India's Indian Ocean Zone of Peace (IOZP) objectives (reducing external military presences while preserving its own options), because some littoral states already suspicious of Indian intentions would be even less agreeable to withdrawal of non-littoral naval forces. Likely reactions from other states might include seeking to keep one or the other superpower in the Indian Ocean, advocating arms reductions among the littoral states themselves, and increasing naval expenditures. In addition, the IOZP concept itself might well receive less public backing from many littoral states. Up to now, it has had almost universal backing as a long-range goal among littoral states since its introduction at the 1970 meeting of non-aligned states in Lusaka.

Even without an expansion of the Indian navy, the IOZP proposal must overcome some major hurdles. There are already differences among littoral states concerning what should be addressed in the IOZP question (e.g., Does it only limit foreign forces or does it also involve the navies of littoral states? Does it forbid nuclear weapons, and if so, only those of non-littoral states, or does it include littoral states as well?). New Delhi surely would not be enthusiastic over an IOZP regime that involved restricting the military and nuclear capabilities of the littoral states. Another (and related) problem regarding littoral support of the IOZP notion is that most littoral states do not perceive the Indian Ocean as a whole, and there is no one nation whose leadership on this (or other) subjects would be accepted. Far more important to most littoral states are events in their immediate vicinity. Indeed, many of them desire a close-by superpower presence as a guarantee against a hostile neighbor(s) or the perceived threat of a superpower.

Regarding superpower approaches to the IOZP issue, the Soviet Union will come out looking better than the United States in public relations terms since Moscow would lose relatively little by reducing its naval presence in the Indian Ocean. The Soviet Union's geographic proximity would enable it to continue exerting pressure on Southwest Asia even if its navy were totally withdrawn from the Indian Ocean. Because of this asymmetry of forces between the United States and the Soviet Union, Washington would be very reluctant to withdraw its naval forces from the Indian Ocean. It is not likely to do so until there is a major change in U.S.-Soviet bilateral relations and until the threat to oil resources subsides. The U.S. reluctance to support an IOZP resolution will undoubtedly cause continuing differences with India, though I doubt that such differences will be on the front burner. U.S. naval forces are focused on the Persian Gulf and the approaches to it—not on South Asia. Pakistan is peripheral on that score. Facilities at the mouth of or in the Persian Gulf itself are far more desirable from a military standpoint than Karachi or Gwadar. Regarding R and R, ports in Pakistan (or other South Asian states) do not offer the kinds of entertainment U.S. sailors would desire. Finally, the chances of the United States deploying SLBMs to the Indian Ocean are receding as SLBM range increases and ASW technology improves.

The United States and India share an interest in keeping open sea lanes of communication and ensuring unimpeded access to Gulf oil. A case could be made positing at least tacit Indian approval of U.S. efforts to safeguard these mutual interests through naval (though not ground) activity. Should there occur frequent random sinking of tankers, causing insurance rates to go up, perhaps prohibitively for many countries, or should some countries (or labor unions) react to uncertainty by prohibiting trade, shortages would develop and prices would go up.[134] The United States possesses one of the few navies in the area with the technological capability of responding to such developments, and it is not totally implausible that India would see its interests served by U.S. mine-clearing operations and by the protection of tankers, some of which might be Indian, from attack. It is instructive that India has not protested the naval protection offered Kuwaiti oil tankers in the Persian Gulf.

Notes

1. The left wing of the Labor Party was concerned about the costs, while the right within the Conservative Party favored a more Europe-oriented defense establishment.

2. Noted in K. R. Singh, *The Indian Ocean: Big Power Presence and Local Response* (Columbia, Mo.: South Asia Books, 1978), p. 54.

3. The three external powers promised to contribute one battalion each to an integrated force to be known as ANZUK. The external powers also contributed to plans for the air and naval defense of the two regional states. In the mid-1970s, however, Australia, New Zealand, and Great Britain decided to reduce their forces in Singapore and Malaysia, retaining a minimum necessary to demonstrate a commitment to honor the agreement. After the escalation of tensions in Southeast Asia in the wake of the Vietnamese invasion of Kampuchea, the FPDA states have attempted to breathe new life into the agreement.

4. A comprehensive description of U.S. submarine Trident developments in James John Tritten, "The Trident System: Submarines, Missiles and Strategic Doctrine," *Naval War College Review*, January–February 1983, pp. 61–74.

5. The Kremlin leadership, however, did not demonstrate interest in the other arms control measures brought to Moscow by Secretary of State Cyrus Vance. Moscow probably accepted NALT because it was the only proposal offering an unambiguous advantage to the Soviets and one that critics of NALT were quick to point out.

6. *FBIS USSR*, April 16, 1984, p. aai. From Moscow TASS 0938 GMT, April 14, 1984.

7. U.S. Senate, Subcommittee on Military Construction of the Committee on Armed Forces; 93rd Congress, 2nd Session; July 10, 11, 12, 18, 1974; p. 106.

8. William F. Hickman, "Soviet Naval Policy in the Indian Ocean," *Naval Institute Proceedings*, August 1979, p. 42.

9. Cited in Dieter Braun, *Indian Ocean: Region of Conflict or 'Zone of Peace'?*, trans. from the German by Carol Geldart and Kathleen Llanware (London: Hurst and Company, 1983), p. 48.

10. Elmo R. Zumwalt, Jr., analyzes the expansion of the Soviet navy under Gorshkov's leadership in "Gorshkov and His Navy," *Orbis*, Fall 1980, pp. 491–500. Figures for the increasing number of ship days from James M. McConnell and Bradford Dismukes, "Soviet Diplomacy of Force in the Third World," *Problems of Communism*, January–February 1979, p. 17.

11. Geoffrey Jukes, "The Indian Ocean in Soviet Naval Policy," Adelphi Paper No. 87 (London: International Institute for Strategic Studies, 1972), p. 22.

12. Information in the following paragraphs is drawn largely from Stephen S. Kaplan, *Diplomacy of Power: Soviet Armed Forces as a Political Instrument* (Washington, D.C.: The Brookings Institution, 1981), pp. 176 ff.

13. With the termination of the British security relationships in the Gulf, the United States on December 23, 1971, concluded an executive agreement with the government of Bahrain for the continued use of the port facilities there. This was renewed in a somewhat modified form in 1977.

14. Probably the best study to date of the growing U.S. involvement in the Indian Ocean is Gary Sick, "The Evolution of US Strategy and the Indian Ocean,"

58   SUPERPOWER RIVALRY IN THE INDIAN OCEAN

in Alvin Z. Rubenstein, ed., *The Great Game: Rivalry in the Persian Gulf and South Asia* (New York: Praeger Publishers, 1983), pp. 49–80.

15. The war ended, however, before the United States had to make a final decision on using the air power on the U.S.S. *Enterprise* on India's behalf.

16. Sick, op. cit., p. 55.

17. The doctrine had its only practical application in the Persian Gulf region, where the United States relied on Iran and Saudi Arabia to maintain stability.

18. Testimony of Ronald I. Spiers before the House of Representatives, Subcommittee on National Security Policy and Scientific Development of the Committee on Foreign Affairs; 92nd Congress, 2nd Session; July 20, 22, 27, 28, 1971; p. 165.

19. Ibid., 171–173.

20. Spiers, op. cit., pp. 183–184.

21. Part of submission of statement by Senator Claiborne Pell, inserted into U.S. Senate Hearings before the Subcommittee on Military Construction of the Committee of Armed Services; 93rd Congress, 2nd Session; July 10, 11, 12, 18, 1974; p. 491.

22. U.S. Senate, Subcommittee on Construction of the Committee of the Armed Services; 93rd Congress, 2nd Session; July 10, 11, 12, 18, 1974; p. 138.

23. Data contained in Message from National Military Command Center, submitted into the record of U.S. Senate, Subcommittee on Construction of the Committee of the Armed Services; 93rd Congress, 2nd Session; July 10, 11, 12, 18, 1974; p. 511.

24. Sick, op. cit., p. 65.

25. Information from U.S. Senate, Committee on the Armed Services; Military Procurements Supplemental Fiscal Year 1974; 93rd Congress, 2nd Session; March 12, 1974; pp. 42–61.

26. J. P. Anand, "Diego Garcia Base," *IDSA Journal*, July–September 1979, pp. 58–85. The article provides a good summary of the Indian reaction to the base.

27. Ibid., p. 71.

28. Ibid., p. 72.

29. Submission of Professor Guy Pauker to House of Representatives, Subcommittee on National Security Policy and Scientific Developments of the Committee on Foreign Affairs; 92nd Congress, 1st Session; July 20, 22, 27, 28, 1971; p. 225.

30. Admiral Gene R. LaRocque, whose arguments set out here were included in the April 14, 1974, issue of his periodical, *The Defense Monitor*.

31. His doctrines are incorporated in three books published between 1963 and 1966, reprinted in *An Introduction to Strategy; Deterrence and Strategy; Strategy of Action* (London: Faber and Faber, 1967).

32. A leading navy spokesman of the "indirect strategy" is Admiral Joire-Noulens. See his "Reflexions sur les missions de la marine," *Armees d'Aujourd'hui* (July 1975), and "Quelle marine et pourquoi fair des le temps de paix," *Defense Nationale*, July 1976.

33. Keith Shreves, "French Frigate 'Babry' at Sea," *Asian Defense Journal*, March 1984, pp. 66–67. For a discussion of the French buildup in the wake of the Iran-Iraq tanker war, see Ronald O'Rourke, "Persian Gulf: U.S. Military Operations" *Library of Congress, Congressional Research Service*, December 23, 1987, pp. 8–11.

34. James F. Kelly, "Naval Deployments in the Indian Ocean," *Naval Institute Proceedings*, May 1983, pp. 174, 176–189.

35. After 1980, Chinese analysts wrote about the "equidistance" of China between the United States and the Soviet Union. However, the continuing convergence of Chinese and U.S. views regarding the Soviet threat in East Asia surely motivated Premier Zhao Ziyang to declare during his 1984 visit to the United States that China's "independent" foreign policy did not imply "equidistance" between the two superpowers. *FBIS China,* January 11, 1984, p. B11.

36. See "The Military Balance 1983–84," *Air Force Magazine,* December 1983, p. 111; and M. Weisskopf, "China Fires a Missile from a Sub," *International Herald Tribune,* October 18, 1982, p. 1.

37. "The Military Balance 1983–84," op. cit.

38. G. Jacobs, "Chinese Naval Force Requirements: The Next Decade," *Asian Defense Journal,* September 1982, pp. 40–46.

39. A systematic study of the various scenarios under which the Chinese might consider deployment to the Indian Ocean in Yaacob Vertzberger, "China in South Asia: Convergence of Interests with the United States?," an unpublished paper presented to the Regional Seminar in Chinese Studies, Berkeley, California, April 6–7, 1984, pp. 28–36.

40. The material in the following two paragraphs drawn from *Jane's Fighting Ships* 1983–84 (Boston: Van Nostrand Reinhold Co., Inc., 1983), p. 95; Paul Wettern, "The PLA Navy," in *Defense: China 1982,* Supplement of *Defense,* nos. 1–2 (1982), pp. 37–59; Bruce Swanson, *Eighth Voyage of the Dragon: A History of China's Quest for Sea Power* (Annapolis: Naval Institute Press, 1982), pp. 277–278; *Far Eastern Economic Review,* June 11, 1982, pp. 21–25.

41. Testimony of Rear Admiral John L. Butts, U.S. Navy, Director of Naval Intelligence to Committee on Armed Services, U.S. Senate; 98th Congress, 1st Session, pt. 6, "Sea Power and Force Projection"; March 14, 22, 23, 24, April 6, 7, 1983; p. 2933.

42. James W. Houck, "The Chinese Navy's Prospects for Growth," *Naval Institute Proceedings,* March 1981, p. 75.

43. Material in this paragraph taken from *Defense of Japan 1983* (Tokyo: Defense Agency, 1983), pp. 321–332; *Soviet Military Power 1984* (Washington, D.C.: G.P.O., 1984), p. 50.

44. According to one study looking at the effects of a complete disruption of oil supplies from the Persian Gulf on seven industrialized states, such a disruption in 1980 would have caused crude oil prices to increase from a base of $30/barrel to as high as $300/barrel. Production of all goods and services would have declined between 12 and 27 percent. *Western Vulnerability to Disruption of Persian Gulf Oil Supplies: US Interests and Options,* Congressional Research Service Report 83–24F (March 24, 1984).

45. For a discussion of the Carter Doctrine and its subsequent elaboration, see William R. Brown, "Middle East Policy and Gulf Defense," *Middle East Insight,* January/February 1983, pp. 39–44. The Carter Doctrine is not a totally new U.S. expression of concern regarding the security of the Persian Gulf region. It was foreshadowed by the March 9, 1957, Congressional Joint Resolution to Promote Peace and Stability in the Middle East (PL 85–7, Jt. Res. 117)—sometimes referred to as the "Eisenhower Doctrine"—affirming the independence and integrity of those nations judged "vital" to the national interest of the United States and authorizing the use of troops to cope with a communist aggression against them. Bilateral agreements incorporating this pledge were worked out with Iran, Pakistan, and Turkey in 1959. However, the Eisenhower Doctrine goes into effect only after

a presidential judgment, including presumably a consideration of the War Powers Act of 1973. The precise wording of section 2 of the Joint resolution, the operative clause, is that "if the President determines the necessity thereof, the United States is prepared to use armed forces to assist any such nation or group of such nations requesting assistance against armed aggression from any country controlled by international communism: provided that such employment shall be consonant with the treaty obligations of the United States and with the Constitution of the United States."

46. For discussion, see Brown op. cit., p. 39.

47. Secretary of Defense Harold Brown's *Defense Annual Report* to the Congress for FY 1982 was inserted into the record of U.S. Senate Committee on the Armed Services; 97th Congress, 1st Session; January 28, 1981; pp. 83–422.

48. Ibid., p. 104.

49. Ibid., pp. 172–173.

50. Ibid., p. 172.

51. A review of the initial steps taken to create a rapid deployment force in Lewis C. Sowell, Jr., *Base Development of the Rapid Deployment Force: A Window to the Future* (Washington, D.C.: National Defense University, 1982), p. 15.

52. Public Broadcasting System, MacNeil-Lehrer Report, July 5, 1979.

53. *Defense Annual Report,* op. cit., p. 173.

54. Sick, op. cit., p. 74.

55. For example, see U.S. Senate, Committee on the Armed Services; 98th Congress, 1st Session, pt. 6, "Sea Power and Force Projection"; March 14, 22, 23, 24, April 6, 7, 1983; pp. 3101–3148, which contains a comprehensive discussion of the goals of USCENTCOM.

56. Ibid., p. 3105.

57. U.S. Senate, Committee on the Armed Services; 98th Congress, 1st Session; pt. 6, "Sea Power and Force Projection"; March 14, 22, 23, 28 and April 6, 7, 1983; p. 3140. General Kingston noted to the committee what types of forces a full USCENTCOM deployment would include:

U.S. Central Command Headquarters (augmented)
U.S. Army Forces Central Command:
Headquarters, U.S. Army Central Command
1 Airborne Division
1 Air Mobile/Air Assault Division
1 Mechanized Infantry Division
1 Cavalry Brigade Air Combat
Rangers and Unconventional Warfare Units
U.S. Navy Forces Central Command:
Headquarters, U.S. Navy Central Command
3 Carrier Battle Groups
1 Surface Action Group
5 Maritime Patrol Air Squadrons
U.S. Marine Corps Forces: 1⅓ Marine Amphibious Forces
U.S. Air Force Central Command:
Headquarters, U.S. Air Force Central Command
7 Tactical Fighter Wings
2 Strategic Bomber Squadrons

58. Sherwood S. Cordier, *U.S. Military Power and Rapid Deployment Requirements in the 1980s* (Boulder: Westview Press, 1983), p. 159.

59. For example, see formulation by then Deputy Secretary of Defense Frank Carlucci in U.S. Senate, Committee on Appropriations; 97th Congress, 2nd Session; pt. 3; May 6, 12, 13, 19, 20, and June 10, 24, 1984; p. 280.

60. U.S. Senate, Committee on Armed Services; 97th Congress, 2nd Session; March 5, 8, 12, 15, 16, 18, 19, 22, 23, 1982; p. 3733.

61. Carlucci, op. cit., p. 280.

62. For example, see James P. Wootten, *Rapid Deployment Force* (Washington, D.C.: Congressional Reference Service, 3/4/80, revised 2/1/84).

63. Ibid., p. 4.

64. Cordier, op. cit., pp. 60–61.

65. Wootten, *op. cit.,* pp. 11–12.

66. *Report of the Secretary of Defense Caspar W. Weinberger to the Congress on the FY 1985 Budget, FY 1986 Authorization Request and FY 1985–89 Defense Programs* (Washington, D.C.: G.P.O., 1984), p. 177.

67. Information on such access and prepositioning agreements, ibid., pp. 214–215.

68. For report on this, see Wootten, op. cit., p. 4.

69. For discussion of the reflagging decision, see "War in the Persian Gulf: The U.S. Takes Sides," U.S. Senate, Staff Report to the Committee on Foreign Relations, October 1987.

70. Four US AWACS based at Riyadh maintain patrol of the northern half of the Gulf.

71. O'Rourke, op. cit., p. 10.

72. Material taken from xeroxed copy of his testimony before the U.S. Senate Foreign Relations Committee, June 16, 1987.

73. *New York Times,* April 7, 1987.

74. *New York Times,* May 3, 1987.

75. *Washington Post,* May 30, 1987.

76. *Washington Post,* June 27, 1987.

77. Wootten, op. cit. p. 9.

78. Ibid.

79. For a discusion of the expanded NATO deployments to the Indian Ocean, see O'Rourke, *op. cit.*

80. This case is perhaps best presented in Robert J. Hanks, "The Unnoticed Challenge: Soviet Maritime Strategy and the Global Choke Points" (Washington, D.C.: Institute for Foreign Policy Analysis, 1980).

81. Ibid., p. 48.

82. Ibid.

83. John R. Thomas, *Political Strategic Framework for Soviet Oceanic Policy* (Washington, D.C.: G.P.O., 1976), p. 29.

84. Albert E. Graham, "Soviet Strategy and Policy in the Indian Ocean" in Paul J. Murphy, ed., *Naval Power in Soviet Policy,* vol. 2 (Washington, D.C.: G.P.O., 1978), p. 281.

85. For a comprehensive argument regarding the largely political orientation of the Soviet navy in the Indian Ocean, see Bruce W. Watson, *Red Navy at Sea: Soviet Naval Operations on the High Seas 1956–1980* (Boulder: Westview Press, 1980), ch. 10.

86. *Defense Monitor,* op. cit., p. 5.

87. *Air Force Magazine,* Sept. 10, 1985, p. 78.

88. *Far Eastern Economic Review,* December 29, 1983, pp. 14–15.

89. G. Jacobs, "The Soviet Navy—Supporting Overseas Deployments," *Asian Defense Journal,* February 1982, p. 44.

90. Following data in this paragraph taken largely from Watson, op. cit., pp. 153–154.

91. Most of the information in this paragraph from presentation of Rear Admiral John L. Butts, Director of Naval Intelligence, inserted in U.S. Senate Committee on the Armed Services; 98th Congress, 1st Session; pt. 6, "Sea Power and Force Projection"; March 14, 22, 23, 24, and April 6, 7, 1982; p. 2975.

92. William L. Dowdy, "Middle Eastern, North African, and South Asian Navies," *Naval Institute Proceedings,* March 1983, p. 48.

93. An analysis of the U.S. advantage vis-à-vis the Soviet Union in Watson, op. cit., pp. 150–151.

94. This data drawn from *Soviet Military Power,* 2nd ed. (Washington, D.C.: G.P.O., 1983), pp. 50–51.

95. This point is persuasively argued by Keith A. Dunn, "Towards a U.S. Military Strategy for Southwest Asia," in Alvin Z. Rubenstein, op. cit., pp. 209–234.

96. For a discussion of Soviet activity in the Persian Gulf, see Robert J. Ciarrocchi, "U.S., Soviet, and Western European Naval Forces in the Persian Gulf Region," (Library of Congress, Congressional Research Service, December 8, 1987), pp. 10–13.

97. Figures from O'Rourke, op. cit., p. 11.

98. Quoted in Joel Larus, "India: The Neglected Service Faces the Future," *Naval Institute Proceedings,* March 1981, p. 81.

99. Norman C. Dodd, "African Navies South of the Sahara," *Naval Institute Proceedings* (March 1984), p. 57.

100. John Moore, ed., *Jane's Fighting Ships 1983–84* (Boston: Van Nostrand Reinhold Company, 1983), p. 411.

101. Dodd, op. cit., p. 57.

102. Ibid., p. 59.

103. Michael Vlahos, "Middle Eastern, North African and South Asian Navies," *Naval Institute Proceedings,* March 1984, p. 51.

104. Dowdy, op. cit., pp. 46–47.

105. Michael Vlahos, "Middle Eastern, North African and South Asian Navies," *Naval Institute Proceedings,* March 1987, pp. 52–56.

106. Vlahos (1984), op. cit., p. 53.

107. *Jane's Fighting Ships, 1983–84,* p. 222.

108. Vlahos, (1987), op. cit., p. 53.

109. Singh, op. cit., p. 39.

110. See analysis of expansion of Indian navy in Gary L. Sojka, "The Missions of the Indian Navy," *Naval War College Review,* January–February 1983, pp. 2–15.

111. Vlahos (1984), op. cit., pp. 53–54.

112. *Jane's Fighting Ships 1983–84* reports possible purchase of two cruisers.

113. Ibid., p. 222.

114. For example, see Joel Larus, op. cit., pp. 77–83.

115. *Jane's Fighting Ships 1983–84,* pp. 227–228.

116. Keith Jacobs, "Pakistan's Navy," *Naval Institute Proceedings*, March 1984, p. 150.

117. A summary of Sukarno's foreign policy assertiveness in Herbert Feith, "Indonesia," in George McTurnan Kahin, ed., *Government and Politics of Southeast Asia*, 2nd ed. (Ithaca: Cornell University Press, 1964), pp. 265–270.

118. The data from *The Military Balance: 1964–65* (London: The International Institute for Strategic Studies, 1964), p. 62.

119. P. Lewis Young, "Naval Developments in Southeast Asian Region: Current Trends," *Asian Defense Journal*, February 1982, p. 21.

120. An analysis of Australia's security concerns regarding Southeast Asia in Michael O'Conner, "Security Cooperation in the Western Pacific: An Australian View," *Asian Defense Journal*, May 1983, pp. 87–88.

121. Quoted in Ray Sunderland, "Australia's Changing Threat Perceptions," Working Paper No. 78 (Australian National University: Canberra, 1984), p. 9.

122. Quoted in "Australian Defense Issues in the Eighties: Part I," *Asian Defense Journal*, February 1983, p. 30.

123. *U.S. News and World Report*, March 4, 1985, p. 31.

124. *Asian Defense Journal*, November, 1984, pp. 21–2.

125. See *Johannesburg Star*, August 15, 1983, pp. 3–4 for an analysis of Australia's Indian Ocean policy.

126. See Ministry of Foreign Affairs News Release, No. 91, June 20, 1984.

127. For an Indian argument against the notion of superpower rivalry in the Indian Ocean, see P. K. S. Namboodiri, "The Indian Ocean: Need for a New Approach," *Strategic Analysis*, April 1979, pp. 42–45.

128. For example, see Mohammed Ayoob, "Superpowers and the Third World: Prospect for the Eighties," *IDSA Journal*, January–March 1981, pp. 339–349.

129. See Hedley Bull, "Sea Power and Political Influence," Adelphi Paper No. 122 (London: International Institute for Strategic Studies, 1976), pp. 7–8.

130. Elizabeth Young, "Military Implications of the Law of the Sea," *Survival*, November–December 1974, p. 276.

131. K. Subrahmanyam, "India's Security in the Eighties," *Strategic Analysis*, September 1983, pp. 420–421.

132. Butts, op. cit., p. 2978.

133. The late spring 1984 escalation of fighting in the Iran-Iraq war over the Persian Gulf led some oil industry experts to announce that oil prices could rise to $50–80/barrel from the then current level of $29/barrel if the situation continued to escalate. As it was, insurance rates on oil tankers sailing to the Persian Gulf tripled in May 1984. *Los Angeles Times*, May 24, 1984.

TABLE 1.1.   Naval Deployment in the Indian Ocean

	United States	Soviet Union
1981/1982*	1–2 carrier task forces (some 12 surface combatants), 7 chartered store ships (Persian Gulf: 1 command ship, 4 surface combatants)	"Detachments from the Pacific Fleet serve in the Indian Ocean" Facilities are located in Aden (Socotra) in South Yemen and Dahlak Island in Ethiopia
1982/1983†	1 carrier task force (some 6 surface combatants), 13 chartered stores ships (Persian Gulf: 1 command ship, 4 surface combatants)	3 submarines, 7 surface combatants, 18 support ships Facilities also in South Yemen (Aden, Socotra) and Ethiopia (Dahlak Island)
1983/1984**	1 carrier battle group (from the 7th Fleet); (some 6 surface combatants), 9 stores ships (Middle East Force in Persian Gulf: 1 command ship, 2 destroyers)	2–3 submarines (on the average), 8 surface combatants, 2 amphibious, 12 support ships Facilities in Aden and Socotra in South Yemen and Dahlak Island in Ethiopia
1984/1985††	Same as 1983/1984 data	Same as 1983/1984 data
1985/1986***	Detachments from the 7th fleet, 11,000; 1 carrier battle group (some 6 surface combatants) Near Term Prepositioning Force (Diego Garcia) (1,300): 3 ammunition, 7 cargo ships, 3 barges, 3 oilers, 1 water tanker. Middle East Force (Persian Gulf/Bahrain) 1 command ship, 4 destroyers/frigates	Detachments from Pacific Fleet (Average 2–3 subs, 8 surface combatants, 2 amphibious support ships normally deployed in the Indian Ocean; facilities also in Vietnam [Cam Ranh Bay] South Yemen, [Aden, Socotra] and Ethiopia [Dahlak Island])
1987†††	6 frigates, 1 destroyer, 1 cruiser, 1 marine amphibious assault carrier, 1 command ship (LaSalle), 1 landing ship dock, 6 ocean going mine sweepers 8 fast patrol boats, 6 river patrol boats, 4 special warfare craft, 2 barges	*Inside the Gulf:* 1 destroyer/submarine which rotates with 2 frigates in the immediate area of the Gulf of Oman/Arab Sea; 3 minesweepers, 1 intelligence-gathering ship *Outside the Gulf:* 1 aircraft carrier, 3 cruiser battleships, 2 auxiliary support craft

Sources:
* International Institute of Strategic Studies, "The Military Balance, 1981/82," in *Air Force Magazine,* December 1981, pp. 58, 60.
† International Institute of Strategic Studies, "The Military Balance, 1982/83," in *Air Force Magazine,* December 1982, pp. 66, 70.
** International Institute of Strategic Studies, "The Military Balance, 1983/84," in *Air Force Magazine,* December 1983, pp. 74, 78.
†† International Institute of Strategic Studies, "The Military Balance, 1984/85," in *Air Force Magazine,* December 1985, pp. 71, 72.
*** International Institute of Strategic Studies, "The Military Balance, 1985/86," in *Air Force Magazine,* February 1987, pp. 65, 69.
††† Information from Clyde Mark, Congressional Research Service, Library of Congress, Foreign Policy Division; unverifiable.

TABLE 1.2. Military Expenditures, Estimated GNP/GDP, Percentages of Military Expenditures to Central Government Expenditures and GNP/GDP, Where Available (Current U.S. Dollars)

Country/Years	Area (sq mi)	Population (000)	Armed Forces	Military Expenditures (ME)	Estimated GNP/GDP	ME GNP/GDP %	ME CGE %
Afghanistan	253,861				(GNP)		
1982		15,360	43,000				
1983		15,500	47,000				
1984			47,000	209.000 mn	3.3 bn	37.5	6.9
1985			50,000				
1986			50,000				
1987		15,531	50,000				
Australia	2,967,741				(GDP)		
1981/1982		14,760		4.472 bn	163.062 bn	3.1	10.2
1982/1983		15,438	72,473	4.492 bn			
1984				4.954 bn	184.000 bn	3.0	
1985			70,400	5.100 bn			
1986			70,500				
1987		16,428	70,500				
Bahrain	231				(GDP)		
1982		400		84.1 mn			
1983		400		253.191 mn			
1984			2700	319.0 mn	4.2 bn	6.3	23.5
1985			2800	111.0		3.0	
1986			2800				
1987		420	2800				
Bangladesh	55,126				(GDP)		
1981/1982				158 mn	11.910 bn		
1982/1983		92,900	77,000	160.898 mn	10.633 bn	1.8	10.9
1984				262 mn			22.0

65

TABLE 1.2. (continued)

Country/Years	Area (sq mi)	Population (000)	Armed Forces	Military Expenditures (ME)	Estimated GNP/GDP	ME GNP/GDP %	ME CGE %
1985			91,300		15 bn		
1986			91,300				
1987		104,235	101,500				
Brunei	2,226				(GDP)		
1982		233	3650				
1984			4100	195 mn		8.1	24.5
1985			4100	305 mn			
1986			4100				
1987		238	4100				
Burma	261,789				(GNP)		
1981/1982			179,000	174.428 mn	5.601 bn		33.5
1982/1983		35,260		175.159 mn			25.6
1984			186,000	245.0		3.9	
1985			186,000	226.0	6.5 bn	3.3	
1986			186,000				
1987		38,457	186,800				
China (PRC)	3,691,501 (includes Tibet)				(GNP)		
1983			4,100,000	12.5 bn (1981)			
1984				6.455	318 bn	1.6	11.9
1985			3,900,000	11.027		2.9	
1986			2,950,000				
1987		1,078,765	3,200,000				
Djibouti	8,996				(GNP)		
1982		315	2400	2.9 mn	357 mn (1981)		
1983			2700				

Country / Year							
1984			3000	27.0 mn	307 mn	8.1	22.4
1985			4500				
1986			4200				
1987							
Egypt	386,872	417			(GNP)		
1981/1982				2.100 bn			
1982/1983		43,000	452,000	2.495 bn		7.4	12.0
1983/1984		46,000	447,000	3.043 bn	29.614 bn		12.0
1984				3.786	33 bn	9.6	19.6
1985			445,000	2.153		8.9	
1986			445,000				
1987		49,500	445,000				
Ethiopia	471,776				(GNP)		
1981/1982		29,695	250,500	377.778 mn	4.466 bn	11.4	28.4
1983		31,500					
1984			217,000	548.0	4.7 bn	9.3	
1985			227,000	310.0			
1986			320,000				
1987		42,600					
India	1,266,596				162.416 bn		17.8
1981/1982		683,900	1,104,000	5.12 bn	(1980)		
1982/1983		723,000	1,120,000				
1984			1,260,000	6.907			
1985			1,260,000	6.320		3.9	19.3
1986			1,262,000			3.2	
1987		779,983					
Indonesia	779,675				(GDP)		
1981/1982		154,360	273,000	2.039 bn	84.309 bn		12.3
1982		160,000	281,000	2.926 bn			
1983				(1982/83)			

TABLE 1.2. (continued)

Country/Years	Area (sq mi)	Population (000)	Armed Forces	Military Expenditures (ME)	Estimated GNP/GDP	ME GNP/GDP %	ME CGE %
1984			278,100	2.420	78.8 bn	3.0	12.4
1985			281,000	2.610		2.7	
1986			284,000				
1987		168,815					
Iran	635,363						
1982/1983		39,665 (1982)		6.9–13.3 bn (total war costs to end of 1982 reported as some $100 billion)	(GDP)		
		41,500 (1983)					
1984			305,000	20.162	162 bn	12.3	42.9
1985			704,500	8.842		10.0	
1986			654,000				
1987		45,200					
Iraq	172,000				(GNP)		
1982		13,835	252,000	7.772 bn			
1983		14,300	517,250				
1984			520,000	13.831		51.1	
1985			845,000			57.1	
1986		15,400					
1987			1,000,000				
Israel					(GNP)		
1982		4000	174,000	8.242 bn	21.770 bn	37.9	40.7

1983		4100	172,000	6.461 bn	21 bn	24.4	39.5
1984				5.798		13.9	
1985			142,000	3.200			
1986			149,000				
1987		4400	141,000				
Japan	142,871				(GNP)		
1982		117,400	243,000	10.36 bn	1,057.616	1.0	5.5
1983		119,400	241,000				
1984				12.018	1.3 tr	1.0	5.8
1985			243,000	12.094		1.0	
1986			243,000				
1987		122,090	246,000				
Jordan	37,297				(GNP)		
1982		3320	67,500	440.091 mn	3.878 bn	11.3	21.5
1983		2469	72,800	465.394 mn			
1984			70,300	533.0	4.2 bn	13.4	28.0
1985			70,200	546.0		13.1	
1986							
1987		2720	80,300				
Kenya 1981/1982	224,960	17,090	16,700	155.186 bn	(GDP) 5.950 bn		
1983		18,000	16,000	285.377 bn			
1984			13,700	243.0	5.7 mn	4.1	15.9
1985			13,700	303.0		4.4	
1986							
1987		20,711	13,400				
Korea (South)	38,022				(GNP)		
1982		38,800	601,600	5.173 bn	68.419 bn	7.6	35.0
1983		39,400	622,000				
1984				4.494 bn		5.4	27.2

TABLE 1.2. (continued)

Country/Years	Area (sq mi)	Population (000)	Armed Forces	Military Expenditures (ME)	Estimated GNP/GDP	ME GNP/GDP %	ME CGE %
1985			598,000	4.621 bn	90.6 bn	5.2	
1986			601,000				
1987		42,126	629,000				
Kuwait	7,780				(GDP)		
1981/1982		1450	12,400	1.561 bn	20.215 bn		8.4
1984				1.638	22 bn	7.6	14.0
1985				1.608		9.1	
1986			12,000				
1987		1710	15,500				
Madagascar	228,000				(GDP)		
1982		8,775	19,550	78.511 mn			
1983		9,350	21,100				
1984				55.0	2.6 bn	2.3	10.9
1985			21,000				
1986			21,000				
1987		10,367	21,000				
Malaysia	128,727				(GNP)		
1982		14,350	99,100	2.077 bn	25.936 bn	8.0	15.2
1983			99,700				
1984			110,000	1.997	29.8 bn	5.9	16.8
1985			110,000	1.604		5.6	
1986		16,176	110,000				
1987			113,000				
Mozambique	303,073				(GNP)		
1982		10,610	26,700	200.918 mn			

Year							
1984		12,650	12,650	231.0		8.4	
1985			15,800	206.0			43.3
1986			15,800				
1987		13,126	15,800				
Nepal					(GNP)		
1982	54,362	14,309	25,000	30.353 mn	2.459 bn		
1983		15,000	25,000	(1982/83)	2.6 bn	1.3	5.2
1984			25,000	30.0			
1985			30,000				
1986							
1987		19,495	31,700				
New Zealand					(GDP)		
1982	103,736	3152	12,913	493.475 mn	24.043 bn		6.2
				(1982/83)	(1981/82)		
1983		3230	12,943				
1984				400.0		1.8	4.4
1985			12,400	504.0		2.1	
1986			12,600				
1987		3317	12,600		23.2 bn		
Oman					(GNP)		
1982		930	18,000	1.714 bn			42.5
1983		970	23,550	1.772 bn	8.8 bn	24.2	49.0
1984				2.131		20.1	
1985			2,500	2.076			
1986		1300	21,500				
1987			21,500				
Pakistan					(GDP)		
1981/1982	310,463	88,950	450,600	1.857 bn	31.0 bn		36.7
1983		89,500	478,600	1.957	35 bn	7.1	39.8
1984							

TABLE 1.2. (continued)

Country/Years	Area (sq mi)	Population (000)	Armed Forces	Military Expenditures (ME)	Estimated GNP/GDP	ME GNP/GDP %	ME CGE %
1985			482,800	2.353		6.9	
1986			480,600				
1987		99,705	480,600				
Philippines	115,800						
1982		50,010	112,800	879.752 mn	(GDP) 39.638 bn	2.2	12.5
1983		50,800	104,800				
1984			114,800	504.0	32.6 bn	1.5	15.0
1985			113,000	463.0		1.4	
1986							
1987		56,371	105,000				
Qatar							
1982		230	6000		(GDP)		
1983		260	6000	165.98 mn	6 bn		
1984				0.0			
1985			6000				
1986			6000				
1987		300	7000				
Saudi Arabia							
1981/1982		10,395	52,200	27.022 bn	(GDP)		27.7
1982/1983			51,500	21.952 bn			
1983/1984		8–12,000		22.674			
1984			62,500	19.860		20.9	36.9
1985			67,500			18.9	
1986		11,600	73,500		98.1 bn		
1987			73,500				

Country / Year							
Seychelles							
1982	225,600				(GNP)		
1983		67	1000	8.0 mn			
1984				8.0			
1985			1200		140 mn	5.6	
1986			1200				7.4
1987		69	1300				
Singapore					(GNP)		
1981/1982		2400	42,000	718.0 mn	12.901 bn		15.8
1982/1983		2500	55,500	851.791 mn	15.125 bn	5.6	17.0
1983							
1984			55,000	1,046.0	16 bn	5.8	15.2
1985			55,500	1,042.0		6.8	
1986			55,500				
1987		2631					
Somalia					(GNP)		
1982		5910	62,550	127.376 mn		11.3	
1983		4–6000	62,550			13.4	
1984			62,700	130.0			40.1
1985			42,700	132.0	1.8 bn		
1986		7010	65,000				
1987							
South Africa					(GNP)		
1981/1982	790,261	29,030	81,400	3.081 bn	75.739 bn		21.1
1982/1983		26,100	82,400	2.769 bn	71.668	3.9	18.7
1983							
1984			106,400	2.634	112	4.1	16.8
1985			106,400	1.726		3.6	
1986		33,642	97,000				
1987							
Sri Lanka					(GNP)		
1982	25,332	14,900	14,840	40.736 mn	4.820 bn		

TABLE 1.2. (continued)

Country/Years	Area (sq mi)	Popula-tion (000)	Armed Forces	Military Expendi-tures (ME)	Estimated GNP/GDP	ME GNP/GDP %	ME CGE %
1983		15,500	16,560	102.0	5.3 bn	1.7	5.1
1984				213.0		3.8	
1985			21,600				
1986			21,600				
1987		16,173	22,000				
Syria							
1982		9,150	222,500	2.548 bn	(GNP)		30.0
1983		9,200	222,200				
1984			402,500	3.372	13.9 bn	15.1	29.9
1985			392,500	1.840		16.3	
1986		11,250	407,500				
1987							
Taiwan	13,887						
1981/1982		18,165	451,000	3.60 bn	(GNP) 46.0 bn		39.4
1982/1983		18,500	464,000	3.323 bn			40.0
1984				3.417 bn	56.6 bn	5.9	
1985			444,000	3.715		6.6	
1986			424,000				
1987		20,352	424,000				
Tanzania	364,943						
1981/1982		19,120	40,400	315.662 mn	(GNP)	2.5	10.2
1983		20,500	40,350				
1984			40,400	103.0	4.1 bn		
1985			40,400	101.0			
1986							
1987		22,710	40,100				

					(GNP)		
Thailand							
1982	198,500	48,890	238,100	1.437 bn	37.320 bn	3.9	21.7
1983		49,750	235,300	1.562		4.2	21.7
1984				1.752	42 bn		
1985		52,863	235,300	1.583		3.9	
1986			256,000				
1987			256,000				
United Arab Emirates							
1982		950	42,500	2.195 bn	(GNP)	8.3	
1983		1130	49,000				
1984					28 bn	8.0	57.0
1985			43,000	2.343			
1986			43,000	2.023			
1987		1300	43,000				
Yemen (North)							
1982		5365	32,100	526.904 mn	2.838 bn	18.6	28.3
1983		7200	21,550				
1984					3.9 bn	17.8	30.1
1985			36,600	598.0		11.7	
1986			36,600	379.0			
1987		9300	36,600				
Yeman (South)							
1982		1955	24,300	159.409 mn	(GNP)	16.3	21.0
1983		2000	25,500				
1984					1 bn		
1985			27,500	194.0			
1986			27,500				
1987		2300	27,500				

Source: "Comparisons of Defense Expenditures and Military Power," *The Military Balance,* London: International Institute of Strategic Studies, Autumn, 1983, Autumn 1984–85, 1985–86, 1986–87, 1987–88.

TABLE 1.3. U.S. International Military Education and Training Program Deliveries/Expenditures, Includes Military Assistance Service Funded (Dollars in Thousands)

	FY 1979	FY 1980	FY 1981	FY 1982	FY 1983	FY 1984	FY 1985	FY 1986	FY 1987	FY 1950–87
East Asia and Pacific	5562	4640	4463	7161	8316	8877	9668	9618	10,557	871,445
Burma	—	30	31	151	196	116	226	260	301	5,537
Indonesia	1848	1858	1724	2252	2438	2233	1705	1859	2070	43,541
Japan	—	—	—	—	—	—	—	—	—	44,589
Korea (South)	1613	1086	1212	1544	1750	1765	1955	1814	3	168,877
Malaysia	516	267	305	492	650	860	969	894	1032	9,156
Philippines	794	559	394	1130	1364	1462	2205	2371	2550	46,453
Singapore	—	—	7	48	52	55	50	47	46	296
Taiwan	—	—	—	—	—	—	—	—	—	103,156
Thailand	791	832	761	1526	1783	2205	2326	2204	2329	88,763
Near East and South Asia	6235	4615	4651	9579	10,060	9217	10,195	9761	10,950	224,297
Afghanistan	9	—	—	—	—	—	—	—	—	5,616
Bangladesh	230	121	131	167	215	263	336	269	296	2,272
Egypt	394	848	730	2337	1899	1458	1402	1672	1816	12,570
India	455	270	4	82	146	129	295	307	202	7,745
Iran	—	—	—	—	—	—	—	—	—	67,442
Iraq	—	—	—	—	—	—	—	—	—	1,487
Jordan	1482	968	775	2147	1213	1701	1828	1752	1977	21,567
Lebanon	544	376	324	544	1733	490	668	460	493	7,454
Maldives	—	—	—	—	—	23	23	31	36	128
Nepal	51	26	62	87	76	108	122	87	105	1,143
Oman	—	10	4	82	106	124	128	41	39	508
Pakistan	463	—	—	573	781	770	973	916	1124	29,679
Saudi Arabia	—	—	—	—	—	—	—	—	—	12,456
Sri Lanka	—	21	67	105	105	144	148	158	160	1,154

Syria	—	—	—	—	—	—	—	—	—	56
Yemen	560	407	924	1155	1213	912	1292	1095	1420	9,991
Africa	2944	2591	3884	5124	7283	8509	10,241	9376	9,220	99,440
Djibouti	—	—	—	32	161	106	117	107	163	662
Ethiopia	—	—	—	—	—	—	—	—	—	22,701
Kenya	395	505	511	934	1372	1500	1685	1516	1051	11,163
Madagascar	—	—	—	—	17	50	55	77	73	272
Somalia	—	—	366	454	603	1023	1096	1091	677	5,192

Totals may not add due to rounding.

Source: Foreign Military Sales, Foreign Military Construction Sales, and *Military Assistance Facts* (as of September 30, 1987), United States Department of Defense, Security Assistance Agency, Washington, D.C. 1, Defense Security Assistance Agency, ch.d.3 (extrapolations from chart), Table 1.3, pp. 76–81.

TABLE 1.4. Military Assistance Program, Includes Military Assistance Service Funded and Excludes Training (Dollars in Thousands)

	FY 1979	FY 1980	FY 1981	FY 1982	FY 1983	FY 1984	FY 1985	FY 1896	FY 1987	FY 1950–87
East Asia and Pacific	30,275	160,377	125,657	131,172	1,295	747	—	10,000	—	29,007,223
Burma	—	—	—	—	—	—	—	—	—	72,134
Indonesia	1900	1735	585	194	15	*	—	—	—	192,200
Japan	—	—	—	—	—	—	—	—	—	810,276
Korea (South)	11,042	121,931	99,660	130,086	10	—	—	—	—	5,471,719
Philippines	15,864	25,205	25,059	760	267	741	—	10,000	—	617,069
Taiwan	14	*	10	—	—	—	—	—	—	2,554,637
Thailand	1455	11,504	344	132	1003	5	—	—	—	1,169,122
Near East and South Asia	41,575	28,220	1212	91	30	75	—	—	—	2,167,214
Afghanistan	—	—	—	—	—	—	—	—	—	2
India	10	—	1	—	—	—	—	—	—	90,256
Iran	—	—	—	—	—	—	—	—	—	766,733
Iraq	—	—	—	—	—	—	—	—	—	45,208
Jordan	41,562	28,210	1207	90	30	75	—	—	—	489,908
Lebanon	—	—	—	—	—	—	—	—	—	13,585
Nepal	—	—	—	—	—	—	—	—	—	1,678
Pakistan	—	—	—	—	—	—	—	—	—	650,281
Saudi Arabia	—	—	—	—	—	—	—	—	—	23,868
Sri Lanka	—	—	—	—	—	—	—	—	—	3,167
Africa	—	—	2669	27	17,224	110	—	10,000	25,000	278,817
Djibouti	—	—	—	—	1475	—	—	—	—	1,475
Ethiopia	—	—	—	—	—	—	—	—	—	182,948

* Less than $500.
Numbers may not total due to rounding.

Source: Foreign Military Sales, Foreign Military Construction Sales, and Military Assistance Facts (as of September 30, 1987), United States Department of Defense, Security Assistance Agency, Washington, D.C. 1, Defense Security Assistance Agency, ch.d.3 (extrapolations from chart), pp. 53–55.

TABLE 1.5. Foreign Military Sales Deliveries

	FY 1980	FY 1981	FY 1982	FY 1983	FY 1984	FY 1985	FY 1986	FY 1987	FY 1950–87
East Asia and Pacific	1,073,621	1,920,254	1,287,969	1,663,232	1,532,536	1,610,410	1,474,216	2,056,304	17,419,819
Australia	150,284	506,226	127,443	151,123	398,245	428,262	370,134	619,350	4,249,647
Brunei	*	*	132	14	72	37	1	48	350
Burma	57	259	743	1,172	1,193	329	43	31	7,525
Indonesia	88,329	63,583	14,611	29,587	15,679	17,953	12,759	24,333	319,725
Japan	84,875	320,431	326,242	435,420	333,325	389,699	151,312	306,242	2,741,803
Korea (South)	295,197	295,449	220,648	304,649	258,016	258,281	387,474	403,928	3,641,664
Malaysia	4,622	28,953	3,642	26,434	28,525	9,114	3,476	3,279	167,599
New Zealand	7,371	8,328	8,908	12,525	11,095	9,301	8,518	10,243	202,145
Philippines	14,326	16,397	21,845	71,433	13,777	16,027	37,343	33,787	287,705
Singapore	17,914	52,755	23,483	85,018	32,848	22,435	134,934	163,192	655,986
Taiwan	209,100	373,749	390,035	434,977	274,896	339,535	248,999	387,058	3,604,605
Thailand	201,523	254,041	149,040	170,262	164,776	118,946	118,470	100,659	1,524,374
Near East and South Asia	2,392,689	3,182,231	4,529,606	6,129,837	3,432,556	3,213,110	3,472,416	6,569,352	55,250,651
Bahrain	1,515	862	2,010	699	1,957	8,522	53,606	170,693	239,986
Bangladesh				—	8	253	543	616	1,439
Egypt	202,929	203,307	989,307	1,004,720	314,992	570,148	607,313	1,135,122	5,258,195
India	6,230	511	582	955	548	114	21	127	78,573
Iran	—	—	—	—	—	—	—	—	10,654,842
Iraq	—	—	—	—	—	—	—	—	13,152
Israel	564,416	1,039,757	924,379	309,075	216,069	483,065	195,803	13,472,282	10,548,220
Jordan	173,212	113,425	123,080	278,927	76,973	122,325	62,766	64,838	1,552,017
Kuwait	77,902	65,317	85,147	72,758	48,738	33,990	71,900	83,059	977,771
Lebanon	15,990	12,783	37,199	189,141	208,480	48,045	12,626	13,818	559,522
Nepal	1	—	—	—	—	—	—	—	73
Oman	7,798	16,850	31,473	21,167	4,313	1,300	756	281	84,483

TABLE 1.5. (continued)

	FY 1980	FY 1981	FY 1982	FY 1983	FY 1984	FY 1985	FY 1986	FY 1987	FY 1950–87
Pakistan	52,635	72,810	146,407	255,975	452,906	357,950	148,159	135,186	1,895,580
Qatar	21	83	278	148	97	144	141	208	1,114
Saudi Arabia	1,151,752	1,451,558	2,092,714	3,888,694	1,932,464	1,369,568	2,242,561	3,254,147	21,561,080
Sri Lanka	—	—	—	—	—	—	—	—	4
Syria	—	—	—	—	—	—	—	—	1
United Arab Emirates	296	1,936	2,742	3,180	12,339	5,068	10,672	241,702	280,533
Yemen	72,254	49,350	24,919	16,542	9,217	8,266	2,454	7,222	298,315
Africa	44,990	69,663	129,248	76,072	78,672	77,444	75,410	70,346	857,571
Ethiopia	—	—	—	—	—	—	—	—	86,561
Kenya	3,901	28,464	23,543	20,060	6,025	8,162	11,006	5,544	143,398
Madagascar	—	*	*	—	—	—	3	90	94
Somalia	—	3	14,334	21,292	20,103	19,814	11,413	13,904	99,449
South Africa	—	—	—	—	—	—	—	—	3,149

* less than $500.
Totals may not add due to rounding.

Source: Foreign Military Sales, Foreign Military Construction Sales, and *Military Assistance Facts* (as of September 30, 1987), United States Department of Defense, Security Assistance Agency, Washington, D.C. 1, Defense Security Assistance Agency, ch.d.3 (extrapolations from chart), pp. 13–19.

TABLE 1.6 U.S. Commercial Exports Licensed Under Arms Export Control Act (Dollars in Thousands)

	FY 1980	FY 1981	FY 1982	FY 1983	FY 1984	FY 1985	FY 1986	FY 1987	FY 1950–87
East Asia and Pacific	500,015	572,725	544,053	635,553	1,036,452	1,828,250	1,658,978	840,804	9,743,920
Australia	51,015	35,244	40,000	40,000	111,540	497,496	418,636	63,316	1,403,315
Brunei	63	569	1,000	1,500	2,104	2,124	1,819	1,731	12,729
Burma	229	203	1,000	1,000	69	1,051	1,350	637	17,706
China	622	—	1,000	2,000	22,732	46,303	54,020	14,576	141,264
Indonesia	6,221	6,673	10,000	10,000	27,197	33,285	15,108	7,964	165,839
Japan	264,892	344,862	300,000	400,000	546,874	708,118	606,635	342,103	4,369,653
Korea (S)	41,459	28,710	25,000	25,000	122,299	210,674	156,562	126,287	1,072,740
Malaysia	19,016	29,522	25,000	25,000	16,811	119,681	41,078	20,142	480,190
New Zealand	6,019	3,709	5,000	5,000	30,179	35,524	19,862	4,582	125,870
Philippines	7,954	967	1,000	1,000	4,018	11,566	2,224	4,862	83,055
Singapore	11,167	22,691	20,000	20,000	45,439	66,963	89,035	28,073	391,852
Taiwan	57,770	66,731	75,000	75,000	70,000	54,463	228,400	210,000	1,128,282
Thailand	13,796	13,526	10,000	10,000	23,453	23,360	11,106	11,784	183,418
Near East and South Asia	403,251	413,432	296,800	315,000	1,068,073	1,233,874	633,586	339,373	7,562,810
Afghanistan	281	—	—	—	—	**	—	—	597
Bahrain	224	1,171	1,000	1,000	1,965	928	1,852	1,227	12,753
Bangladesh	552	474	1,000	1,000	323	1,114	257	259	5,284
Egypt	6,530	4,052	15,000	30,000	69,307	151,882	71,051	22,250	452,839
India	2,833	4,643	5,000	5,000	23,234	18,615	27,414	24,878	157,551
Iran	7,036	—	—	—	—	—	—	—	670,767
Iraq	1	—	—	—	13	120	1,178	—	1,552
Israel	271,805	267,337	150,000	150,000	417,513	599,930	290,847	136,360	3,383,208
Jordan	53,638	41,653	50,000	50,000	17,340	19,460	23,247	13,409	264,211
Kuwait	232	1,307	5,000	5,000	60,794	4,617	13,455	1,437	102,793
Lebanon	768	1,050	1,500	1,500	1,209	2,079	914	113	20,279

Table 1.6. (continued)

	FY 1980	FY 1981	FY 1982	FY 1983	FY 1984	FY 1985	FY 1986	FY 1987	FY 1950–87
Nepal	67	—	—	—	4	3	6	1	143
Oman	186	661	1,500	3,000	5,313	5,623	3,960	5,150	33,927
Pakistan	4,670	11,108	5,000	5,000	35,153	21,935	54,145	15,404	209,406
Qatar	1,818	1,002	2,000	2,000	3,790	1,678	597	427	16,033
Saudi Arabia	28,985	71,540	50,000	50,000	359,600	307,996	91,992	108,563	1,686,142
Sri Lanka	33	—	—	—	378	1,324	412	1,717	3,931
Syria	1	—	—	—	6	132	—	—	1,529
United Arab Emirates	5,085	3,937	2,000	5,000	9,346	28,501	26,501	5,141	91,377
Yemen	14	4	100	1,000	276	1,322	14	24	2,456
Africa	7,257	2,359	10,450	11,750	102,097	11,254	69,220	9,593	362,464
Djibouti	—	—	—	—	—	—	*	—	12
Ethiopia	—	—	—	—	2,335	—	—	—	3,856
Kenya	197	165	300	800	219	100	407	6,863	16,226
Madagaskar	10	—	—	—	*	—	—	—	574
Mauritius	—	—	—	—	12	7	—	—	168
Mozambique	—	—	—	—	2	38	26	2	516
Reunion	—	—	—	—	4	—	—	—	5
Seychelles	—	—	—	—	*	2	—	*	42
Somalia	—	—	—	—	1,811	59	3	177	6,290
South Africa	—	—	—	—	3,482	1,612	148	—	38,729
Tanzania	598	23	50	100	3	112	9	54	3,317

* less than $500.

Totals may not add due to rounding.

Source: Foreign Military Sales, Foreign Military Construction Sales, and Military Assistance Facts (as of September 30, 1987), United States Department of Defense, Security Assistance Agency, Washington, D.C. 1, Defense Security Assistance Agency, ch.d.3 (extrapolations from chart), pp. 37–43.

TABLE 1.7.   Attacks on Ships in the Persian Gulf

Number of ships attacked	1981	1982	1983	1984	1985	1986	1987
By Iraq	5	22	16	53	33	66	62
By Iran	0	0	0	18	14	45	61

Source: Washington Post, October 3, 1987.

2

Emerging Security Issues in the Indian Ocean: An Indian Perspective

M. P. AWATI

The emergence of an unrestrained superpower military competition in the Indian Ocean/Persian Gulf region poses increasingly serious dangers both for the superpowers themselves and for the littoral states. With its carrier task force and a growing network of bases to serve the Rapid Deployment Force (RDF), the United States deploys substantial capabilities to safeguard its oil supplies and sea lanes against what it sees as potential threats from the Soviet Union and local powers. The Soviet navy, for its part, perceiving a threat from China as well as the United States, maintains a significant naval presence of its own to preserve access to the region from the Mediterranean and the Pacific for transit and for onshore facilities. Apart from the possibility of a direct superpower clash in the region incidental to a global military confrontation, the littoral states are concerned that Washington and Moscow might be drawn into conflicts between regional powers by manipulative local elites. More important, there is a widespread fear in the region that the superpowers might seek to pursue their foreign policy objectives by engaging in gunboat diplomacy, intervening in support of their clients in civil conflicts. Such anxieties are present in many unstable Third World areas but are peculiarly acute in the strife-torn Indian Ocean region.

This essay will present an Indian perspective on the regional military environment, first analyzing the threat perceptions and force deployments of extra-regional powers and then examining the postures of regional powers, with special emphasis on India. It will then assess the conflicts and complementarities in the interests of the powers concerned as the prelude for a discussion of the desirability of resuming regional arms control efforts.

The United States

American Interests in the Indian Ocean

The Suez crisis in 1956 "more than anything else epitomized the changing Afro-Asian ocean scene" that persuaded Washington to establish a naval presence in the Indian Ocean.[1] The growing evidence of diminishing British potency, accompanied by the end of French colonial rule over Madagascar in 1958, prompted U.S. defense planners to foresee a possible power vacuum in the region.[2]

The United States had long regarded a British presence in the East as very important for the non-communist world. In fact, it offered to share part of the cost for Britain's presence in the Indian Ocean as early as the Kennedy Administration.[3] Washington subsequently proposed the idea of joint staging posts in the Indian Ocean in its strategy to build them up into a chain of small islands.[4]

The British Indian Ocean Territory (BIOT) was created as a result of these early perceptions. The idea was to ensure the availability of strategically located "real estate" for future joint military uses. After the announcement of BIOT in the British Parliament on November 10, 1965, British officials visited Washington to discuss what was reported as "the nuts and bolts of Anglo-American defense coordination east of Suez."[5] The details of the U.S. decision to participate in the east of Suez presence are still not known precisely, as much of that discussion has been kept secret at the request of Britain.[6]

When the British finally did decide to withdraw from the Indian Ocean in January 1968, the limited Soviet naval entry into the region that followed in March was seen in Washington as part of a calculated Soviet move to "fill the vacuum" created by the withdrawal.[7] In U.S. eyes, Soviet naval expansion in the Indian Ocean dramatized the global reach of its navy and was seen as an indication of a general effort of the Soviet Union to expand its political influence. Soviet prominence in the Indian Ocean was also seen as a possible temptation to the Soviet leaders to take additional risks in the pursuit of targets of opportunity.[8] A U.S. presence was therefore seen as a deterrent against any disruption of vital sea lanes.

Interest in the Indian Ocean was also accelerated by the changed atmosphere after Vietnam, marked by general overseas rollbacks, sharply reduced foreign commitments, the declining usefulness of overseas bases, and the Nixon Doctrine.[9] Military analysts contended that through its seapower the United States would be better equipped to deal with small "brushfires," which were predicted in great numbers in and around the Indian Ocean. Although aircraft carriers have become increasingly vulnerable to missilery, it was argued, they would provide the U.S. navy with unrivaled flexibility for limited faraway engagements.[10]

From the start of its plans for Indian Ocean deployment, the United States perceived, though did not acknowledge, the strategic utility of the ocean. The establishment of the North West Cape facility in Australia for submarine communications coincided with the introduction of Polaris A-3 SLBMs. A congressional study revealed that the United States possessed a "potential strategic nuclear military objective" of deploying, when necessary or convenient, ballistic-missile submarines targeted on the Soviet Union.[11]

A U.S. naval presence in the Indian Ocean was thought to permit the United States to exercise its nuclear deterrent with fewer nuclear submarines. The range of Polaris and Poseidon missiles is relatively limited, and while Trident signifies a marked improvement in that respect, their presence in the Indian Ocean would greatly aggravate Soviet ASW problems. Simultaneously, U.S. targeting flexibility would be enhanced vis-à-vis some targets in the Soviet Union.[12] The Indian Ocean was thus regarded as an attractive deployment site for U.S. SLBMs because the Soviet Union would find it most difficult to deploy adequate ASW forces there to contain the U.S. threat of attack from the sea.[13]

American strategic bombers based in the Indian Ocean also appeared advantageous because the targets on Soviet Central Asian territory were considered to be readily accessible from that region. American defense specialists also believed that strategic bombers could support the general-purpose naval forces in a conventional war.[14]

The other U.S. security interests in the Indian Ocean defined as military objectives for U.S. conventional forces include the capability to: (1) protect U.S. economic interests in the Persian Gulf region; (2) employ or threaten force in support of U.S. diplomatic objectives in the Middle East; (3) secure the Indian Ocean air and sea routes against harassment or interdiction; (4) intervene in support of other objectives in the littoral; (5) related to all these, balance Soviet forces in the region and attain superiority in a crisis; and, finally, (6) provide ready protection to "friendly democratic" regimes on the littoral and in the hinterland.[15]

The last objective arises from a perception that although U.S. military strategy has deterred direct Soviet attack for many years, it has not prevented indirect incursions within the less-developed world. So an important purpose of U.S. armed forces is to counter Soviet expansionist activities, particularly "those aimed at limiting U.S. and allied freedom of access throughout the world."[16] At the same time it is admitted that the principal threat to U.S. interests in the Indian Ocean region arises out of political instability "fed by Soviet intrigue," leading to "unexpected transitions" and thus complicating relations between Western and local governments.[17]

The unsettled Iranian situation added another important dimension to U.S. security perceptions in the region. The Pentagon believes that should the Soviet Union decide on further military moves in Southwest Asia, one scenario could include a full-scale invasion of Iran. In its view, the prospect of actual combat with the United States and its allies may be the ultimate deterrent to such a Soviet move[18]—the "trip-wire" strategy.

American Capabilities

The origins of the American military presence in the Indian Ocean can be traced to 1948, when a U.S. naval station was established in the former British base of Bahrain. Beginning in the 1960s, major U.S. naval units had been frequently entering the Indian Ocean. These visits were "markedly political" in character.[19] In 1962, at the time of Sino-Indian border war, a task force of the 7th Fleet was "ordered to move" into the Bay of Bengal.[20] In 1963, an aircraft carrier, submarines, and other vessels took part in CENTO maneuvers in the Arabian Sea off Karachi, though the United States was not a member of CENTO.[21]

In late 1963, it was revealed that a decision was taken to set up a special command for the U.S. forces in the Indian Ocean. The Chairman of the Joint Chiefs of Staff declared the intention in 1963 to station special U.S. naval units in the Indian Ocean independent of local ports and composed of an aircraft carrier, some escorts, and supply ships.[22] By April 1964, the "Concord Squadron" was sailing the Indian Ocean waters. A joint U.S.-Iranian exercise was held in 1964 in which 2300 U.S. paratroopers were dropped on the continental part of Iran and a marine force landed on an Iranian island in the Persian Gulf. Hundreds of planes and 6800 U.S. officers and men took part in the exercise.[23]

When Britain proposed to withdraw from east of Suez, the suggestion came up for an Anglo-American "joint defense zone" that was to involve Saudi Arabia, Iran, Iraq, Kuwait, Pakistan, and Turkey, but the littoral states rejected the plan.[24]

For the first time, a carrier task force from the 7th Fleet entered the Bay of Bengal in December 1971 at the time of the Indo-Pakistani war. In 1972, the U.S. navy declared that the Indian Ocean was included in the "zone of responsibility" of the Pacific Fleet. The American Secretary of Defense said in 1973 that visits of U.S. naval forces to the Indian Ocean would be "more frequent and more regular than in the past."[25] The Arab-Israeli war in October 1973 and the oil crises dramatically altered the strategic situation in the Indian Ocean. The U.S. navy received instructions to conduct regular deployments with the intention to deprive the Soviet navy its countervailing capability, which it had demonstrated in 1971 and 1973, of neutralizing a reinforced U.S. naval presence.[26]

U.S. naval units took part in the biggest exercise until then, the CENTO MIDLINK maneuvers. It was held in 1974, covered the entire Arabian Sea, and involved some 50 ships and two nuclear submarines, among others. The aircraft carrier U.S.S. *Constellation* made a significant visit to the Persian Gulf. In January 1975, a task force of the Seventh Fleet headed by the U.S.S. *Enterprise* appeared in the Indian Ocean for another exercise that involved landing on a Persian Gulf island under the UAE.[27]

In 1977 alone, U.S. ships passed through the Indian Ocean three times, with the *Enterprise* and *Midway* involved on two occasions. They took part in the joint naval exercises of the United States, Great Britain, Iran, and Pakistan, including the MIDLINK-77, carried out in the northern part of the Arabian Sea, the Gulf of Oman, and the Strait of Hormuz.[28] Between 1971 and 1979, the Indian Ocean was visited by some 20 American carrier groups.[29] Both during the Iranian revolution in early 1979 and the U.S. hostage incident later that year, the U.S. naval presence in the region increased, reaching a peak of U.S. and allied presence of over 80 warships in the wake of the outbreak of the Iraq-Iran war in September 1980.

In the fall of 1979, the U.S. administration undertook to establish a new security framework in the Persian Gulf following the Iranian events and their perceived impact on the region in the context of Western dependence on Gulf oil. Soviet capabilities also became a factor in the new security outlook, which prompted new initiatives such as a regional focus for the RDF and a significant increase in naval presence in the Indian Ocean.[30] These new commitments were announced in the form of the Carter Doctrine in early 1980.

By January 1983, a new command structure, the U.S. Central Command (USCENTCOM), the first-ever regional command in 30 years, came into being. It evolved from the Rapid Deployment Joint Task Force, in existence since 1979, and is charged with ensuring U.S. security interests "focused exclusively" on Southwest Asia.[31] It has assumed all of the functions of a regional unified command, including a security assistance function. US-CENTCOM is assigned an area of responsibility that previously had been divided between U.S. European and Pacific commands. It has operational command of army, air force, and naval components headquarters as well as of those U.S. forces earmarked for the region that are located *primarily* in the United States.[32]

According to U.S. defense assessments, the regional naval support facilities and access to facilities ashore for prepositioning equipment and supplies have been increased. Initiatives afloat include a 13-ship near-term prepositioning force. By 1987, prepositioned ships containing equipment and supplies for three Marine Amphibious Brigades will replace part of the near-term prepositioning force, providing U.S. forces with a "dramatic increase in both sustainability and deployability." Prepositioning plans ashore include plans for obtaining POL support from U.S. allies and friends. Agreements are being sought with numerous countries for additional facilities that could increase en route, overflight, and recovery access.[33]

A major part of the visible U.S. power projection efforts center around the RDF/USCENTCOM strategy, vis-à-vis the Diego Garcia facility and other secondary facilities.

Until 1977, the U.S. military posture seemed to imply that the purpose of power projection in the Indian Ocean area would be served largely by naval deployments. The successful military use by the Soviet Union of an ally, East Germany, and friend, Cuba, in Angola and Ethiopia in 1976–77, probably convinced the Pentagon of the need for a force dedicated for intervention in Third World situations.

In fact, the United States has been in the rapid deployment and power projection business for a long time (the marines are more than two centuries old). It has been a part of U.S. military doctrine to be ready to fight in contingencies in remote areas.[34] In the 1960s, the United States created a "Strike Command" that had at its disposal a 100,000-strong army corps and tactical air force command units with a total strength of 50,000 men. According to then Secretary of Defense Robert McNamara, the command's task was to be a combat-ready force capable of rapid deployment in reaction to "crises situations at levels below a full-scale nuclear war."[35] However, the need for a truly awesome and effective force and the further need for publicity of such a force seems to have emerged in the later 1970s.

Thus, shortly after taking office, President Carter ordered a far-ranging review of U.S. national security commitments and capabilities. The exercise resulted in a series of Presidential Review Memoranda (PRMs), one of which, PRM-10, describing U.S. force commitments worldwide, became the basis for the Presidential Directive 18, setting up the RDF.[36]

In September 1977, addressing the National Security Industrial Association, Secretary of Defense Harold Brown described several highlights of the new U.S. decision.[37] He stated that the United States must continue to maintain a defense posture that permitted it to respond effectively and simultaneously to both relatively minor as well as major military contingencies. The requirements for such a posture, over and above the forces programmed for Europe, were a limited number of light land combat forces, naval and tactical air forces, and strategic mobility. The initial geographic areas of concern were Korea, the Middle East, and the Persian Gulf.[38]

The fall of the Shah of Iran in early 1979 and the Soviet entry into Afghanistan at the end of that year not only quickened the pace of the RDF buildup, but also caused the United States to shift its focus exclusively to that part of the Indian Ocean region now known as Southwest Asia.[39] Along with the new command structure for the RDF, and USCENTCOM, the strength of forces assigned to them has grown from what President Carter estimated as "from a few ships or air squadrons to formations as large as 100,000 men together with their support"[40] to nearly 400,000 men, if reserves are included.[41] In the period 1984–88, spending on RDF will total $13.6 billion.[42]

The RDF is qualified as the "cutting edge" of America's total power projection system,[43] and such a force is intended to maintain an "intervention capability" for the United States "to be used unilaterally" if necessary in Third World contingencies.[44] General Bernard Rogers, the U.S. Army Chief of Staff, suggested that the RDF was being created in response to the U.S. President's desire for a specialized force "to handle conflicts in the Third World." Therefore, it has been further argued that the unusually high "teeth to tail," or support-to-combat, ratio of the RDF force structure is justified in view of the situation that the force would be primarily deployed in areas lacking any but the most rudimentary forms of logistical infrastructure.[45]

In an emergency, specific units in all services designated as RDF units will revert to USCENTCOM, which will report directly to the organization of the Joint Chiefs of Staff. USCENTCOM has a hold on five army and two marine divisions, plus the equivalent of ten air wings. With support units, the RDF numbers about 220,000 men.[46]

Logistics appear to create formidable problems for the RDF strategy. For the United States, Southwest Asia poses a challenge of nearly 7000 miles of an air line of communication (LOC) and 8000 miles of sea LOC via the Suez Canal, which if closed would add another 4000 miles. During the 1973 Arab-Israeli war, for every ton of American cargo delivered to Israel, over six tons of fuel was used in the air LOC. When, for political reasons, the United States decided to fly 12 F-4s, with their support nonstop from the East Coast to Cairo, it took 28 C-5s, 4 C-141 loads, and 32 KC-135 refuelings.[47]

The Americans are attempting to overcome this strategic mobility problem with a new concept of maritime prepositioning, both offshore and onshore. The initial maritime positioning ships containing the heavy equipment and supplies for a 12,000-man Marine Amphibious Brigade are deployed off Diego Garcia. The embarked equipment will support ground combat operations, the essential functions of marine aviation, and the air–ground logistics system. In addition, a 30-day contingency block of consumables, spares, and replacements will be included.[48]

As more of these ships become available, they could be based in other places, such as in Norway, Great Britain, the Philippines, the Mediterranean, or friendly ports along the Indian Ocean littoral. They would be able to sail separately on a routine basis, or in company with the forward-deployed amphibious-ready groups. In the event of a crisis, the personnel to operate the equipment could be flown in Military Airlift Command aircraft to the region to join the waiting prepositioned ships.[49]

The periodical exercises conducted by U.S. combined forces with local forces provided clues to gaps in future integrated operations such as the RDF use. After Bright Star '82, General Kingston, the present USCENTCOM Commander, said that a certain amount of warning time was essential to the RDF mission. He stated, for example, that with adequate advance notice of four or five days, he could get an airborne brigade "on the ground" in the Persian Gulf region in 48 hours, and an airborne division in 10–14 days.[50]

Three contingencies would activate the RDF: Soviet intervention, regional aggression, and civil strife. The Soviet threat is the "least likely to occur" and also not the threat that worries the local states, which are concerned with regional rivalries.[51]

First and foremost, the RDF is intended as a deterrent. The decision about its size, combat equipment, and mobility are influenced by its expected impact on the "international behavior of other states and/or groups."[52] In a supportive role, the RDF is expected to intervene within a matter of days to bolster a regime faced with an external threat or internal anti-regime challenge.[53] In a coercive interventionary role, it must be prepared to fight its way in and establish an operating area and a fairly rigorous line of resupply, probably by sealift.[54]

Even before the later significance of Diego Garcia became obvious, the atoll figured prominently in the navy's and the DOD's "strategic island concept" plan as early as the 1950s.[55] Initially the island was being canvassed as a "modest communication base," as an alternative to the U.S. station in Eritrea (Ethiopia). The Congress supported the idea since the cost of funding for Ethiopian forces as a consideration for the Eritrean base was escalating.[56]

The communication station became operational on March 23, 1973. Though there was no official announcement, it was described as an essential development to help control the future movement of American ships and planes through the area.[57] A *New York Times* report declared that it opened a new chapter in America's involvement in the Indian Ocean. Diego Garcia became an important link in the U.S. Worldwide Military Command and control systems. The facility was designed to fill a long-felt gap in high-frequency radio coverage in the area. Diego Garcia receives its information from the Defense Satellite Communications System and relays it to the naval and air units in the region.[58]

Following the 1973 Arab-Israeli war and the oil crises, the defense planners put forward an expansion plan for Diego Garcia and a $29 million authorization. The Defense Department justified it along the following lines:[59]

MISSION AND PROJECT:

The Naval communication station provides Fleet broadcasts, tactical ship-to-shore and point-to-point communications and is a critical link in the Defense Communication system.

A new mission is being assigned to this station to support periodical presence of an Indian Ocean Task Group. The project provides facilities to improve Diego Garcia for logistically supporting the Task Group.

IMPACT IF NOT PROVIDED:

If this project is not provided, there will be no fixed site to support carrier task force operations in the Indian Ocean area.

As early as 1968, the U.S. Chief of Naval Operations, Admiral Thomas Moorer, suggested that Diego Garcia should serve as a base for aerial reconnaissance, headquarters for a small permanent staff, and facilities for servicing one aircraft carrier on special occasions. Two further functions were added by the Joint Chiefs of Staff: the building of a modest communications center and facilities for receiving strategic submarines. However, the Senate did not approve of the funding plan.[60]

The situation changed by the mid-70s. Concomitant with the Nixon Doctrine and to ensure the maintenance of a viable defense posture in the overall Indian Ocean region, the "strategic mobility" concept received increased emphasis. The expanded facility at the atoll was viewed as central for peacetime projections as well as wartime assignments of the U.S. navy for the area.[61] However, even as late as 1973, the Pentagon reiterated in the Congress that "there were no plans to transform Diego Garcia into a base facility from which forces could be projected or that would provide a location for basing of ships and aircraft."[62]

With the prospects for access to facilities in the littoral states diminished, Diego Garcia assumed greater importance in U.S. strategic considerations. Further, an added military justification for upgrading the facility arose in the form of Soviet facilities in Berbera (Somalia). Contrary to the view that Western facilities in the Indian Ocean constituted a "far more substantial infrastructure than the Russians have been able to assemble,"[63] assertions were made that Diego Garcia alone "would not even equal the Soviet facilities in Somalia."[64]

Thus, a new Anglo-U.S. agreement was signed providing for expansion of the existing facility into a "logistics facility," the scope of which included an anchorage, airfield, support and supply elements and ancillary services, personnel accommodation, and transmitting and receiving services.[65]

The expansion was to facilitate an extended and semi-continuous American presence in the Indian Ocean. The 12,000-foot runway, the dredged harbor, and the lagoon would enable the United States to use the facility for strategic units.[66] The runway can be used by almost any aircraft in the world, including the U.S. B-52 strategic bombers and the KC-135 plane used for refueling them, even if the B-52s are fully loaded.[67] In March 1974, Admiral Moorer, then Chairman of the Joint Chiefs of Staff, admitted in Senate testimony that Diego Garcia would accommodate B-52s,[68] and a congressional report confirmed that in 1979.[69] In early 1980, Japanese sources reported that beginning in January 1980, the United States began flying regular B-52 missions from Diego Garcia.[70] Officially, two squadrons of B-52s are assigned to USCENTCOM as part of the U.S. air force's "strategic power projection force,"[71] and they have participated in combined military maneuvers in the Southwest Asian theater.[72] Meanwhile, Diego Garcia was being used as transit base for long-range reconnaissance P-3 and SR-71 planes flying between the Philippines and Kenya.[73]

The protected harbor at Diego Garcia is capable of harboring an aircraft carrier (CVAN) and support ships, that is, a carrier task group. The fuel storage capacity on the atoll, 380,000 barrels of aviation fuel and 320,000 barrels of fuel oil, is enough to supply a carrier task group for about 39 days. In addition, the harbor contains both an anchorage and 550 feet of berthing facilities for loading and unloading fuel.[74]

Diego Garcia is thus pivotal to the military and strategic measures decided upon at the beginning of the 1980s, for example, securing of rights to use military facilities in the littoral states, the deployment of marines, advance storage of arms on ships for use by the RDF. Former constraints limiting the offensive capabilities of Diego Garcia have been dropped.[75] The deployment of up to 30 U.S. naval units (including two aircraft carrier task groups) on standby in the Gulf region in recent crises considerably increased the importance of Diego Garcia.

Apart from Diego Garcia, there is evidence that the United States intends to have a permanent presence in the Gulf backed by access to facilities in countries that have regimes sympathetic to such a presence.

Confusion persists as to the exact operational distinction between "bases," "facilities," "access agreeements," and "host-nation support." This confusion is further compounded by official disclosures that the United States in many instances—indeed, in most—seeks not formal, public guarantees and agreements, but rather the establishment of "quiet consultation and of quiet building of an ability."[76] Further, crucial details of various arrangements the United States has concluded with some of the regional states are missing even in congressional reports, some of which are cited below:

> *Kenya:*[77] The June 1980 agreement provides (*security deletion*). The United States will give to Kenya a total of $50 million in economic and food aid and $27 million in foreign military sales credits over 1981–82.

> Given the consistently friendly relations between the two nations, Kenyan officials felt that a formal agreement was not necessary (*security deletion*).

> The agreement involves (*security deletion*). The projects will provide the United States (*security deletion*).

> Mombasa and adjacent port and airfield facilities should clearly enhance the operational facility of the U.S. fleet. Also, the Nanyuki air base is only 1900 air miles from the nearest Gulf shore, compared to 2700 miles from Mombasa, which is only 4–6 days sailing time to the Strait of Hormuz.

> *Oman:* The U.S. provided $25 million in Foreign Military Sales to Oman in 1980 and again in FY 1981 . . . (*security deletion*).[78]

> The former RAF base at Masirah has been made available to U.S. forces. A new U.S. facility came up at Juff, on the Gulf of Oman, in 1978. Another U.S. facility was completed in Al Qasab, on the extreme finger of Oman jutting into the Strait of Hormuz.[79]

> The 1800-strong amphibious marine task force and the USCENTCOM command ship, the U.S.S. *LaSalle,* are headquartered in and around these facilities.[80]

> The Defense Department has announced its plan to build a "brigade staging facility" at Thumrait in Oman and has asked for appropriate funding in FY 1985 and 1986.[81]

> *Bahrain:* Under the terms of the agreement with Bahrain, the United States has contracted for limited repair, refueling, and replenishment for Mideast for (*security deletion*). Because of the sharp increase in the volume of U.S. naval forces in the region, U.S. policymakers might have to reexamine the adequacy of logistical capabilities in Bahrain (*security deletion*).

> Drydocks of various sizes exist there, some of which may be of political utility to the navy. The largest of the Bahrain drydocks was constructed under the aegis of the OAPEC and is reportedly capable of handling vessels the size of large oil tankers (*security deletion*).

> *Somalia:*[82] The August 1980 agreement provides for U.S. use of Somali facilities in Mogadishu, but particularly in Berbera, including (*security deletion*).

Unlike Oman and Kenya, who prefer a limited U.S. military presence and low profile on implementing access agreements, Somalia welcomes a large number of Americans and extensive high-visibility use of Somali facilities. Somalia will probably also (*security deletion*).

Barbera is 600 miles closer to Gulf than Mombasa and Diego Garcia. It has an excellent 2.5-mile runway, fuel storage tanks, and ample open space for extensive prepositioning of equipment. Bunkers exist for 12 fighter aircraft and there are a limited number of general operations and support buildings.

Australia and the Philippines have provided the traditional U.S. naval bases that have now grown in importance due to increased U.S. naval interest in the Indian Ocean. At a meeting of ANZUS foreign ministers in Washington in early 1980, the Indian Ocean was formally included in future ANZUS activities. Australia later sent some naval units and the carrier *Melbourne* to the Strait of Hormuz and took part in joint naval exercises there and in the eastern Indian Ocean.[83] Australia also agreed to incorporate the Darwin air force base into the B-52 strategic bomber network and appeared prepared in principle to open the naval base at Cockburn Sound on the Indian Ocean to the U.S. navy, possibly with a view to the more long-term home-porting of personnel. Australia's air force uses Diego Garcia for long-distance reconnaissance over the Indian Ocean.[84]

Three most important military installations impinging on the strategic balance of the superpowers have been in operation in Australia from the late 1960s and have since been expanded:

1. The Exmouth Communication Center (North West Cape), which specializes *inter alia* in very-low-frequency communication with submerged submarines;
2. The Nurrungar Early Warning Satellite Station, which has the task of detecting enemy missile attacks; and
3. The Pine Gap Reconnaissance Station, which is linked to a geostationary satellite looking into Soviet and Chinese territories—this is a communication and EW interception facility.[85]

The recent New Zealand government policy of banning nuclear-armed ships from its ports may lead to a "reappraisal" of the ANZUS, according to Australian Prime Minister Robert Hawke.[86]

The bases in the Philippines, primarily Clark Field, an air force base, and Subic Bay naval base, are valuable to U.S. Indian Ocean strategy. They provide key logistics and supply facilities that permit transshipment between the Western Pacific and the Indian Ocean areas and thus help maintain a continuous U.S. military presence in these regions.[87]

In fact, in the entire Indian Ocean region, the ports of only two countries—Iraq and South Yemen (PDRY)—are not open to U.S. warships.[88]

The United States had "voluntarily denied itself" access to ports in India since 1971, when India instituted a requirement that naval vessels visiting Indian ports specify whether they were carrying nuclear weapons. In 1972, this was modified to a simple request that host facilities in Indian ports not be sought for vessels carrying nuclear weapons.[89] However, of late there seems to be some change in the situation. For the first time in 14 years, a U.S. warship, the U.S.S. *Lewis B. Puller,* arrived in Bombay on May 21, 1984, on a three-day goodwill visit.[90] She also visited Cochin.

The Indian Ocean in Emerging U.S. Strategy

The United States says that it is preparing to face challenges in the Indian Ocean ranging from the containment of crises in peacetime to general warfare and from direct confrontation with the Soviet Union to conflict with nations that are dubbed as its clients in what have come to be known as "proxy" wars.[91] To confront these challenges, it is said, "maritime superiority" is crucial and is derived from the balance of naval forces "in being"—both naval and merchant ships, aircraft, munitions, and manpower—as well as from logistics, training, tactics, operational experience, and overseas support structure.[92]

Possible U.S. naval missions in the Indian Ocean are listed as deterrence, strategic nuclear capability, sea control, projection of power ashore, support of allies, and peacetime presence.[93] The goal of the naval presence is defined as "the use of naval forces short of war to achieve political objectives" and diplomatic advantage.[94]

In the strategic realm, the Indian Ocean provides the United States with an ideal spot for deployment of sea-based missiles aimed at the Soviet Union. The geographic location of waters, especially around the Red Sea, the Persian Gulf, and the Arabian Sea, provide some of the best locations for U.S. sea-based missile deployment as a deterrent against the Soviet Union.[95] The U.S. interest in the defense potential of the Indian Ocean is also apparent in the fact that ocean engineering in the United States is still primarily military oriented. Washington appreciates the enormous importance of oceanography and approaches it as a "necessary support element in all warfare areas."[96] As land-based missiles become increasingly vulnerable, undersea long-range missiles have become the key to U.S. strategic offense and defense. The U.S. navy, as Admiral Zumwalt noted, has come to view its assignment as The Strategic Force as its primary responsibility.[97]

The determination of American strategic planners to continue using the sea-based strategic potential was also evident from the American opposition to additional constraints on the strategic use of the seabed in the Seabed Arms Control Treaty. Although the treaty forbids "the emplacement of nuclear weapons or other weapons of mass destruction on or in the seabed beyond a 12 mile maritime zone," submarines and other such vehicles that can navigate beneath the waters, but above the seabed (without being in contact with the seabed), are viewed by Washington as any other ship and thus not subject to the prohibition of the treaty.[98] The Joint Chiefs of Staff openly warned that "any additional constraints on military use of the seabed beyond the prohibitions contained in the treaty" bear a potential for "grave harm to the U.S. national security interests."[99] The thrust of the American forward naval strategy is well expressed in the following jingle:[100]

> Keep deterrence out at sea
> Where the real-estate is free
> And it is far away from me.

The full potential of the conventional capabilities of U.S. forces in the Indian Ocean area has not yet been realized. Maximum effective use of all facilities contracted for in Kenya, Somalia, and Oman and on Diego Garcia, for instance, will not be possible for several years because of the extensive work still required,[101] which is estimated to cost another $1 billion in addition to the RDF cost of $13.6 billion. For the future, two proposals have been discussed to improve RDF effectiveness. One is prepositioning of armor and other heavy equipment "close to or in the Persian Gulf area itself." The other is a permanent U.S. military presence in the area.[102] At the same time, the U.S. military assistance to and cooperation with Gulf states are so designed as to be "helpful to the United States in a time of conflict."[103]

However, such cooperation itself seems to have generated further security needs. The massive transfer of the most sophisticated weapon systems into the West Asia–Persian Gulf region and the presence of U.S. personnel in that area related to this militarization were the subject of a 1977 U.S. Congress Staff Study, which estimated that there were 100,000 Americans (30,000 in Saudi Arabia and 70,000 in Iran) in mostly "defense-related activities." It observed that this developing situation posed particular policy problems for the United States. The estimate then was that there would be over 150,000 Americans living in the Gulf by 1980.[104] The Iranian revolution may have drastically cut this figure, yet it continues to be substantial.

In a contrary view, it has been argued that the basic U.S. national interest of maintaining access to Gulf oil at tolerable prices, both for the United States and its allies, could be promoted by maintaining a series of close relationships with the oil states,[105] and not exclusively by military means.

The Soviet Union

Soviet Interests in the Indian Ocean

Soviet interests in the Indian Ocean center on countering U.S. military and political thrusts in the region, thwarting possible American plans to pose a strategic missile threat from that front, securing its long sea lanes, and extending assistance to friendly countries in the littoral, especially in times of threats to their security. All these make the Soviet presence in the Indian Ocean area an "essentially defense oriented" one.[106]

The principal reason for the Soviet Union's initial involvement in the Indian Ocean region was the need for reciprocal arrangements with littoral states that would assist its attempts to break through the Western containment of its long southern flank, effected in the 1950s, principally through the Baghdad Pact and, to a lesser extent, SEATO.[107] By 1968, after a major building program, Moscow was able to establish its access to the region.

One important political function of the Soviet navy in the Indian Ocean was to provide support for the regional states threatened with "imperialist intervention." Both in the 1971 Bangladesh conflict and in the 1973 Arab-Israeli war, the Soviet fleet, after swift reinforcement, took up positions that countered U.S. naval movements and projected an image of active support for the interests of Third World states.[108]

Throughout the 1970s, Soviet pronouncements explaining the presence of its fleet in the Indian Ocean contained constant references to the threat to Soviet territory, posed in the first instance by American submarines with nuclear missiles operating from the Indian Ocean, combined with the offensive capability of U.S. aircraft carriers.[109] Since Washington has not expressly ruled out deployment of strategic submarines in the Indian Ocean, the Soviets do not exclude such a threat, especially when the imminent introduction of Tridents would probably make this a reality.[110] The Trident, with its more sophisticated support systems, will be able to stay longer on Indian Ocean missions than the current Polaris and Poseidon submarines, which must make costly trips back and forth to Guam. In Soviet calculations, the Indian Ocean provides certain geographical advantages for U.S. targeting. From the Pacific, for example, even with its increased range (over 6000 miles), the Trident D-5 missile could reach only the central part of the Soviet Union via "a narrow strip along the coast," whereas such missiles fired from the vast Arabian sea and the Bay of Bengal could strike Soviet targets "on a much wider front."[111] Moscow might perceive greater danger in what American "navalists" are fond of advocating—that "the U.S. navy must make an ally of surprise." One could plausibly argue that the deployment of the Trident in the Indian Ocean could be perceived by the Russians as giving to the United States an enhanced first-strike capability.

The Soviet Union, as a nation continually in need of food supplies, has extensive fishing fleets in the Indian Ocean. Historically, warships follow these fishing fleets simply to ensure their safety and add some weight to their right to be where they are.[112]

Although in the 1950s and 1960s, the military components of Soviet policy in the Indian Ocean region were still "on the whole reactive" vis-à-vis the overwhelming influence of the West, by 1970 these circumstances had changed somewhat.[113] However, in most Western analyses of the military element of Soviet policy in the area, the navy has been accorded undue emphasis. In the Soviet Union's two most important military operations in the Indian Ocean region so far—the Big Lift to Ethiopia to win back the Ogaden at the end of 1977 and the beginning of 1978 and the intervention in Afghanistan—the fleet has played only a peripheral supporting role.[114]

Further, the concern in America, and in the West generally, over oil supplies has its counterpart in the Soviet Union in the form of the threat represented by the "China syndrome." The image of a Soviet Union moving nearer the Gulf and spreading its military net in an ever widening circle, against a background of instability in Iran and in the Arab Gulf states, is qualitatively equivalent to the Soviet image of increased rapprochement between China and America (as well as Japan and Western Europe). Both developments raise the superpowers' perception of threat—in the United States on the basis of the formula "oil dependence plus the Soviet Union," and in the Soviet Union according to that of "collusion between the main adversaries."[115]

Soviet Capabilities

Since its first entry, in 1968 into the Indian Ocean region, the Soviet navy has steadily increased its presence there. But Moscow has been unable to obtain versatile base facilities comparable to those available to the United States. Prior to 1977, the only permanently based Soviet vessel was a repair ship at Berbera. Many Soviet efforts to acquire bases, such as the 1978 bid for Gan in the Maldives, did not prove fruitful.[116] The Soviet navy used to maintain deep-sea buoy moorings or anchorages, described as berthing stations or floating bases by the West, off the coast of Mauritius in international waters, which provided rendezvous points for replenishment of ships operating in the area.[117] Their present status is not known.

Aden in South Yemen has witnessed the heaviest Soviet buildup, particularly after the Soviet withdrawal of naval and air force equipment from Somalia at the end of 1977. In May 1979, the Soviet Union conducted a naval demonstration off Aden. Aircraft from the carrier *Minsk* performed vertical takeoffs and landings and the amphibious assault ship *Ivan Rogov*, with 499 marines on board, was put through its paces.[118] The Ethiopian ports of Assab and Massawa are open to the Soviet navy, but these lie in Eritrean territory and hence not far from the areas of fighting. Massawa is a deepwater port and suitable for enlargement for military purposes. Since 1980, the Dahlak islands off Massawa have been extended for military uses by the Soviet Union. The Soviet Union makes use of harbors in Mozambique (Maputo, Beira, Nacala), which could come to play an important role if the conflict in Southern Africa were to intensify.[119] In India, the Soviet navy has no exclusive right of access, but in the event of an international conflict it would most probably invoke the 1971 bilateral treaty under which it could obtain such rights, always provided that this was also in India's own interests.[120] The Soviet Union has important military facilities for its navy and air force outside the Indian Ocean, in Vietnam (Cam Ranh Bay and Da Nang) and hence within reach of the Malacca strait and providing a geostrategic link between its Pacific harbors and those in the Indian Ocean.[121]

Given its lack of base facilities, Soviet supply lines stretch from Vladivostok—an incredibly long distance—through areas that could easily be interdicted. Alternatively, they have to come through the Dardanelles, the Suez Canal, and the narrow Straits of Jubal, "again a most dangerous route in the event of hostilities."[122] It has therefore been contended that the Soviet increase of ships in the Indian Ocean is merely "part and parcel" of the increase of the Soviet navy in all oceans, and that this general buildup in turn is merely part of the total increase in Soviet naval strength since the Cuban missile crisis proved to the Soviets the value of a stronger fleet.[123]

However, there is another consideration that determines the Soviet naval behavior in the region. Besides providing a countervailing presence, as in the case of 1971 and 1973 crises, the Soviet naval factor has, in fact, been invoked in the contexts of regional conflicts as well. Thus, in 1973, Moscow sent a naval contingent to Iraq during the latter's border clash with Kuwait. In 1977 and 1978, the fleet provided support for the air bridge operations in the Ogaden war. Amphibious assault ships bought in material and Soviet units operated just outside the harbor at Massawa, which had been cut off by Eritrean rebels. And at the beginning of 1981, the Soviet Union reinforced its naval presence in Mozambique in response to a South African incursion there.[124]

As a result, though the size of the Soviet naval force regularly fluctuated from 1968 to 1973, the strength of both major and interim groups steadily increased. In the summer of 1973, the Soviet Union deployed twice as many surface combatants to the Indian Ocean (up to 30) as they had done in the previous summer. Moreover, they deployed a submarine, and instead of departing after the usual five or six months, most of the interim group remained in Indian Ocean almost an entire year.[125] This increased naval presence was the beginning of what is now a continuous year-round force, with units normally relieved on a one-to-one basis.[126] Units generally assigned to the Soviet Indian Ocean squadron in the beginning of the 1980s numbered between 20 and 22 ships. The force is usually composed of one or two major combatants, four minor combatants, one or two amphibious units, one submarine, and various support, research, and space-related ships.[127]

The overriding limitations of the Soviet navy seem to dissipate its challenges to the West, both at the tactical/regional level and in the global/strategic context. It has, therefore, been forcefully argued that the Soviets just cannot afford to hurt critical Western interests in the Indian Ocean area. In a purely maritime worldwide conflict between NATO and the Warsaw Pact nations, the Soviet Union could use its forces in the Indian Ocean to hinder Western oil supplies. But the very existence of a Soviet Indian Ocean squadron would increase the dispersion of Moscow's naval forces, which are already divided between Murmansk and Vladivostok.[128] "According to all traditional criteria of naval power," claims one analyst, "the Indian Ocean squadron would be a source of weakness rather than strength, and isolated squadrons are unlikely to play any major disruptive role."[129]

It has been argued that in the event of a general war, the greater the number of Soviet ships located in the Indian Ocean—rather than in the Atlantic, the Mediterranean, or the Pacific—"the better it would be for the West." Though the Soviet ships could hinder or even halt Western oil supplies from the Gulf, in the crucial first weeks of the war this would be a less important threat to the West than attacks on troop convoys across the Atlantic; and, in any case, Soviet ships would not be ideal for attacks on commerce because of their limited gun armament.[130] In a scenario including

U.S. occupation of oil fields and a subsequent intervention by Moscow, the Soviet navy would probably be given tasks only in connection with air operations over the oceans to be conducted mainly from Soviet territory.[131]

Nor is the picture of naval interdiction that much brighter for the Soviet side, for the ASW balance would swing against the Soviet navy, which— using a submarine/bomber combination—could sink only 30 percent of the tanker traffic using the Gulf sea lanes.[132] Soviet naval deployment in the Indian Ocean—particularly submarines, depends on long-range reinforcement, which consumes both time and resources.

As for naval capabilities against U.S. carrier task forces in the Indian Ocean, the Soviet navy could commit currently at most some 10 submarines and about 100 naval bombers. The transit of the *Ivan Rogov,* an amphibious assault ship, in May 1979 with its naval infantry battalion of 400 men "hardly tips the balance in any disastrous sense." Nor are there any signs that the Soviet Union is developing a major capability in the American style. If anything, Soviet naval developments appear to be designed to "frustrate the preferred American mode [naval intervention], rather than to compete with it."[133]

The Indian Ocean in Emerging Soviet Strategy

Significant developments in Soviet naval construction now taking place could affect the naval balance in the Indian Ocean. The Pentagon's suspicion[134] that the Soviets are building a larger conventional aircraft carrier with a full-length flight deck has already been proved correct.[135] This ship is nuclear-powered, displaces about 70,000 tons, has catapults and arresting gear, and carries high-performance conventional takeoff and landing aircraft.

Another recent development that the U.S. Defense Department considers "most significant" is the Kiev-class carrier, the first Soviet-built ship to carry fixed-wing aircraft.[136]

With a displacement of 28,000 tons, the nuclear-powered guided-missile cruiser KIROV is considered the largest combatant other than aircraft carriers built by any country since World War II. Another type of multi-purpose guided-missile cruiser, tentatively designated the BLK-COM-1, is also under construction. Both cruisers represent a departure from the Soviet special-purpose cruiser designs of the 1960s and 1970s.[137] Perhaps they have a raider role.

Extensive Soviet ship-borne air defense capabilities would increase the effectiveness of surface combatants when operating beyond the range of land-based fighter planes. However, the lack of adequate Soviet carrier-based fighters would remain a weakness in the short run.[138] Moreover, the open-ocean effectiveness of Soviet naval forces is adversely affected by geographic constraints that are likely to remain unmitigated. The four Soviet fleets—Northern, Baltic, Black Sea, and Pacific—are widely separated and must either traverse considerable distances or transit through choke points to reach the open ocean. To enter the North Atlantic, the Northern Fleet (based along the

Barents Sea) must transit more than 1500 miles through waters bounded by potentially unfriendly nations. The Baltic Fleet has access to the oceans only through the narrow, easily mined Skagerrak dominated by Sweden, Denmark, Norway, and West Germany. The Black Sea Fleet can reach the Mediterranean Sea only by transiting the Bosphorus and the Dardenelles, which are also narrow and easily mined and are controlled by Turkey.[139]

These constraints could be offset somewhat by prehostilities deployments, but this would provide significant strategic warning to the United States and its allies.[140]

The Soviet Pacific Fleet is concentrated at Vladivostok, on the Sea of Japan, and Petropavlovsk, in the northwest Pacific Ocean. Forces at Vladivostok have ready access to the Sea of Japan, but to reach the Pacific Ocean they must pass through the strait of Tsushima close to Japan and South Korea, waters readily accessible to Western forces. Although the fleet at Petropavlovsk has easy accress to the Pacific Ocean, Petropavlovsk itself is located in the Kamchatka Peninsula, which is remote from the Soviet heartland and not easily resupplied. Thus, the Soviet navy would have difficulty in maintaining operations out of Petropavlovsk unless major sea lanes of resupply could be sustained.[141]

Such is the Pentagon's own assessment of the Soviet naval capability.

India

India is by far the strongest military power in the Indian Ocean littoral and also the most potent naval power. Since the early 1970s, the Indian navy's share in the defense budget of the country has steadily increased. But the navy has suffered significantly from unplanned growth. It could not have been otherwise, given the narrow base and the organizational disruptions of the immediate post-independence years, its overwhelming dependence on the Royal Navy for doctrine as well as for leadership, and the resultant subordination of purely Indian interests to the concepts of an imperial—albeit vanishing—strategy.

The acquisition of hardware from wherever it was available and, most important of all, the neglect of its submarine arm until well into the 1960s contributed further to this unplanned growth. The meager 4 percent of the defense budget that was the navy's share until well after 1960, despite the vociferous declamations in Parliament and the press in support of a strong and self-reliant naval force, typified a pervasive lack of understanding of maritime affairs and strategy in general and of naval affairs in particular.

There has of course been a compensating advantage in this slow and often faltering buildup of the Indian navy. It is that the naval personnel have had time to become well grounded in their profession and have had the benefit of a long and mostly beneficial stewardship of senior officers of the Royal Navy. This may explain the relatively faster growth of recent years, which has been astonishingly smooth and free of any upheavals among the navy's personnel, and the transformations in command and control that became necessary to cope with the needs of a high-technology, three-dimensional Naval force.

The dawn of the 1970s was a period of change and innovation. By consensus of the lower deck, the traditional uniform, the square rig and the sailor's cap, underwent a metamorphosis. Everyone preferred to wear a peak cap and abandon the bell-bottom trouser. It heralded the new, high-technology era of the submarine and the missile, the gas turbine, and an almost total break from the apron strings of the Royal Navy, its tactical doctrine and methods of training and management. With increasing acquisition of Soviet hardware, this had become inevitable. But the Indian navy did not forsake its language nor did it abandon the hallowed traditions and several quaint customs that were the legacy of its long and fruitful association with Britain and her Royal Navy.

The naval war in 1971 against Pakistan was won essentially by fast-moving, hard-hitting coastal forces. Surprise was the essential factor responsible for such heavy casualties on the opponent in the west. The carrier-centered task force in the east played its appointed role in the blockade of erstwhile East Pakistan and helped in neutralizing Pakistani air power around Dacca and Cox's Bazar. The one gaping shortcoming in this short, swift campaign was the navy's (and the army's) gaucherie in amphibious operations. In the amphibious landings attempted at Cox's Bazar, one LCT went aground and a few obedient, heavily equipped Gurkha troops drowned in deep water when they stepped off their landing craft in the semi-darkness of dawn in what should have been waist-deep water. The operation was hastily abandoned. The lack of amphibious capability is still the most glaring gap in the navy's capability in 1987.

Since the Bangladesh watershed and what could have been an epochal encounter with the U.S.S. *Enterprise,* India has become much more conscious of its shortcomings at sea. The importance of maritime power in all its multitudinous manifestations is being daily driven home—through the new Law of the Sea Convention, the continuing debate concerning Diego Garcia, the Soviet presence in Afghanistan and what it may portend in the Persian Gulf and the Arabian Sea, and the increasing naval clout of the sub-continental neighbors.

Maritime power is the sum total of several constituent capabilities. Naval forces are only a part of the total formulation, which consists of a country's industrial capacity and its resultant economic strength, the strength of its merchant fleet, the quality of its ports and harbors and of its shipbuilding and ship repair facilities, the productivity of its fishing fleet, and its technological and hydrological capacity to exploit the resources to be found in its economic zone. India's relative lag in its shipbuilding and ship repair industry—notwithstanding the fact that it is among the very few countries that build their own warships—has undoubtedly affected India's stature at sea. At the other end of the spectrum, India's advance in ocean sciences, the explorations carried out by its oceanographic ships, its acceptance as a pioneer investor in the seabed mining enterprise, and its recent participation in the councils of the Antarctic Treaty countries have all contributed to her standing as a resurgent maritime nation.

The Indian navy is not well served by bases on the mainland if one excludes Visakhapatnam, and even that base has its geographical and hydrographic limitations, most of them quite severe. In almost every case the Indian navy has to share its base ports with commercial traffic for the simple reason that the almost smooth and unindented coasts of India are poorly served by natural, deep-water harbors. In Bombay the security of the navy's little niche at the southern end of the Island of Bombay is distorted by the fact that the naval dockyard and berths for both surface vessels and submarines are located in the midst of the metropolis' bustling business district. The situation in Goa and Cochin is not much better. It is well known that in December 1971 the Pakistani submarine *Ghazi* attempted to lay mines in the narrow entrance channel of the harbor at Visakhapatnam to bottle up the fleet. Fortunately, the fleet was elsewhere, safely anchored.

It is my view that the Indian navy must give priority to establishing safe and secure bases for its fleet. Very properly, the many large and secluded anchorages in the Andaman and Nicobar Islands come to mind. A large, well-supported, and equally well-defended naval base in the Andamans will have the added advantage of overlooking the strategic Strait of Malacca, one of the historic choke points of the Indian Ocean. As the naval activities of the extra-regional powers are stepped up in the Southwest Pacific and spill over into the Indian Ocean, the significance of an Andamans complex will increase. Efforts to develop such a complex were initiated in 1986 and should be accelerated. In the west, Bombay must be replaced as the main naval base if the fleet is to operate with any safety in times of tension and near-war situations. The decision to establish a new base at Karwar is a welcome one. It acquires compelling logic from the increased activities of extra-regional navies in the Arabian Sea as well as from the potential Pakistani naval threat.

Some observers have argued that the Indian navy should break away from its Pakistan-centered policies and tactics. My own view is that until the end of this decade, at least, our problem at sea will mainly be Pakistan. Neither the United States nor the Soviet Union is going to apply its naval forces directly against India. Attempts will be made to use a proxy. That proxy will be Pakistan. The Indian navy will therefore have to keep a very close watch on the manner in which Pakistan's naval armory is being replenished and modernized. It will have to negate the enemy's most formidable weapons, for if the potential opponent has weapons of equal destructiveness, the decisive advantage will go to the side that first creates a suitable defense.

Abiding by this rule, the Indian navy must take note of the recent acquisition by Pakistan of additional destroyers equipped with surface-to-surface Harpoon missiles as well as sub-surface–to–surface Harpoon missiles of extremely high sophistication that can be fitted to its submarines. China, too, has shown increasing interest in the Indian Ocean an to Pakistan, Sri Lanka, and Bangladesh in 1986. The Chinese have also transferred naval vessels to these countries and developed military-aid relationships with them.

The Harpoon-equipped submarine poses a threat not only to naval vessels but also to vital shore-based facilities such as nuclear power plants, oil refineries, and other industrial installations. The Pakistani submarine threat is not limited to the west coast of India; it could be projected to the east coast as well. Moreover, future trends point to submarines being fitted with longer-range cruise missiles.

The presence of submarines of extra-regional powers in the waters around India further complicates the Indian security effort. This foreign presence has aroused concern about possible intelligence-sharing arrangements between Pakistan and the U.S. Central Command involving hydrographic and other data relevant to submarine operations around Indian waters. This concern has now been compounded by the projected American sale of AWAC planes to Pakistan.

Given the emerging security environment in the Indian Ocean, the Indian navy defines a fourfold mission:

1. To safeguard the Indian coastline and vital installations in the vicinity of the coastline against both surface and submarine threats.
2. To safeguard the flow of trade into and out of Indian ports during limited war situations.
3. To restrict the naval activities of the potential adversary—in this case Pakistan—during limited war.
4. And to be in a position to assist island republics of the Indian Ocean— notably Mauritius, the Seychelles, Sri Lanka—in case they seek Indian assistance, particularly against threats of subversion. The Sri Lankan intervention beginning in 1987 illustrates this mission, and the Seychelles has been subjected to two coup attempts since 1982.

Focusing on anti-submarine operations, India has modernized its existing aircraft carrier, the *Vikrant,* and has acquired a second aircraft carrier (*Hermes,* renamed *Virant*) from Britain. These ships will carry anti-submarine helicopters and provide air cover with British VTOL Harriers for anti-submarine task forces. Two aircraft carriers are necessary at this stage—first, to ensure that at least one will be available at all times and, second, because India's two seaboards, extending over 7500 miles, make it necessary to have two task forces built around carriers. In fact, for optimum coverage a much larger number will be needed. The Indian plan is to build air-capable ships in the country in the future, and the present purchase of a second aircraft carrier is only an interim step.

The second component in augmenting anti-submarine warfare capability is to acquire modern submarines. The German-designed, HDW type-1500 submarines are being constructed in India and two are being acquired from Germany. India has also acquired the first Kilo-class Soviet submarine as the first step in progressively replacing its eight older, F-class Soviet submarines. It is likely that three to six Kilo-class submarines may be acquired.

India is attempting to develop a nuclear-propelled submarine and leased one from the U.S.S.R. in 1988.

The third component of an anti-submarine capability is the versatile, all-purpose frigate. Having started with the licensed production of the British-designed Leander-class frigate (of which six were built in India), the next logical step was to move to the indigenously designed Godavari-class missile frigate. Two of this class have been commissioned and one more is being built. A new, improved category of missile frigate is now under design and the keel of the first such vessel is expected to be laid next year. Altogether, India has 24 frigates of mixed size and origin. Indigenous efforts are being supplemented by the acquisition of three Kashin II–class missile destroyers from the Soviet Union, and three additional improved Kashin-class destroyers are to join the Indian navy. The first arrived in late 1986. Supplementing these will be a line of corvettes that are also being built in India in accordance with a design purchased from France.

The fourth component is India's maritime air reconnaissance and strike capabilities, which are based on long-term maritime reconnaissance and strike aircraft and helicopters. At present, India has two Soviet IL-38 maritime reconnaissance squadrons. These are becoming obsolete and may be replaced by the Soviet SU-12. The helicopters are the British Sea Kings. The coast guard air patrol has been standardized with the German Dornier aircraft, which is being produced in India under license.

The Indian naval buildup is planned to be increasingly based on indigenous design and construction. Indian naval construction has been diversified to include missile frigates, type-1500 submarines, and corvettes. Future air-capable ships and naval missiles are proposed to be designed in India. India has been eclectic in its acquisition of technology and has incorporated Soviet, British, German, Dutch, and French technologies in its indigenous construction. In addition, an agreement has been concluded to produce General Electric LM-2500 marine-adapted gas-turbine engines in India, and various other technologies are on request from the United States.

Neither the size of the Indian navy nor its composition as it can be visualized in the foreseeable future will come anywhere near the extra-regional naval capabilities deployed in the Indian Ocean or India's optimal requirements in terms of its obligations arising out of its island territories, its vast coastline, its increasing off-shore petroleum and seabed mining assets and overseas trade, already totaling more than $20 billion annually, as well as its broader threat perceptions. The Indian navy has had a low priority in resource allocation among the three defense services. In the 1960s, it declined to as low as 4 percent of the defense budget. Since the late 1960s, however, efforts have been made to increase this allocation steadily, and it reached 13.2 percent of the 1986–87 defense budget. There is consciousness among defense planners in India that this has to be steadily stepped up to 20 percent over the next 10–15 years if the modest tasks envisaged for the navy are to be effectively managed. But the modernization programs of the other two services present very severe competition. While I am not aware of the naval staff's projection of future force levels, I would guess that by 1995 it could involve a frigate force twice as powerful as the present one and a submarine strength, as noted, of at least 12 fleet boats.

Though the naval threat to India is not wholly attributable to the presence of extra-regional navies in the Indian Ocean, as has been spelled out earlier, they do have a complicating effect on the task of the Indian navy; and the superpower rivalry does lead to the inflow of equipment to potential adversaries of India, such as Pakistan. The transfer of the Harpoon missile and refurbished Gearing-class destroyers has been justified on the basis of the role Pakistan is expected to play as part of the U.S. strategic consensus in the area. Hence the Indian interest in ensuring the Indian Ocean as a Zone of Peace in addition to its broader political objective of insulating the area from a superpower confrontation.

A standard principle that guides naval doctrine is the concentration of force, that is, launching attacks with overwhelming forces at the outset of hostilities. This principle was used during India's 1971 operations against Karachi and, when combined with surprise, achieved signal success. When dealing with superpowers, the Indian navy would quite rightly adopt different tactics—tactics that will perhaps persuade the superpower to leave well enough alone for two very good reasons.

One reason is the Indian navy's demonstrable capability to inflict unacceptable damage if the superpower pursued a course of action considered by India to be inimical to its interests. Another is that the other superpower would in all probability intervene on India's side and thus raise the stakes. This presupposes that the political leadership in New Delhi will prove itself adept at keeping the two superpowers equally interested and committed to India's interests and accept India's primacy in the sub-continental context.

There is unlikely to be a consensus between the superpowers on India's approach to the problems of the Indian Ocean waterspread and related matters. Thus, the Indian naval leadership must clearly explain to Indian political leaders what India's current naval capabilities are and how far they can be stretched in pursuit of Indian aims. The naval leadership will surely have learnt a lesson from the totally unprofessional manner in which the army leadership submitted to a manifestly uninformed political decision in 1962 in the Himalayas.

This brings me logically to the command and control of naval operations in India's sea areas. Any future naval operation will most likely be a joint operation with the air force or the army (amphibious) or one with all three services involved. The navy is unlikely to go it alone, except in small local operations involving mine countermeasures or harbor defense patrols. Although we do have a system of joint services consultations and planning, such joint methods of working have yet to become thoroughly accepted practice.

The imperatives of naval operations make it urgent for India to formulate an effective joint services doctrine, install machinery in New Delhi to direct the doctrine, and constitute joint operational commands to implement it. Given the geographical advantages with which peninsular India is endowed and its essentially maritime character, I would make a bold suggestion for the constitution of a Peninsular Command, encompassing the three naval commands, the present Southern Command of the Army, not including Rajasthan, and the Southern Air Command. The Joint Forces Commander-in-Chief (CinC Peninsular Command, or COMSULAR) would have the two Naval Commanders (East and West) and the two Fleet Commanders (East and West), the Army Commander in Pune, and the Air Force Commanders in Bangalore and Trivandrum under him. The COMSULAR would rotate among the three services and would be responsible to the Chiefs of Staff in New Delhi for the planning and conduct of all operations in his command in accordance with national directives. He would be responsible for all maritime operations in the Indian Ocean area.

With respect to the crucial issue of an amphibious or marine force, while the navy has been crying for the establishment of such a force, the army response has been tardy. The army attitude is that any line battalion with a crash course in dry and wet shod training is capable of carrying out marine operations. Such a view stems from an overall lack of exposure to a maritime environment. Moreover, even army officers who see the need have expressed reservations in private on the management of such a force. Should it be under army or naval control? This is the same question put forth by India's air force regarding the employment of attack helicopters.

The importance of an amphibious capability was demonstrated in the Falklands campaign, as was the need for integrated air cover for a fleet in distant operations. It is only when such unresolved issues are effectively addressed that India's naval potential will be fully realized. But much has been accomplished.

Other Powers

France

Like other great powers, France also has maintained its capability to intervene militarily in the Indian Ocean. During the sub-continental war in 1971, France dispatched a naval unit of five warships with a marine unit to register its presence. Throughout the 1970s it maintained a significant presence of 15 naval units, claiming a traditional mission and a need to protect its territorial possessions.[142] It continued its flag-showing mission from the Gulf and the Red Sea down the east coast of Africa as far as the more distant French possessions in the southern Indian Ocean and the Antarctic.

Since the independence of the Comoros and Djibouti and the termination of agreements covering use of military facilities in Malagasy, La Réunion has emerged as France's single most important remaining possession, and the headquarters of the French Indian Ocean forces were transferred there after Djibouti became independent. But several units of the French Indian Ocean fleet still regularly use Djibouti's dock facilities.[143] Other possessions include Mayotte, the disputed island belonging to the Comoros group. On Mayotte are located airfields that would play a key role in the surveillance of the Mozambique channel and in complementing France's network of outposts and landing facilities.[144] Aircraft can refuel on the island.

In 1981, the French Indian Ocean presence in the strategic triangle between Djibouti, La Réunion, and Mayotte (including the Mozambique channel) consisted of some 20 vessels, the most important of these being a guided-missile frigate (the *Duquesne*), five other frigates, and five minesweepers. When fighting broke out between Iran and Iraq, several additional naval units, including the *Suffren,* France's most modern guided-missile destroyer, were sent to the area, where they were involved in "increased technical consultations" with other naval formations from the West (the United States, Great Britain, and Australia).[145]

France is building an RDF, the Force d'Action Rapid, of 47,000 men that will be considerably better equipped than its present force and will be organized for independent employment. It includes an air mobile division, a light infantry division, a parachute division, a marine infantry division, an Alpine division, and a logistics brigade.[146]

Great Britain

When Britain redefined its strategic frontiers in the 1960s, it withdrew nearly 80,000 troops it had maintained east of Suez. Before withdrawal, it established a defense cooperation agreement with the United Arab Emirates and a five-power defense pact with Malaysia, Singapore, Australia, and New Zealand. Britain also set up the BIOT with a clear intention to assist its allies in the Indian Ocean. In 1975, Great Britain also gave up its defense cooperation with South Africa along with the use of the Simonstown naval base.

Britain took part in the annual CENTO Midlink naval maneuvers in the Gulf region along with the United States until 1977. These maneuvers were resumed in the autumn of 1980 after the outbreak of hostilities between Iran and Iraq. CENTO had ceased to exist by then. Meanwhile, British access to both the Bahrain naval base and the Masirah air base was handed over to the United States. Britain maintains a token presence on Diego Garcia and was a party to its expansion.

At the beginning of 1980, there were British officers assigned to most of the Gulf states. The highest number (around 140) was in Oman, and there were about as many more directly commissioned by Oman. A total of 311 British instructors, most of them officers on assignment, were in Kuwait, Bahrain, Qatar, Saudi Arabia, Oman, and UAE.[147]

A British RDF of 5000 men became operational in 1985.[148] The then British Foreign Secretary, Lord Carrington, stated that his government was ready to use armed force in support of the U.S. troops in the Gulf and elsewhere.[149]

West Germany

For the first time, the Federal Republic of Germany sent a naval unit (two destroyers, a tanker, and a supply ship) to the Indian Ocean in 1980, calling at several ports (Pakistan, India, Sri Lanka, and Kenya, as well as Diego Garcia). Bonn does not have any possessions in the region and its dependence on oil from the Gulf comprises approximately 40 percent of its total imports. It is therefore significant to note that the Federal Republic considers Soviet influence in the vicinity of the Gulf to be a potential threat, and it is not possible to rule out a German "military contribution" within the framework of an expanded commitment to intervene on the part of NATO.[150]

China

Though not a littoral country, China has shown interest in the littoral states' naval capabilities through active defense cooperation. Thus, it has supplied missile boats to Sri Lanka, Tanzania, Egypt, Pakistan, and Bangladesh, and submarines to Egypt. Submarine deals with Bangladesh and Thailand have also been reported. It has a policy of friendly relations and active cooperation with countries like Sri Lanka and Maldives. Beijing's most substantial aid program has been in Pakistan, which can offer access to the Indian Ocean via the Karakoram Highway.[151]

China's present capabilities do not allow a naval power projection into the Indian Ocean. But it might develop a strategic interest through the future deployment in the Arabian Sea and the Bay of Bengal, of submarine-launched ballistic missiles directed at Soviet targets.

Japan

Japanese security stakes in the Indian Ocean are obviously the oil routes and shipping lanes. But it cannot safeguard these interests by itself and therefore depends on U.S. capabilities in the region. In return, Japan seems to be preparing for a significant naval expansion, under American pressure, so that it can assume some of the U.S. navy's Pacific responsibilities. Indirectly, therefore, increased Japanese naval power will have an impact on the naval balance in the Indian Ocean. But a direct Japanese presence is only a remote possibility at this time.

Indonesia

The Indonesian navy is halfway through a two-year modernization plan for revamping its numerically strong yet largely obsolete navy of ships of Soviet origin obtained in the 1950s and 1960s. Major equipment such as frigates, fast attack craft, and maritime patrol aircraft are being procured from West European countries and from the United States. A fut from now, to undertake limited and independent naval operations in the area of the Bay of Bengal is a distinct possibility.

Pakistan

Since the renewal of the U.S.-Pakistan military relationship, as noted earlier, there has been an emphasis on naval modernization. Pakistan has acquired Gearing-class destroyers and anti-ship missiles from the United States and missile boats from China. The transfers of U.S. naval equipment to Pakistan have been justified before the American Congress on the grounds that the United States envisages a role for the Pakistan navy in the Persian Gulf/Indian Ocean region. Recently there have been reports of Pakistani interest in Britain's Type-2 frigates, both for outright purchase and for construction in a Karachi dockyard.

The Persian Gulf

Despite a considerable scaling down of the ambitious naval plans of the Shah, Iran is still the dominant naval power in the Gulf. However, its role beyond the Gulf is doubtful in the immediate future, and even within the Gulf Iran is presently overshadowed by the U.S. presence.

Saudi Arabia is building a navy from scratch. Although in time it might develop into a force in the Gulf, it is unlikely to play a significant role outside the Gulf and the Red Sea. However, Saudi naval development plans give added momentum to U.S. naval plans in the region, since both are to a great extent linked.

South Africa and Australia

In the southern Indian Ocean, the South African navy is unchallenged and could play an increasingly crucial role in the event of turbulence in southern Africa and the adjoining islands. Though the West has formally ended its defense cooperation with South Africa since the British withdrawal from Simonstown, both the Simonstown and the Durban naval bases would be available for Western navies in any future contingencies, such as the closure of the Suez.

On the other side of the southern Indian Ocean, the Royal Australian Navy is equally unchallenged. At the time of writing, the navy is going through a minor upheaval in the wake of the government's decision to scrap its only aircraft carrier, the *Melbourne,* without replacement. The navy is contesting this decision. The air force, however, is more than happy to receive the funds thus released to fund its expansion program. It is planning to introduce 40 F-18s and some additional Orions for long-range maritime work and it has assured air cover to the navy "within the Australia Moat."

For oceanic operations, the Australian air force at least is of the view that the navy should operate as part of a U.S. naval task group. Whatever the inter-service arguments over the Indian Ocean and the nature of the threat to Australia from the sea, it is apparent that in any general war situation Australia would be firmly on the side of the United States. The combined power of Australia, New Zealand, and the United States is more than adequate to meet any Soviet challenge to the West's sea lines of communication in the southern Indian Ocean, between Australia and the East Indies. The very substantial contribution of Australia to the United States in the provision of bases and facilities has already been discussed.

Moscow, Washington, and Indian Ocean Arms Control

Undoubtedly it is the United States that has set the pace of the cold war in the Indian Ocean/Persian Gulf region and would have to initiate any movement toward détente. While nominally conceding strategic parity to the Soviet Union, the overriding preoccupation of U.S. security policy appears to be keeping Americans far ahead of the Soviets in terms of global capabilities. Obviously, the U.S. military has appropriated to itself considerable resources to deal with what official U.S. jargon describes as the "non-Soviet threats"; yet there is need to depict in public the overall buildup solely as directed against the Soviet threat. The U.S. Secretary of Defense Caspar Weinberger made this clear in his Annual Report to the Congress for FY 1983:

> We recognize that several important foreign policy and military problems are not the result of any Soviet initiative. But this recognition must not divert us from the fact that it is the Soviet military effort, its direction and its nature, that drives our defense budget. When it comes to planning our military forces and defense strategy, it is clear that Soviet capabilities—present and potential—must be the dominant consideration.[152]

Thus, the dominant consideration of the American strategic planners in the Indian Ocean is the Soviet challenge, if not from its navy, then from the Soviet landmass. In the fall of 1980, when the Western naval presence reached a peak, it was in response not to any Soviet moves but to a regional event, the Iran-Iraq war. A new argument was then advanced, that the Western naval presence in the Indian Ocean was necessary to confront Soviet power based on the Eurasian continental mass. In other words, the early twentieth-century geostrategic doctrines of Mackinder were being revived to justify the emerging Western naval strategy: the Eurasian power is to be hemmed in from all sides—across the Arctic ice cap, from the West, from China, Japan, the Pacific, and from the Indian Ocean.[153] To outsiders this looks like a revival of the Dullesian doctrine of containment.

Furthermore, in the superpower nuclear strategy, the indivisibility of the ocean is a fundamental principle. Neither the United States nor the Soviet Union is—in contrast to the situation in the Atlantic and Pacific—an Indian

Ocean power from the territorial point of view. Rather, the Indian Ocean is viewed as a potential offensive field for the Americans and a defensive one for the Soviets.[154] The U.S. Navy League magazine *Sea Power* acknowledged in early 1974 that the communication station at North West Cape was sending "classified messages to Polaris/Poseidons" while the units are deployed in the Indian Ocean,[155] hinting at the possibility that this offensive potential at least has been confirmed by actual, perhaps trial, deployment. Countering the threat of strikes from the sea, therefore, becomes an important mission of the Soviet forces, and of the navy in particular, although there is some argument as to the priority now accorded this mission.[156]

Besides strategic containment, the U.S. military moves into the region appear to upset major Soviet stakes. While the Indian Ocean region as a whole serves as an area of competition among the Soviet Union, China, and the United States for world influence, its northern part is particularly important in terms of Sino-Soviet rivalry, with the Kremlin concerned to physically counter Chinese expansion while protecting itself from being outflanked to the south.[157] The Soviet stake in the Indian Ocean as a waterway is enormous. In peacetime, its Asian provinces are supplied by rail, but in the event of war with China, the Trans-Siberian railway could be cut and military supplies to the far eastern front would have to be moved by sea. If possible, these would pass via the Suez Canal. But if that were closed, they could transit overland to the Persian Gulf or the Arabian sea.[158] However, the Soviet Union is much more at the mercy of the littoral countries, both for access to the ocean from the Mediterranean and the Pacific and for onshore facilities. Its position is therefore much more vulnerable than that of its superpower rival.[159]

The irony of the Soviet threat has largely been that its nature, dimensions, and consequences have often been perceived and propagated by the Western strategic community in terms that constitute self-fulfilling prophecies. In May 1976, former U.S. Ambassador to Saudi Arabia James E. Akins testified in the Senate that in early April 1975, in response to reports of Soviet activities in Berbera, Saudi Arabia offered to pay the necessary aid to Somalia for a Washington effort to reduce Soviet influence there. Akins told the Senate that Saudi Arabia was prepared to offer the same amount of economic aid that the Soviets were offering to Somalia and also offered to pay for arms sales by Washington to Somalia, in an effort to reduce Somalian dependence on the Soviets.[160]

However, in the face of opposition from the Department of Defense, which was relying heavily on the alleged Soviet buildup in Berbera to facilitate congressional passage of its Diego Garcia expansion plan, the Department of State did not respond to the Saudi offer. The administration's refusal to accept the Saudi offer was seen by many as indicating that the United States was not serious about reducing Soviet inroads in the area, since such an attempt might make an expanded Diego Garcia facility appear not absolutely essential.[161] In a crude sense, therefore, the United States has been provoking the Soviets so that each of their responses to U.S. provocations would reinforce the rationales for further militarization of the Indian Ocean. When the Saudis finally won over the Somalis, the Soviet response was to switch their support to Ethiopia.

An American Enterprise Institute study pointed out that even an immensely greater Western deployment would not have discouraged a Soviet presence and, in fact, the strengthening of Western forces might actually have encouraged Moscow to deploy more units and to acquire the use of facilities from some littoral states. The largest number of Soviet ships appeared in the Indian Ocean after the arrival of U.S. carrier forces. The Soviets introduced an ASW capability in anticipation of SLBM deployments by the United States. The study also observed that, politically and psychologically, the Soviet Union earned undeniable dividends from U.S. actions, at least partly because of the high visibility of U.S. carrier task forces and the Diego Garcia base.[162]

While there is a real element of risk that direct conflict may result from the rival military thrusts into the Indian Ocean, no less worrisome for the littoral states is the prospect of application of the superpower interventionary capabilities against them. Whereas in a nuclear age a superpower need not have a large fleet and bases all over the world to be insulated from military challenges,[163] it has been forcefully argued that such an approach ignored the political benefits that can accrue to a country with the capability of employing its naval forces in support of its foreign policy.[164]

However, the reemergence of the old-style bipolar confrontation has added a new element of uncertainty into the traditional exercise of armed suasion. If either superpower were to exploit the opportunity offered by depolarization to apply coercive pressures on the small powers of the Third World, it may discover that this would suffice to destroy the very setting that made the move possible in the first place.[165] Therefore, as Professor Edward Luttwak points out, in many ways the risks of the former bipolar world, with its clear lines of demarcation, were "both less insidious and more manageable," since a direct confrontation in the old style was at least simpler to control than the "systemic disruption" that may now result if the superpowers act to defend their interests.[166] And they appear to be determined.

To forestall domestic criticisms, President Carter declared, when announcing the RDF decision in December 1979: "We must understand that not every instance of the firm application of power is a potential Vietnam."[167] To allay Third World fears, then Secretary of Defense Harold Brown stated in his FY 1981 defense posture report:

> None of this [RDF plans], however, should be taken to suggest a U.S. intention to threaten the sovereignty of any country or to intervene where we are not wanted. Rather, mobile, well equipped and trained conventional forces are essential to assist allies and other friends should conditions so dictate and should our assistance be needed.[168]

However, no intervention has ever been in violation of "sovereignty," whatever the technicalities of the term might imply, or unwanted in the calculations of the intervening state. Besides, force can always be applied without its actual use and bring about the desired outcome.

Admiral Gorshkov has recognized with professional admiration the capabilities of the U.S. navy in the fighting of limited wars. Restricted capability, lack of experience, and the Soviet calculus of interests might suggest that Soviet leaders will not use their navy as the vehicle for large-scale intervention. However, now that the Soviet Union has at least an "embryonic intervention capability," it may become involved in supporting local clients in coups and in protecting pro-Soviet governments.[169] Should the Soviet squadron in the Indian Ocean participate in some action, it is more likely that such a move would be carried out in support of a "national liberation movement" or in support of one of the friendly littoral powers in order to protect it against foreign aggression. This is a possibility that cannot be totally excluded, but it might take place only when essential Soviet interests were at stake, and then only when Moscow could be certain that no American counteraction was to be expected. Probably, any such initiative will remain a "naval demonstration" only, a part of "gunboat diplomacy," which belongs to the area of political, rather than strictly military, use of the navy.[170]

While the competitive naval presence of the superpowers in the Indian Ocean has not so far proved to be the best means of influencing the course of events in the regions of the Indian Ocean littoral, nonetheless this presence has added to the general atmosphere of insecurity and anxiety in the area.[171] Many American ships were present in the Indian Ocean in February and March 1979, but they could not save the Shah's regime. Their presence would not have overawed the Shah's opponents, and if they had intervened with force to prop up the Shah, it is doubtful whether they would have been successful. Twenty thousand Cuban soldiers have had a far greater effect on the complexion of African regimes than all the Soviet and American naval ships in the Indian Ocean put together.[172] These facts, however, are very much in the calculations behind the present preparations, which are meant to prevent further such occurrences. In preparing an RDF for physical intervention in Third World situations, the United States may have such calculations in mind.

Meanwhile, forward deployments, particularly of naval units, pose other grave consequences. In recent years, ship movements of the Sixth and Seventh Fleets in crisis situations have been first ordered on the initiatives of local commanders.[173] Some of the dangers of forward deployment were seen in the attack on the Liberty in June 1967. With a different set of personalities, the escalatory potential would have been awesome, for, as then Secretary of Defense McNamara subsequently said: "I thought the Liberty had been attacked by Soviet forces. Thank goodness, our carrier commanders did not launch immediately against the Soviet forces who were operating in the Mediterranean at that time."[174] Even the handling of the Cuban missile crisis, that supposedly model example of clinical crisis management, showed some of the tensions that can arise between political leaders primarily concerned with the "wider issues" and images and naval commanders on the spot directly concerned with their men and ships and their reputations for operational success.[175]

The Soviet navy is a powerful force in absolute terms, though it does not match the U.S. navy's greatly superior capability to operate in distant waters. The major danger is that at a time when Third World conflicts are on the increase, a greater Soviet naval strength creates a higher risk of clashes, accidental or deliberate, arising out of the superpowers' pursuit of their respective interests.[176] Such a danger is greater in the Indian Ocean because of its inherent instabilities and rivalries. As relatively new naval powers, the Soviets and Americans are still learning the limitations that such regional disputes place on their freedom of action.[177] The possibility, therefore, arises that forward deployment might be manipulated by local powers for their own political survival purposes, resulting in the power concerned being dragged into local conflicts. Before the superpowers moved into the Indian Ocean, it was relatively easier for them to stay out of local quarrels. However, with naval units just on or over the horizon, the pressure for some intervention in local disputes will be greater, from local associates, and also because "weapons shape the will to use them." Thus, forward deployment does increase the possibility of involvement and risk of escalation.[178]

For instance, to the extent that two of the U.S. facilities agreements are with long-standing adversaries that have a festering border dispute, such as Somalia's claims to Kenyan territory, the United States is in a precarious position. Any serious crisis between the two countries, especially action involving the use of American arms supplied under the agreement, could result in the abrogation of agreements with the United States and, ultimately, a "serious undermining of the U.S. ability to fulfill primary U.S. objectives in the Persian Gulf,"[179] not unlike what happened to the Soviets in Somalia in 1977.

The American involvement in the military modernization process in the region has important implications for the United States as well as for the states of the Persian Gulf and Red Sea areas. For Washington, the participation in military affairs in the Gulf has political and economic underpinnings and strategic and security implications, both globally and regionally. For the Persian Gulf states, these military modernization programs have—in addition to their security implications for the entire area and for each state—"broad social, economic and political effects" on each state.[180] The dimensions of these programs are truly staggering. In 1977, a congressional staff study reported that if Saudi Arabia were to stop receiving military equipment, it would have still taken six years for its personnel to be trained in all aspects of equipment already bought, resulting in the need for continuing outside support.[181] Similar factors operated in other Gulf areas that have received further massive doses of military supplies since 1977.

Controlled and measured military sales as well as technical and logistical training and support to friendly governments could help U.S. policy goals in the region. However, the Iranian experience indicates the serious potential pitfalls in using military sales and/or aid as an instrument of policy.[182] In fact, U.S. experience by and large has been a trifle unhappy in the area of military assistance to "friendly" countries.

Given the situation in the area and its importance to the United States and its allies, implementation of the "containment" strategy to its fullest extent might require increased U.S. naval deployment and coverage of the area's vital sea lanes by whatever means available. On the other hand, if the United States chose to pursue the "regional partnership" strategy, it would logically make a concerted effort to assist the local states in strengthening their own capacity to resolve disputes in a peaceful manner and to enhance their ability to guarantee that the vital oil transshipment routes in the area would be kept open, instead of emphasizing a major military buildup in the region to ensure that they remain open.[183]

The Indian Ocean has a "limited military importance" to the United States. It does not figure directly in the American forward defense in the way the Atlantic and Pacific oceans do. Nor does seapower deployed in the Indian Ocean have much effect on the events in the littoral states, most of whose vital interests are primarily influenced by adjacent littoral or hinterland states. Moreover, the growth of naval power of important littoral states such as Iran and India and the substantial naval force of South Africa, France, Australia, and, potentially, Indonesia greatly reduces the feasibility of the control of the area by a single outside power,[184] as happened during the days of the British Empire.

The increasing capabilities of the Soviet navy also place limits on the potential role of the United States for intervention in the region. Previous events have clearly shown that each surge of U.S. military power into the Indian Ocean has been matched by a temporary surge of Soviet forces and a longer-term Soviet naval presence, albeit on a lower scale. With a navy that is still declining in number of ships, the United States, in the opinion of many military authorities, is ill-equipped to engage in a naval arms race in the region with the Soviet Union.[185] Given the long distances and the long supply lines for ships in the Indian Ocean, both Washington and Moscow could find advantages in agreeing to a naval limitation in the area. A Rand Corporation paper, while advocating a naval limitation, views an oil embargo as the first link in a chain of circumstances "whose final end is hidden in obscurity" and therefore argues in support of the facility on Diego Garcia, which dominates the oil routes, as a deterrent for "those who visualize hasty action" in the area.[186]

The crucial consideration for the United States and its European and Japanese allies is that the most important nations in the Indian Ocean region are naturally inclined toward a fairly close integration with the Western economic system. The markets of industrialized countries, Western technology, and capital are crucial to the developing countries of the region.[187] In the Indian Ocean region, therefore, the United States has only a limited need of seapower to influence the desired economic and political orientation of littoral states. These capabilities are not necessarily required in the region on a permanent basis.[188]

For all these reasons, it would appear that the "wisest U.S. policy in the Indian Ocean would be to negotiate an arms limitation agreement," or "an agreement to disengage gradually." If the superpowers cannot agree on zero deployment of combatants, they might agree to limit the number to perhaps "six to eight" and "prohibit aircraft carriers and nuclear ballistic missile submarines."[189] The conclusion of an arms limitation agreement could reduce the cost to the United States of expanding Diego Garcia and other Indian Ocean–related military costs and reap "political dividends" from the littoral states by promoting a "joint zone of peace or a policy of limited presence." The Soviets have already limited their naval presence to facilities and anchorages of low visibility. An agreement would also provide a "good barometer of Soviet intentions" in regard to their intentions in the Indian Ocean region.[190]

While the cold war and the global arms race are anathema to the concept of non-alignment to which almost all states of the Indian Ocean are committed, the realities of the situation demand that the search for an identity of interests need not be concentrated solely on the "peace zone" idea, which envisages total elimination of all military presence conceived in the context of super-power rivalry. Alternatives contributing to reducing the militarization of the ocean could be examined. As an American Enterprise Institute study points out:

> Much has been said about the crucial geographic position of the Indian Ocean. Some have contended that the region is destined to be a chessboard for superpower rivalry, but, just because the chessmen are poised, the game need not be played. Others have argued that the dominant naval power in the region will be able to influence the policies of the littoral states, but there is no necessity for an outside naval power to dominate any region.[191]

The U.S.-Soviet talks between June 1977 and February 1978, according to Soviet sources, "showed some promise of success: there emerged the idea to agree, at the first stage, to 'freeze' the armed forces in the Indian Ocean at their present level, and then to go on to scale down military presence in the region." Among the early results of the consultations were "the start of discussion on the text of the future agreement" by working groups of experts.[192] The successful beginning of the consultations was also reported in official communications of the two sides to the Chairman of the U.N. Ad Hoc Committee on the Indian Ocean.[193] It soon emerged that the United States and the Soviet Union did in fact acknowledge each other's strategic interests in the Indian Ocean and that in the event of a reduction of military forces, Diego Garcia's role, at least as a center for surveillance, would be retained.[194]

The reasons for the unilateral American withdrawal from the talks are claimed to be related to the events in Ethiopia. In fact, they lay elsewhere. Partly, it was due to a "rapid deterioration" in the general global climate for negotiations between the superpowers dating from the end of 1977.[195]

But more crucial perhaps was the Pentagon's stand on any arms limitations in the Indian Ocean. The U.S. navy's view was crudely and typically reflected in former Chief of Naval Staff Admiral Zumwalt's description of the Zone of Peace as a "very dangerous idea."[196] As became known later, even before the first round of talks began, the Joint Chiefs of Staff had declared its objections to any agreements on limiting military activity in the Indian Ocean. However, when the negotiations did start, the Chairman of the Joint Chiefs, in a special memorandum of August 9, 1977, expressed his disagreement with the essence of the proposals being considered by the two sides. When signs of progress appeared at the negotiations, he issued a new statement, on January 30, 1978 (just before the start of the fourth round), recommending that the White House suspend the negotiations, a recommendation ultimately accepted.[197]

To the superpowers themselves, arms control in the Indian Ocean is secondary to the global arms control dialogue. But to the littoral states, the growing tensions in the Indian Ocean underline the urgency of a regionally focused superpower dialogue that could set the stage for a larger accommodation.

Notes

1. Manoranjan Bezboruah, *U.S. Strategy in the Indian Ocean: The International Response* (New York: Praeger, 1977), p. 35.

2. Ibid.

3. Ibid.

4. Ibid.

5. Ibid.

6. Ibid.

7. Ibid.

8. Ibid., p. 36.

9. R. D. Heinl Jr., "American Defense Policy and Strategy for the 1970s," *Brassey's Annual*, 1972, p. 34.

10. Bezboruah, op. cit., p. 52.

11. *United States Foreign Policy Objectives and Overseas Military Installations, Committee on Foreign Relations*, 96th Congress, 1st Session, 1979, p. 88.

12. Alvin J. Cottrel and Thomas H. Moorer, *U.S. Overseas Bases: Problems of Projecting American Military Power Abroad* (London: Sage Publications, 1977), p. 35.

13. I. Redko et al., *The Indian Ocean: A Sphere of Tension or a Zone of Peace* (Moscow, Nauka Publishing House, 1983), p. 30.

14. Ibid.

15. *United States Foreign Policy Objectives and Overseas Military Installations*, op. cit., p. 88.

16. *U.S. Military Posture, FY 1984*, Organization of the Joint Chiefs of Staff, p. 3.

17. *U.S. Military Posture, FY 1982*, pp. 11–13.

18. *U.S. Military Posture, FY 1984*, p. 25.

19. Redko et al., op. cit., p. 27.

20. Ibid.

21. Ibid.

22. Ibid., p. 28.

23. Ibid.

24. Ibid.

25. Ibid., p. 29.

26. Dieter Braun, *The Indian Ocean: Region of Conflict or Zone of Peace?* (London, C. Hurst, 1983), p. 41.

27. Redko et al., op. cit., p. 29.

28. Ibid., p. 56.

29. Ibid., pp. 29–30.

30. *U.S. Security Interests in the Persian Gulf. Report of a Staff Study Mission,* 97th Congress, 1st Session, 1981, p. 1.

31. *U.S. Military Posture, FY 1984,* pp. 56–57.

32. Ibid., p. 56.

33. *U.S. Military Posture, FY 1983,* p. 40.

34. Testimony by Walter Slocombe, Deputy Under-Secretary for Policy Planning, Department of Defense, in *U.S. Security Interests and Policies in South West Asia,* Hearings Before the Committee on Foreign Relations, 96th Congress, 2nd Session, 1980, p. 306.

35. D. A. Quinlan, "The Marine Corps as a Rapid Deployment Force," *Marine Corps Gazette,* March 1980, pp. 38–39; quoted in Redko et al., op. cit., p. 26.

36. D. A. Quinlan, *The Role of the Marine Corps in Rapid Deployment Forces* (Washington, 1983), pp. 1–2.

37. Ibid.

38. James P. Wootten, "Rapid Deployment Force," Issue Brief No. 80027, updated 16.7.84, Congressional Research Service, Washington (Mimeo), p. 1.

39. For a discussion on force planning and ship building in this context, see testimony of Adm. Thomas B. Hayward, Chief of U.S. Naval Operations, in *National Policy Objectives and the Adequacy of Our Current Naval Forces,* Hearings Before the Committee on Armed Services, House of Representatives, 96th Congress, 2nd Session, 1979, pp. 101–137.

40. Department of State Bulletin, 1980, No. 2035, Vol. 80, Spl., p. 1.

41. Wootten, op. cit., p. 6.

42. Ibid., p. 1.

43. Quinlan (1983), op. cit., p. 14.

44. Ibid., p. 3.

45. Ibid., p. 7.

46. James P. Wootten, op. cit., p. 8.

47. *Defense Sealift Capability,* U.S. Congress, Hearings, 1981, pp. 5–6.

48. Quinlan (1983), op. cit., p. 18.

49. Ibid.

50. Wootten, op. cit., p. 4.

51. Ibid., p. 3.

52. Ibid.

53. Ibid., p. 4.

54. Ibid.

55. Bezboruah, op. cit., p. 53.

56. Ibid., p. 110.

57. *New York Times,* June 18, 1973; quoted in ibid., p. 68.

58. Bezboruah, op. cit., p. 68.

59. Senate Committee, quoted in ibid., pp. 69–70.

60. Braun, op. cit., pp. 40–41.

61. Bezboruah, op. cit., p. 53.

62. Ibid., p. 93.

63. Tom Farer, *War Clouds on the Horn of Africa: A Crisis for Detente* (New York: Carnegie Endownment for International Peace, 1976), quoted in Cottrel and Moorer, op. cit., p. 33.

64. Cottrel and Moorer, op. cit., p. 33.

65. Bezboruah, op. cit., p. 75.

66. Ibid., p. 84.

67. U.N. Secretary-General's Report, a/Ac. 159/1, p. 12.

68. Quoted in P. K. S. Namboodiri, J. P. Anand and Sreedhar, *Intervention in the Indian Ocean* (Delhi, 1982), p. 172.

69. *United States Foreign Policy Objectives and Overseas Military Installations,* op. cit., p. 102.

70. Quoted in Namboodiri et al., op. cit., p. 34.

71. Secretary of Defense Caspar Weinberger's Annual Report to the Congress. 1984.

72. Namboodiri et al., op. cit., p. 195.

73. Braun, op. cit., p. 42.

74. *United States Foreign Policy Objectives and Overseas Military Installations,* op. cit., p. 96.

75. Dieter Braun, op. cit., p. 43.

76. Testimony by Walter Slocombe, op. cit., p. 307.

77. *U.S. Security Interests in the Persian Gulf,* op. cit., pp. 43–44.

78. Ibid., p. 19.

79. Namboodiri et al., op. cit., p. 73.

80. Ibid., p. 74.

81. Wootten, op. cit., p. 5.

82. *U.S. Security Interests in the Persian Gulf,* op. cit., pp. 50–51.

83. Braun, op. cit., p. 121.

84. Ibid.

85. Ibid.

86. *Defense Week* (Washington), August 27, 1984, p. 10.

87. *U.S. Military Posture, FY 1984,* p. 26.

88. *United States Foreign Policy Objectives and Overseas Military Installations,* op. cit., p. 99.

89. Ibid.

90. *Statesman* (New Delhi), May 23, 1984.

91. Statement by Vice Admiral M. S. Holcomb in *National Policy Objectives and the Adequacy of Our Current Naval Forces,* op. cit., p. 75.

92. Ibid.

93. *Proposed Expansion of U.S. Military Facilities in the Indian Ocean,* U.S. Congress, House Committee on Near East and South Asia, Committee on Foreign Affairs; 93rd Congress, 2nd Session, 1974, p. 135; quoted in Bezboruah, op. cit., p. 53.

94. Admiral John McCain, USN (Ret.), quoted in Bezboruah, op. cit., p. 57.

95. Bezboruah, op. cit., p. 41.

96. Ibid.

97. Quoted in ibid., p. 41.

98. *Seabed Arms Control Treaty,* U.S. Congress, Committee on Foreign Relations, 93rd Congress, 2nd Session, 1974; quoted in Bezboruah, op. cit., p. 42.

99. Bezboruah, op. cit.

100. Ibid.

101. *U.S. Security Interests in the Persian Gulf,* op. cit., p. 3.

102. Ibid., p. 13.

103. Ibid., p. 4.

104. *United States Arms Policies in the Persian Gulf and Red Sea Areas: Past, Present and Future,* Report of a Staff Survey Mission, 95th Congress, 1st Session, 1977, pp. 12–13.

105. *U.S. Security Interests in the Persian Gulf,* op. cit., p. 14.

106. Bezboruah, op. cit., p. 117.

107. Braun, op. cit., p. 23.

108. Ibid., p. 65.

109. Ibid., p. 63.

110. Ibid., pp. 44, 64.

111. Redko et al., op. cit., p. 30.

112. James H. Hayes, *Indian Ocean Geopolitics,* Rand Paper No. P–5325–1, 1975, p. 5.

113. Braun, op. cit., p. 63.

114. Ibid., p. 61.

115. Ibid., p. 25.

116. *Statesman Yearbook* 1979–80, p. 884.

117. Namboodiri et al., op. cit., p. 10.

118. Braun, op. cit., pp. 65–66 n.

119. Ibid., p. 66.

120. Ibid.

121. Ibid.

122. Hayes, op. cit., p. 5.

123. Ibid.

124. Braun, op. cit., p. 65.

125. *United States Foreign Policy Objectives and Overseas Military Installations,* op. cit., p. 91.

126. Ibid.

127. Ibid.

128. Philip Towle, *Naval Power in Indian Ocean: Threats, Bluffs and Fantasies* (Canberra, 1979), p. 34.

129. Ibid.

130. Ibid.

131. Braun, op. cit., p. 65.

132. Statement by John Erickson in *Afghanistan: The Soviet Invasion and its Consequences for British Policy,* House of Commons Foreign Affairs Committee, 5th Report, (London: 1980), pp. 235ff.; quoted in Braun, op. cit., Appendix D, pp. 211–212.

133. John Erickson, op. cit., p. 50.

134. *U.S. Military Posture, FY 1984,* p. 29.

135. *Jane's Defense Weekly,* London: Jane's Publishing, July 28, 1984, p. 8.

136. *U.S. Military Posture, FY 1984,* p. 29.

137. Ibid.
138. Ibid.
139. *U.S. Military Posture, FY 1984*, p. 29.
140. Ibid.
141. Ibid.
142. Braun, op. cit., pp. 100–103.
143. Ibid., p. 102.
144. Ibid., p. 101.
145. Ibid., p. 103.
146. Wootten, op. cit., p. 9.
147. Ibid., p. 98 n.
148. Wootten, op. cit., p. 9.
149. Redko, op. cit., p. 12.
150. Braun, op. cit., p. 108.
151. Ibid., p. 81.
152. Secretary of Defense Caspar Weinberger's Fy 1983 Department of Defense, *Annual Report* to the Congress, p. II–3.
153. K. Subrahmanyam, *Indian Security Perspectives* (New Delhi, Lancer International, 1982), p. 36.
154. Ference A. Valid, *Politics of the Indian Ocean Region: The Balance of Power* (London: Collier Macmillan, 1976), p. 39.
155. February 1974, p. 5. Also see U.S. Congress, House Committee on Armed Services, Military Posture and HR 11500, Part 4 of 5 parts; 94th Congress, 2nd Session, 1976, p. 61; quoted in Bezboruah, op. cit., p. 154.
156. Michael MacGwire, "The Proliferation of Maritime Weapon Systems in the Indo-Pacific Region," in Robert O'Neill (ed.), *Insecurity: The Spread of Weapons in the Indian and Pacific Oceans* (Canberra, Australian National University Press, 1978), pp. 121–22.
157. Ibid., p. 130.
158. Ibid., p. 135.
159. Mohammed Ayoob, "The Indian Ocean Littoral: Intra-Regional Conflicts and Weapons Proliferation," in O'Neill (ed.), op. cit., pp. 102–4.
160. Bezboruah, op. cit., p. 121 n.
161. Ibid.
162. Dale R. Tahtinen, *Arms in the Indian Ocean: Interests and Challenges* (Washington; American Enterprise Institute, 1977), p. 24.
163. Ibid., p. 44.
164. Cottrel and Moorer, op. cit., p. 35. See also Edward Luttwak, *The Political Uses of Seapower* (Baltimore, Johns Hopkins University Press, 1974), p. 47. In the context of naval forces planning, Luttwak pleads for a less sophisticated but more visible power since, for instance, one does not need a powerful sonar under the hull or a digital data system in the superstructure "to frighten South Yemen or encourage the Sheikh of Abu Dhabi."
165. Luttwak, op. cit., p. 68.
166. Ibid., p. 69.
167. Quoted in Quinlan (1983), op. cit., p. 10.
168. Testimony by Walter Slocombe, op. cit., p. 334.
169. Booth, op. cit., p. 232.
170. Vali, op. cit., p. 181.
171. Ayoob, op. cit., p. 106.

172. Towle, op. cit., p. 101.

173. Booth, op. cit., p. 104.

174. Quoted in ibid.

175. Ibid.

176. *Strategic Survey* (London: International Institute of Strategic Studies, 1979), p. 24.

177. Towle, op. cit., p. 36.

178. Booth, op. cit., pp. 105–106.

179. *U.S. Security Interests in the Persian Gulf,* op. cit., p. 3.

180. Ibid., p. 13.

181. Ibid., p. 39.

182. *United States Foreign Policy Objectives and Overseas Military Installations,* op. cit., p. 7.

183. Ibid.

184. Ibid., p. 84.

185. William J. Barnds, "Arms Race or Arms Control in the Indian Ocean," quoted in ibid., p. 91.

186. Hayes, op. cit., p. 6.

187. *United States Foreign Policy Objectives and Overseas Military Installations,* op. cit., p. 100.

188. Ibid., p. 101.

189. Tahtinen, op. cit., pp. 41–43.

190. Ibid., p. 42.

191. Ibid., p. 44.

192. Redko, et al., op. cit., p. 57.

193. Doc. UNA/AC.199/SR.3.P.12, quoted in ibid.

194. See J. Fuller, "Dateline Diego Garcia: Paved Over Paradise," *Foreign Policy,* No. 28 (Autumn 1977), pp. 175–186.

195. Braun, op. cit., p. 27.

196. *Defense Monitor* (Washington), No. 4 (1974), p. 1.

197. Department of Defense authorization for appropriations for FY 1981, Hearings before the Committee on Armed Services, U.S. Senate; 96th Congress, 2nd Session, 1980, pp. 7–9; quoted in Redko et al., op. cit., pp. 56–57.

TABLE 2.1.   Fifty Years of Gunboat Diplomacy: 1919–69

A total of 151 incidents of gunboat diplomacy have been identified in which 63 of the victims were non-European states outside the alliances in Asia, Africa, and Latin America. The assailants in these incidents are listed and also the number of incidents in which they are involved.*

United States	60
Britain	55
France	14
Soviet Union	4
China	2
Others**	45

Notes:
* The number of incidents do not tally with the number of assailants because of involvement of more than one assailant in each of many incidents.
** Others include mainly ex-colonial powers like the Netherlands, Spain, Portugal, Italy, Germany, and Japan.

Source: K. Booth, *Navies and Foreign Policy* (London: Croom Helm, 1977), App., pp. 177–229

TABLE 2.2.   Great Power Naval Position in the Indian Ocean

U.S. Deployments in the Indian Ocean
(Regular)

Indian Ocean Detachment from 7th Fleet:
1 Carrier battle group (about 6 surface combatants)
9 Stores/Replenishment vessels

Middle East Force:
1 Command ship
2 Destroyers

Marine Amphibious Unit (MAU)* (1800)
deployed intermittently (*MAUs are embarked in Amphibious Ready Groups [ARG], comprising 4–7 amphibious ships, with a reinforced infantry battalion, including tanks and artillery, a composite air squadron [including helicopters], and a logistical group)

Bases and facilities:
Diego Garcia and Subic Bay (outside the Indian Ocean)
Mombasa port and airfield and Nanyuki air base in Kenya
Berbera and Mogadishu in Somalia, Masirah and Muscat in Oman and Bahrain
Saudi Arabia, Sinai, and Egypt
Singapore
N.W. Cape and Cockburn Sound in Western Australia

Soviet Indian Ocean Deployment
(Regular)

Detachments from the Pacific Fleet serve in the Indian Ocean, the average strength being:
2–3 Submarines
8 Surface combatants

TABLE 2.1.   (continued)

2 Amphibious ships
12 Support ships

Bases and facilities:
Da Nang and Cam Ranh Bay (outside the Indian Ocean)
Aden, Socotra in South Yemen
Dahlak Island in Ethiopia, Massawa, and Assab

French Forces in the Indian Ocean
(Frequent)

Task force led by aircraft carrier/guided-missile frigate

South Indian Ocean:
1 Para regiment
1 Infantry regiment
1 Marine regiment   } 2700 personnel
1 Infantry company

Dijibouti
6 Infantry companies
4 armored squadrons
2 Artillery (1AA) batteries   } 3250 personnel
1 Mirage III squadron with 10 aircraft
    Naval elements

Bases and facilities: Djibouti, La Réunion, and Mayotte

British Presence
(Intermittent)

1–2 Destroyers/Frigates

2 Support ships

1 Naval detachment on Diego Garcia

Bases and facilities: Access to Gulf base in Oman, Singapore, Malaysia

TABLE 2.3. Indian Ocean Littoral Naval Balance

	Australia	Bangladesh	India	Indonesia	Malaysia	Pakistan	S. Arabia	S. Africa	Thailand
Navy Personnel	17,000	5,300	47,000	42,000	8,700	11,000	2,500	5,000	32,200
Aircraft Carriers	—	—	1	—	—	—	—	—	—
Patrol Submarines	6	—	8	2(1)	—	6+ 5(small)	—	—	—
Cruisers	—	—	—	—	—	1	—	—	—
Destroyers	3	—	3(+3)	—	—	7	—	—	—
Frigates	10(+2)	3	21(2 + 3)	10(+3)	2(+2)	—	(4)	1	6
Corvettes	—	—	3(+3)	—	—	—	4	—	(2 + 1)
Fast Attack Craft:									
Missiles	—	4	8	4(4)	8(4)	4	9	9(1)	6
Torpedo	—	2	—	2	—	4	3	—	—
Gun	—	8	—	(2)	6	12	—	—	—
Patrol Craft	22(2)	13(2)	4	22	22	5	36	35	94
Naval Air Arm:									
Personnel	1,650	—	2,000	1,000	—	—	—	—	—
Combat A/c	9	—	36	8	—	3	—	—	15
Combat Hel.	6	—	26	10	—	6	—	—	11
Bases	Sydney Melbourne Jervis Bay Brisbane Cains Darwin Cockburn Sound	Chittagong Dacca Khulna Chalna	Bombay Goa Cochin Vishakapatnam Port Blair	Jakarta (Tanjung Priok) Surabaya	Woodlands Kuantan Lebuan Lumut	Karachi Port Cassim	Jeddah Al Qatif/Jubail Ras Tanura Damman Yanbu Ras al Mishab	Simonstown Durban	Bangkok Sattahip Songkla Phangnga

Figures in parentheses as: (4) building
(+4) proposed
(4 = 4) building and proposed

TABLE 2.4. Major Naval Armaments of Indian Ocean Littoral States

---

Australia

3 Destroyers with Standard SAM; 2 Ikara ASW
2 Frigates with 1 Harpoon SSM, 1 Standard SAM, 2 helicopters
6 River frigates with 1 × 4 Seacat SAM/SSM, 1 Ikara ASW

Air arm:
1 Composite squadron with 7S–2G, 2 HS–748 (ECM)
1 ASW helicopter squadron with 6 MK–50 Sea Kings

On order:
2 FFG–7 frigates
6 PCF–420 large patrol craft
2 MCM catamarans
7 Harpoon SSMs
2 Phalanx 20mm AA systems
6 AS–530 Ecurewil
2 Sea King helicopters

India

3 Modified Kashin II destroyers with 4 Styx SSM, 2 × 2 SA–N–1 SAM, 1 Ka–25 Hel.
21 Frigates; 1 Modified Leander (Godawari class), 6 Leanders with 2 × 4 Seacat SAM, 1 helicopter, 2 Whitly class with 3 Styx SSM; 10 Petya–II, 2 Type 41 AD frigate
3 Nanuchka corvettes with 4SS–N–2 SSM, 1 SA–N–4 SAM
8 Osa–I (6 FAC(M), 2 FAC), 8 Osa–II with 4 Styx SSM

Air arm:
1 Attack squadron, 8 Sea Harriers
1 ASW squadron with 5 Alize 1050
2 MR squadrons with 2 Super Constellation, 5 GL–38
5 ASW helicopter squadrons with 12 Sea King, 5 Ka–25 Hormone (on Kashins), 11 Alouette III
1 Search and Rescue (SAR)/liaison helicopter sqn. with 10 Alouette-III

On order:
4 Type–1500 submarines
3 Kashins
5 Godawari and Improved Godawari frigates
2 Nanuchka corvettes
3 IL–38 MR a/c
10 AM–39 Exocet ASM
5 Sea Eagle ASM

Indonesia

9 Frigates: 3 Fatahilla with 4 Exocet SSM (1 with Wasp helicopter), 2 Riga Class
4 FACs Dagger with 4 Exocet SSM

On order:
Frigates and FACs

Air arm:
1 ASW helicopter squadron with 10 Wasps
2 MR squadrons: 2 Nomad N–223

TABLE 2.4. (continued)

Malaysia

1 Frigate with 1 × 4 Seacat SAM; 1 Type–41
8 FAC with 4 or 2 Exocet SSM

On order:
4 Spica FAC(M) with MM–40 Exocet SSM

Pakistan

1 County-class destroyer with 1 Sea King, 2 × 4 Seacat SAM,
   1 helicopter
5 U.S. Gearing with 1 × 8 ASROC ASW, three type 21 on order
   from Vosper Thorney Craft
1 Battle-class destroyer

Air arm:
1 ASW/MR squadron with 3 Atlantic with Exocet ASM
2 ASW/SAR helicopter squadrons with 6 Sea King ASW with
   AM–39, 4 Alouette–III.

On order:
Harpoon ASMs

Saudia Arabia

Corvettes with 2 × 4 Harpoon SSMs
FACs with 2 × 2 Harpoon SSMs

South Africa

FAC with 6 Skerpioen (Gabriel-type) SSMs

Thailand

1 Frigate with 1 × 4 Seacat SAM
3 FAC with 4 Exocet SSM
3 with 5 Gabriel SSM

On order:
5 Harpoon SSM
10 MM–39 Exocet coast defense missiles

TABLE 2.5.   Value of Arms Imports into the Indian Ocean Area (1976–80)

Recipients	*Suppliers/Million Dollars (Current)*						
	US	*USSR*	*France*	*UK*	*FRG*	*Others*	*Total*
Africa							
Botswana	—	—	—	20	—	5	25
Ethiopia	80	1900	10	—	5	230	2225
Kenya	50	—	30	40	—	60	180
Malagasy	—	60	10	—	—	10	80
Mali	110	—	—	—	10	—	120
Malawi	—	—	10	10	5	5	30
Mozambique	180	—	—	—	—	95	275
Niger	—	—	40	—	10	—	50
Nigeria	40	90	50	110	50	—	340
Somalia	—	150	40	10	10	540	750
Sudan	140	10	5	—	360	60	575
South Africa	20	—	200	—	—	250	470
Tanzania	—	320	5	10	—	135	470
Uganda	—	40	—	5	—	10	55
Zambia	—	220	—	20	5	100	345
Zimbabwe	—	—	40	—	—	50	90
Total Region	620	2790	440	225	455	1550	6080
East Asia							
China	—	220	50	400	—	20	690
Indonesia	220	—	40	40	20	510	830
Japan	1000	—	—	20	—	—	1020
Malaysia	170	—	110	50	—	185	515
Singapore	160	—	10	10	—	75	255
Thailand	525	—	5	10	—	180	720
Vietnam	—	1900	—	—	—	—	1900
Total Region	2075	2120	215	530	20	970	5930
Middle East and Gulf							
Bahrain	5	—	20	—	—	25	50
Egypt	430	20	600	180	370	300	1900
Iran	6200	625	200	250	380	650	8305
Iraq	—	5000	950	90	160	1560	7760
Israel	4300	—	—	60	—	30	4390
Jordan	725	—	—	280	5	50	1060
Kuwait	390	50	130	220	—	10	800
Lebanon	40	—	10	20	5	10	85
Oman	10	—	—	400	—	10	420
Qatar	5	—	70	90	—	10	175
Saudi Arabia	2000	—	700	975	350	660	4685
UAE	20	—	450	60	40	20	590
South Yemen	—	775	—	—	—	10	785
North Yemen	170	625	80	—	10	205	1090
Total Region	14,295	7095	3210	2625	1320	3550	32,095
Oceania							
Australia	575	—	—	190	140	100	1005

TABLE 2.5.   (continued)

Recipients	Suppliers/Million Dollars (Current)						
	US	USSR	France	UK	FRG	Others	Total
South Asia							
Afghanistan	—	450	—	—	—	10	460
Bangladesh	—	20	—	10	—	30	60
India	50	2300	50	160	10	180	2750
Nepal	—	—	—	—	—	—	—
Pakistan	220	20	390	20	50	360	1060
Sri Lanka	—	10	5	10	—	5	30
Region Total	270	2800	445	200	60	585	4360
Region-Wide Totals							
Africa	620	2790	440	225	455	1550	6080
East Asia	2075	2120	215	530	20	970	5930
Middle East and Gulf	14,295	7095	3210	2625	1320	3550	32,095
Oceania	575	—	—	190	140	100	1005
South Asia	270	2800	445	200	60	585	4360
Grand Total	17,835	14,805	4290	3770	1955	6755	49,470

Note: Totals do not tally due to rounding off and approximations.

Source: World Military Expenditures and Arms Transfers, 1971–80 (Washington: U.S. Arms Control and Disarmament Agency, 1981), pp. 20–30.

TABLE 2.6. Incidents of "Gunboat Diplomacy" in the Indian Ocean Area (1971–81)

Year	Assailant	Victim	Size/Type of Force	Deployment Area	Explanation
December 1971	U.S.	India	Task force of 7th Fleet; Carrier U.S.S. *Enterprise*, amphibious assault ship with a battalion of marines, and 7 destroyers.	Bay of Bengal	"To deter India" and "to show solidarity with China" during the India-Pak conflict[1]
1973	Soviet Union	Kuwait	Naval contingent		During border conflict with Iraq[2]
October 1973	U.S.	Arab States of West Asia	Task force led by U.S.S. *Hancock* carrier	Western Indian Ocean	It is acknowledged that "force was used in a vague coercive fashion," and that the deployment was meant as "reinforcement" for U.S. diplomatic initiatives.[3]
July 1976	U.S.	Uganda	—	East coast of Africa	In the wake of the Entebbe raid, to warn Uganda against an attack on Kenya, which facilitated raid.[4]
1976	U.S.	Uganda	—	East coast of Africa	To counter Idi Amin's threat against Americans residing in Uganda.[5]
May 1977	France	Somalia/Ethiopia/Djibouti	18 warships including two aircraft carriers	Off Red Sea coast	To "deter the grab" of Djibouti by Somalia and Ethiopia.[6]
1977–78	Soviet Union	Somalia	—	—	Ships helped air force operations/ amphibious ships brought war material for Ethiopia during the Ogaden war.[7]

TABLE 2.6. (continued)

Year	Assailant	Victim	Size/Type of Force	Deployment Area	Explanation
February 1979	U.S.	North Yemen	Task group led by U.S.S. *Constellation*	Dispatched to the Arabian Sea	At the time of the Yemeni war, after sending two E-3A AWACS from Okinawa and 200 military technicians to South Yemen.[8]
December 1979	U.S.	Iran	—	—	U.S. naval capability was demonstrated as a means of "trying to put the squeeze on Iran."[9]
1981	Soviet Union	South Africa	—	Mozambique Channel	Reinforced presence in response to South African incursions into Mozambique.[10]

Notes:

1. *United States Foreign Policy Objectives and Overseas Military Installations*, Committee on Foreign Relations, 96th Congress, 1st Session, 1979, p. 90.
2. Dieter Braun, *The Indian Ocean: Region of Conflict or "Zone of Peace"* (London, 1983), p. 65.
3. *United States Foreign Policy Objectives*, p. 89 and 89n.
4. Ibid., p. 90.
5. Ibid.
6. P. K. S. Namboodiri et al., *Intervention in the Indian Ocean* (Delhi, 1982), p. 46.
7. Braun, op. cit, p. 65.
8. Namboodiri et al., op. cit, pp. 144, 157.
9. *National Policy Objectives and the Adequacy of Our Current Navy Forces*, Hearings before the Committee on Armed Services, House of Representatives, 96th Congress, 2nd Session, 1979, p. 23.
10. Braun, op. cit, p. 65.

132

3

Emerging Economic Issues in the Indian Ocean: An American Perspective

JOEL LARUS

While the Indian Ocean is the world's third largest ocean, the economic diversity of its littoral and hinterland states may be without equal. Few statements regarding industrial-agricultural conditions and development programs can be made that apply equally to all sectors or even to the several states within a particular sector. Here can be found some of the world's most densely populated countries, as well as island nations whose total population is well under 100,000. The level of agricultural development ranges from countries that are involved in carrying out a green revolution to others whose farming methods have changed little in the last several hundred years. The scientific, technological, and business communities of the most progressive states are sizeable and have realized notable accomplishments; other governments have to depend on a handful of men and women with modest educational backgrounds. In the Persian Gulf, there are oil-rich states that have sufficient financial resources to provide each citizen with exceptionally liberal educational, medical, and social benefits; several hundred miles away there are countries, lacking oil-gas reserves, whose populations are poorly housed and clothed and must struggle daily to obtain minimal quantities of food.

Such sharp contrasts and uneven tempos of development mean that discussion and analysis about the economic goals of the 36 littoral and 11 hinterland states that make up the so-called Indian Ocean community must be approached with caution. For example, a modernization program that excites the imagination of officials of an island nation may be discounted by bureaucrats of its nearest neighbor as being unrealistic, impractical, and wasteful of public funds. And, of course, states receiving aid and assistance from one superpower may be praised or attacked by leaders with a differing economic orientation.

Perhaps there is only one economic objective that is common to all Indian Ocean states, no matter where they are located or the level of their economic progress: Every government is committed to developing its diverse economic resources in a manner that holds out the most likely prospects for improving the general welfare of its citizens, and doing so in the most expeditious manner possible. Disagreements and tensions arise when discussion turns to the specific means that will lead to economic growth. Then the aforementioned diversity of the regional states comes into sharp focus.

While one should not discount their parochialism, the regional states somewhat recently have come to recognize that the approximately 30 million square mile area of the Indian Ocean is a commonly shared resource, one that could be instrumental to their respective economic development efforts. The long-negotiated, now drafted, but not operative Law of the Sea Convention (LOSC) has given each littoral and hinterland state a variety of new rights and duties, both within the 200-mile exclusive economic zone (EEZ) as well as on the seabed beyond the limits of national jurisdiction.[1] Some LOSC provisions, more and more local capitals are realizing, hold out the promise of facilitating new industrial enterprise, reducing chronic unemployment, correcting unfavorable balance-of-payment gaps, and, not the least important, improving the diet. These states now are engaged in policy discussions of how best to utilize the ocean's mineral and living marine resources. Concomitantly, they also have begun to consider the most appropriate means to explore and exploit the mineral and living marine resources of the continent of Antarctica and its surrounding waters. (Whether or not the ocean space below 60° south latitude—where Antarctica is located—is or is not a part of the Indian Ocean is a question better left to geographers and oceanographers.) Here is located one of the world's last common spaces, a continent where territorial claims are ill-defined or in dispute and an area where great proven as well as enormous potential resource wealth exists.

These two related topics—how best to apply key provisions of the LOSC for the economic development of regional states, and whether or not to challenge the existing Antarctic regime—are issues of great moment to these countries. A common policy on either topic will not be forthcoming; the region's diversity precludes such agreement. Some local states have announced that they would not ratify the LOSC, thus ending what was thought to be a chance at unanimity.[2] Other governments are expected to take a similar stand. The debate over whether the Antarctic Treaty should or should not be amended to reflect better local economic priorities and development programs is currently taking shape both within the U.N. General Assembly and elsewhere. Here, too, regional consensus is highly improbable.

This paper, accordingly, will attempt to deal selectively with four key economic issues relating to the Indian Ocean and its future. They are issues that will have an important impact on U.S. relations with the states of the

Indian Ocean region as a whole, and in particular on U.S. relations with India. These issues are:

1. The exploitation of living marine resources in the EEZs of the littoral states;
2. The exploration and exploitation of mineral resources, particularly oil and gas, in the same areas;
3. The recovery and utilization of the polymetallic nodules that are located on the deep seabed;
4. The exploration and exploitation of both the mineral and living marine resources of Antarctica.

In both a geographic and economic sense, India occupies the control position throughout the Indian Ocean. Not only is it the regional country that has been most successful in industrializing and modernizing, but its development is also one of the principal keys to the region's future economic growth, particularly if this development is connected to resources of the ocean. New Delhi's several oceanic programs, as will be discussed, are imaginative and broad ranging, and almost all appear to hold out the promise of being successful. Unquestionably, the effectiveness of the oceanic programs of the remaining 35 coastal states is closely related to what New Delhi does or does not realize in executing its comparable programs. In such matters, India's leadership role increasingly is being recognized and its goals respected.

To analyze India's oceanic policies and programs without first discussing the common-heritage-of-mankind concept and its application to both the LOSC and Antarctica would be imprudent. It is a concept that Indian leaders for years have championed in the United Nations and other international forums, but never under the political-economic pressures that exist today. Accordingly, the concept will be examined critically before discussing its implications for Indo-U.S. relations.

The United States, for its part, cannot be indifferent to the economic dimension of the Indian Ocean and, above all to India's oceanic activities. The Persian Gulf–Arabian Sea sector has been declared to be vital to American security; Washington has friends and allies throughout the region. Currently, the governments of India and the United States do not share similar views on some of the aforementioned four topics to be examined in this paper. If future, serious disagreements on oceanic economic policies and programs are to be avoided, it is a propitious time to consider the points of divergence and work for compromise solutions, if possible.

The 200-Mile Exclusive Economic Zone

Whether or not the LOSC enters into force, international lawyers generally agree that the 200-mile EEZ is now a customary rule of law. Today the area considered as the high seas has shrunk one-third while the hydrospace and seabed under national jurisdiction of coastal states has been enlarged manifold. (See Table 3.1.) For example, Mauritius (population 997,000) claims sovereign rights to the seventeenth largest EEZ in the world, or some 345,000 miles of ocean; Maldives (population 157,000) is twenty-third on the EEZ list; and the Seychelles (population 68,000) controls over 380 thousand square miles of EEZ space. India has become an EEZ giant. It now has 800 thousand square miles of ocean where it may exercise sovereign resource rights, thus ranking it twelfth in a worldwide listing.[3]

Within the newly created zone, a 200-mile corridor seaward of the baseline of the territorial sea of a coastal state, a government has sovereign rights to explore and exploit the living and non-living resources, as well as the duty to develop programs designed to better manage, conserve, and utilize the ocean under its control.

The worldwide acceptance of the EEZ concept as an integral part of contemporary international marine law must be considered one of the most significant accomplishments of the prolonged LOS negotiations. In most practical and utilitarian ways, it has completely altered ocean management and development. It also offers Third World states that border on ocean space an unprecedented opportunity to increase national income, raise foreign exchange earnings, and improve national diets. The policies and programs adopted by each coastal state to maximize its benefits from EEZ use will be somewhat different, reflecting the level of industrial development, economic objectives, defense needs, and the domestic political situation. In turn, each venture will have a series of different political-economic (and possibly military) effects. But some general observations concerning Indian Ocean states and their EEZ opportunities can be offered in the two most important areas of activity, namely, fishing and oil-gas recovery.

EEZ Fishing Expansion

Marine experts estimate that, as a result of the 200-mile rule, 99 percent of the world's fish resources are located in ocean space under national control. For the first time in history, foreign fishing vessels can be excluded from sectors of the ocean that earlier had been available and, conversely, coastal states can now contract with foreign fishermen for their mutual economic advantage.

The fishing states of the Indian Ocean are in as good a position as any nation in the world to take advantage of the new rule. For well-established historical, cultural, and technological reasons, local fishermen traditionally have tended to concentrate their efforts in offshore, coastal fishing rather than sail hundreds of miles from land and risk the dangers to life. Conversely, fishermen from non-regional states—notably French, Japanese, South Korean, Soviet, Spanish, and Taiwanese—have been most prominent in harvesting migratory and non-migratory species. The result has been that the annual catches of foreign vessels in Indian Ocean waters have been substantial, but the harvests of local fishermen are much less impressive.[4] A recent report on "The Fishing Industry in the Indian Ocean" calls attention to this imbalance in a dramatic fashion. In comparison to the Atlantic and North Pacific areas:

> . . . the Indian Ocean has been relatively neglected for a long time. . . . it is an extremely under-exploited area. Catches in 1982 only represented close to 5% of worldwide production; 3.74 million tonnes . . . out of a world total of 76 million tonnes (including aquaculture).

The essay then concludes with the observation that a large proportion of Indian Ocean fish is harvested by "the two huge fleets that comb the area—the Japanese and Soviet fleets."[5]

Fishing statistics of regional states during the post–World War II period are unreliable and difficult to locate. But recent tonnage figures of what may be considered a typical local situation are revealing. In a 1971 survey of the Seychelles, one author reported:

> Inshore fishing produces an estimated 1000–1500 tons per annum, which provides for minimal local needs and some export. . . . Efforts are being made to develop the rich potentials of the surrounding seas with colonial development and welfare funds.[6]

A report on the Seychelles fishing industry that was issued 13 years later bears no resemblance to the earlier situation. Reporting on the opportunities that would accrue to coastal states prepared to capitalize on their EEZ sovereign rights, the July 1984 survey noted: "Only a few years ago, the Seychelles were having to import large quantities of fish, but the country is now on the way to becoming one of the largest fishing centres in the Indian Ocean."[7] In offering reasons for such a turnabout, the editors reported that in January 1984 the government of the Seychelles exercised its sovereign rights over the 200-mile EEZ and negotiated a licensing fee and royalty arrangement with European fishermen for the right to harvest catches in its waters.

Depending on its location, the size of its EEZ, the marketability of the species, and the like, every coastal state of the Indian Ocean has a comparable opportunity either to develop its indigenous fishing industry or to lease to a foreign vessel(s) the right to operate in its waters, or possibly a combination of the two.

India, because of its geographical and technological advantages, should be among the region's most progressive and successful fishing nations, but it has been slow to develop its potential.[8] According to a 1982 article written by an Indian reporter, the country's fishing fleet consisted of approximately 16,000 mechanized boats plus hundreds of traditional catamarans. Only 57 trawlers were equipped for deep-sea fishing. The author also stated that India's 1982 total catch was about 1.5 million tons, of which an estimated 99 percent came from coastal waters and the remaining amount from the deep sea.[9] Approximately a year later, another report, dated July 1983, characterized the country's fish production as "stagnant." It continued:

> . . . state corporations in the field are running at a loss and unable to raise the finance for expanding operations; and the traditional fishermen

. . . have been increasingly threatened by the expansion in number of mechanised fishing boats.[10]

Several months ago, New Delhi released figures regarding the nation's 1983 catch. Indian fishermen harvested an all-time high of 1.6 million tons, a 1.1 percent increase over the previous year but an amount that nevertheless continues to represent "an under-exploited national resource."

The negative results of India's efforts to organize and manage a dynamic and growing fishing industry can be found in *The Yearbook of Fisheries for 1984,* the latest compendium of statistics assembled by the United Nations Food and Agriculture Organization. In 1980, India's total production of fish (fresh/chilled/frozen) was 22,629 metric tons. The following year it had fallen to 8769 metric tons, and in 1982 it was further reduced to 6760 metric tons. There was a major increase in 1983 to 19,094 metric tons, or an amount somewhat comparable to the nation's catch in 1980.

Additional facts about India's fishing industry help explain its sluggish performance. The country's principal harvest is shrimp, a catch that consistently represents about 85 percent of the total annual marine product. In 1982–83, for example, out of a gross seafood export of Rs 361 crore (approximately $3.6 million), the value of shrimp was Rs 316 crore (approximately $3.2 million.[11] Export sales in such amounts, as a United Nations study revealed, makes India the largest volume exporter of shrimp in the world.[12]

Such figures are not grounds for optimism since India's shrimp industry is facing a very troubled future. Indian marine biologists have expressed concern that the possibilities for increased shrimping are not only limited but possibly also fading rapidly. So intensively have local inshore fishermen exploited the nation's shrimp beds that today there is genuine concern that the coming years may be marked by serious depletion, shortages, and local hunger. In 1982, an Indian editorialist, Rahmatullah Khan, wrote:

> According to reliable FAO estimates, India's shrimp stock has already reached the 'full exploitation' status—which in layman's language means that any increment in effort (increase in the number of trawlers, for instance) will drag it into the 'depletion' status, or put it on the endangered species list.[13]

Other problems abound in the industry. Japan, India's principal shrimp importer, discontinued large purchases in September 1983 because of pricing disagreements. Within a few weeks the country was heavily overstocked with frozen shrimp and no foreign market. The dispute has since been resolved, but tensions remain. Also, the United States, which at one time imported a substantial quantity of Indian shrimp, became concerned in recent years with the problem of salmonella. In October 1979, the Food and Drug Administration placed the import on its "block listing" register, a designation that requires all such products to receive special inspection. The block listing remains in force. In short, India's leading item of exported fish products, namely, shrimp, is in jeopardy. The industry needs governmental assistance on every level of operation, beginning with a program designed to protect existing beds from being over-fished and ending with the actual processing of the product for the export market.

A different, but related, complicating problem for India's fishing industry—and almost every other littoral state of the region—is the paucity of data concerning the physical makeup of the EEZ. On this topic, Khan wrote:

> On the state of knowledge of the resource potential, one needs to note that there is a good deal of guessing game involved. There has never been an accurate and scientific survey made of all of India's 7,100 km coastline to evaluate the stock situation, population dynamics, migration patterns etc., of the living resources, which alone can lead to meaningful resource estimates. . . . There has been little of commercially relevant, resource-related research on fisheries in India.[14]

The other fishing-related problems that Indian Ocean states will have to deal with add up to a sizeable list. Patrols must be enlarged and strengthened so that they are better able to stop poaching by unauthorized vessels, currently a heavy drain on local catches. Fleets must be expanded and mechanized; on-board processing facilities must be modernized. The rights and interests of the traditional fisherman, unable or unwilling to change occupational patterns of a lifetime, need to be protected. The on-shore infrastructure for processing and retailing (locally and abroad) will have to be brought up to date.

In pursuing their various programs to exploit their respective EEZs under national control, and to build up a greater fishing capability, the Indian Ocean states have, at the same time, shown a willingness to work cooperatively. Encouraging signs of moves toward accommodation were evident at the July 1984 conference on the development of the world's fishing industry, a meeting held under the auspices of the Food and Agricultural Organization of the United Nations. A leading topic for discussion and analysis was the Indian Ocean and how coastal states and island nations could increase annual harvests. The press reports suggest that apparently there was greater interest than ever before in the Indian Ocean Fisheries Committee, an agency established by the Organization in 1968 but not operative until 1981. It was the delegates' recommendation that the Committee develop multilateral programs as expeditiously as possible to make the fishing industry of the Indian Ocean states scientifically and technologically on a par with operations in the world's leading oceans and by its leading fleets.[15]

If such goals become a reality, foreign assistance will be required. In developing an appropriate strategy, the Indian Ocean Fisheries Committee should give careful attention to an earlier recommendation of another multinational body. In May 1983, the 39-nation Asia-Africa Legal Consultative Committee held a session in Tokyo and considered, at length, how best to organize a program of cooperation among member states so that they could acquire and apply modern methods of fish harvesting. The Asia-Africa

Legal Committee expressed the opinion that unless member states "appropriately guarantee" foreign investments, it would be difficult to attract the funds required for modernization.[16]

In summary, very great economic opportunities exist for Indian Ocean states to exploit the fish found in EEZ waters provided they formulate policies that are realistic and reflective of the experiences of the leading non-regional fishing nations.

EEZ Oil and Gas Exploration

According to a 1973 U.N. analysis, a significant 87.5 percent of the world's offshore oil reserves are located in the seabed of the 200-mile EEZ. The remaining 12.5 percent, the report added, is located at such great depths below the floor of the high seas that it is unlikely it ever will be recovered. In one sense, therefore, the exploration and exploitation of energy resources within a state's 200-mile EEZ, sometimes designated the continental margin resources, represents a domestic policy matter and involves questions that are within the exclusive purview of the local government. It has two policy alternatives. First, it can go it alone, excluding foreign participation in all (or most) phases of its energy development program and relying on its own financial resources, personnel, and equipment to the greatest extent possible. Such a policy decision relieves it of sharing gas or oil, if located and recovered. Its alternate choice is to enter into a joint arrangement with a foreign oil corporation, farming out bloc(s) of offshore sites, relying on its experience and expertise, and dividing in an equitable manner whatever oil and gas are produced. The specific terms and conditions of such joint ventures vary considerably; each party is entitled to press for the most favorable economic arrangement attainable. There is no treaty or other international agreement that lists the norms or standards that apply in such situations.

Viewed from a different perspective, however, offshore energy exploration and exploitation do have an international dimension, one bearing on complex international economic problems. More specifically, a state's economic development is tied directly to whether its oil and gas supplies come from local and/or foreign fields. The state that is self-sufficient or nearly so is well situated. To the extent that a nation's bill for imported energy represents a disproportionate amount of its hard currency outflow, on the other hand, it may have to curtail industrialization, limit agricultural modernization programs, and slow down the upgrading of its infrastructure. Also, there is a high probability that such a state will have to seek out funds from an international bank or other lending agency or request assistance from a friendly government. The state, particularly the Third World state, that experiences a continuous cycle of heavy oil-gas imports and difficult balance-of-payment problems almost invariably can expect to remain poor and undeveloped, in spite of often desperate and heroic efforts. The politics of development, it is widely recognized, have become a key aspect of international affairs.

To a greater or lesser degree, the coastal states of the Indian Ocean have been attempting, since the energy crisis of the early 1970s, to locate offshore oil-gas fields in order to cut down on costly imports. The programs of India and Indonesia until the last several months have markedly differed in their willingness to seek out and join in partnership ventures with foreign oil corporations, taxation arrangements, profit sharing, and other basic terms of production. Their respective policies, therefore, stand as contrasting regional case histories of how programs designed to realize energy self-sufficiency can be planned for and executed. If recent press reports are accurate, the participation of foreign oil companies appears to lead to a more sanguine result.[17]

The establishment of the 200-mile EEZ has resulted in a sizeable number of territorial disputes in the Indian Ocean. When coastal states began to extend the area of national jurisdiction beyond traditional 3- to 12-mile range, governments became increasingly attentive to claim as large an area of the ocean as possible and, concomitantly, determined to limit or cut back the ocean space that neighboring nations claimed or utilized. The possibility of locating oil and gas to help reduce imports sometime in the future was sufficiently intensive to result in an indeterminate number of bilateral and multilateral disagreements over where maritime boundary lines were to be located. Because of the somewhat sketchy rules governing the establishment of the 200-mile EEZ, states laid claim to long-ignored, sometimes uninhabited, minuscule points of land, thus adding to the general instability and tensions in some sectors of the region.

Again, India has been among the leading states peacefully adjusting its marine boundaries. In 1974, for example, it settled its boundary with Indonesia in the Andaman Sea. Four years later, India and Thailand concluded a similar delimitation agreement, which, in turn, led the three countries to sign the so-called Tripartite Agreement, which established a fixed, trilateral seabed boundary line in the Andaman Sea.[18] New Delhi also has taken the lead in removing the possibility of maritime quarrels with Sri Lanka by concluding an agreement with that government in 1976, as well as one with the Maldives in 1979.[19]

In one sector of the Indian Ocean, however, maritime boundary controversies remain unresolved. One such quarrel is over Tromelin, a one-mile-long and 700-yard-wide, uninhabited islet in the western sector of the ocean. France, Madagascar, and Mauritius all claim territorial rights to Tromelin and the controversy appears one that may have to be resolved in an international court.

The Deep-Seabed Mining of Nodules

The Common-Heritage-of-Mankind Concept

In August 1967, Arvid Pardo, Malta's Ambassador to the United Nations, called to the attention of the General Assembly the fact that "the known resources of the seabed are far greater than the resources known to exist on land."[20] He requested member states to open negotiations for a new Law of the Sea, one consistent with current uses of the ocean and emerging technological processes. Following an in-depth analysis and debate, in December 1970 the General Assembly adopted Resolution 2749 (XXV), entitled "Declaration of Principles Governing the Seabed and Ocean Floor, and the Subsoil thereof, Beyond the Limits of National Jurisdiction." Seeking to lessen the economic and social inequalities between developed and developing states, Article 7 of the resolution included a revolutionary concept: "The exploration of the area [i.e., the seabed beyond the limits of national jurisdiction] and the exploration of its resources shall be carried out for the benefit of mankind as a whole, irrespective of the geographical location of States, whether land-locked or coastal, and taking into particular consideration the interests and needs of the developing nations."

Article 7 reflected two complementary objectives of the early advocates of a new Law of the Sea. First, it would create an international maritime regime authorized to explore and exploit the mineral and living marine resources of the seabed for the general benefit of the world and for the particular benefit of states struggling to modernize, industrialize, and create more equitable societies. Second, the article was intended to rebut the claims of states seeking broad extensions of the traditional territorial seas, notably those asserting a 200-mile or wider band as their jurisdictional maximum. By incorporating the common-heritage concept and holding out a promise of economic benefit to developing nations, the resolution's principal sponsors hoped to convince all member states that it was in their individual and collective interests to agree on very modest, frequently mentioned 12-mile limits of national jurisdiction on the sea.

While a number of commentators have written favorably about the General Assembly's declaration and analyzed the rationale of the several states that were instrumental in securing its passage, few writers have mentioned an even earlier policy statement of the United States. Washington's pronouncement not only has historical significance, but, as will be shown, may have current application in discussions of revised or future new applications of the common-heritage concept.

In May 1970—seven months before the United Nations acted and approved of Resolution 2749—the Nixon Administration demonstrated its acceptance of the common-heritage concept and proposed its application. Today, perhaps more than in past years, this proposal is significant because it reveals an American government willing to accept the principle that what belongs to all should be for the benefit of all. The proposal also disproves the implied charge of critics that the U.S. government in 1970 was intent on exploiting the planet's common space resources for its own economic gain, regardless of the needs of developing states.

According to the record, the Nixon Administration, following Ambassador Pardo's initial call, undertook a broadly based, in-depth study of all aspects of traditional rules of the Law of the Sea and whether or not these rules should be revised. The study determined which rules were in the national interest of the United States and which no longer served its political, economic, and security interests. Details of Washington's first policy declaration regarding a modern sea law were made public in the early spring of 1970. Nations were called upon to renounce national claims over the natural resources of the sea and seabed beyond the point where the high seas reached a depth of 200 meters (656 feet), and to regard all marine resources beyond this point as the common heritage of mankind. Specifically, such resources were to be exploited for the benefit of mankind as a whole. The area was to be designated an international trust zone; coastal states were to be the managing trustees; and, more important, the fees and royalties collected by the trustees were to be dedicated primarily to aid the developing states. When the plan was initially unveiled, Washington proposed that 66 percent of all funds collected by the trustee-states were to be distributed to Third World governments to assist their development programs. Somewhat later, and after the Nixon proposal had been debated by American mining leaders who were involved in the recovery and processing of land-located minerals, the announced schedule of common-heritage payments was revised downward. The new proposal called for between 50 percent and 33 percent of the total funds realized from the high-sea trust zone to be applied to the common-heritage distribution scheme. "At issue," stated President Nixon, "is whether the oceans will be used rationally and equitably and for the benefit of mankind or whether they will become an area of unrestrained exploitation and conflicting jurisdictional claims in which even the most advantaged states will be losers."[21]

The 1970 Nixon proposal was not a fanciful bargaining ploy that the administration planned to discard when serious negotiations took place. It was a thoughtfully drawn plan that complemented three principal American maritime objectives. First, because of its extensive maritime frontiers and the dynamics of its free enterprise system and the need for foreign markets, the United States historically has championed freedom of the seas and policies backing unencumbered, non-regulated navigation—especially the right of innocent passage. The Nixon proposal sought to minimize the area of the high seas where littoral states legally could assert jurisdictional control. It would have secured America's freedom of navigation in a fashion acceptable both to U.S. commercial shipping interests and to the Department of Defense. Second, the proposed system of licensing a specified area of the high seas and making fee payments for the right to explore and exploit whatever resources were located there did not violate free market, free enterprise principles concerning the establishment of a secure and satisfactory investment climate. Such arrangements were long familiar to American corporations. They offered a realistic opportunity for profit and industrial growth without the program being burdened with unacceptable, inequitable regulations. Finally, if the 1970 American proposal had been adopted, the United States would have become a leader in the recovery and processing of polymetallic nodules.

As the United States and other nations became active in such operations, it should be added, the trustee-states would have had, within a relatively few years, an important and substantial source of funds for distribution to developing countries. This application of the common-heritage-of-mankind concept today might be an accepted norm of international affairs and a standard easily transferred in whole or part to other common space areas of the world.

Washington's policy initiative died a quick death at the United Nations as well as in Law of the Sea negotiations. The proposal was a casualty of the Third World's aversion to the West's private enterprise system cojoined with a strong suspicion of programs of economic development emanating from the United States. Leading the attack were the diplomats of those littoral states determined to secure a legal right to exploit a 200-mile coastal zone of ocean space so that they would have to share only minimally with other countries the varied resources located on the continental shelf and beyond. Allied with them were a number of Third World delegations committed to applying the common-heritage concept in the most ambitious fashion possible so that it would accelerate the much-proclaimed need to bring about a redistribution of wealth between the industrialized North and the impoverished, economically weak South. The latter group of Third World states, all advocates of a New International Economic Order (NIEO), was determined to use its majority power to win approval of an international deep-sea mining regime that would create for the first time a supra-national agency designed to produce and distribute wealth in accordance with NIEO criteria of international equity. This agency was to be highly structured and have the power and administrative organization to engage in nodule mining operations on a par with, and perhaps even better equipped and better financed than, similar private enterprise operations. As has been widely reported, Part 11 of the pending LOSC did in fact incorporate these values and ideas.

While the Nixon trust zone proposal today is a mere footnote to early sea law negotiations, perhaps it deserves a less obscure fate. It reveals the United States as an early proponent of the common-heritage concept, and that position is a creditable one. Of far greater long-range importance, however, it outlined an economically realistic way to exploit the resources of common space for the developing nations. This latter aspect, particularly the percentages of fees and royalties that were advocated for distribution to Third World states, will be recalled in the sections of this paper dealing with the current unsettled situation regarding nodule mining of the seabed and also with the emerging issue of how best to exploit the resources of Antarctica.

The Part 11 Regime

Part 11 of the LOSC creates an International Seabed Authority (ISA) that is composed of an Assembly, an Executive Council, a Secretariat, and an operating arm known as the Enterprise. Together they have the legal right to organize and manage all aspects of mineral exploration and exploitation beyond the limits of national jurisdiction. The powers of each body are carefully delineated. The Assembly, composed of all treaty parties, is the supreme body of the ISA. Its voting pattern is on a one nation–one vote basis rather than a weighted voting arrangement that would have given leading investor states more of a say as to the conduct of operations. The 36-member Executive Council grants licenses, decides mining operational plans, and formulates rules. No signatory state is to have a permanent or guaranteed representation on the Executive Council. The Secretariat is the administrative arm of the regime and is given the customary rights and duties of such a body.

The Enterprise is by far the most controversial feature of Part 11 because its broad and far-ranging economic powers exceed those ever previously granted to a public international agency.[22] The statesmen who drafted the provisions of the LOSC that dealt with the rights and duties of the Enterprise were attempting to meld the economic interests of private mining corporations with those of the international agency; this arrangement generally is known as the parallel system of the LOSC. However, the drafters of Part 11 ignored or minimized some of the most basic principles of free economy operations as well as the essentials of any venture capital undertaking.

In general, the most vocal American detractors of Part 11 have expressed the most serious misgivings about three of the Enterprise's grants of authority. These, they contend, are so biased in favor of a non-capitalistic economic regime that they would give the Enterprise a decided advantage over corporate miners, thereby imperiling the economic success of such corporate undertakings.

First, they faulted the provision of Part 11 that requires a private corporate or a public financed corporation to provide the Enterprise with a detailed profile of two sites on the high seas, each with an area of 150,000 square kilometers (58,000 square miles), where it had located nodules and wished to operate. The geological profile was to be sufficiently precise and in-depth for Enterprise officials to make an informed decision as to which of the two offered locations it wished to select for Enterprise mining operations and which was to be licensed to the applicant-miner. Such a profile would be very costly, yet it was to be made without charge to the Enterprise. As some Western corporate mining officials have noted, the profile would double their initial cost of commencing nodule recovery operations, thus giving the Enterprise a decided monetary advantage.

A second requirement of Part 11 that, in the opinion of America's leading association of corporate miners, is unacceptable deals with the transfer of technology from the licensee-miner to the Enterprise to request any and all seabed mining technology purchased or developed by a licensee-miner. Provided that the miner is legally entitled to make such a transfer, the technology must be made available if the Enterprise is unable to secure the same—or equally efficient and useful—technology on the open market. When such a transfer is negotiated, the Enterprise is required to pay "a fair and reasonable" fee for the acquired technology. If the technology cannot be transferred legally because of restrictions imposed by the inventor-patentee or by the owner-manufacturer, the private corporate miner is required to secure for the Enterprise a similar technology. If such alternate arrangements cannot be made, the licensee-miner must discontinue use of the technology in question and shift to other mining procedures.

Each of these stipulations was debated intensively during the negotiations concerning Part 11 of the convention. Those advocating the mandatory-transfer provisions argued that all technological advances, regardless of their source or finance, constitute part of the universal human heritage and, as such, should be treated as a property right to be made available to would-be users who were prepared to offer a fair and reasonable compensation. Opposed were those who maintained that such universal sharing obligations do not exist and violate cardinal Western standards regarding the patent rights of a property holder. They also contended that such transfers potentially could be economically ruinous of their entire investment programs in nodule mining and processing.

A third notable feature of the parallel system, one that applies to the common-heritage-of-mankind concept most dramatically, concerns royalty payments that the licensee-miner is required to make to the Enterprise. The financial terms are exceedingly complicated: they distinguish between a miner-operator from a socialist country and one from the capitalist world. The former is taxed between 5 and 12 percent of the market value of the metals it extracts from the recovered and processed nodules. The miner from a capitalist country, in contrast, pays two taxes, both of which are determined on a sliding scale. The first is a production tax of either 2 or 4 percent, depending on the time period of production; the second is an attributable net proceed tax that ranges from a minimum of 35 percent to a maximum of 70 percent, depending on the overall profitability of the operation. Such two-tier taxation, it has been noted, handicaps the deep-seabed miner from a capitalist nation to such an extent that serious questions arise if any such operation can be conducted profitably. Another controversial taxing provision of Part 11 cited by anti-LOSC groups grants the Enterprise a 10-year tax holiday before it is required to contribute to the common-heritage fund but denies the same privilege to the private corporate miner.[23]

Assuming that the ISA regime becomes functional before the end of the century, approximately how much income might be available to it for distribution to the developing countries? One sketchy answer has been provided in a recent publication by R. R. Churchill and A. V. Lowe. They state:

> It is difficult to estimate the resultant income to the Authority, since much depends upon movements in metal prices, interest rates and other imponderables. But estimates made in 1978, based on similar systems proposed in the past, suggest that an average operation, having development costs of about $559 million, annual operating costs of about $100 million, and annual gross proceeds of about $258 million, might yield sums of the order of $200 or $300 million during the estimated twenty-year life of a mine

site. Currently it is being suggested that there could be about a dozen mine sites by the end of the century.[24]

U.S. Rejection

On July 9, 1982, President Reagan publicly announced that the United States had decided to reject the now completed convention and that American diplomats would neither participate in signing ceremonies scheduled for the following December in Jamaica nor participate as observers in the work of the Preparatory Commission.

Somewhat earlier, on January 29, 1982, President Reagan had released a list of general issues of concern to the United States, which were described as "unacceptable elements" of the then pending convention.[25] A more precise roster of Washington's "serious concerns" appeared in a so-called White House Fact Sheet released the same day.[26] All of the administration's reservations centered on the articles dealing with the Enterprise's operations. The first items objected to dealt with several operating provisions, including the possible economically destructive effects of seabed mining on the economies of land-based producers of the same metals. Other, perhaps even more serious objections related to procedural matters such as the voting arrangements in the Assembly, representation in the Executive Council, and future amending procedures and their relationship to American constitutional law.

It has been argued that the provisions of Part 11 that the Reagan Administration found unacceptable and not in the national interests of the United States could have been amended to meet Washington's objections if the Law of the Sea negotiators had persisted in their efforts. There appears to be some truth to this position. However, had such revisions been made and each one of the aforementioned provisions rewritten to reflect the American position, the Reagan Administration's last objection would have remained unanswered. That objectionable element of Part 11 could not be eliminated, amended, or reinterpreted without destroying the very essence of the Enterprise regime.

In listing the final "unacceptable elements," President Reagan called upon the negotiators to amend the draft treaty so that it "not set other undesirable precedents for international organizations." Freed of stilted, bureaucratic phrasing, Washington served notice that the United States declined to accept, in whole or in part, the philosophy of Part 11 as a stage in the growth of international economic institutions. That is, the Enterprise represented an unacceptable response by the Third World for a NIEO.[27] To the Reagan Administration, Part 11 signified the first global attempt to create a collectivist economic enterprise, one antithetical to the free market system and about which the American people had strong views. As such, it was an economic doctrine that had to be checked, lest its concepts be applied elsewhere by those favoring them.

The January 1982 statement made no mention of Antarctica or the so-called Moon Treaty.[28] It is conceivable nevertheless that the American administration had the future of the continent and the moon in mind when the President noted the "undesirable precedents" for international organization in his statement. As will be shown, some developing nations by this time had begun discussing the extreme and far-reaching application of the common-heritage concept to the mineral and living marine resources of Antarctica. Thus, President Reagan's detailed statement may have served notice to the world community that in the eyes of the American government an Enterprise-type regime was not an acceptable model for Antarctica or the Moon Treaty.

India and Seabed Mining

Since the early 1980s, India has been engaged in a broadly conceived, costly program to establish itself as the leading Third World state in the exploration and exploitation of polymetallic nodules.[29] No other developing country of the Indian Ocean area or beyond approximates India's interest in and commitment to deep-seabed mining and the processing of the metals for industrial use.[30] As V. V. Eswaran noted in his essay on the nation's ocean policy, India maintains a "unique position befitting its technological and scientific advancement."[31]

To date, the results of New Delhi's foresight and of the high professionalism of the men and women assigned to the program are impressive. In January–February 1980, for example, a locally built research vessel, the *Gaveshani,* located an area particularly rich in manganese, iron, cobalt, and nickel nodules while conducting the country's first scientific examination of the central sector of the Indian Ocean. Two other *Gaveshani* expeditions followed, each approximately 1360 miles from the Indian littoral and 10 degrees south of the equator. So successful were these voyages that in April 1982, India brought its nodule program to the attention of the Law of the Sea Conference. By the end of that year, New Delhi announced, it would be able to make the minimum $30 million budgetary allocation for seabed mining operations required for countries seeking pioneer investor status under Part 11 of the pending treaty. India did make the requisite investment and was granted pioneer status accordingly; to date, India remains the only Third World state so recognized.

During the next 12 months, Indian marine experts scanned 1 million square miles of the central Indian Ocean seabed before deciding to concentrate on two specific ocean sectors each 150,000 square kilometers as called for in a Part 11 provision. The Indian team began a systematic mapping and exploration program designed to assemble as detailed a profile as feasible of the potential nodule reserves at both sites. When, and if, the LOSC becomes operative, one of these sites will be assigned to India and the other will be taken over by the Enterprise. The transfer of the data base of the second site would be made without charge to the Enterprise. The cost to India of mapping a total of 300,000 square kilometers of ocean floor is not public information; however, *The Statesman* reported in November 1983 that "the country has already invested more than Rs 800 million ($80 million) in exploring 2.6 million square kilometers [1.1 million square miles] of the ocean floor." For a nation struggling so determinedly with poverty and a low per capita income along with so many other diverse socio-economic problems, such allocations of public funds are one of the clearest indicators of the government's determination to industrialize and realize self-sufficiency in metal supplies.

The relatively new administrative agencies established by New Delhi to develop and manage its marine programs are expanding rapidly. In July 1981, Indian officials approved the formation of the Department of Ocean Development (DOD), as well as a reorganization and expansion, but not elimination, of the 17-year-old National Institute of Oceanography. Recent press reports have stated that in the next several years the DOD expects to include a staff of at least 3000 geologists and marine engineers, as well as an undetermined number of support staff. Its 1983–84 budget has been placed at $32 million, almost twice the previous year's allocation of $17 million, albeit far less than the original DOD request of $45.35 million. The largest segment of the funds appropriated, $14.5 million, has purchased additional oceanographic vessels. Of the remaining funds, $9.6 million has been assigned to further explore the seabed in order to gain greater information about the characteristics of prime nodule locations, and the remaining $7.9 million for unspecified but necessary administrative costs.[32]

These are yearly appropriation figures. As a line item of the country's Sixth Five Year Plan (1980–85), New Delhi authorized the expenditures of Rs 1 billion ($100 million) for "major oceanographic facilities," a figure that the Indian press once characterized as "only a fraction of what the entire project is estimated to cost."[33] The Seventh Five Year Plan (1985–90) currently is being debated and allocations determined. When made public, it is very likely that the DOD will receive a percentage increase as great as, if not greater than, any of India's other leading public financed endeavors.

These costs must be considered as first-stage expenditures. If India's mining of the seabed program is to be successful, much greater allocations must follow. As reported, the Indian government has entered into contractual arrangements with West Germany[34] and the Netherlands[35] to acquire vessels built in those countries in order to accelerate the tempo of its exploration efforts. Also reported are plans for construction of land facilities capable of processing 10,000 tons of nodules daily, the amount estimated to be needed to operate a commercially successful operation.[36]

India's most generous financial commitment to nodule mining indicates the paucity of the country's present metal and mineral inventory. Currently India imports 60 percent of its copper requirements, a figure that is likely to increase as local mines are depleted and as the expanding economy grows more metal intensive. India's small supply of manganese—another metal essential to a modern, high-technology economy—is inadequate for the country's anticipated industrial expansion. Also, India lacks nickel and cobalt.

By undertaking a mining program at a seabed site while comparable operations are being conducted simultaneously at offshore locations in its territorial sea and/or EEZ, India probably will realize three highly desired national goals. First, it will cut down significantly the expenditure of national funds on imported metals and minerals. Second, India will be assured of a nearly inexhaustible supply of these key elements, a factor that will greatly advance the national drive toward self-sufficiency and maximum reliance on local resources exploited by Indian nationals. Finally, by attaining recognition of its pioneer investor status and thereafter developing a seabed mining industry, India will demonstrate strikingly its regional and global leadership in science and technology.

One undeniable conclusion arises from the foregoing survey: Based on the scope and goals of its programs, India is not a typical developing nation insofar as seabed mining is concerned. One must consider the billions of rupees of public funds expended by New Delhi to be competitive with Western mining consortia;[37] one must also consider the all-but-certain future allocations that will be made. Indian leaders are being shortsighted if they continue to regard their country as a typical Third World nation as far as this particular, ultra-sophisticated emerging industry is concerned. More accurately, India is a newly industrializing country.

If the foregoing analysis is correct, then there is good reason to question India's support for the provisions of Part 11 of LOSC. For example, every developing state in the world, except India, someday can expect to realize—cost free—material benefits from the Enterprise's mining operations, operations that will be based on the initiative, creativity, and venture capital of leading industrial nations of the West *and India*. It never will be one of these beneficiaries because its financial/personnel commitment to a national seabed mining operation in no way resembles the policy of any other Third World state. The input of all but a very few other developing states will be nil, but India is expected to spend as much as $1.5 billion of public treasury funds to bring each of its central Indian Ocean sites into full operation. Such monetary outlay of public funds places India in an ambiguous position: It is a developing nation, but in this ocean mining industry India is spending and behaving like an industrialized state.[38]

Expressed somewhat differently, India decided as early as 1981 that it would undertake a very expensive program of oceanic exploration and nodule exploitation. At some point during the last two years, the nation's total cost of seabed operations—including funds allocated, personnel assigned to DOD and related marine agencies, and vessels and on-land facilities—began to resemble comparable outlays of foreign private corporations engaged in the same marine technology.

As India becomes more active and involved in seabed mining, its national policy goals and its position regarding Part 11 of the LOSC are less likely to match the perspective of other Third World states. As has been cited, an Indian-researched site of 150,000 kilometers of the ocean will be transferred to the Enterprise without charge. An even more costly and complicated issue may arise in the future. If LOSC comes into force, the Enterprise will have the right to require licensee-miners to make transfers of technology. India could easily be a leading candidate to be selected to make such technology transfers.

According to leading Indian papers, the DOD has agreed with foreign corporations to work jointly with Indian personnel to develop the machinery and instruments necessary for successful seabed operations. For example, the DOD is known to have under consideration a program that will give India the technology to construct in local shipyards a number of foreign-designed submersibles that are essential for nodule recovery. Such arrangements have been a common practice in India's industrial history and a prime reason for the country's economic strength. If the submersible program becomes operational, Indian scientists and related experts may be expected in due time to improve the vessel and to become state-of-the-art inventors and developers in their own right. Thus, a foreign-designed, foreign-equipped vessel may eventually be superseded by a submersible that is distinctly Indian and has cost the Indian taxpayers heavily.

The history of India's program to refine and upgrade the British-designed Leander frigate is a case in point. The keel of the first locally constructed version, the I.N.S. *Nilgiri,* was laid in 1966 at Mazagon Docks, Bombay. In structure, in instrumentation, and in military performance this vessel bears little similarity to the 1980 version, the I.N.S. *Vindhyagiri,* or to the more recent frigates of the Godavari class.

The issue of India's improvements of foreign purchased technology has been addressed by V. V. Eswaran. Regarding the country's goal of industrial self-sufficiency as applied to its seabed mining programs, he said, in part:

> To be self-reliant, such technologies have to be largely developed, tested and operated indigenously. Technologies relating to instrumentation, diving systems, position fixing and position maintenance, materials development, oceanic data collective devices, anti-corrosion capabilities, submersibles, energy and energy saving devices are priority items [for Indians themselves to perfect and/or develop].[39]

Under proposed LOSC provisions, it will be recalled, the Enterprise will have the right to call upon New Delhi to transfer Indian technology considered desirable by Enterprise officials if such technology or equally efficient and useful technology is not available on the open market and if there is no legal impediment to such a transfer. The LOSC stipulates "a fair and reasonable" fee be paid for the transferred technology; but it should be noted that considerable disagreement almost invariably arises between disputant parties when this standard is applied. There is little reason to believe that the transfer of nodule mining technology would proceed without such conflict. India's monetary loss, if such an Enterprise-instigated transfer took place, could be substantial. Equally severe could be the loss of India's property rights and commercial advantage.

Modifying the Common-Heritage Concept

In 1980, the United States passed the Deep Seabed Hard Mineral Resource Act. While it was called an "interim measure," this legislation signaled U.S. disenchantment with the proposed provisions of the ISA regime and with proposed American obligations to the Enterprise and its future operations. It also served as notice of U.S. determination to protect the rights and investments of domestic corporations that had invested in exploratory seabed mining ventures. The act defined the rules and regulations that were to apply to American nationals (corporations included) engaged in high-sea nodule mining. West Germany, Great Britain, France, Japan, and a number of less prominent, sea-oriented industrial states acted in a similar fashion. That is, the domestic legislation of each of these countries was deliberately drafted to match the American law; therefore, currently there is in force what is generally designated as a seabed mining mini-treaty, or Reciprocating States Regime (RSR).

The RSR, as might be predicted, protects both the mining rights of the corporate investor as well as all property rights. The regime thus offers substantial assurance that corporate investors will be able to conduct mining operations without being encumbered with obligatory loans to an international agency, mandatory transfers of technology, and the like. In essence, RSR establishes a traditional commercial arrangement whereby national mining corporations are licensed and required to conduct operations beyond national jurisdiction according to time-tested rules and regulations. The corporate-licensees, in turn, are taxed for the right to engage in seabed mining, but the designated levy is extremely modest. Miners must pay their national governments a 3.75 percent tax on the value of all nodules recovered or, if that value cannot be determined, a 0.75 percent tax on the value of the metals processed from the nodules.

Further, the RSR specifies that if the LOSC comes into force, the licensing state will be required to transfer all collected fees to the ISA for distribution. On the other hand, if the LOSC is not made operative, the funds will be distributed according to the preferences of each mining state. Only the West German legislation stipulates that such money be ear-marked to aid developing nations.[40]

It has been estimated that between 5 and 10 years will pass before the fate of LOSC ultimately is determined, and no one can predict with any certainty whether it will come into force or not. But the next decade promises to be one during which Third World states will be calling for development loans, gifts, and grants from the industrialized states and/or from international monetary agencies. If the inequities between the developed and underdeveloped world are not to grow more severe, greater success than in the past must be realized in meeting the funding requests of the Third World. Governments, such as the United States, committed to the progress and modernization of the underdeveloped nations should examine the common-heritage-of-mankind concept once again in order to determine if it cannot be applied more judiciously and more successfully than was done in Part 11 of the LOSC.

The principles incorporated in the RSR arrangement, if modified some-what, suggest an appropriate course of action: The RSR relies on sovereignty and is attentive to the demands of international corporations engaged in risky capital-intensive ventures. With a nominal amount of revisions, this regime could be broadened to apply the common-heritage-of-mankind concept to the deep-seabed mining activities of all participating states. In its most basic outline, an amended RSR would set up an authority with the right to collect fees at three levels. First, it would have authority to grant explora-tory licenses to interested parties, granting them prospecting rights prior to auction. When sufficient time had passed for determining the nodule reserves in a designate site, the RSR authority would hold a public auction for the right to prospect for the nodules. The successful bidder, after paying an exclusive prospecting fee, would have a legally protected license to establish operations within the designated area for a predetermined number of years. The licensee-miner would be appropriately and sufficiently taxed for every ton of nodules recovered from the seabed floor, such taxes being due when the vessel transporting the nodules reached its home port or first port of call. In its determination of the royalty levy, the authority should take into con-sideration the market limits on new sources of production. Finally and central to the theme of this paper, on an annual or semi-annual basis, the authority would be required to turn over a minimum of 50 percent of all such collected funds to a board or committee made up exclusively of developing states. In turn, the developing states would distribute the funds to whatever countries and in whatever amounts the board considered wise and prudent. Such an arrangement would generate funds for the developing states almost as soon as deep-seabed mining operations got under way, in amounts directly related to the quantities recovered.[41]

Thus, Nixon's 1970 proposal for distributing profits from maritime com-mon space suggests a standard for benefiting Third World states that is worthy of reexamination. States that participated in the updated RSR re-gime—and, hopefully, India would be one—would give new, realistic mean-ing to the common-heritage-of-mankind concept, and, as the next section will explain, this may be carried over and be applied to the future development of Antarctica.

The Antarctic Treaty

In February 1956, when Arthur Lall was Permanent Representative of India to the United Nations, he circulated a memorandum proposing that the Gen-eral Assembly examine the feasibility of neutralizing the entire continent of Antarctica and utilizing its resources for the benefit of the entire world. Un-less prompt and imaginative action was initiated, he argued, the continent was most likely to become an area of American-Soviet rivalry and tension, possibly a site for nuclear weapons testing.[42] The Lall memorandum was the first statement made by a public official asserting that Antarctica was a potential trouble spot that required the Assembly's consideration. Because of Washington's opposition, as well as that of several Latin American states, the Lall proposal ultimately was withdrawn and the Antarctica issue languished for 27 years before it finally was put on the agenda of the General Assembly.

Although the Eisenhower Administration was opposed to a U.N. discussion on the future of Antarctica, it was neither indifferent nor unresponsive to the issues raised by Ambassador Lall. In 1958, only two years after opposing action in the General Assembly, the State Department invited the seven states asserting territorial claims to Antarctica (Argentina, Australia, Chile, France, New Zealand, Norway, and Great Britain), plus the four states engaged in scientific work there (Belgium, Japan, South Africa, and the Soviet Union), to join the United States in drafting a treaty that would ensure the preservation of the polar continent as an international laboratory for scientific research and peaceful purposes, an area of 5.5 million square miles and larger than India and China put together.[43]

India was not invited to the Washington meeting, as Ambassador Lall regretfully notes in his recent summary of his early contribution to the genesis of the Antarctic Treaty. Rightfully, he chides the State Department for lifting "parts of my own explanatory memorandum to the UN General Assembly without, of course, quotation marks or any other acknowledgement of my penmanship."[44] Nevertheless, the meeting of the 12 invited states did take place and was a success.

Since becoming operative in 1961, when it was ratified by all original initiating states—now designated as the Consultative Parties—the convention has succeeded beyond all expectations in implementing its three designated, principal objectives.[45] The continent remains demilitarized: No military base or fortification has been located on Antarctica and there never has been a military maneuver conducted on land or in its adjacent waters. Second, an extensive program of peaceful scientific investigation and cooperation has been carried out that has amassed very large quantities of information regarding the continent's ecological system. Third, the several countries making territorial claims—some claims competing, all claims a potential source of international conflict—have not pressed their respective causes. Without prejudicing any of the rights of claimant states or narrowing their differences in any way, the treaty put aside the entire territorial issue until 1991 at the earliest.

Several other features of the Antarctic Treaty are germane to American-Indian economic relations. All recommendations and programs of the Consultative Parties are realized by consensus.[46] The older Consultative Parties expect a newly admitted member state to approve of the recommendations previously agreed to and operative. Finally, although the treaty applies to the area south of the 60° parallel, including the ice shelves, it makes no provision for setting up an EEZ or for including other offshore rights and duties of a littoral that are found in the LOSC.

Today Antarctica looks forward to an economic development program not imagined when the 1959 treaty was first drafted. A growing body of evidence suggests that the continent proper or its immediate offshore waters contain the world's greatest undiscovered, unrecovered storehouse of mineral and energy resources. In 1979, for example, an official of a leading American oil corporation stated that he believed there might be 50 billion barrels of oil there, an amount comparable to the reserves of Saudi Arabia.[47] Another source predicted that as much as 115 trillion cubic feet of natural gas would be discovered on the shelf. Still others have spoken with considerable conviction of the probability of recovering coal, iron ore, uranium, gold, lead, cobalt, silver, and titanium on the Antarctic continent.[48]

To date, none of these forecasts have materialized and, although earlier optimism has waned, the world's scientific community continues to expect significant discoveries. However, most experts also call attention to the fact that there is no technology currently available that could make commercial exploitation of such geographically inhospitable mineral and energy resources feasible for approximately 15 to 25 years. But oceanographic and seismic work conducted by some of the world's most aggressive petroleum corporations throughout the region is an additional indication of the anticipated resource wealth of the continent. "All this activity would not be taking place," a former British diplomat has observed, "in the absence of a real possibility of major oil and gas finds."[49]

The possible discovery of polar minerals inspires great speculation, but there is no question whatsoever regarding the abundance of Antarctica's living marine resources. In 1977, its surrounding waters were estimated to be four times more productive of fish reserves than any other comparable marine area in the world.[50] Antarctica's seals, whales, and squid are well-established economic assets, and the fishing fleets of a number of states long have been active in local waters. Leading the list of the most intriguing, as yet unexploited, new food source is krill, a 2-inch-long crustacean. It physically resembles shrimp, feeds on diatoms and other phytoplankton, and is basic to the marine food chain of the entire area and beyond. Nutritionists have determined that krill contains roughly the same protein content by net weight as beefsteak or lobster. Because of its super-abundance in offshore waters, it has stimulated considerable global interest regarding all aspects of its life cycle as well as the most promising processes for its commercial exploitation. Such unusual interest in krill is understandable since some believe that a sustainable krill recovery on an annual basis could double the world's total marine harvest, thus making available 70 to 150 tons of edible fish. Because it is not yet known exactly how many tons of krill can be harvested yearly without endangering the species or threatening the well-being of other, higher forms of local marine life, a reasonably modest krill fishing program currently is in force. The FAO's *1984 Yearbook of Fishery Statistics* highlights how aggressive the fleets of the Soviet Union and Japan have been in harvesting Antarctic krill. For example, in two of the leading areas of krill fishing in Antarctica, the Soviets in 1984 reported a total catch of 74,366 metric tons. In the same two areas, Japan harvested 49,145 metric tons. Officials of the fishing industry in both capitals have said that their respective catches would be significantly greater if and when technicians learned how to process and market krill for general consumption and the public came to appreciate its high protein characteristics.[51]

As has been made public, the Consultative Parties discussed in their closed meetings for several years the questions of both mineral and living marine resources in an attempt to determine policies that would safeguard the continent's potential wealth as well as protect its ecosystem. Responding first to the more immediate problem of developing new food supplies for the world, they concluded in 1980 a Convention on the Conservation of Antarctic Marine Living Resources, which became operative in April 1982.[52] The Parties agreed that they would (1) prevent a decrease in the size of any harvested population of fish to unstable levels; (2) maintain the ecological relationship between harvested, dependent, and related populations of Antarctica's living resources; and (3) prevent change or minimize irreversible risks to the marine ecosystem. In order to implement these objectives, the Consultative Parties authorized the creation of a Commission for the Conservation of Antarctic Marine Living Resources, headquartered at Hobart, Tasmania. While the Commission's potential role in managing the continent's living marine reserves is both extensive and important, it has only limited powers to enforce compliance with a recommendation. A member state unwilling to accept a particular recommendation of the Commission legally is entitled to give notice within 90 days of its refusal to comply.

Presently under way are efforts to establish a comparable regime for the continent's mineral and energy resources. In July 1981, the Consultative Parties declared it a "matter of urgency" to conclude a convention that dealt with land-located mineral and energy reserves along with those located in the offshore waters. Accordingly, the Consultative Parties have held a series of special meetings to draft a set of rules that will govern the exploration and extraction of such resources yet ensure that the pristine environment of the continent is disturbed minimally. Because all Consultative Party deliberations are secret, the specifics for the mineral regime are not yet public.

In their substantive decisions as well as in the procedures they have employed, the Consultative Parties increasingly have displeased a number of concerned, excluded nations. Particularly offended are a number of developing countries. Complaints were made at Law of the Sea negotiations and in speeches in the General Assembly about the exclusivity of the Antarctic regime and about the need to establish a more internationally democratic management for exploitation of the continent and its resources. To date, these protests have not been acted on by the Consultative Parties. A more specific complaint was included in the Economic Declaration that was issued at the close of the summit of non-aligned nations in New Delhi in March 1983. This resolution called on the General Assembly to undertake a comprehensive study of Antarctica. Furthermore, the states insisted that "in the interest of all mankind, Antarctica should continue forever to be used exclusively for peaceful purposes, should not become the scene or object of international discord and should be accessible to all nations." The resolution then continued: "They [the non-aligned nations] agreed that the exploration of its resources shall be carried out for the benefit of all mankind, and in a manner consistent with the protection of the environment of Antarctica."[53]

The next development was inevitable. Despite some opposition from the Consultative Parties, the General Assembly agreed in September 1983 that the item "Question of Antarctica" should be considered by the First Committee. The topic was debated, with a lack of enthusiasm by several Consultative Parties still much in evidence. The Committee nevertheless passed a resolution requesting that the Secretary General prepare for the next session of the General Assembly (September 1984) a comprehensive, factual, and objective study of Antarctica. Thus, 27 years after Ambassador Lall first attempted to introduce the question of Antarctica, the continent and the regime created as a result of the 1959 treaty became a concern of the United Nations.[54]

India and Antarctica

Under the provisions of the 1959 treaty, Consultative Party status is open to a new state that has demonstrated "substantial scientific research activity" on the continent. In August 1983, the government of India not only adhered to the treaty but applied for and was granted Consultative Party status the following month. The distinction accorded India, the first Third World state to conduct the stipulated level of scientific work on the continent, was a result of the two expeditions sent to the Queen Maude sector by the DOD and from India's decision to establish a permanent manned scientific weather station there. Once admitted as a Consultative Party, India joined the 15 other signatory states that collectively have the power to manage the continent's affairs and to decide by consensus on the rules that will determine its future.

The press has reported that Indian officials have participated in Consultative Party meetings since its September 1983 election, but New Delhi's specific policy positions on nearly all agenda items remain unclear at this time. Because discussions of the 16-member group are closed to the media, there has been considerable public speculation about New Delhi's views on pending issues, particularly its stand on applying the common-heritage-of-mankind concept to the resources of Antarctica. One Indian commentator has suggested that the government ought to apply the concept in a very liberal fashion, implying that the provisions written into Part 11 of the LOSC should be used as the model. Discussing possible policy alternatives the country's representative should take at Consultative Party meetings, he argued, "The role of India as a representative of the Third World Countries is to establish the principle of 'Common Heritage of Mankind,' not to make special claims."[55] More revealing of the government's hesitation to commit itself on this issue, however, were the remarks of India's representative at the United Nations' First Committee meetings when the "Question of Antarctica" was discussed in late November 1983. He summarized India's long-standing concern for developing Antarctica's potential; he pledged to the Secretary General India's full cooperation in carrying out the proposed study of the continent; and he assured the delegates of his country's future commitment to Antarctica affairs. However, unlike most other Third World diplomats who spoke, India's representative avoided any mention whatsoever of the desirability of applying the common-heritage concept to the case of Antarctica.[56] The omission did not go unnoticed in capitals of the other Consultative Party states as well as those of the third world.

Except for indirect signals in the form of statements concerning its fishing plans in the Antarctic,[57] India continued to maintain a posture of calculated ambiguity throughout the Indira Gandhi period. Mrs. Gandhi spoke publicly only once about India's emerging role and responsibilities in the Antarctica system. Addressing the issue of the future development of the continent, she was quoted as declaring that "there is no reason why part of the world should be reserved for rich nations."[58] Her comment was interpreted by some as notification that her government intended to challenge the entire 1961 treaty arrangement. Others, more favorable to the existing system, maintained that the prime minister was serving notice that India planned to assume its rightful place as an Antarctica power.

The administration of Rajiv Gandhi had assumed power when the First Committee (Political and Security) of the United Nations began in late November and early December 1984 the first of five sessions devoted to the Antarctic Treaty. For many Third World states, the key issue was whether New Delhi would speak in favor of applying the common heritage principle to the continent's mineral and marine resources and argue that the current arrangement was discriminatory in nature.

In the First Committee debate, India's position became known when it joined all other Consultative Treaty Parties in refusing to participate in the discussion of the two key pending resolutions. The first resolution called for the updating and expansion of the United Nations' study on Antarctica; the second resolution dealt with inviting the Consultative Parties to set up a minerals regime. One section of the latter resolution called for the international management and equitable sharing of the benefits of exploiting the continent's resources, that is, for application of the common heritage principle. In explaining India's non-participation, its delegate announced that New Delhi was opposed to all initiatives to revise the Antarctic Treaty or to drastically alter its format; such changes were unnecessary and would lead to international discord, as well as revive disputes concerning conflicting territorial claims. The Indian government preferred to consider the Antarctica system as an evolving arrangement whose structural and organizational framework could and should be applied in a flexible manner.

The states that found the existing system unacceptable and called for its dismantlement did not respond publicly to India's new conservatism, but it is not too difficult to imagine their disappointment. In any event, in December 1985, India did break ranks with the other Consultative Parties when it voted in favor of South Africa's exclusion from participation in the meetings of the Consultative Parties. Here India was joined by China, also a Consultative Party. It was the first time since the Antarctica question was placed on the agenda of the United Nations some three years earlier that there was a lack of consensus on the issue.

At this writing, many questions remain unclear about India's future in the Antarctica system. At meetings of the Consultative Parties, decisions are reached by consensus so that the policy positions taken by India regarding Antarctica have global significance. New Delhi appears to have decided not to be the leading spokesman for the common heritage principle insofar as the exploitation of Antarctica's resources are concerned, but rather to support more traditional, economically sound, and tested principles of development. This could mean that reaching consensus in future Consultative Party meetings will be far less difficult than would have otherwise been the case.

An LOSC-Antarctica Linkage

The debate already is under way as to whether to apply the common-heritage-of-mankind concept liberally or conservatively to programs to exploit the resources of Antarctica.[59] If the Consultative Parties are pressed to favor an approach similar to the provisions written for the LOSC-Enterprise, there is, without question, going to be a hopeless deadlock in their discussions, one that could bring about the collapse of the Antarctic regime. With the Reagan Administration's policy stand on the LOSC in mind, it is a reasonable assumption that the United States will be among the leading opponents to such an approach, and for reasons similar to those offered when Washington declined to sign the Law of the Sea Convention.

Billions of dollars will be required to invent and perfect the techniques necessary for the recovery, processing, and distribution of the various resources found on or about Antarctica. The head of the Juridical Department of the French Ministry of External Relations, Mr. Gilbert Guillaume, called attention to this issue when he stated in February 1984 in New Delhi that, at present, the technology required for commercial exploitation of the continent's mineral and energy wealth does not exist.[60] Also, Antarctica's climate and working conditions are as inhospitable as any in the world; therefore, the amount of investment capital needed to establish a working oil field or coal mine will be extremely high. A corporate investor that undertakes such projects must be prepared to accept the risks of such high-cost ventures and have sufficient resources to carry out its programs. It is most unlikely that such an investor would agree to commit funds if the operation was burdened with the provisions of Part 11. Corporate officials contemplating such programs almost certainly would insist on greater security and protection of their venture capital than provided for by an Enterprise-type regime.

On the other hand, if the Consultative Parties unanimously agree to a more conservative, business-like application of the common-heritage idea, then their decision could enable the developing states to realize Antarctica-generated development funds. More specifically, an Antarctic authority that assumed jurisdictional control over all the continent's resources—mineral and living marine—below the 60° parallel could negotiate with interested parties for the right to explore and exploit such potential wealth. It could levy fees and royalty taxes for such rights provided they were not destructive to the investment capital. Such an Antarctic authority would be required to distribute a minimum of 50 percent of all collected funds to the developing states, such distribution again to be according to the decisions of the Third World states.

The fate of the Antarctic Treaty could well be decided within the coming five years. The present arrangement obviously has not satisfied the aspirations of some governments, particularly those committed to a centrally planned and managed world economy. Nevertheless, the Consultative Parties have so far successfully divorced the continent from the East-West arms race, frozen the potentially disruptive territorial claims, and made immeasurable contributions to the world's scientific knowledge. This impressive 24-year-old record of the Antarctic Treaty should not be dismissed lightly. As the Australian Delegate to the 1983 Consultative Party conference observed:

> We have no problem at all with . . . the need to ensure that activities carried out in Antarctica are for the benefit and in the interest of mankind as a whole, but this must be achieved by building on the Antarctic Treaty and the system of measures, instruments and actions in furtherance of it and not by beginning from scratch, or trying to begin from scratch, with some new instruments.[61]

Redesigning the "Common Heritage" Concept

A revolutionary international proposal, fundamentally meritorious and timely, albeit too far-reaching in its application, should not be discarded because it failed the first time it was applied by states championing its adoption. Twentieth-century foreign relations are replete with novel policy suggestions that initially were rejected. After being reinterpreted and amended to reflect more accurately global political and economic conditions, sometimes the revised proposal won sufficient international approval to come into force.

The common-heritage-of-mankind concept may be such a proposal. The time may be propitious for states committed to the economic development of Third World nations to come forward with a more limited, functional application of the distribution of profits from the exploitation of the resources of common space. Such a revision would have to be (1) more responsive to the legitimate prerequisites of entrepreneurial capital, whether from the private or public sector, and (2) less threatening to the concept of state sovereignty and a state's rights and duties in today's international system.

Applying these observations to the future of deep-seabed mining of polymetallic nodules and also future Antarctica development, three conclusions follow from the material presented.

First, economic progress in developing states is best ensured and the prospects for industrial-agricultural modernization most sanguine if such governments receive continuing, substantial funds for projects that they determine will advance their national interests. It cannot be stated too often: Funding is the all-important, key factor in helping to build a sound and solid economic foundation and reduce the disparity in the standards of living currently prevailing in different parts of the world. If developmental funds are unavailable, insufficient, or vary greatly from year to year, then the Third World's varied programs must be cut back, if not discontinued. Therefore, the principal objective of any new application of the common-heritage concept must be designed to distribute the greatest possible amount of money to developing nations while keeping administrative and bureaucratic costs to a minimum, and to do so in a politically acceptable manner to the international community of sovereign states.

Second, some current arguments put forth by developing states concerning the need for technological transfers appear to lack relevance. With some exceptions, developing states appear to have only a remote, tangential need to gain access to extremely sophisticated, exotic state-of-the-art technologies, particularly those technologies awaiting invention and relating to speculative ventures that could prove to be commercial disasters. Governments pressing for the mandatory sharing of super-modern technologies within the context of a transnational regime may act from motives they regard as enlightened internationalism, but it is doubtful that practical business considerations have been given comparable weight. The scientific and technological goals of the developing states should be of a modest nature. Their individual or collective modernization policies do not appear to be much advanced if the overall project is based on unprecedented concessions from the industrial states, leading ones of which are opposed to the proposed arrangement.

Industrialization and modernization are processes marked by a distinctive tempo. During the past century, many nation-states have moved successfully from backwardness and poverty to positions of economic strength and industrial growth. They have succeeded, in part, because they have favored domestic economic policies that reflected a well-conceived, orderly evolution. The speed of industrialization and modernization can be accelerated considerably with the help of outside aid, and the so-called leapfrogging principle of economic development may be applied with dramatic results; yet, there still remain innumerable slowly changing, local limitations that help determine a society's advancement. For example, infrastructure deficiencies, personnel gaps, and cultural restrictions may require gradual modifications or corrections. There exists a built-in logic of modernization. A nation or group of nations that disregards this logic and tries to race ahead toward developmental goals not commensurate with its current level of progress or maintains that the traditional tempo of modernization is out of fashion in today's nuclear world faces great domestic disappointments, failures, or loss of income, or all three.

Specifically, the most prudent course for Indian Ocean coastal states may be to work individually and collectively to develop modern, mechanized fishing vessels while at the same time helping traditional fishermen become more efficient and better informed about local maritime conditions. Such a policy would allow Indian Ocean fisheries to exploit the maritime areas under national jurisdiction and to begin to realize immediate economic benefits. On the other hand, any government that expects Enterprise-like operations to generate profits that will be distributed for modernization projects may have to wait years; worse, profits may be entirely illusory. These states have a great need for immediate funds and aid, and encouragement should be given to policies that will increase the annual fish harvests of EEZ areas. International programs calling for the redistribution of wealth via transnational agencies that are based on questionable economic concepts are far less likely to receive funding and the backing of key industrial states than development plans designed to produce new wealth.

Third, the international system continues to be made up of sovereign state actors. This may be disconcerting to those who work to redefine the United Nations and its associated bodies into a growing transnational system empowered to facilitate the redistribution of wealth among the developed and developing states. International organization today bears no similarity to a federal government in which the national legislature has the constitutional right to determine and enforce policies for the common good. As has been true for the preceding 300 years, and probably will remain true far into the future, the national interest of a sovereign state, unilaterally determined, will be the ultimate standard by which that state will accept or reject a proposal. In the General Assembly or in the course of diplomatic negotiations, a government may decide whether to vote in favor of or against a pending resolution or a proposed treaty provision on the basis of what is fashionable, timely, or in accordance with previously determined group principles. However, it invariably decides whether to implement the resolution or to ratify the convention on the basis of self-interest.

Non-traditional global or regional systems of international organization therefore need to be responsive to traditional norms of sovereignty. They need to be formulated and applied in such a manner that they do not threaten the values and practices of the sovereign state in commerce and finance, as in all other areas of state interaction.

Notes

1. For text, see *The Law of the Sea: United Nations Convention on the Law of the Sea* (New York: United Nations, 1983).

2. Mauritius announced in June 1984 that it would not ratify the LOSC.

3. See Wil D. Verwey, "The New Law of the Sea and the Establishment of a New International Economic Order: The Role of the Exclusive Economic Zone," *Indian Journal of International Law* 21, 3 (July–September 1981), pp. 387–423.

4. "The estimates of potential fish yield from the Indian Ocean vary from

about 7 million to 17 million tons. Of this potential, India's contribution is expected to be of the order of 5–9 million tons. Thus a four-to-sixfold increase over the existing production is envisaged." See S. Z. Qasim, "A Technological Forecast of Ocean Research and Development in India," *Impact of Science on Society,* Nos. 3–4 (1983), p. 467.

5. *The Fishing Industry in the Indian Ocean: Special Report* (Paris: The Indian Ocean Newsletter, June 6, 1984). Also see issues of July 7 and July 21, 1984, for concluding sections of the Report. See also Elizabeth Cheng, "Underpaid, Second-Class Citizens—That's Fishermen," *Far Eastern Economic Review* 125, 31 (August 2, 1984), pp. 35–57.

6. Theodore L. Stoddard et al., *Area Handbook for the Indian Ocean Territories* (Washington, D.C.: Government Printing Office, 1971), pp. 69–70. Also see the 1982 edition, Frederica M. Bunge, ed., *Indian Ocean: Five Island Countries,* which states (p. 216), "The immense fish resources estimated to lie in and around the nation's self-proclaimed 200-nautical mile EEZ were virtually untapped by Seychelles."

7. *The Fishing Industry in the Indian Ocean: Special Report* (Paris: The Indian Ocean Newsletter, July 7, 1984), p. 8.

8. Qasim, op. cit., p. 467, states that the estimated fish production from India's EEZ is expected to be about 3 million tons. He then adds, "The projected fish requirements of India's population by the year 2000 are estimated to be 11.4 million tons. Of this, 60–75 percent is expected to come from the sea and the rest from fresh water sources."

9. Rahmatullah Khan, "Ocean Resources Development—India's Options," *Indian Journal of International Law* 22, 4 (July–December 1982), p. 451.

10. "A Poor Catch," *India Today,* July 31, 1983, p. 108. Also see the remarks of Agriculture Minister Rao Birendra Singh at the first all-India conference of maritime states and Union territories at Hyderabad on June 26, 1983, when he "lamented that although India, with its long coastline, had the potential to become a major maritime country, the vast marine resources remained largely unexplored and unexploited." *The Statesman,* June 27, 1983, p. 11.

11. "India Big Shrimp Exporter," *India Abroad,* August 10, 1984, p. 4.

12. Ibid. Also see "Dangerous Dependence," *India Today,* December 15, 1983, p. 129.

13. Khan, op. cit., p. 452.

14. Ibid., p. 451.

15. There is growing evidence that regional countries will cooperate in fishery development and extension programs. In September 1984, seven Bay of Bengal littoral states (Bangladesh, Sri Lanka, Maldives, Thailand, Indonesia, India, and Malaysia) held a five-day meeting at Bangkok to discuss common programs to improve harvests.

16. *The Statesman,* May 22, 1983, p. 7.

17. See Mohan Ram, "India's Lonely Oil Search," *Far Eastern Economic Review* 116, 15 (April 9, 1982), p. 66; Mohan Ram, "Hounded by Bad Luck," *Far Eastern Economic Review* 119, 74 (March 3, 1983), p. 9; Jon Sikes and Patrick Smith, "Oil Exploration," *Far Eastern Economic Review* 121, 37 (August 25, 1983), pp. 39–78; Meenakshi Behara, "Ready for an Oil Rush," *Far Eastern Economic Review* 123, 1 (January 5, 1984), pp. 50–51.

18. See "India, Indonesia and Thailand Sign Agreements on Seabed Boundaries," *Indian & Foreign Review,* July 1, 1978, p. 7.

19. See, for example, "No, Man, It's My Island," *Time,* December 26, 1977, p. 32, and *Foreign Report,* September 15, 1983, p. 6.

20. See Arvid Pardo, "Future Prospects for Law of the Sea," *Oceans: Our Continuing Frontier,* H. William Menard and Jane L. Scheiber, eds. (Del Mar, California: Publisher's Inc., 1976), p. 227.

21. Ann L. Hollick, "The Law of the Sea and U.S. Policy Initiatives," *Orbis* 15, 2 (Summer 1971), pp. 670–686.

22. Not even the International Atomic Energy Agency's powers are as extensive as those granted the Enterprise, and it, since the mid-1950s, has been considered the organization with the widest range of functions, limiting the sovereignty of member states.

23. See R. R. Churchill and A. V. Lowe, *The Law of the Sea* (Manchester: Manchester University Press, 1983), p. 170.

24. Ibid.

25. Department of State Bulletin 82, 2 (March 1982), pp. 54–55.

26. Ibid.

27. For a negative evaluation of NIEO and LOSC, see Richard J. Payne and Jamal R. Nassar, "The New International Economic Order at Sea," *Journal of Developing Areas,* No. 1 (October 1982), pp. 31–50.

28. The Moon Treaty stipulates that "for the purposes of this agreement, the moon and its natural resources shall be considered the common heritage of mankind." See United Nations, General Assembly, A/34/20 Annex 2 (1979). For background information on the stalled Moon Treaty, see "Tentative Draft Agreement States Moon is Common Heritage of Mankind," *UN Chronicle* 15, 5 (May 1978), p. 25.

29. Whether or not India has nodules within its 200-mile EEZ appears to be not yet determined with finality. An October 1982 statement of the Minister of State for Science and Technology in the Rajya Sabha stated categorically that nodules did not exist within the zone. See *The Statesman,* October 21, 1982, p. 10. Other officials, however, recently have privately questioned the accuracy of this determination and cite a number of foreign-made vessels that DOD is to acquire that are specifically designed to operate within the EEZ.

30. India, however, soon may not be the only regional state to be engaged in exploring for seabed nodules. According to the August 18, 1984, issue of *The Indian Ocean Newsletter,* the Seychelles' government requested assistance from the Soviet Union to "plan the development of the seabed and its other maritime resources." In response, Moscow dispatched the R.V. *Vinogradov,* carrying 64 scientists from 14 different Soviet institutes and universities, and a joint operation got under way on August 2.

31. V. V. Eswaran, "India's Ocean Policy," *Indian & Foreign Review,* April 1, 1983, pp. 11–13.

32. See Department of Ocean Development, Press Release, June 14, 1983.

33. *The Statesman,* November 3, 1983, p. 12.

34. In June 1983, the West German–built vessel *Sagar Kanya* arrived at Bombay and the following month began its research studies in the Arabian Sea. It is described as costing $40 million and "one of the most modern oceanographic research vessels with advanced facilities for working in various disciplines of oceanography." See "Oceanography—Rapid Development in India," *Indian & Foreign Review,* reprinted in *India News,* July 16, 1983, p. 4.

35. In January 1984, it was announced that India will acquire two coastal vessels from the Netherlands for mineral exploration in its EEZ.

36. See M. K. Tikku, "Poor but Resourceful," *Far Eastern Economic Review* 117, 28 (July 9, 1982), p. 54.

37. In discussing the overall cost to India of its seabed mining program, M. K. Tikku, op. cit., p. 50, has written: "A major part of the estimated Rs 12 billion set aside for infrastructure is to be spent on a decade-long program of building facilities—offshore and on."

38. For a negative evaluation of the wisdom of India's seabed mining program, see Khan, op. cit. He argues (p. 454) that "it is a certainty that deep seabed mining technology is not going to be available for commercial transfer to the developing countries. In such circumstances, is it advisable for India to venture into the ocean depths at great costs? Hardly."

39. Eswaran, op. cit., p. 13.

40. Churchill and Lowe, op. cit., pp. 173–174. For a recent survey of the problems associated with seabed mining, see David L. Larson, "Deep Seabed Mining: A Definition of the Problem," *Ocean Development and International Law,* Vol. 17 (1986), pp. 271–294.

41. Others have examined the feasibility of alternate proposals for the common-heritage-of-mankind concept. See Arvind Khilnani, "Fishery Resource Conflict Resolution under Law of the Sea," *Economic and Political Weekly* 18, 24 (June 11, 1983), pp. 1049–1050.

42. Arthur Lall, *The Emergence of Modern India* (New York: Columbia University Press, 1981), pp. 139–140.

43. See R. D. Hayton, "The Antarctic Settlement of 1959," *American Journal of International Law* 54, 2 (1960), pp. 354 ff.

44. Lall, op. cit.

45. For text, see United Nations, *Treaty Series,* Vol. 402, No. 5778. (The treaty entered into force on June 23, 1961.)

46. Concerning voting in Consultative Parties meetings, Finn Sollie has written, "Recommendations adopted by Consultative Meetings . . . are mere recommendations to the governments. They become effective if and when approved by all parties with consultative status. Thus, the unanimity rule does apply to such measures. However, under the rules of procedure, adoption of recommendations at Consultative Meetings requires a unanimous vote and consequently it is a rare event indeed that an adopted recommendation is not subsequently approved. . . ." "Trends and Prospects for Regimes for Living and Mineral Resources in Antarctica" (Norway: The Fridtjof Nansen Foundation, 1978), p. 7 (mimeographed).

47. Barbara Mitchell, "The Politics of Antarctica," *Environment* 12, 1 (January–February 1980), p. 13.

48. For a recent survey of the continent and its resources, see Garry D. McKenzie, "Geopolitical and Scientific Roles of the United States in Antarctica" (Mershon Center, Ohio State University, October 1983) (mimeographed).

49. *New York Times,* October 15, 1982, p. 10.

50. See M. A. McWhinnie, "Marine Biology," in D. H. Eliot, ed. *A Framework for Assessing Environmental Impacts of Possible Antarctic Mineral Development* (Columbus, Ohio: Ohio State University Institute of Polar Studies, 1977), p. 9.

51. Also see McKenzie, op. cit., p. 34. He also notes that "In 1977, the reported catch by East Germany, Poland, and the USSR was about 280,000 tons."

52. For a discussion on the convention, see James N. Barnes' "The Emerging Conservation of Antarctic Marine Living Resources: An Attempt to Meet the New Realities of Resource Exploitation in the Southern Ocean," *The New Nationalism and the Use of Common Spaces,* Jonathan I. Charney, ed. (Totowa, New Jersey: Allanheld, Osmun, 1982), pp. 239–275. Also see M. J. Peterson, "Antarctic Implications of the New Law of the Sea," *Ocean Development and International Law,* Vol. 16 (1985), pp. 137–170.

53. See letter request of Government of Malaysia and the Government of Antigua and Barbuda to Secretary General Javier Perez de Cuellar, dated August 11, 1983, requesting inclusion in the agenda of the 38th General Assembly the supplementary item "Antarctica," EK.42/83, p. 2.

54. See Peter J. Beck, "Antarctica: A Case for the UN?" *The World Today* 40, 4 (April 1984), pp. 165–172.

55. G. Oommen, "Antarctica Treaty: A Critique," *Mainstream* 21, 47 (July 23, 1983), p. 30.

56. United Nations, General Assembly, *Question of Antarctica* (A/C.1/38/ PV.44, November 29, 1984), pp. 3–5.

57. In September 1984, India announced that it would fish for krill for the first time with the help of a special vessel to be acquired from Denmark. According to the DOD announcement, the vessel is equipped with on-board deep-freeze equipment and a processing factory. When an official of the National Institute of Oceanography was questioned about the progress of the project in December 1986, he stated that, although unexpected problems had arisen, he believed that positive results would be forthcoming "before too many years."

58. See Oommen, op. cit., p. 30. When she addressed the Lok Sabha on February 24, 1982, on the Antarctica issue, Mrs. Gandhi said, "We do not subscribe to the view that only a few very rich countries have the right to such uninhabited and other places." See Khan, op. cit., p. 456.

59. See, for example, K. S. R. Menon, "The Scramble for Antarctica," *South,* April 1982, pp. 11–13, and "Icebox Hotting Up," *The Economist,* October 8, 1983, pp. 37–38.

60. Gilbert Guillaume, "La France et l'Antarctique," address presented February 15, 1984, New Delhi, by France's Director of Legal Affairs, Ministry of Foreign Relations. Ministère des Relations Extérieures No. 283-DJ/JFD/VP/PI, undated. Also see *The Statesman,* February 16, 1984.

61. United Nations, General Assembly, *Question of Antarctica* (A/C.1/38/ PV.45, November 30, 1984), p. 20.

TABLE 3.1.   Maritime Claims

Country	Territorial sea (nmi)	Fishing zone (nmi)	Area within 200 nmi coastal zone (nmi^2) [*includes non–Indian Ocean coastline]
Australia	3	12	2,043,300*
Bahrain	3	3	1,500
Bangladesh	12	200	22,400
Burma	12	12	148,600
Comoros	12	12	undetermined
Egypt	12	12	50,600*
Ethiopia	12	12	22,100
French Territory of the Afars and Issas	12	12	1,800
India	12	12	587,600
Indonesia	12	12	1,577,300*
Iran	12	50	45,400
Iraq	12	12	200
Israel	6	6	6,800*
Jordan	3	3	200
Kenya	12	12	34,400
Kuwait	12	12	3,500
Madagascar	50	50	367,800
Malaysia	12	12	138,700*
Maldives	2.77–55.0	100–150	279,700
Mauritius	12	12	345,500
Mozambique	6	12	163,900
Oman	12	50	163,800
Pakistan	12	50	92,900
Qatar	3	3	7,000
Saudi Arabia	12	12	54,300
Seychelles	3	12	undetermined
Singapore	3	3	100
Somalia	200	200	228,300
South Africa	6	12	296,500*
Sri Lanka	12	12	150,900
Sudan	12	12	26,700
Tanzania	50	50	65,100
Thailand	12	12	94,700*
United Arab Emirates	3 and 12	3 and 12	17,300
Yemen (Aden)	12	12	160,500
Yemen (Sana)	12	12	9,900

Source: Indian Ocean Atlas, Central Intelligence Agency, 1976, p. 12.

4

Emerging Economic Issues in the Indian Ocean: An Indian Perspective

C. RAJA MOHAN

Surprisingly, while Indian observers have often questioned the American strategic rationale for the projection of U.S. military forces in the Indian Ocean, they have not challenged the American economic rationale. Indian writings on the Indian Ocean region have often echoed the conventional wisdom in the United States that "vital" economic interests in the region necessitate the American military presence. Yet, closer examination leads one to reconsider the related assumptions that the West is dependent on the petroleum and strategic minerals of the region and that the security of the sea lanes there is threatened.

After reviewing the emerging economic importance of the oceans for mankind as a whole, this essay will assess potential conflicts over ocean resources in the Indian Ocean and the Gulf. I will then examine the relationship between seapower, strategy, and resources in the region, focusing especially on the issue of Gulf oil and U.S. security. One section analyzes in detail the popular myths concerning U.S. dependence on the non-petroleum strategic minerals of the region. Finally, I discuss Indian Ocean non-living ocean resources and fisheries and the future economic exploitation of the Antarctic in the context of India's ocean development policy.

The Future in the Oceans

Mankind appears all set to return to the primeval soup of the oceans, from which its own biological evolution began.[1] Since time immemorial, man has used seas as a source of food, as a means of communication and trade. However, it was only since the dawn of the renaissance and the age of discovery that the world's oceans have begun to assume a significant role. The European search for spices and other exotic goods, the evolution of modern seafaring, and the "discovery" of new lands enormously enlarged the role of the seas. The industrial revolution, the search for cheap raw materials and markets for industrial goods, the manifold increase in sea-borne trade, and the colonization of non-European societies and siphoning off their surpluses interacted with each other to tremendously enhance the role of sea and seapower in history.

These now traditional uses of the sea are as a medium of trade and commerce, the military activity to protect them, a dumping ground for waste from human habitations, a source of food through fishing, and a space for the projection of military power and browbeating of other nations. But the planet's seascape—its economic character—and, consequently, the configuration of its seapower might be in for rapid transformation. It appears that we are on the verge of a veritable revolution in the way mankind interacts with the ocean space of the planet. The cumulative advances in ocean sciences and engineering have made this revolution possible. In at least three specific areas—energy, food, and the extraction of minerals—the contours of the new uses of oceans can be visualized.

In the energy sector, the increasing exploitation of hydrocarbons from the sea is of course the most significant. Offshore oil development has steadily inched forward from drilling in shallow coastal waters to the current depths of up to 5000 feet. The production of offshore oil, too, has increased at a steady pace. In 1969, the worldwide offshore crude production of about 2.26 billion barrels comprised nearly 15 percent of the total production. By 1980, the world offshore production of crude rose to 5 billion barrels, or nearly 23 percent of the total. It is expected that most of the future discoveries of hydrocarbons would either be in the sea or in hitherto unexplored Third World regions. It has been estimated that by the end of this century, nearly 50 percent of the world's oil could be extracted from the seas.

Offshore hydrocarbons are associated chiefly with the continental margins that constitute 25 percent of the total ocean area. And the exploitation of this offshore oil is knowledge-intensive. A comprehensive understanding of the ocean environment and its effect on marine operations, equipment, and permanent structures is essential to carry out offshore exploration, drilling, and production activities. Offshore oil extraction is dependent on a large body of structural engineering technology needed to design, fabricate, transport, and install offshore structures. The technological developments have successfully coped with a number of challenges, such as the harsh operating environment of the North Sea. With the advances in manned and remotely operated submersible systems, the development of sub-sea oil production systems, and the like, the exploitation of oil resources at deeper depths would be facilitated.[2]

Besides energy potential, the world's ocean space is a vast treasure house of food. The world demand for food and its production are hanging on a delicate balance. This is so in spite of the near doubling of food output in the third quarter of this century, a remarkable feat achieved through the spread of the high-yielding varieties, the expansion of irrigation, and a six-fold growth in the use of fertilizers. In the coming years, the maintenance of the past rate of growth of food production would be difficult and constrained by limits of available land, water, and energy and also by biological limits on food-producing species. Despite the unrealized food-producing potential in the Third World, the conditions for expansion of food production might be unfavorable. Moreover, tremendous pressure is being exerted on just one region—North America—for meeting world demand for food. Since the end of World War II, not one new country has emerged as a significant cereal exporter. As the renowned food expert Lester Brown says: "The worldwide shift of countries outside of North America from export to import status is a well-travelled one-way street."[3]

Can the sea fill the increasing food needs of man? By 1980, the annual world fish catch totaled 65 million metric tons (mmt) and was worth nearly $20 billion. This amount can be considered insignificant since it provided only about 1–2 percent of the calories of food available to man. Its value, however, can be better appreciated by the fact that fish is the source of about 13 percent of the world's animal protein—about three-quarters as much as provided by beef and more than three times that supplied by poultry.[4]

The hopes that the sea could be a major contributor to world food output received a setback in the mid-1970s, when the world fish catch began to stagnate. The main reason for this is the character of man's fishing activity, which is extremely inefficient. Our fishing has been similar to the hunting of land animals by our ancestors. As pointed out by Arnold Toynbee, the historian, fishing has been a practice of "skimming the sea by the paleolithic method of hunting." This inefficient form of fishing, coupled with over-fishing in the last three decades, has often led to great fishing disasters. The most dramatic of these was the collapse in 1972 of the anchovy fishery of the coast of Peru in South America. Just before is collapsed, this fishery was the world's largest and contributed one-fifth of the world's catch.

Food production from the seas could dramatically improve if only we can devise appropriate fishery management policies and quicken the transformation from "hunting" to "farming" of the seas. To quote Toynbee again, he called for abandoning hunting of seafood in favor of "farming the sea by cultivating edible seaweed and breeding and shepherding fish as we breed and shepherd sheep."[5] A technology of *aquaculture* (or *mariculture*, with special reference to ocean waters)—the cultivation of marine plants and the husbandry of marine animals, is now at hand. The evolution of aquaculture matches the emergence of agriculture on land 10,000 years ago, and involves the transition from "capture to culture" of fish.[6]

Though aquaculture has a long history—particularly in China, Japan, and Europe—it is now being modernized and spread. The worldwide fish production from aquaculture in 1980 was estimated to be over 8.7 million tons. About 75 percent of this came from the farming of the seas, especially in coastal areas. Compared with 1975, when the total production was about 6.1 million tons, there was an increase of some 42 percent in overall aquaculture production in five years. The aquaculture production in 1980 formed only about 12 percent of the total output of fishery, but this percentage is likely to grow rapidly, provided the scientific and technological inputs are increased.[7]

Seaweed culture, as part of aquaculture, is also gaining importance. Seaweed culture has a long tradition in East and Southeast Asia. Four major species of seaweed have already been domesticated, and the Chinese production of seaweed has rapidly risen in the last two decades. But, as yet, seaweed and algae are largely untapped resources that can be developed for human food and cattle feed, energy and fertilizer, and a variety of chemicals and drugs. They can be cultured, selected, genetically improved, and grown anywhere in the ocean, if there is a suitable infrastructure.[8]

A perhaps disproportionate amount of attention of the world has centered on the prospects of deep-seabed manganese nodules. These nodules, containing various metals, were among the most contentious issues of the LOS Treaty. The creation of the International Seabed Authority to regulate the exploitation of the manganese nodules saw the expenditure of considerable international legal acumen and diplomatic skills, but still proved unacceptable to some big powers. But even before the convention was signed in December 1982, the manganese nodules lost some of their century-old glamor to the newly discovered polymetallic sulfides, the discovery of which is changing perceptions of seabed mining.[9] These rich sulfide nodules are expected to be found all along the globe-girdling ridges on the ocean floor, located at only half the depth of manganese nodules.

The spectacular metallic sulfides (also called hydrothermal ore sulfides) are far from being understood. The first deposit was found in the central Red Sea in an area of hot brines at a depth of about 6000 feet. The multicolored muddy sediments contained iron sulfides and hydroxides, manganese, copper, zinc, lead, silver, and gold. Comparable muds were also discovered in the late 1970s on the East Pacific Rise at the mouth of the Gulf of California, where enormous quantities of hot water escape from the ocean floor, carrying similar metal sulfides.

The most dramatic discovery of these deposits, by the U.S. manned submersible *Alvin,* was announced in October 1981 by the U.S. National Oceanographic and Atmospheric Administration. The U.S. geologists found several mineral zones between the Galapagos Islands and Ecuador in the Pacific. They are estimated to contain 25 million tons of polymetallic sulfides. The concentration of copper and tin in these deposits is said to be high, calculated at around 10 percent each. Also present in these deposits are lead, molybdenum, vanadium, zinc, tin, cadmium, silver, gold, and platinum. The total value of the deposits is estimated at $3 billion. The leader of the U.S. team that discovered these deposits, Dr. Alexander Malahoff, reported on the significance of the new discoveries:

> Manganese nodules . . . may no longer mark the prime mineral resource of the ocean floor and may be overshadowed by the probably renewable polymetallic sulphide deposits. . . . The relatively simple geochemical composition of the polymetallic sulphides as compared to that of manganese nodules taken together with the availability of land-based plants currently processing polymetallic sulphides may make the ocean floor polymetallic sulphides even more an attractive proposition. . . . Polymetallic sulphides on the ocean floor may leave lasting effects upon the international minerals industry. . . .[10]

There are also other, less spectacular mineral resources—such as placer deposits—available from the seas. The placer deposits obtaining in the coastal waters contain varying amounts of gold, platinum, tin-iron, zirconium, titanium, rare earths, and diamonds. Though some of these have been mined for a long time (tin in Southeast Asia, for example), many are still to be explored.[11] Since placers occur in coastal and near-shore waters at depths usually not exceeding about 60 feet, they will be explored and exploited within the EEZ. Some of the mineral occurrences in the seas are listed in Table 4.1.

At the same time, more exciting methods of extracting large amounts of seawater minerals are being explored. Two examples based on the significance of aquatic weeds and algae are illustrative. Experiments are under way to develop hybrid green algae that absorb and accumulate the uranium in concentrations several thousand times that in normal seawater. In another case, the U.S. NASA has been experimenting with water hyacinth, which has the ability to absorb through its roots heavy metals such as mercury, cadmium, nickel, and lead, and even gold and silver. These metals can be recovered from the harvested plants. If the experiments succeed, water hyacinth and other plants would have a great potential in mineral extraction from the seas.[12]

Conflict Over Ocean Resources

The fears of depleting resources on land and a rising consciousness of the importance of ocean resources, coupled with the clamor of the developing countries to create a new order in the oceans, has culminated in the negotiation of a new legal regime for ocean space. The new dispensation replaced the traditional laissez-faire system of the freedom of the seas with a new international regime for nearly four-fifths of the planetary surface. It placed 40 percent of the ocean and its bottom adjacent to the coasts of the continents and islands under the jurisdiction of the states in possession of these coasts. It reserved the other 60 percent of the ocean surface and the water below for the traditional freedom of the seas; but it declared the wealth of the ocean floor outside the coastal state jurisdiction as a common heritage of mankind. It also created a unique international mechanism, the International Seabed Authority (ISA), to govern the exploration of seabed resources. The ISA has the theoretical capacity to generate income, the power of taxation, and some domain over ocean-exploiting technologies. The new regime affirms the 12-mile limit of the territorial sea as well as a 12-mile contiguous zone. Beyond these limits, it gives the coastal states sovereign rights over the use of natural resources in the newly created 200-mile exclusive economic zone (EEZ) and, in addition, a set of other rights in regard to such activities as scientific research. Where the continental shelf extends beyond 200 miles, the EEZ rights with respect to resources on the shelf are extended with it, but not beyond 350 miles. The coastal state does not hold territorial sovereignty over its economic zone, but a new kind of "functional sovereignty."

What sort of military situations could this enormous expansion of coastal state jurisdiction over oceans and "imposition" of collective sovereignty over the seabed resources lead to? What would be the new relation between maritime powers and the coastal Third World states? It has been suggested by Robert Osgood that in the earlier era, fishing and shipping had been causes of conflict, but "not generally on such a scale as to impinge on the wealth or security of nations, and never on a scale that threatened the prevailing legal regime, except in the case of shipping, temporarily during wars."[13] However, Osgood argues, with the great expansion of economic activities in the ocean space—oil extraction and fishing—the conflicts over ocean resources are likely to grow.

Many coastal states are increasingly getting into conflicts on claims over island territories and delimitation of EEZs in the desire to expand their respective stakes in ocean wealth. These disputes are unlikely to remain local and could involve big extra-regional maritime powers with security and basing interests in the region. The corporate actors of technologically advanced countries are also likely to be involved. These conflicts could be most acute in regions of southern, Southeast, and East Asia.

A number of nations have put forward competing claims to hitherto unclaimed obscure islands, reefs, and atolls in order to extend their EEZs as much as possible. "In a number of cases competing claims, security interests, national pride and economic interests have come together to create disputes and some actual conflicts concerning the ownership of previously obscure islands."[14] The state of political relations also clouds the possibility of settling the disputes amicably. For example, the disputes between Vietnam and ASEAN nations over certain South China Sea islands must be seen in the context of wider disputes over Kampuchea; and so must be viewed the Sino-Vietnamese dispute over the Paracel Islands. Similarly, the difficulties of India in resolving its maritime boundary disputes with Pakistan and Bangladesh must be viewed in the context of the uncertain political relations in South Asia.

Of greater significance is the likelihood of big-power involvement in Asian maritime disputes, given the fact that most of the Asian countries are linked to outside powers through treaties. As pointed out by Young:

> The dispute between Vietnam and Malaysia over the ownership of Amboyna Cay and Terumbu [Layang] has implications for Malaysia's allies in the Five Power Defense Arrangement (Britain, Australia, New Zealand, Singapore) and for Vietnam's ally, the Soviet Union.
> The dispute between Communist China, Taiwan, the Philippines and

Vietnam over the Spratly group of islands has its implications for a large number of nations, including the superpowers, given that the U.S.S.R. has a treaty with and is establishing bases in Vietnam and that the United States has a treaty with and well developed bases in the Philippines.[15]

The multinational oil companies and consortia are also likely to get involved in these conflicts. "Nations with conflicting EEZ claims have used survey area concessions to such companies as a means of furthering their claims. The oil companies, keen to better their competitors and ingratiate themselves with governments, have often been willing pawns in these disputes."[16]

The more significant cause of conflict in the utilization of ocean resources could be the refusal of the United States and a few other Western maritime powers to join the Law of the Sea Treaty. In a situation where the United States is not part of the treaty system, John Norton Moore points out, "We [the United States] might feel compelled to take measures to protect our interests in ocean resources in a fashion that would possibly engender more intense conflicts between the United States and others."[17]

Another possible form of conflict could be offshore maritime terrorism.[18] Against the background of increasing terrorist activities worldwide, offshore oil platforms could be attractive targets. The greater the economic value of the platform and the larger the dependence of a state on a particular set of platforms, the higher the incentive to terrorists and other hostile groups to strike. However, Western literature neglects to mention that these offshore installations could also be attractive targets to covert-action agencies of the big powers.

The rising economic importance of the ocean space and its large-scale enclosure by coastal states need not necessarily lead to hostile relations between big maritime powers and coastal Third World states. It could also lead to dominance-dependence relationship with the complete cooperation of the ruling elites in the Third World. The new legal regime on the oceans cannot transcend the power structure that gave rise to it. Even though the coastal developing states have acquired economic sovereignty over large tracts of coastal waters, they lack the scientific, technological, and industrial means of utilizing the ocean resources. Most of them also lack the capacity to defend and protect these resources. The temptations to "rent out" the EEZs could be irresistible to the coastal developing states. It would be hardly surprising if, ultimately, coastal states with Exclusive Economic Zones exploited the resources not just in their own EEZs, but also those in the EEZs of the developing coastal states. It would be supremely ironic if the movement for the enclosure of oceans ended up advantageously for those states that have been opposing it. It appears possible that the maritime powers and their large corporations could soon make appropriate bilateral arrangements with coastal developing states, paying them rent or royalties in return for the use of EEZs. As in the case of land resources in weaker countries, so in the case of ocean resources: The corporations from the advanced countries in possession of technological know-how and skills are likely to acquire the legal possession of these resources for a pittance.

Seapower, Resources, and Strategy in the Indian Ocean

Seapower is an old and enduring concept, despite all the semantic confusion surrounding it. The concepts of seapower and sea control have acquired a new urgency in the last decade as the importance of ocean resources and ocean politics began to dawn upon the world. The new urgency was strongly felt in Western strategic thinking, thanks to the emergence of the blue-water capability of the Soviet Union and the increasing economic confrontation between the North and the South. The specters of a "Soviet naval threat" and the resource denial by the Third World now threaten to haunt Western strategic thinkers for quite some time to come.

In this context, all encompassing definitions of seapower have become common: "a nation's seapower is determined not only by the weapons and armed forces with which it can affect events at sea but also by its merchant marine, its fishing and oceanographic fleets, and its maritime outlook and tradition."[19] Admiral Sergey Gorshkov is one of the more recent exponents of this all-embracing concept of seapower:

> In the definition of the seapower of the state we include as the main components possibilities for the state to study (explore) the ocean and harness its wealth, the status of the merchant and fishing fleets and their ability to meet the needs of the state and also the presence of a navy matching the interests of this state, since antagonistic social systems exist in the world.[20]

Along with the new awareness of the importance of seapower, there has been a great revival of reverence for Admiral Alfred Thayer Mahan, at least in the United States. Admiral Mahan's teachings—stressing the importance of seapower to great nationhood—evoke grandiose feelings in a militarily resurgent United States. It is not as if the current U.S. naval strategic thinking is looking back to Mahan for any specific principles or guides to current action. As Geoffrey Kemp notes:

> The most important legacy of Alfred Mahan is not to be found in his technical writings or even in his classical work *The Influence of Seapower Upon History*. His great relevance today is his political vision, his sense of destiny, and his efforts to persuade his own government that its future greatness lay in further exploration of its maritime assets. His message for today would be that unless the United States has greater sense of purpose and seeks practical ways to fulfill it, it will surely decline as a world power.
>
> What does this mean for the United States?
>
> First, the United States has abundant maritime assets that it can and should exploit, ranging from further development and control of its own immensely rich offshore maritime technology for both military and nonmilitary purposes. Second, in a sense most applicable to Mahan's basic message, the United States must make greater effort to extend and exploit its lead in air and space technology, for it is in this medium—especially in outer space—that important determinants of international power will be decided in the twentieth century. In fact, it would be appropriate to modify

the catchwords of earlier geopolitical strategists, such as Sir Halford Mackinder and Giulio Douhet, and propose the dictum that in future the
country that controls outer space will control the maritime environment,
and the country that controls the maritime environment will control the
world. The third message derives from the second: The United States must
discover the political will necessary for new progress to be made.[21]

The fascination with Mahan is so great that Admiral Gorshkov is grudg-
ingly complimented by Elmo Zumwalt as the "20th century Mahan."[22]

The rationale for the strengthening of American seapower, as put forward by its modern proponents, consists of two factors. One is the Soviet
threat to American naval supremacy, unchallenged since the 1940s. Hedley
Bull refers to the "righteous indignation" in the United States that the existing distribution of power should be disturbed. The American argument
is that the United States stands at the center of an alliance system that
depends vitally on sea lines of communication, while also being heavily dependent on trade herself. The Soviet Union, as a self-sufficient economy, is
not in this position. Bull argues that this thesis is quite correct, but only on
the assumption that the existing power structure should not be disturbed.[23]

The second factor is the Third World control over vital natural resources—such as oil and minerals—and the debilitating consequences on
Western security of the denial of the resources by the developing countries.
Thus, the strategic need for ensuring the security of these natural resources.[24]
The struggle of Third World nations for a new international economic order
and the fight for better control over the appropriate price for their natural
resources was likened in the West to the nineteenth-century trade union
movement in the West and required the urgent development of doctrine, plans,
weapons, and force structures in anticipation of possible uses of military force
in some novel crisis situations.[25] Force projection through seapower naturally
would have to play a major role in this.

This argument of the "dangerous dependence" on Third World resources
was put at its poignant best by an American admiral:

> We were once a nation which produced more raw materials than we
> consumed. Because this is no longer true, we must look elsewhere for raw
> materials, often vital and strategic raw materials, to supply our defense
> and economic needs. In time of war, strategic raw materials will be critical
> to the sustenance of our war-fighting capability. . . . In peacetime, the
> uninterrupted flow of raw materials is required to support *our way of life*.
> This tender relationship has been most recently and dramatically observed
> when *Americans altered their life styles one way or another* as the flow of
> oil to our nation was affected by political or economic variables. For some
> Americans, adjustments to the turns of the international oil spigot meant
> little more than frustrating times in long gas lines. Others changed their
> driving habits. Some Americans lived, and a few died, in cold unheated
> rooms in homes during winters when heating oil was unavailable or un-
> affordable.
> The shortage of fossil fuel has underscored our national dependence
> on the sea. We rely on raw materials which are dispersed globally and

which must reach us by way of the sea. The world ocean has no rival in the effective transportation of bulk materials, and it is across salt water that we draw our vital national lifelines.[26] (emphasis added)

Thus, seapower and its projection across the globe are vital for the very survival of the American "island state" and the "American way of life"! The Rapid Deployment Force, the 600-ship navy, and the U.S. Central Command are the products of the new strategy of seapower, based on the above apocalyptic perceptions, which appear deep-rooted in the United States.

The new U.S. seapower doctrine, however, would have to operate under the maritime environment—which includes the need to protect its own large "offshore estate,"[27] the opportunities of new economic activities in the ocean space, the constraints of the Law of the Sea and the growth of regional naval powers. Given the all-embracing nature of the new concept of seapower, the creation of a new American national ocean policy in relation to its naval strategy becomes imperative. A vision of the U.S. ocean policy–naval strategy matrix is given in Table 4.2.

How are the current U.S. plans to strengthen its seapower, and the new U.S.-Soviet naval rivalry, viewed in the Third World? In the words of an Indian observer:

As in the colonial past, at stake are the economic and commercial interests of the advanced industrial nations. . . . For the West, the real target of the rivalry is the resources of the Third World, while for the East the objective is to expand its sphere of influence to the developing parts of the world and deny it to the extent possible to the West.[28]

The proposed new contingencies for the use of force against the Third World states are not entirely novel to the observers in the Third World. Their own colonization has been achieved through the use of seapower, and even after their independence they have lived with "gunboat diplomacy." Out of the 215 instances of an American demonstration of force, at least 71 percent involved the use of naval power, mostly against the developing countries.[29]

We must now examine how the new U.S. seapower doctrines and the developing-country responses relate to the specific situation in the Indian Ocean region. The bone of contention between the United States and the littoral countries like India is the projection of American seapower into the Indian Ocean. The United States states that the projection of its seapower into the area is to defend its allies and its own vital interests in the region. This perception of vital interests can be briefly summarized as follows.

The volume of maritime traffic in the Indian Ocean is the third largest in the world.[30] The predominant portion of the Indian Ocean littoral trade is with the United States and its allies: In the mid-1970s, it totaled 33 percent with West Europe; Japan, 19 percent; and the United States, 13 percent. The Eastern bloc share was only 5 percent. There are well-developed sea lanes in the region, through which annually pass some 30,000 ships, about 1500 of which are tankers. Most of these sea lanes traverse such choke points as the Suez Canal, the Bab-el-Mandeb Strait, the Hormuz Strait, the Mozambique

Channel, the Eight Degree Channel above the Maldives, and the Malacca Strait, Selat Sunda, and Selat Lambok. Oil is, of course, the most important material exported from the region; the volume of oil exported constitutes one-third of the world's supply. In addition, there are other, non-fuel minerals whose production is concentrated in the Indian Ocean region. The unhindered supply of these minerals is crucial for the survival of the civil and defense industries of the West.

It is thus postulated that the security of the supply of oil and other strategic materials is the basic rationale for the projection of U.S. seapower to the Indian Ocean. The threats to this resource security are visualized on two levels: The threat to the sea lines of communications is either from the Soviet Union or from the regional powers.

The Soviet interdiction of the Western sea lines of communication has been the most cited threat in U.S. and Western security literature. However, some Western strategists have themselves discounted this threat as exaggerated. For example, Ken Booth has written:

> The Soviet threat to these areas, the Cape of Good Hope route, for example, is often asserted without any reference to the resupply problems which Soviet units would face in any sustained campaign against Western shipping in that distant area, operating in a hostile environment, remote from their bases, and with inadequate afloat support.[31]

It is now argued, in an elegant transformation, that the Soviet threat is not so much to the sea lanes but to the source itself. One U.S. Admiral says: "Our greatest vulnerability is Soviet disruption at the source of our supply of critical raw materials; not the sea lanes, but the source. Soviet air strikes, mining operations, or ground attacks aimed at those oil terminals would constitute a threat to the flow of oil in the event of major hostilities."[32] This logical jugglery is carried one step further by Geoffrey Kemp:

> In fact, the least vulnerable stage of the oil flow from the Gulf is currently the transoceanic stage. This could become more vulnerable if the balance of power at sea changed, but . . . this would require major geopolitical shifts and changes in the landmass of Asia and Africa that would result in the construction of maritime bases along the littoral.
>
> No sensible Western maritime strategy can be envisaged that does not also take into account the *environment on the landmass* from which most of the resources come. In the Persian Gulf, in the absence of overall strategy for using military power in the Gulf, a forward-based U.S. maritime posture will not be used to cover some of the most likely military contingencies in the region and certainly not the most serious ones—namely a Soviet invasion of the Gulf.[33] (emphasis added)

This shift in the focus of U.S. attention from the sea lines of communication to the "environment of the landmass" itself is seen as a most irksome development by India. "It is no secret that the U.S. policy is directed as much towards domestic upheavals in the Third World nations [of the Indian Ocean region] as towards Soviet intervention, the former being more probable than the latter."[34] The Indian fear is that the U.S. power would not be confined to the sea, but would inevitably encroach onto the landmass, and not just against a Soviet threat.

Oil, the Gulf, and U.S. Security

Ever since the oil crisis of October 1973, American strategic thinking has been obsessed with the issues of energy security, oil dependence on the Gulf, and the protection and securing of these resources in the Gulf. This concern with Gulf oil has been, and continues to be, the predominant motor of U.S. Indian Ocean policy. The oil crisis itself was over-dramatized by the American media, and the reaction was near hysterical. The Western reaction went further than this, with undertones of racist attacks against Arab oil exporters and threats of military action by U.S. politicians. In fact, the so-called crisis of 1973 was nothing but a culmination of the actions of the oil exporters, begun in 1960, to get a better deal for their product and arrest the decline in real terms of oil prices. What they did in October 1973 was to take control over their oil resources and ensure themselves the power to formulate and implement pricing and production policies, without submitting to the power of the Western oil companies (see Table 4.3).

Because Arab oil export policies were seen as an aspect of Arab-Israeli politics and the imposition of an oil embargo on the United States and the Netherlands spurred concern about the political use of economic power by Arab oil producers, fears of a possible oil strangulation appear to have been highly exaggerated. Recent Western studies of the Saudi behavior in OPEC reach some interesting conclusions:

> . . . if the Saudis were to behave as purely economic beings, acting solely to maximize profit, how would their behaviour differ from what it has been? The answer . . . is: very little, if at all. Throughout, their decisions have been made on the basis of economic self-interest, not political issues. Saudi oil pricing and production policies can be explained without reference to the Arab-Israeli conflict, arms sales or any other political or diplomatic issue. Of course, Saudi policy is often expressed politically, since the Saudis want to earn political credit where possible. But where economics and politics conflict, it is clear that the former has been decisive.[35]

The perceptions of oil power were reinforced by the second oil crisis, in 1979. But today's emerging economic issue is the current crisis for Gulf oil producers. The oil glut is a crisis for the oil producers because there is a drop in demand, a drop in production, and consequently a drop in export revenues. While the new oil crisis has hit all the oil producers, the Arab members of OPEC have suffered a much greater cutback in their production and revenues, absolutely and relatively, than the non-Arab members.[36] The crisis in the oil market was dramatized in the winter of 1985–86, when oil prices collapsed from their peak of over $40 a barrel in 1980–81 to less than $12.[37]

Before we examine the implications of the new crisis, it is necessary to understand its causes. First is the fall in the world energy consumption, which declined from 6947 million tonnes oil equivalent (mtoe) in 1979 to 6870 mtoe in 1982. In 1985 and 1986, consumption picked up, but primary energy consumption in the OECD countries remains well below the level of 1979, indicating that energy consumption is rising essentially in the communist and developing worlds. As stated, worldwide oil consumption declined sharply between 1979 and 1982, and it continues to remain below the 1979 level (see Table 4.4). World oil production, which peaked in 1979, also remained below that level in 1986[38] (see Table 4.5).

This decline in energy and oil consumption and production has been explained by some as a result of a worldwide recession that began in the late 1970s. But it appears that the decline is due to more basic, long-term developments, such as weakening of the so-called historical link between economic growth and energy consumption in the industrially advanced countries of the West. In the United States, over the last decade, the amount of energy used to produce a given amount of goods and services has fallen by at least 20 percent, and this trend is expected to continue[39] (see also Figure 4.1). In the main, this has been due to increased energy conservation measures and a greater efficiency in the use of energy. Even if the worldwide economic activity picks up, the energy efficiency trend would not be reversed. Furthermore, most future growth is likely to be in such high-tech industries as microelectronics, computers, and communications, which are not energy intensive.

The decline of oil imports has also been the result of the increased use of non-oil energy sources, stimulated by the high price of oil. Coal has made an impressive comeback, the share of nuclear energy has steadily advanced, and the search for alternative sources, such as solar energy, has intensified.

Significantly, though worldwide oil production has declined, there has been a great rise in oil production outside OPEC, and the OPEC share of worldwide oil production shrank to a significant extent (see Table 4.5). Total non-OPEC oil production rose by 35 percent from 1973 to 1983.[40] And OPEC's share of world production dipped from 53 percent in 1973 to 33 percent in 1982, and dropped to about 28 percent in 1985. This rise of non-OPEC oil production was spurred by the high price of oil, which led to (1) making the development of high-cost, hitherto uneconomic, reserves economic; (2) encouraging the exploration of many new areas for new sources of oil; and (3) the development of new, exotic techniques of oil production. The rise of non-OPEC oil production also meant that an increasing number of producers were competing for a shrinking market.

The cutbacks in oil imports by the major oil-importing countries have been striking. The United States, whose oil imports rose from 6.3 millions of barrels per day (mb/d) in 1973 to 8.7 mb/d in 1977, began to reduce its imports and in 1983 imported only 4.9 mb/d. The imports of Western Europe fell steadily from 15.4 mb/d in 1973 to 8.7 mb/d in 1983. And Japan managed to cut its imports from 5.5 mb/d in 1973 to 4.1 mb/d in 1983.[41]

All these factors have led to a decline in the importance of Gulf oil and

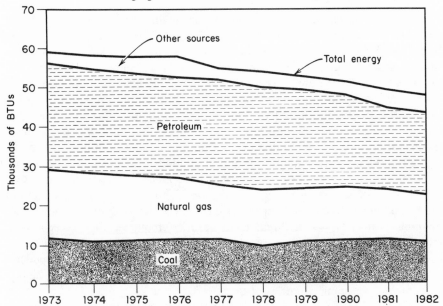

FIGURE 4.1. U.S. Energy Consumption Per Dollar of Real GNP, 1973–1982

to the current crisis (for the producers). As Table 4.6 indicates, the flow of oil from the Persian Gulf/Middle East to the oil-importing nations of the "Free World" has steadily declined. By 1983, the dependence on Middle East oil had been reduced to 11.6 percent for the United States, 39.4 percent for Western Europe, and 65.8 percent for Japan. Reports in 1987 indicate there has been a further reduction in that dependence: 5 percent for the United States, 26 percent for Western Europe, and 50 percent for Japan.[42]

Thus, fundamental changes in the character of world energy consumption and structural changes in the world oil industry had major consequences. First, the argument that the political power of OPEC Gulf states is being used to deny oil to the Western powers can no longer be sustained. OPEC's declining exports and falling revenues do not allow such a freedom of action to oil producers. The capacity of OPEC to impose selective embargoes to derive political advantage appears far-fetched.[43] In fact,

> the use of economic power by OPEC as a political weapon is largely an imaginary threat, and even the power of OPEC on economic issues is slowly but surely eroding as a result of forces set in motion by its own actions. On both grounds it appears that the influence of oil politics in the 1980s, and beyond, will recede and leave the oil politics of 1970s as a passing and somewhat arcane chapter in international politics. Should the present trends continue, by the end of the decade 'oil power' may be re-reduced to a rather marginal aspect of the international system, despite the continued dependence of the industrialized countries on imported energy.[44]

In such a situation, the argument by the United States of the need "to guarantee access to oil in Southwest Asia," and to "defend Gulf oil," cannot be accepted without reservation. Yet the U.S. strategic thinking continues to revolve around the vital importance of Gulf oil—or, rather, the reserves of oil. The argument is now based on the fact that the Gulf contains nearly 50 percent of the world's proven oil reserves, and that its reserves-to-production ratio is still the highest in the world. "It therefore remains a key element of U.S. foreign policy to preserve Western access to these reserves, and in particular the reserves of the Arabian peninsula. . . . Saudi stability is of prime concern to U.S. policymakers."[45] While these kinds of justifications based on oil security can be unending, they cannot hold much water, given the above examination of structural changes in the world oil market. The tendency in the United States to cite any dependence of its economy—however small and marginal it may be—as a threat to its security, requiring the projection of military power, cannot be acceptable to the rest of the world, or at least to India. The use or threat of use of force in an economically interdependent world—projected in a one-sided way—is inimical to the interests of highly vulnerable developing countries of the world.

Two other reasons—cited in relation to oil dependence—may lead us to a greater appreciation of the possible real motivations behind the U.S. Indian Ocean policy. One is the threat of local conflict among the countries of the region or from internal upheavals in the countries leading to a cutoff in the supply of oil. The experience of the unending Iran-Iraq war, however, shows that there has been no dramatic impact of the war on the oil supplies from the region. According to oil industry analysts, even the tensions that were building up in the Gulf during mid-1987 following the *Stark* incident, the U.S. decision to protect reflagged Kuwaiti tankers, and the Western naval buildup might not lead to a crisis of oil supplies.[46] To the extent that a limited threat to oil security has existed, it has arisen from the supply of a new generation of arms during the conflict by some Western powers. The fears related to internal conflicts are also untenable. Even if there is a dramatic and radical change in the nature of the power elites of the local states, given the dependence of these states on a single commodity for economic survival, economic necessity would make an oil cutoff unlikely. These arguments cannot mask the real nature of the projection of force into the Indian Ocean—and that is to assure local allies that the security threats to them from within and without would be countered, a capacity much vaunted in the Iran crisis. Another aim of the power projection is to prevent any radical regime change in the region and to ensure a continuous capability to influence political and economic developments in the region.

The second reason cited by U.S. strategists is the Soviet threat to the Gulf oil supplies. At one time in the early 1980s, the United States was arguing two issues simultaneously: on the one hand that the Soviet Union was seeking to export energy to Western Europe in order to lure the U.S. allies into energy dependence on the Kremlin and, on the other, that the Soviet Union was exhausting its domestic energy supplies and might prepare to invade the

Gulf to acquire the oil resources there. It is obvious that both sets of arguments cannot be true at the same time. The continual refrain about the ever-growing Soviet threat to the Gulf appears to be an obsession of some groups of conservative U.S. ideologues. This refrain does not evoke much credibility even within the United States, if one goes along with the evidence presented by Daniel Pipes.[47] Himself a virulent anti-Soviet ideologue, Pipes argues that there has been an enduring "non-ideological" basis in U.S. policy in the Middle East, and that the Soviets recognize this. He suggests that, in contrast to all other regions, "the Middle East appears to offer a unique opportunity for U.S.-Soviet cooperation."[48]

While Professor Pipes is correct in envisaging possibilities for superpower cooperation in the Middle East, he misses the overall thrust of the U.S. strategic policy of which Southwest Asian policy is an integral part. The U.S. force projection into the Indian Ocean region is part of the evolving military strategy directed against the Soviet Union, in the context of the new cold war. The strategy is based on the perceived need of the Reagan Administration to correct the earlier assumption that deterrence in Europe was sufficient to keep the Russians at bay in the rest of the world too. The doctrine now appears to be that deterrence must be extended to all the regions around the Soviet Union. The aims of the new strategy, as spelled out by Caspar Weinberger, are:

> Deterring Soviet aggression is our biggest challenge . . . the Soviet and their allies have a significant advantage of proximity to several critical theaters. In addition they are enhancing the ability to transport their own surrogate forces to areas far from both the Soviet Union and the United States.
>
> As a result of these Soviet gains, the demands on our projection are greater today than ever before. We must be prepared to dispatch forces promptly to any of a number of regions around the world possibly simultaneously.[49]

This new strategy has been described as a shift from the U.S. military strategy of the 1970s of "one and a half wars" to one of "three and a half wars." In sum, the new strategy implies that

> the Soviets are to be simultaneously and forcefully engaged on several fronts on or along the Eurasian landmass. The defense of Europe is, of course, important, but in a worldwide war with the Soviet Union, Europe will be only one of several theaters of operations and not necessarily a decisive one. Prospects for a conclusive counteroffensive in Europe are less promising than in other regions of the world where the military balance is more favourable to the United States.[50]

It is this perceived imperative of a new military strategy that propels U.S. forces toward the Indian Ocean, and the issues of energy and economic security in relation to Gulf oil are only peripheral and serve propaganda purposes. The capacity to use this force against regional powers of course is a bonus.

The real problems of oil and economic security are for the littoral countries. Their dreams of unlimited economic prosperity and political power began to vanish in the early 1980s along with declining oil exports, and revenues from them (see Tables 4.7 and 4.8). By the mid-1980s, it was evident that a serious fiscal crunch was at hand. Overambitious budgets had to be slashed, projects canceled, and austerity measures introduced. The large foreign exchange reserves held by the industrialized countries—$224 billion in 1984—give these countries powerful economic leverage over Middle East and Gulf oil producers who had reserves of only $58 billion in that year.[51] Internally, the strategy of petroleum-led development—using oil revenues as the engine of growth and diversification—remains only on paper. The advance being made in downstream processing could be of limited value given the worldwide excess capacity in oil refining. For the oil-exporting countries, investment and development priorities did not result in the building of national and regional productive capabilities—even in those sectors requiring simpler technologies. The lack of effective institutions and the inadequate availability of skilled manpower coupled with overambitious budgets resulted in excessively costly and wasteful plans and programs. How the oil-exporting countries adapt to the new situation remains to be seen, but their past record does not offer much hope.

The declining economic fortunes of Gulf oil producers are likely to have an impact on the advanced countries of the West as well as on the littoral countries of the region. For the Western countries, the end of the boom in the oil-producing countries implied a shrinking market for Western exports there. In 1982, exports to the Middle East and North Africa from the six major OECD suppliers totaled $85.5 billion; in 1984, the figure dropped to $67 billion.[52] The oil-importing developing countries paid a high price for skyrocketing oil bills. But some of them gained from the economic boom in the Gulf. This was mainly through the export of labor, and some technologically advanced countries like India received construction and other contracts. Within the Arab world, some of the non-oil-exporting countries emerged as labor exporters—notably Egypt, Sudan, Syria, South Yemen, North Yemen, and Jordan. Inter-Arab remittances from labor exports were said to be more than $6 billion in 1980.[53] The real transfers will be higher than what cash figures indicate, because of transfers in kind. Migration from Asia—mainly from South Asia, but later from the Philippines and South Korea—has been a growing segment of labor composition in the Gulf region. By 1980, Asia accounted for approximately one-third of the foreign labor force in the region. The downturn in economic activity in the Gulf is bound to lead to a shrinking of the remittances to the oil-poor countries of Asia, which had benefited considerably from labor exports. Besides the loss of revenue, the absorption of returning migrants could be a major problem.[54]

The Mythology of Strategic Minerals

In 1979, *Business Week* sounded the following alarm:

Now the Squeeze on Metals

America's industrial might—already threatened by the deepening energy mess—is in for another resource crunch. . . . All signs point to longer-range problems in U.S. mineral supply that will not be solved by cyclic swings in the economy. If not solved, those problems could make U.S. business less competitive, lower America's standard of living, and endanger the national security.

Most ominous is the growing U.S. dependence on foreign supplies. . . . By the mid-1980s, experts warn, the U.S. will be dangerously dependent on foreign sources for a significant portion of its total metals requirements.

All this amounts to a strategic threat every bit as damaging as the energy squeeze.[55]

Thus began a new campaign in the United States warning of a possible "resource war," of a Soviet threat to U.S. mineral supplies and a possible Third World denial of these vital resources. While the idea of a spectacular resource war was new to the U.S. media, it was not so to U.S. strategic thinking. Western writing on the Indian Ocean is littered with references to the rich mineral resources in the Indian Ocean and Western and U.S. dependence on these minerals. Access to these non-fuel raw materials has been a major underpinning (along with access to oil) of the articulation of U.S. strategy in the Indian Ocean. The security of the supply of these raw materials has always been considered a major objective of the U.S. force projection into the region. These concerns, of course, received a boost with the success of the Marxist regimes in Angola and Mozambique and the Soviet support to these regimes.

A recent analysis suggests that "strategic minerals should now be viewed as a central factor in possible scenarios of conflict in some form, especially in the Middle East and Southern Africa. They could also play a part in causing or contributing to conflicts in a number of other areas, for example, North Africa and Southwest Asia."[56] And these potential conflicts could be between superpowers, between a superpower and a regional state, between regional states that may or may not be supported by superpowers, or even between regions or provinces within a state.

Surprisingly, such strategic perceptions are widely shared by Indians writing about the Indian Ocean. For example, one writer points out, "The countries around the Indian Ocean possess raw materials which are vital for the growth and development of the major manufacturing industries of the big powers."[57] Another says, "The interrelationship between the U.S. military strategy and America's dependence for resources on other countries has to be taken note of since that gives a clue to the real nature of U.S. objectives in the Indian Ocean region and elsewhere in the Third World."[58]

The intervention in 1977 and 1978 by Western and pro-Western powers (the United States, France, Belgium, Morocco, Senegal, and Saudi Arabia) in the Shabah Province of Zaire against the Congolese National Liberation Front might be seen as an operation intended to secure access to mineral resources, thus bearing out the shared perceptions of Western and Indian theorists. While the partial validity of this perception is to be accepted, the strategic importance of mineral resources has been exaggerated. Before we explain this, we must examine some of the basic trends in the mineral industry.

First is the declining importance of metals, at least the base metals, for the industrially advanced countries due to some basic structural changes in their economies. In the advanced Western industrial societies there has so far existed a one-to-one relationship between growth in real GDP, the rise in industrial production, and the consumption of metals. In the past decade or so, secular trends have been widely observed that indicate a severing of these one-to-one relationships. From 1950 to the early 1970s, the OECD countries experienced unprecedented growth rates in GDP. In this period, industrial production grew at higher rates than the GDP. Since the early 1970s, however, the trend has been reversed. The leading role of industry in economic growth has been taken over by the services sector, and the OECD economies have been said to enter "the post-industrial era."

The industry sector, besides experiencing a reduced significance, has undergone an important structural change. Until the mid-1960s, demand for base metals and materials developed more or less parallel with overall industrial expansion. Since then, the growth of the consumption of commodities like copper and steel has slowed down. In fact since 1973 the demand for these two products has been completely stagnant. As a noted mineral economist writes:

> With increasing sophistication and extended value added in industry, the requirements for base materials per unit of final output have gradually contracted. Between 1964 and 1982, the industrial output in the OECD area increased by 88%—consumption of copper and steel expanded, by no more than 40% and 13%, respectively, over the same years. In 1982, steel consumption in the area was 310 million tons. If demand had grown in line with total industrial output since 1964, then the use of steel would have reached 525 million tons, 215 million tons above the actual figure.[59]

He concludes that it is this structural change in mineral consumption, and not the low growth rates of GDP and industrial output, that is responsible for the minerals crisis in the West.

That the crisis in the minerals industry is deeply rooted is confirmed by the fact that the recent partial recovery in the U.S. economy has bypassed the metal industries. In these industries, inventories have continued to pile up, demand is slack, sharp production cutbacks have taken place, and the competition is intense from foreign suppliers.[60] Take the case of the ferroalloy industry in the United States. While the total capacity of this industry in the United States has remained relatively constant since 1979, capacity utilization for the bulk ferroalloy industry dropped from 82 percent in 1979 to 35 percent for the first eight months of 1983, according to the U.S. Bureau of Mines.[61] In fact, ferroalloy capacity in the United States had fallen below 20 percent in 1982. The major portion of the decline in domestic capacity is due to low-priced imports. Import penetration of the domestic bulk ferro-alloy market increased from 46 percent in 1979 to 60 percent during the first half of 1983. Imports have been increasing because they are cheaper than the domestic product.[62]

The U.S. copper industry's plight is worse, with U.S. domestic production sharply cut due to a flooding of the U.S. market with imported copper.[63] As a result, the U.S. copper industry reduced its production by about a quarter in 1982, and again by one-tenth in 1983. About 40 percent of U.S. copper mining capacity is out of action and 180,000 miners are said to be out of work.[64] But the massive cuts in North American copper production were offset by increases in production elsewhere, mostly in developing countries, and the prices continued to drop. As copper prices dropped, Third World producers increased their output to make up for lost revenues and maintain their overall export revenues (which are heavily dependent on copper exports). The Third World copper producers also resorted to devaluing their currencies to increase the competitiveness of their exports. This pushed down the price of copper well below the break-even point for the best U.S. mines.[65]

The situation in American aluminum and lead industries was only a little better. And the production rates of iron and steel continued to be low. Capacity utilization in the iron and steel sector averaged about 48 percent in 1983. In overall terms, despite the strong gains for the U.S. economy in 1983, capacity utilization in the metal/materials sector was 63.8 percent compared to 77 percent for total manufacturing.[66] The U.S. mining interests' anger was directed against foreign suppliers, considered the chief villains responsible for their plight. These interests were outraged at the U.S. involvement in foreign mineral loans by multinational lending institutions such as the IMF. Some recent loans include $327 million to Chile from the IMF; $268 million from the Inter-American Development Bank to Condelco, a Chilean copper company; and $75 million to a Zambian copper company from the IBRD. The American domestic copper mining companies saw this as a strangulation of domestic producers at the expense of foreign competitors and tried to block these loans through congressional action.[67] But their pleas for protection from foreign supplies has not cut much ice with the Reagan Administration.

But cheap foreign supplies are only part of the problem. A number of other factors are also responsible for the state of the U.S. minerals industry. The projections of growth rates in metal consumption made in the 1960s and 1970s turned out to be too high, and this resulted in many new projects coming on-line just when the market needed them least. Projects were begun despite the depressed prices, contributing further to the situation of oversupply. Second, the general recession in the industry encouraged downstream metal-consuming manufacturers to look closely at ways of cutting costs through higher recycling rates and by reducing the quantities of metal used per unit through improvements of technology and higher efficiency. Third, metals have increasingly come into conflict with each other; the battle between copper and aluminum in the electrical cable business was perhaps the most dramatic example. There are a host of other conflicts in which one metal's gain has been another's loss.[68]

Fourth, and most important in the long term, there has been tremendous competition to metals from other, new materials, such as plastics, composites, optical fibers, and ceramics, which have continued to invade the traditional metal-consuming market. For example, the copper industry faces a major competition from optic fibers. In the advanced countries, the electrical equipment sector currently accounts for about 50 percent of copper consumption. According to one estimate, over the next 10 years the industry will lose as much as five million tons of copper sales to optic fibers and, in addition, will be faced with some one million tons of additional surplus from scrapped copper cables.[69] Aluminum is facing competition from plastics in such low-tech industries as packaging and from composites in high tech industries such as aerospace.[70] The U.S. aerospace industry used $1.1 billion worth of composite parts in 1983. The costs of composites are still very high, and the composite content of Boeing Aircraft's commercial planes in 1984 was less than one percent. Still, as prices moderate, aerospace industry sources forecast a spurt to 60 percent by 1990.[71] Lead is another metal whose traditional markets are under threat; the current drive in the West to introduce unleaded gasoline would make a serious dent in the consumption of lead.[72] Ceramics—silicon nitrides and carbides—have shown great promise for replacing superalloys based on cobalt and nickel, so critical for various applications, particularly in aerospace. Ceramics permit higher operating temperatures than metals and thus higher efficiencies. Though ceramic use is still plagued by some problems such as brittleness, their application will continue to rise.[73] According to a U.S. ceramics expert, the worldwide ceramics industry has already touched the $50 billion per-year mark. Ceramics are also finding increasing application in cutting machine tools, rotors, turbines, valves, pistons, among other areas. And there is a fear that Japan is likely to overtake the United States in ceramics research. Japanese funding of ceramics R & D has increased 55 percent between 1981 and 1983, a record unmatched by the United States.[74]

The revolution in the science and technology of new materials has only just begun to unfold. As composites, ceramics, polymers, and other materials based on biotechnology—such as biomaterials and renewable materials—begin to develop, the very nature of the "material" basis of advanced industrial societies is likely to undergo a profound transformation. Traditional metals and materials are bound to decline in their importance, yielding way to new materials.

Given this evolving nature of the world minerals industry, what is the validity of the concern over a "resource war," a war to be created by the Soviets, their surrogates, and other Third World countries to strangulate the West by withholding their minerals? Since 1979, the "atmospherics" in the United States surrounding the scare about vulnerability to imported raw minerals appears to have been inspired more by domestic economic concerns than by particular international developments. The conservative U.S. mining industry interests, unable to adjust to the structural changes in mineral consumption, have sought to raise this bogey of dependence to protect their own markets and profits. The fact of the matter was that there have been no shortages, but an oversupply of materials, and that the U.S. industry could not compete with cheap imports from abroad. The bogey of a Soviet-inspired resource war was only too convenient. However, U.S. companies with interests in worldwide mining, such as AMAX, take a different view. A top executive of this company, in testimony before the Senate Committee on Energy and Natural Resources in June 1983, stated that the OPEC-inspired mentality over dependence on foreign sources of supply for critical material has "engendered a xenophobic shortage mentality in which dependence has come to be equated with vulnerability."[75] Evaluating the Reagan Administration's policy on strategic minerals, a U.S. GAO study is reported to have said that the administration focused almost exclusively on "national security" aspects of the materials and minerals issues, while ignoring economic factors and industrial production and paying insufficient attention to R & D in high-technology materials.[76] A close reading of the U.S. debate reveals the role played by James Watt and his enthusiasts at the Department of Interior in pushing the interests of domestic miners on the basis of a non-existent resource war.

Contrary to the widespread belief in the West that it is becoming increasingly dependent on the developing countries for essential mineral commodities, the share of the world output from the developing countries has not appreciably increased for most of the so-called strategic metals (see Table 4.9). One exception is nickel, where the rise of Cuba, Indonesia, and the Philippines as producers and the expansion of output in New Caledonia, a French-occupied territory, have increased the developing countries' output. With this exception, basic shifts have occurred in the location of world mining activity over the last three decades. The noted minerals economist John Tilton[77] delineates some of these for the four strategic metals—cobalt, copper, manganese and nickel. (1) The developed countries have maintained, and in some cases expanded, their share of the world mine output of the four metals, not because the United States and other major industrialized countries have expanded their domestic production, but rather because of increased production from Australia, Canada, and South Africa. (2) Over the last few decades, the number of important metal-producing countries has increased. Australia, Finland, and the Philippines have become significant producers of cobalt; Australia, Peru, the Philippines, Poland, and South Africa, of copper; Australia and Gabon, of manganese; and Australia, Cuba, Indonesia, the Philippines, and South Africa, of nickel. Tilton points out that the entry of new countries, coupled with the decline of the major traditional producers, has reduced the level of country concentration. This, along with a parallel decline in the concentration at the firm or enterprise level, has strengthened competition and made it even more difficult in the cobalt and nickel industries for the dominant producers to control market price and to earn excess profits over a prolonged period of time. *These trends complicate the formation and maintenance of producer cartels and hence reduce the likelihood of such collusive efforts among producers.* They also enhance the security of supply of the major consuming countries, for now an interruption in output from any particular producing countries can more easily be made up by other suppliers.[78]

This situation is not limited to the above four metals alone. In general, a secular trend is visible. The Western mining interests have shifted away from the developing countries, to such "safer" countries as Australia, Canada, and South Africa, thus leading to the decline of the role of mining in the Third World.[79] An examination of American and European mining investments abroad reveals this (see Table 4.10). It is clear that over the last few years an increasing share of U.S. direct foreign investment in mining and smelting has been made in the developed countries—particularly Australia, New Zealand, Canada, and South Africa. From 1968 to 1978, the share of U.S. direct investment in developing countries in this sector decreased from 42 to 32 percent. The decrease is even more dramatic when we consider the fact that in 1950, the Third World's share of U.S. foreign investment in the mining sector was 60 percent.[80] The decline in the share of investment in the developing countries was not limited to the United States. European investment and exploration in the minerals sector of the developing countries fell even more sharply, from 57 percent in 1961 to 13.5 percent during 1973–75.[81]

How credible, then, is the question of Western strategic mineral dependence on the Third World in general and on the Indian Ocean region in particular? Are the so-called challenges to resource security just a bunch of "mineral myths"?[82] In fact, there is no consensus even within the United States over what constitutes "strategic" minerals. The U.S. strategic stockpile comprises 60 materials. Various other U.S. sources—including private sector consultants—list between 18 and 31 strategic minerals. But, going along with Rae Weston,[83] we shall count 21 strategic (for the United States) minerals (see Table 4.11). Over the years, the word "strategic" has often been misused to exaggerate the importance of these minerals. "These minerals bear the title strategic not because they are critical in certain defense-related uses. The United States could lose a substantial portion of its strategic mineral imports without facing any threat to its national security."[84] The word "strategic" has also been used to imply some kind of Soviet threat, based on worst-case scenarios and the improbable effects of supply disruption.

Table 4.11 lists the U.S. dependence on strategic mineral imports. These figures, published every year by the U.S. Bureau of Mines, have been used by international relations theorists both in the United States and outside to suggest the degree of U.S. dependence on mineral resources from the Indian Ocean littoral. However, the use of these figures has been done uncritically and without any relation to the nature and character of the dependence. Before we examine these features, it is necessary to note that the concern over dependence on foreign minerals is not new. Throughout World War II and later, every single U.S. administration was concerned with resource dependence and strategic stockpiling, but the issue never became a matter of grave national security. And most of the U.S. assessments—from the government and others—were reassuring. Yet the fears have continually been raised to suit some political or economic objectives.

The Bureau of Mines figures are based on "apparent consumption," which ignores the impact of the recycling of metals—a trend on the rise. The consideration of recycling would lead to a finding of a declining dependence on imports. Second, the location of mining and the calculation of world reserves are based on current economic decisions and do not necessarily indicate the physical existence or the availability of the ore in various areas of of the world. Therefore, availability is much larger than the figures of current reserves indicate.

From Table 4.11 it is clear that the predominant U.S. dependence is on South Africa and Australia, the two white-settler states in the Indian Ocean region. The usual threat of supply disruption of strategic minerals is in relation to South Africa. Indeed, as we noted earlier, the relative importance of South Africa as a supplier of minerals has increased. This fact is often used in the West to propagate soft policies toward South Africa, to the detriment of human rights and democracy in southern Africa as a whole. But the presumption that a regime change in South Africa would lead to supply disruptions is untenable. The example of Angola, where despite a radical regime change U.S. oil interests were protected, is a significant pointer. With the great dependence of the South African economy on extractive industries and the sale of the minerals in external markets to finance domestic consumption, it is extremely unlikely that any regime in South Africa could force a supply disruption.

Assuming that such a disruption would indeed take place, either in South Africa or in its mineral-rich neighborhood, what would be the consequences for U.S. security? Let us examine the cases of two metals, cobalt and chromium.

Cobalt shows an extreme degree of concentration in two countries in terms of both production and reserves—Zaire and Zambia. The United States imports more than 90 percent of its cobalt requirements. Zaire supplies 52 percent of the world's cobalt and Zambia, an additional 11 percent; these two countries also possess more than 50 percent of world reserves. Cobalt is critical for the aerospace, electrical, and metal-cutting industries. In 1981, in the United States, 40 percent of cobalt consumption was for the production of super-alloys mainly for the aerospace industry (in aircraft gas turbine engines), 15 percent for magnetic materials, and another 10 percent for metal-cutting and mining tool bits; the remaining 35 percent went for other uses.[85] Despite this tremendous significance, a supply disruption of cobalt would not severely affect U.S. national security, because of recycling substitution and new sources, among other factors. There has been an increasing recycling of cobalt, and currently about 15 percent of U.S. cobalt comes from recycled sources. There is already a decreasing U.S. consumption of cobalt—from 18 million pounds in 1978 to 13.6 million pounds in 1981.[86] The U.S. National Material Advisory Board found that in the making of super-alloys, significant amounts of cobalt can be substituted with other non-strategic materials, such as ceramics or other metals.[87] Similarly, substitutes have been found for cobalt in magnetic materials.[88] If the price of cobalt goes up dramatically—say, through a disruption or cartel action—the now closed cobalt mines in Idaho would become economical. If the price of cobalt goes up to $20 per pound from the current range of $7–$12, the U.S. mines would become economical.[89]

Such is the case of chromium. The United States ceased all production of chromium in 1962 and today depends on foreign suppliers for about 90 percent of domestic consumption. South Africa alone supplies 44 percent of the chrome ore and 71 percent of ferrochrome imported by the United States, and Zimbabwe supplies an additional 7 percent.[90] In the United States, the metallurgical industry used 57 per cent of imported chromium, the chemical industry 25 percent, and the refractory industry 18 percent. According to the U.S. Bureau of Mines, scrap recycling of chromium has reached 9 percent of demand in 1980. The Bureau also pointed out that 73,000 tons of chromium in scrap was lost annually in the United States—and this could be recovered.[91] Substitution possibilities do exist for chromium. The U.S. National Bureau of Standards, in a technical report on the use of chromium in the steel industry, concluded that "although no other element is known to produce corrosion resistance comparable to that imported by chromium, the chromium content of the most widely used stainless steels, austenitic stainless steels, can be reduced without impairing corrosion resistance in many applications for which the traditional 18 percent is unnecessary." The NBS also found that "for many specific application of these materials, other materials without chromium are commercially available or appear feasible."[92] Thus, it appears that "concerns over chromium availability may be overblown when the full range of substitution, conservation and improved materials management is considered."[93]

The two examples of cobalt and chromium indicate quite clearly that Western civilization and the American way of life are not at risk because of their dependence on the supply of minerals from the Indian Ocean littoral. The mineral producers have been unable to form cartels and exercise any kind of political or economic power, as the oil producers have done. And such a prospect does not appear feasible. The preceding analysis shows that the importance of traditional strategic materials is on the decline. As the materials revolution unfolds, new materials based on emerging breakthroughs in science and technology will rise in importance. It would be the producers of traditional minerals—being unable to diversify their economies into modern sectors—who would be caught in the bind of shrinking Western markets for these materials. The growth of traditional materials can only take place in the socialist bloc and the newly industrializing countries of the Third World. But the entry of new producers like China are likely to further complicate the traditional metal markets.

To be sure, the Western economies will continue to find useful the cheap minerals from the Indian Ocean littoral. But to suggest that these resources are so vital and are at such risk to warrant massive force projection into the region is untenable. "Interdependence," to use a favorite Western academic term, in resource endowment has been with us for a long time. However, it is easy and convenient to project this economic interdependence in a one-sided way to justify a strategic and military posture and mobilize support internally and externally for predetermined politico-strategic policies based on certain a priori considerations. But these justifications do not survive the real test—that of the marketplace for both traditional and non-traditional metals.

The preceding two lengthy sections on oil and mineral resources were necessary to clarify the real nature of Western economic interests—often termed vital—in the Indian Ocean littoral. It is obvious that these economic interests have been overemphasized by Western and Indian writings on the Indian Ocean. The articulation of these interests is not supported by the emerging economic patterns. The sooner this self-imposed straitjacket of economic interests is cast away, the better the understanding of the Indian Ocean situation would be. After the examination of the emerging patterns of traditional economic issues, we must now move toward the likely conflicts over new economic uses of the Indian Ocean.

Non-Living Resources in the Region

The new regime of the oceans has greatly expanded coastal state jurisdiction through the concept of the exclusive economic zone (EEZ). Within the Indian Ocean littoral, the largest beneficiaries of the new regime have been Indonesia, India, Madagascar, Australia, and South Africa. The smaller island states, such as Sri Lanka, Maldives, Mauritius, and the Seychelles, have EEZs relatively large in comparison to their land areas. A few countries have benefited from the possession of island territories far from the mainland—India (Lakshadweep, and Andaman and Nicobar), Australia (Cocos Islands), and South Africa (Prince Edward Islands). More interestingly, territorial possessions of extra-regional powers have also resulted in extensive EEZs relative to the size of the territories. Great Britain (and the United States) benefits from the possession of the British Indian Ocean Territory; and France, from the possession of various islands in and around the Mozambique channel—the Europa, Bassas da India, Juan deNova, Mayotte, Glorieuses, Tromelin, and La Réunion. The French benefits are even more significant in the southern Indian Ocean, via the islands of Crozet Kerguelen, Amsterdam, and Saint Paul. The economic significance of the EEZs of these extra-regional powers is not clear and is likely to unfold only in the future. Figure 4.2 indicates the distribution of non-living resources in the Indian Ocean.

Of primary interest among these resources would be, of course, offshore hydrocarbons, mostly occurring on the continental margins (which fall under the EEZs). Table 4.12 indicates the trends in offshore oil production in the Indian Ocean littoral. A large fraction of this offshore production, of course, comes from the Persian Gulf, and the decline in 1981 of offshore oil pro-

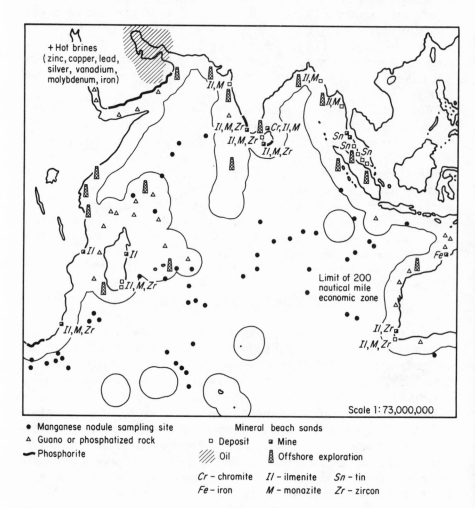

FIGURE 4.2. EEZs and Natural Resources in the Indian Ocean

duction is also due to cutbacks from this region. What is more significant is the emergence of new offshore producers such as India, Indonesia, Malaysia, and Brunei, among others. There are many reasons to believe that despite a glut in the world oil market and an excess capacity, interest in offshore hydrocarbons will continue to rise in the Indian Ocean littoral. This region has not been fully explored for hydrocarbons and it is expected that there is considerable potential there. Second, oil consumption in the developing countries of this region will continue to grow at a rapid pace. Unlike in the West, where the demand for oil is declining, oil needs will rise in this region.[94] This is particularly true of the high-growth economies of Southeast Asia, and also of South Asia. A vast majority of the countries in the region, other than those of the Gulf, are oil importers. The high prices of oil imports impose a heavy burden on their economies, so the incentive for domestic production of oil is very high. Oil exploration activity in the seas of the Indian Ocean is on the rise, and will continue to be very significant.[95]

For example, India has undertaken a massive offshore oil development program through its state company, the Oil and Natural Gas Commission (ONGC). Though the Indian offshore oil exploration commenced in 1962, it was only in the 1970s that it was taken up in earnest. With the discovery in 1974 of the hydrocarbons at Bombay High, a large area located 70–120 miles northwest of Bombay, India's offshore oil production began to surge. From zero oil production in 1975–76, it rose to an estimated 20.8 million tons in 1985–86, providing almost two-thirds of the total crude oil production in the country.[96]

The ONGC has been conducting extensive seismic surveys in the Indian continental shelf, an area of 145,000 square miles, and the continental slope, 155,000 square miles. The success ratio of exploration drilling is said to be encouraging.[97] Besides the Bombay offshore region, where the majority of reserves lie, the ONGC has discovered oil in the Godawari, Krishna, and Palk Bay basins and gas in Andaman offshore. Indications of gas have also been discovered in structures off Pondicherry. Most of the gas is only now being put to good use. The gas from Bombay High is being used to generate electricity at a 240-MW power station near Bombay and being fed to a number of chemical and fertilizer plants. It is also being used to run a large 500-MW power station in Bombay. Work has begun on a gigantic cross-country gas pipeline that will feed natural gas from the Western offshore to six fertilizer plants and three power stations.

The current Indian strategy is aimed at building self-reliance in offshore oil exploration and development. Though much more needs to be done, India has already acquired significant capabilities from its initiation of oil exploration and the construction and installation of offshore platforms.[98] India has also begun, with Japanese collaboration, the construction of highly sophisticated and technologically complex drill ships at its yard in Vishakapatnam. By 1988, India owned 20 drill ships and jack-up rigs, ten of which had been manufactured in the country.[99] India has an ambitious oil development program for its Seventh Plan, proposing to invest about Rs. 18,000 crores ($13.8 billion), a significant portion of which would go for offshore development.

There has been a considerable rise in the offshore oil development activities of other countries of the region, particularly in East and Southeast Asia. The excitement about oil potential in the South China Sea has been dampened by discouraging results from exploratory drilling activity. Further, the collapse of oil prices also meant a waning of enthusiasm among the Western oil companies that dominate offshore oil exploration in Asia. With their limitations of their investment budgets, they focus only on areas where drilling risks are lower and costs cheaper. However, few Asian areas fit this description.[100]

Nevertheless, the offshore oil resource development in the South China Sea holds the potential of regional conflict, which could end up being internationalized with the intervention of extra-regional powers. A large number of unresolved disputes over island territories and maritime boundary limitation among the states of the region cast a long shadow over oil resource development there.[101] The riparian states and territories of the South China Sea are: the Peoples' Republic of China, Taiwan, the Philippines, Malaysia, Brunei, Indonesia, Singapore, Vietnam, Macao, and Hong Kong. (Thailand and Kampuchea also enter the picture, if the Gulf of Thailand is taken into account.) While the eventual Chinese control of Hong Kong and Macao appears assured, Taiwan is likely to remain an intractable issue.

The unique geography, the long history of the ebb and flow of control over the South China Sea, coupled with the expanding jurisdictions under the new Law of the Sea regime have created a host of overlapping claims and counter-claims over territory. The sheer complexity of these claims over islands can be seen in Table 4.13. Two Chinese claimants and three other disputants are involved. The competition for resources has aggravated already serious Sino-Vietnamese political and military tensions. The efforts of the riparian states in relation to offshore hydrocarbon development have differed from country to country, but for each of them, offshore exploration and jurisdictional disputes have been interwoven. A discovery or claim in one area of the region has stimulated activity elsewhere, boosting the spiral of claims and counter-claims.

Of particular interest is the policy of China, which dramatically expanded its offshore activity since the late 1970s. Chinese offshore oil activity is not only integral to its planned rapid growth and access to Western technology, but also helps it in buttressing its claims to disputed territories:

> Foreign firms leasing in disputed areas confer legitimacy on Beijing's claims and prevent the same firms from becoming involved in prospecting for other claimants. Should oil companies lease tracts that only partially overlap disputed zones far offshore, in deep water, the firms would be relatively secure in proceeding to drill in the high-potential, near-shore areas. The Chinese would benefit by having leased an area that extends

into disputed waters and thus obtained "international" recognition of their claims.[102]

Among the other factors bordering the South China Sea, Indonesia, Malaysia, Brunei, and the Philippines already obtain significant amounts of their oil production from offshore areas. If they extend their activity farther ashore, they would enter disputed zones. The Philippines has reportedly drilled, though without much success, in the disputed Reed Bank area. Indonesia has begun development of areas in the South China Sea. Its efforts near the Natuna Islands have stimulated counter-claims by Vietnam and China.

After unification, Vietnam arranged for three Western companies to explore the offshore area south of Vietnam. While the Western companies have reduced their efforts, the Soviet Union has now entered the fray. In 1981, the Soviet Union and Vietnam set up a joint enterprise to conduct surveys in the areas as well as elsewhere in Vietnam. Parts of this area South of Vietnam has overlapping Chinese, Thai, and Indonesian claims. The Chinese pursuit of offshore oil in ever more hostile environments such as the Gulf of Tonkin has rekindled jurisdictional disputes there. Although there is no confirmation of serious Vietnamese exploration in the Gulf of Tonkin, Chinese finds in the vicinity are likely to provoke tensions.

While the potential for oil-related conflicts is latent in the South China Sea, there has also been interest in cooperative ventures in offshore development in the region. Malaysia and Thailand on the one hand and Vietnam and Indonesia on the other are considering such possibilities.

Maritime conflicts are also likely over South Asian waters. In the Andaman Sea to the west of Thailand, a Thai dispute remains with Burma but has not intensified in view of the disappointing results from recent drilling in Burma's own offshore waters. In the South Asian waters, India is yet to complete the process of delineating its maritime boundaries with all of its neighbors. During 1975–76, India and Sri Lanka settled their maritime boundaries in Palk Bay, the Palk straits, and the Gulf of Mannar; in 1977, India and Indonesia demarcated the 300-mile long maritime boundary between them; in 1978, India and Thailand settled the 94-mile-long boundary line between them; in 1979, India signed an agreement with the Maldives on the maritime border;[103] and in early 1984, India demarcated its maritime boundary with Burma.

However, until now India has not succeeded in its attempts to resolve the maritime boundary issues with Pakistan and Bangladesh. Discussions with Pakistan on the delineation of the maritime boundary in Sind and Gujarat waters have not yielded fruit. Maritime relations with Bangladesh have been tense. In 1981, Bangladesh challenged India's right to ownership of the newly emerged New Moore Island off the Sunderbans. Bangladesh deployed gunboats against an unarmed Indian survey ship, and India in turn deployed the I.N.S. *Andaman*. While this situation has been defused, no solution is in sight to resolve the basic dispute on delimitation. Given the current state of political unease, it does not appear likely that India can quickly resolve the maritime disputes with Pakistan and Bangladesh. As all three countries step up their offshore oil exploration activities, there are possibilities of tensions rising. For example, Pakistan alleged in July 1984 that an Indian drilling rig was operating in its area.[104]

Besides oil, the other major issue in non-living resources is the development of manganese nodules on the deep seabed in the Indian Ocean. Table 4.1 shows the location of manganese nodules on the Indian Ocean floor. However, the Indian Ocean is not as rich in manganese nodules as the Pacific Ocean (see Table 4.14). Also, the content of the metallic nodules of the Indian Ocean is not as rich as those in the Pacific Ocean (see Table 4.15). But the Indian Ocean nodules are superior to those in the Atlantic in nickel, cobalt, and copper content.

India has launched a massive program for the exploration of manganese nodules and their eventual mining. It is one of the few countries to have qualified for the "Pioneer Investor" status under the new Law of the Sea regime. It is also the only country in the Indian Ocean littoral evincing interest in deep-seabed mining. India dramatically entered the international arena of seabed mining in 1981, when its research vessel *Gaveshani* scooped up manganese nodules from the Indian Ocean floor. From then on, the *Gaveshani* and two other hired research vessels have carried out extensive surveys in the Indian ocean for the nodules.

Under the regulations of the Preparatory Commission (Prepcom) for the International Seabed Authority (ISA), a nodule mining site should have a minimum nodule abundance of 5 kq/sq. m. and preferably more than 10 kg/sq. m.; should possess at least 2.47 percent of nickel, copper, and cobalt; and the minimum reserves should total about 60 million tons. The Indian Department of Ocean Development, which has been appointed by the government of India as the "Pioneer Investor," has submitted proposals on a mining site to the Prepcom. While the exact coordinates are confidential, the site is said to be in the Central Indian Basin. The ISA would divide the site into two areas of equal commercial value and keep one for itself.

The main rationale for seabed mining in India is its continuing shortage of non-ferrous metals. For example, in 1978 India imported all its requirements of nickel and cobalt, 77 percent of copper, and 50 percent of zinc. The mining of polymetallic nodules would in time affect these figures. But the costs of ocean mining ventures could be daunting. According to some estimates, India would have to invest Rs. 1000 ($768 million) in order to acquire the capacity to mine and process a million tons of these nodules. It has been argued by some that the benefits of such an investment might not be commensurate with its magnitude.[105] It has also been argued that current international prices of the metals to be mined may not justify seabed mining.[106]

However, there are valid reasons to support a continued Indian R & D program in seabed mining. The wealth of scientific and engineering knowledge obtained from the program would be of immense value in the overall ocean development activity. Secondly, the R & D effort would suitably position India to take advantage of seabed mining if and when it becomes commercially viable.

And India has been stepping up its R & D effort. With the acquisition of a sophisticated oceanographic research vessel, the *Sagar Kanya,* from West Germany in mid-1983, at a cost of Rs. 12 crores ($9.2 million), the exploratory part of the program is strengthened. Samples of nodules collected have been analyzed and a laboratory scale method has been attempted for efficient recovery of metals; and plans are on to move to the pilot-plant level. Insofar as the crucial mining part is concerned, India is reviewing the technologies already available and expediting the development of a most efficient design for mining.[107] The Indian Council of Scientific and Industrial Research has undertaken a massive multi-agency and multi-institutional project, with over 19 laboratories participating in the nodule program and with the National Institute of Oceanography (NIO) as the lead institution. According to current plans, India hopes to commission a prototype seabed mining system by 1996, and commercial mining is projected to take place by about 2010.[108]

In its seabed mining efforts, India is unlikely to get into conflict with any littoral state. The conflict with the United States is not specific but stems from the U.S opposition to the Law of the Sea Treaty and the International Seabed Authority. The Reagan Administration and the Thatcher government have remained steadfast in their opposition to the Treaty. At the 1982 UNCLOS, a number of Western mining companies were allowed to be named as Pioneer Investors as a concession to the West and as an inducement for the United States to sign the Treaty. With some of the Western powers (the United States, Great Britain, West Germany, Italy, Belgium, and the Netherlands) refusing to join the Treaty, the status of the Pioneer Investors (in which category the companies of the above states participate) has come under a cloud. The LOS rules require that the nine Pioneer Investors—four Western consortia, one Japanese consortium, plus the four state-owned companies of the Soviet Union, France, China, and India (see Table 4.16)—should settle overlapping seabed claims among themselves before the permission to mine is given by the ISA. But permission is granted to only those countries (and their consortia) that have signed the Treaty. The Treaty will come into force after 60 countries have formally ratified it. And once this happens, the Pioneer Investors of those states that have not signed it will be reckoned out of bidding. While the U.S. companies (and perhaps the British ones too) can hope to "rely on the U.S. Navy to back their claims," the other European powers are not so sure.[109] In August 1987, India became the first investor to be formally registered by the U.N. Preparatory Commission for the Seabed Authority. India has thus obtained exclusive rights to an area of about 20,000 square miles in the Indian Ocean.[110] The overlapping claims of the Soviet Union, Japan, and France in the Pacific have reportedly been resolved, and the three countries' claims are expected to be registered by the end of 1987.

Living Resources in the Region

Among the living resources, fisheries is the most important emerging issue in the Indian Ocean region. Unfortunately, until today the Indian Ocean has not proved to be a productive fishing ground. It only contributes about 5 percent of the world's fish catch; in contrast, 53 percent of the catch comes from the Pacific and 40 percent from the Atlantic (see Table 4.17). Compared to the current catch of about 3.5 million metric tons (mmt), the estimates of potential catch vary from 7 mmt to 17 mmt.[111]

However, fishing capabilities in the Indian Ocean are very low (see Table 4.18) when compared with the capabilities of South Korea (873 trawlers and vessels of 329,109 gross registered tons (grt) and 31 factory ships of 68,452 grt) and Taiwan (266 trawlers and vessels of 81,913 grt). A considerable portion of the catch in the Indian Ocean has been taken by non-local fleets—namely, those of Japan, South Korea, and Taiwan. For example, in 1972, out of 2.6 mmt of Indian Ocean catch, 0.29 mmt was taken away by the non-local fleets. With the proclamation of EEZs, the situation has changed.[112] Now large fishing nations like South Korea are acquiring fishing concessions from coastal states in the region.

Although India was in the top ten fishing nations of the world during 1978–81, there is considerable potential for improvement. The Indian marine catch doubled from 1.4 mmt in 1981 to 2.8 mmt in 1985.[113] However, fishing operations are largely inefficient and limited to coastal areas. Higher levels of future expansion would have to be based upon scientific exploration and mapping of fishery resources. At the end of 1984, India acquired a new vessel, the *Sagar Sampada,* for fisheries and oceanographic research from Denmark at a cost of Rs. 15.29 crores ($11.5 million).[114] Future expansion would also be based on an increased emphasis upon mariculture, whose potential is enormous along the Indian coast.[115]

Indian fishery objectives do not clash in the long term with Western powers, who do not fish in the Indian Ocean. It might come into conflict with the fleets of South Korea and Taiwan. One other potential source of conflict could be the large number of unsettled maritime disputes in the South Asian and Southeast Asian waters, which we had noted in relation to offshore oil.

Antarctic Issues

Hitherto, the problems of an Antarctic regime have had little or no impact on the Indian Ocean debate. However, with the focusing of world attention on Antarctica—at the United Nations, NAM, and other fora and by the countries of the Indian Ocean littoral—Antarctic problems are likely to assume greater significance. The permanent presence of India now on the southern continent underscores the country's interest. Antarctic resources are drawing worldwide attention, and the expectations have been high regarding the "last great land rush" on our planet.[116] The Antarctic krill has already emerged as the basis of a major world fishery. There is also rising interest in the Antarctic mineral resources, which include hydrocarbons and precious metals.

Until the early 1980s, Antarctic affairs were largely insulated from world politics and quietly managed by the 14 Antarctic Treaty powers. The Antarctic Treaty of 1959 was a compromise worked out between seven claimant states—Great Britain, France, Norway, Australia, New Zealand, Argentina, and Chile—and five non-claimants—the United States, the Soviet Union, Belgium, Japan, and South Africa—to further scientific cooperation achieved in Antarctica during the International Geophysical Year (1957–58). The claims were frozen, no new claims were to be made, and the continent was denuclearized and demilitarized. But the Treaty had a peculiar two-tier structure. The decision making was concentrated in the 12 original parties—called consultative members—each of whom had veto power over any decision. All the states were welcome to join the Treaty and abide by the decisions of the consultative parties, without any say in the decision making. Consultative status was open only to those states undertaking substantive scientific research on the continent. Two states—Poland and West Germany—were given the status in the late 1970s.[117] The condition for membership was a capacity to undertake technologically sophisticated and financially expensive expeditions to the continent, beyond the reach of most countries. The exclusivity and high price demand for membership drew increasing criticism from the developing states, who wanted internationalization of the continent by declaring it the common heritage of mankind. This demand from the South grew strident in the late 1970s and early 1980s, and the Antarctic powers became concerned.

It was at this stage that India entered the scene, in 1981–82, when the first Indian expedition reached Antarctica. While the Indian government maintained that its interest was purely scientific,[118] the West was apprehensive of its real intentions.[119] Indian observers themselves believed that India would challenge the dominance of Antarctica by a few nations and take up the cause of the common-heritage principle on behalf of the Third World.[120] And when India joined the Treaty and was immediately granted consultative status, there was disbelief even in India. But it appears that India kept its options open from the outset regarding joining the Treaty. Mrs. Gandhi told the Parliament in February 1982 that India had no "political motives" in sending the expedition, but she did not think "any part of the globe should be reserved for any affluent country." At the same time, she stated that "there must have been some good reason" for not signing the Treaty earlier, but she also indicated that the matter would be "gone into again."[121] Thus, the question of joining the Treaty was kept open.

The Treaty powers themselves were keen to deflect criticism of the Treaty and expand the participation to include at least those countries that could not be stopped for too long. Thus, both India and Brazil were granted consultative status, and they were followed by China. In the eyes of other third world countries, India had defected to the side of the advanced countries by joining the treaty.[122] While this is not correct, India is indeed in a delicate position. India is committed to the Economic Declaration of the 1983 NAM summit, which for the first time included a reference to Antarctica, urging that the continent be "accessible to all nations" and that "the exploration of the area and the exploitation of its resources shall be carried out for the benefit of all mankind."[123] The final phrasing is said to be a toned-down version of Malaysia's proposal to declare the area as a common heritage of mankind. By the time the United Nations took up the issue for debate for the first time, in December 1983, India was already a member of the Treaty. But, unlike the other members of the Antarctic club, India supported the Malaysian resolution urging the U.N. Secretary General to undertake a comprehensive study of the Antarctica issue.

The challenge before the Indian Antarctic policy is to evolve a flexible posture avoiding a confrontation between North and South over Antarctica and at the same time utilize its position within the Treaty to expand the interests of the Third World states in Antarctica.[124] That India is trying to steer this difficult course was indicated by the state Minister for Science and Technology in 1984, at a New Delhi conference on Antarctica.[125]

India's Ocean Policy and the United States

Though India has had a long maritime tradition, it declined as a maritime power and Indians came to regard themselves as a nation of "landlubbers." Thanks to a long coastline and 1200 islands in two stretches on either side, India has acquired economic sovereignty over a vast stretch of the ocean surface. Unlike most other states of the Indian littoral, India has woken up— although belatedly—to the great possibilities in the oceans. India has launched a multifaceted ocean development program that is far-reaching in scope and ambitious in terms of objectives. The achievements till now in offshore oil development, seabed mineral exploration, Antarctica, and fisheries are considerable.

Coordinating the overall maritime development activity in India is the Department of Ocean Development (DOD). Set up in July 1981, the Department was entrusted with the planning and coordination of oceanographic research and development, establishment of research facilities, management of ocean data, and development of manpower and marine technology. An ocean policy statement issued in November 1982 called for a "coordinated, centralized and highly sophisticated response" to the challenge of ocean resource development, optimum utilization of ocean resources while protecting its maritime environment, and the acquisition of basic knowledge and the development of appropriate ocean technology for Indian needs. Self-reliance was stated as a major objective in ocean development. "An important component of the development program should be the acquisition of technology.

To be self-reliant, such technologies would have to be largely developed, tested and operated indigenously."[126]

Although India's maritime achievements are already considerable, its requirements and needs are many. Ocean development will have to be based on advanced science and high technology, and India will have to do extensive surveys of surrounding seas in order to obtain the knowledge and skills upon which exploitation has to be based. Survey ships, modern oceanographic instrumentation based on sophisticated electronics, computer capacity to process ocean data, a research base, and trained manpower are important requirements for the development of the ocean sciences in India. And for exploitation of ocean resources, India will need a wide range of capabilities—ships and various offshore platforms, as well as underwater technology, particularly subsea systems and submersible vehicle technology.

Although self-reliance is the objective, India will certainly require scientific and technological assistance from outside, at least in the initial phases. And India has been scouting for technological cooperation with various advanced maritime powers. A number of countries—including France, Germany, Norway, Denmark, and Japan, among others—have been eager to participate in India's ocean development activity. But, surprisingly, the United States has shown little or no interest in cooperating with India. More than that, the United States has refused to provide the C-130 transport aircraft for India's Antarctic missions. It might be wrong to conclude that the United States was blocking India's scientific development, but the fact remains that an opportunity for cooperation was missed. It was indeed a surprising change in the attitude of the United States, which had eagerly cooperated with India in the early phases of atomic energy and space development.

As the Indian Ocean development activity unfolds, the Indian profile in the area will be more visible. The current plans call for a great expansion of Indian economic activities in the Indian Ocean, thus increasing its stake in the ocean and the demand for peace and stability in the region. As its "offshore estate" becomes larger, its navy too will be more visible and take on the new role of not only protecting the offshore estate, but also providing scientific and technical support. As Indian naval visibility expands along with its expanding economic interest in the Indian Ocean, it is likely to raise concerns among its neighbors, who would most certainly regard it as a naval threat from India. Given the linkages of India's neighbors to the United States, America could be tempted to expand naval military assistance to its neighbors, thus increasing the tension in the seas. For reasons dealt with by Subrahmanyam in Chapter 5, the idea of a maritime threat from India is not a credible one and therefore should not form the basis of a security relationship between extra-regional powers and littoral nations. India has a modest program of cooperation with other neighboring countries in regard to ocean development. For example, India plans to conduct EEZ surveys of the Seychelles and train its manpower in Indian institutions; and India offered a seat to Mauritius on the second Indian Antarctic expedition, of which Mauritius could not avail itself but has decided to do so in the future.

And India has already begun cooperation in ocean research with Sri Lanka. Two Sri Lankan scientists participated in one of the *Gaveshani*'s cruises in 1983–84. In the same year, India sent two scientists to Sri Lanka to assist in the development of its marine science infrastructure.[127] India is also assisting the island state of the Seychelles in the survey of its EEZ area and in the development of seaweeds.[128]

Our review of the emerging Indian economic interests in the Indian Ocean shows no direct clash with U.S. economic interests in the region. In fact, there are opportunities for cooperation. In some areas the interests are complementary, such as stability and security in the Persian Gulf region. The real Indian conflict with the United States is on the issue of U.S. naval force projection into the region, its overall strategy toward the landmass of the littoral, and the U.S. stand on the Law of the Sea Treaty, which had been drafted after seven years of meticulous effort of U.S. negotiators like Elliott Richardson. The U.S. force projection into the region has always been justified on the grounds of vital U.S. economic interests in the region. As we have seen, the issues of energy security and resource security of the United States and its allies in the region have been overblown. The rhetoric on oil and resource security does not match the reality. The expansion of the U.S. force projection into the Indian Ocean at a time of its declining dependence on oil and other resources of the region cannot be rationally explained by economic interests and motivations. The real reasons appear to be different from the declared ones—namely, pursuit of a neo-Dullesian policy of containment of Soviet landmass.

Insofar as the emerging economic issues of the region are concerned the future will most probably be unlike the past:

Oil and the Gulf. The issue will not be energy security but maintaining the Gulf boom, an important market for Western Goods and regional labor. The collapse of the oil market will have profound consequences for the world economy in new and unforeseen ways. There have been suggestions from the Indian Prime Minister on an international conference of producers and consumers of oil and offers from Soviet President Brezhnev and Premier Gorbachev to negotiate on Gulf security and Indian Ocean force reductions. The total lack of response from the United States on these two proposals will raise problems of credibility about the U.S. energy security concerns.

Non-fuel resources. The issue would no longer be "access" to non-fuel minerals, but markets for these minerals, produced in Indian Ocean region.

Offshore oil and fisheries. The priority would be to create an appropriate political climate for resolving the maritime disputes in the South China Sea and South Asian waters, which have the potential of exploding into wider conflicts.

Seabed minerals and Antarctica. The challenge is to evolve a global approach to manage these resources, a process made difficult by the U.S. rejection of the Law of the Sea Treaty after it had been negotiated.

The growing militarization of the Indian Ocean, and the increasing U.S. tendency to view all the regional issues through the prism of strategic confrontation with the Soviet Union offer little hope that the emerging economic issues of the Indian Ocean region will be dealt with in a constructive spirit in the near term.

Notes

1. Elizabeth Mann Borgese, "The Sea and The Dreams of Man," *Impact of Science and Society* No. 3/4 (1983), pp. 479–490.

2. For a competent review of energy production from the sea, see L. Donald Maus, "Energy From the Oceans: Its Development and Delivery," in J. J. Bartell, ed., *The Yankee Mariner & Sea Power* (Los Angeles: University of Southern California Press, 1982), pp. 195–221.

3. "Food and Population: A Time for Reassessment," in Ritchie Calder, ed., *The Future of a Troubled World* (London: Heinemann, 1983), p. 73.

4. Clarence P. Idyll, "Food From the Sea," in Bartell, op. cit., p. 243.

5. For a detailed status of aquaculture, see T. V. R. Pillay, "Return to the Sea—Not as Hunter But as Farmer," *Impact of Science on Society,* No. 3/4 (1983), pp. 445–452.

6. Elizabeth Mann Borgese, "The Future in the Oceans," in Calder, op. cit., p. 83.

7. Pillay, op. cit., p. 448.

8. For an examination of seaweed culture, see Akio Miura, "Seaweed Cultivation: Present Practices and Potentials," in Elizabeth Mann Borgese and Norton Ginsburg, eds., *Ocean Yearbook 2* (Chicago: University of Chicago Press, 1980), pp. 57–68.

9. David Dickson, "Deep Sea Mining: United States Rethink," *Nature* (London), Vol. 295 (January 21, 1982), pp. 182–183.

10. Alexander Malahoff, "Polymetallic Nodules from the Oceans to the Continents," *Sea Technology,* January 1982, pp. 51–55.

11. Peter Rothe, "Marine Geology: Mineral Resources from the Sea," *Impact of Science on Society,* No. 3/4 (1983), p. 363.

12. Elizabeth Mann Borgese, "The Future of the Oceans," in Calder, op. cit., p. 83.

13. Robert E. Osgood, "Military Implications of the New Ocean Politics," *Power at Sea: The New Environment,* Adelphi Paper No. 122 (London: IISS, 1975), p. 10.

14. The following account is heavily borrowed from P. Lewis Young, "The Law of the Sea and Potential Conflicts in Asia," *Asian Defence Journal* (Kuala Lumpur), No. 4 (1984), pp. 26–33.

15. Ibid., p. 28.

16. Ibid., p. 30.

17. John Norton Moore, "Ocean Resource Competition as a Source of Conflict" in W. J. Taylor and S. A. Maaranen, eds., *The Future of Conflict in the 1980s* (Lexington, Mass.: D.C. Heath, 1982), p. 47.

18. Christopher C. Joyner, "Offshore Maritime Terrorism: International Implications and the Legal Response," *Naval War College Review* 36, 4 (July–August 1983), pp. 16–31.

19. Hedley Bull, "Sea Power and Political Influence," *Adelphi Paper,* No. 122, (London: International Institute of Strategic Studies, 1981), p. 1.

20. Adm. S. G. Gorshkov, *The Sea Power of the State* (Oxford: Pergamon, 1979, p. 1.

21. Geoffrey Kemp, "Maritime Access and Maritime Power: The Past, the Persian Gulf and the Future," in Alvin J. Cottrell et al., *Sea Power and Strategy in the Indian Ocean* (London: Sage, 1981), pp. 45–46.

22. Adm. Elmo R. Zumwalt, "20th Century Mahan," *Proceedings of the U.S. Naval Institute,* November 1974, pp. 70–73.

23. Bull, op. cit., p. 4.

24. Geoffrey Kemp, "Scarcity and Strategy," *Foreign Affairs* 56, 2 (January 1978), pp. 396–414.

25. See Guy Pauker, *Military Implications of a Possible World Order Crisis in the 1980s,* Rand Report, R-2003AF, 1977.

26. Vice Adm. Edward S. Briggs, Deputy Commander-in-Chief, U.S. Pacific Fleet, "New Directions over Old Sea Lanes," in Don Walsh and Marjorie Cappelari, eds., *Energy and Sea Power: Challenge for the Decade* (Oxford: Pergamon, 1981), p. 50.

27. Geoffrey Till, *Maritime Strategy and the Nuclear Age,* 2nd ed. (London: Macmillan, 1984), pp. 203–205.

28. P. K. S. Nambooridi, "Intervention in the Indian Ocean," in K. Subrahmanyam, ed., *The Second Cold War* (New Delhi: ABC, 1983), p. 57.

29. B. M. Blechman and S. S. Kaplan, *Force Without War: U.S. Armed Forces as a Political Instrument* (Washington, D.C.: Brookings, 1978).

30. This and the following facts are from Dieter Braun, *The Indian Ocean: Region of Conflict or Zone of Peace* (New Delhi: Oxford, 1983), pp. 8–9.

31. Cited in Briggs, op. cit., p. 58.

32. Ibid.

33. Kemp, "Maritime Access and Maritime Power," op. cit., pp. 63–64.

34. K. Subrahmanyam, op. cit., p. 19.

35. Alan Dowty, "Oil Power in the 1980s," *Jerusalem Journal of International Affairs* 6, 3 (1982–83), p. 87.

36. See Yusif A. Sayigh, "Arab Economic Strategy in a Changing World Oil Market," *Third World Quarterly* 6, 1 (January 1984), p. 43.

37. See Edward L. Morse, "After the Fall: the Politics of Oil," *Foreign Affairs* 64, 4 (Spring 1986), pp. 792–811.

38. *Petroleum Economist,* August 1987, p. 324.

39. Danny J. Boggs, Deputy Secretary, U.S. Department of Energy, in *Economic Impact,* No. 3 (1984), p. 32.

40. "Oil and the Gulf—A Survey," *The Economist,* July 28, 1984, p. 14.

41. Ibid.

42. "Supplies of Oil 'Secure' Despite New Tension," *Financial Times,* August 5, 1987, p. 1.

43. Fred S. Singer, "An end to OPEC? Bet on the Market," *Foreign Policy,* No. 45, pp. 115–121.

44. Dowty, op. cit., p. 90.

45. Thomas H. Moorer and Reginald Brown, "The Persian Gulf: Upheavals, Instability and Preventive Presence," *Sea Power,* April 15, 1984, p. 21.

46. See Mark Potts, "No World Oil Crisis Seen in Gulf Tension," *International Herald Tribune,* August 12, 1987; Lee A. Daniels, "Despite Gulf Tensions, Oil Stockpiles Point to a Price Decline," ibid., August 14, 1987.

47. Daniel Pipes, "Breaking All the Rules: American Debate Over Middle East," *International Security* 9, 2 (Fall 1984), p. 140.

48. Ibid., p. 144.

49. Caspar Weinberger, *Annual Report to the Congress FY 1985*, February 1, 1984, p. 173.

50. Jeffrey Record, "Jousting with Unreality: Reagan's Military Strategy," *International Security* 5, 3 (Winter 1983–84), p. 10.

51. *International Financial Statistics Yearbook* (Washington: International Monetary Fund, 1985), pp. 37, 39.

52. "Changing Business Climate: No More Quick Returns," *Middle East Review, 1986*, 12th Ed. (1985), pp. 23–25.

53. Fred Halliday, "Labour Migration in the Arab World," *MERIP Reports*, No. 123 (May 1984), pp. 7–8.

54. For an analysis, see Nazli Choucri, "Migration in the Middle East: Transformation and Change," *Middle East Review* 16, 2 (Winter 1983–84), pp. 16–25.

55. *Business Week,* July 2, 1979, p. 46.

56. Robert A. Kilmarx, "Strategic Minerals Competition as a Source of Conflict," in Taylor and Maaranen, op. cit., p. 49.

57. S. S. Bhattacharya, "Economic Interests of the Big Powers in the Indian Ocean Region," *IDSA Journal* 10, 3 (January–March 1978), p. 262.

58. Namboodiri, op. cit., p. 59.

59. Martin Rodetzki, "Economic Maturity Recession and Consumption of Base Materials," *Resources Policy* 9, 2 (June 1983), p. 75.

60. For a general overview, see "Metals: A Survey," *Financial Times*, October 9, 1984.

61. *Strategic Materials Management,* March 1, 1984, p. 3.

62. Ibid.

63. "Industry Outlooks: Nonferrous Metals," *Business Week*, January 9, 1984, p. 49.

64. "Metals: A Survey," op. cit.

65. Ibid.

66. *Strategic Materials Management,* January 15, 1984, p. 4.

67. *Strategic Materials Management,* April 15, 1984, p. 4.

68. "Metals: A Survey," op. cit.

69. Ibid.

70. "Alloy Makers React to Composite Gains," *Aviation Week & Space Technology,* September 24, 1984, pp. 57–63.

71. "Composites Have Sikorsky Flying High," *Business Week,* July 9, 1984, p. 51.

72. "Metals: A Survey," op. cit.

73. U.S. National Science Foundation, *The Five Year Outlook: Problems, Opportunities and Constraints in Science and Technology*, Vol. II (Washington; NSF, 1980), p. 191.

74. Summary of Prof. James Mueller's briefing to the U.S. National Strategic Materials and Minerals Program Advisory Committee on September 19, 1984, in *Strategic Materials Management*, October 1, 1984, p. 5.

75. Quoted in *Strategic Materials Management*, July 1, 1983, p. 1.

76. *Strategic Materials Management, April 15, 1984, pp. 3–4.*

77. John E. Tilton, *The Impact of Seabed Nodule Mining: A Qualitative*

208   SUPERPOWER RIVALRY IN THE INDIAN OCEAN

Analysis, RR-83-83 (Laxenberg, Austria: International Institute for Applied Systems Analysis, December 1983), pp. 6–9.

78. Ibid., p. 8.

79. Michael Tanzer, *The Race for Resources: Continuing Struggles over Minerals and Fuels* (London: Heinemann, 1980), pp. 201–209.

80. Amos A. Jordan and Robert A. Kilmarx, "Strategic Mineral Dependence: The Stockpile Dilemma," *Washington Papers,* no. 70; (London: Sage, 1982) "Nonfuel Minerals: U.S. Investment Abroad," *Washington Papers,* No. 23 (London: Sage, 1975).

81. Jordan and Kilmarx, ibid. (1982), p. 30.

82. Michael Shafer, "Mineral Myths," *Foreign Policy,* no. 47 (Summer 1982), pp. 154–171.

83. Rae Weston, *Strategic Materials: A Survey* (London: Croom Helm, 1984), pp. 1–10.

84. Shafer, op. cit., p. 159.

85. Weston, op. cit., p. 18.

86. *Strategic Materials Management,* August 15, 1983, p. 1.

87. Ibid.

88. *Strategic Materials Management,* March 1, 1984, p. 4.

89. *Strategic Materials Management,* August 15, 1983, p. 2.

90. Shafer, op. cit.

91. Weston, op. cit., p. 95.

92. Quoted in *Strategic Materials Management,* September 1, 1983, p. 5.

93. Ibid.

94. *Petroleum Economist,* August 1984, p. 285.

95. *Petroleum News* (Exploration Annual, 1984) 14, 10 (January 1984).

96. Planning Commission, *Sixth Five Year Plan: Mid Term Appraisal* (New Delhi, 1983).

97. A. K. Malhotra, "India's Offshore Oil Program," *India International Centre Quarterly* 10, 3 (September 1983), p. 22.

98. Ibid., p. 24.

99. A spokesman for the Indian Embassy, Washington, provided this estimate. See also *The Statesman,* March 29, 1984.

100. *Asia Yearbook,* 1987 (Hong Kong: Far Eastern Economic Review, 1986), p. 77.

101. See Young, op. cit.; see also Choon-Ho Park, "Offshore Oil Development in the China Seas: Some Legal and Territorial Issues," in Elizabeth Mann Borgese and Norton Ginsburg, eds., *Ocean Yearbook 2* (Chicago: University of Chicago Press, 1922), p. 101.

102. Daniel J. Dzurek, "Boundary and Resource Disputes in the South China Sea," in Elizabeth Mann Borgese and Norton Ginsburg, eds., *Ocean Yearbook 5* (Chicago: University of Chicago Press, 1985), p. 263.

103. J. P. Anand, "The Law of the Sea: India and the Indian Ocean," *IDSA Journal,* July–September 1981, p. 31.

104. *The Statesman,* August 2, 1984, p. 5.

105. Editorial in *Times of India,* October 28, 1983, p. 6.

106. Editorial in *The Statesman,* October 21, 1983, p. 8.

107. Department of Ocean Development, *Annual Report of 1983–84* (New Delhi, 1984), p. 38.

108. Government of India, Department of Ocean Development, *Annual Report 1986–87* (New Delhi, 1987), p. 27.

109. Deborah Mackenzie, "Law of the Sea Flounders in Geneva," *New Scientist*, August 30, 1984, pp. 3–4.

110. *Times of India*, August 19, 1987.

111. S. Z. Quasim, "A Technological Forecast of Ocean Research and Development in India" *Impact of Science on Society*, No. 3/4 (1983), p. 467.

112. K. C. Lucas and T. Loftas, "FAO's EEZ Program," in Elizabeth Mann Borgese and Norton Ginsburg, eds., *Ocean Yearbook 3* (Chicago: University of Chicago Press, 1983), p. 55.

113. *Yearbook of Fishing Statistics*, Food and Agriculture Organization (Rome), Table A-2, p. 88. B. Ramachandra Rao, "Man and the Ocean: Resources and Development," *Strategic Digest* (New Delhi), September 1983, p. 609.

114. *DOD, Annual Report 1983–84*, p. 53; and *Annual Report 1986–87*.

115. S. N. Dwivedi and N. P. Dunning, "Progress and Potential of Aquaculture," in Elizabeth Mann Borgese and Norton Ginsburg, eds., *Ocean Yearbook 4* (Chicago: University of Chicago Press, 1984), pp. 60–74.

116. M. J. Peterson, "Antarctica: The Last Great Land Rush on Earth," *International Organization* 34, 3 (Summer 1980), p. 41.

117. For a comprehensive discussion on Antarctica, see F. M. Auburn, *Antarctica: Law and Politics* (Bloomington: Indiana University Press, 1982).

118. *Times of India*, February 18, 1982.

119. *The Hindu*, February 20, 1982.

120. Rahmatullah Khan, "India and Antarctica Treaty," *Hindustan Times*, p. 9, March 18, 1982; K. J. S. R. Kapoor, "The Antarctica Treaty: India's Refusal to Sign," *Business Standard*, p. 7, July 16, 1983; and C. Raja Mohan, "Land Grab at Antarctica: Need for an Indian Initiative," *Indian Express*, p. 10, August 2 and 3, 1983.

121. *The Hindu*, p. 8, February 20, 1982.

122. Barbara Mitchel, "Has Antarctica Split the South?" *The Telegraph*, p. 6, September 23, 1983.

123. Economic Declaration of the New Delhi Summit, paras. 122–123.

124. Joel Larus, "India Claims a Role in Antarctica," *The Round Table*, No. 289 (January 1984), pp. 45–56.

125. Statement of Shivraj Patil at New Delhi on September 17, 1984; see *Times of India*, September 18, 1984.

126. Government of India, *Ocean Policy Statement*, November 7, 1982.

127. Department of Ocean Development, *Annual Report 1983–84*, pp. 55–56.

128. Department of Ocean Development, *Annual Report 1986–87*, p. 62.

TABLE 4.1.   Main Types of Mineral Resources on the Sea Floor

Type of Deposit	Materials for Elements	Geological Setting	Law of the Sea Setting
Placer deposits	Iron, gold, platinum, tin, diamonds, rare earths, zirconium, titanium, and others	Coastal and near-shore	EEZ
Hydrocarbons	Petroleum, gas	Mainly passive continental margins and back-arc basins	Mostly EEZ
Hydrothermal ore deposits	Iron, managanese, copper, zinc, lead, silver, and others	Fracture zones, spreading centers, back-arc basin (?)	Mostly Area (deep seabed)
Manganese nodules	Managanese, iron, cobalt, copper, nickel, titanium, molybdenum, and others	Deep sea (14,000 feet)	Mostly Area
Phosphorites	Phosphorous, uranium, rare earths, and others	Coastal (locally continuation of land resources) and near-shore; submarine plateaus	Mostly EEZ

Source: Peter Rothe, "Marine Geology: Mineral Resources of the Sea," *Impact of Science on Society,* Nos. 3/4 (1983), p. 360.

TABLE 4.2. U.S. National Ocean Policy–Naval Strategy Matrix

Ocean Use	National Ocean Policy Action	Related Naval Strategic Activity
Seabed mining	Deep-seabed mining; encourage commercial activity; LOS Treaty	Strategic mineral usage; protection of miners
Offshore/deep sea, oil and natural gas	Hydrocarbon recovery; new technology; encourage activity; LOS Treaty	Strategic hydrocarbon usage, protection of sites
Strategic passage for naval forces	Interface with LOS Treaty; other Treaty activity on peaceful uses	Sea control/power projection/choke points
Trade routes	Commercial shipping; movement of imports/exports, raw materials	Sea lines of communications; raw materials
Fisheries	Expanding U.S. deep-sea fishing; source of protein; industry jobs; new technology	Protection of operations; some EEZ patrol exclusion
Scientific research	Joint projects, investigation areas; encourage development of new technology	Military application, possible protection
Environmental	Resource control; environmental control; LOS Treaty interface	Rules apply to ships; possible police action
Ocean energy	Potential energy source (OTEC*: wave current), new technology	Protection in deep water
Arctic/Antarctic	Possible commercial activity; research; joint projects; new treaties	Strategic sites for various new equipment, R&D, transit strategic
Strategic forces	Treaty implications; possible havens	Critical mission possible haven concept
Post development coastal/deep water)	Trade; processing; artificial islands	Forward basing; home ports overhaul; POMUS (pre-positioned overseas materials in unit sets) sites
Marine technology	New commercial application; trade, transfer; LOS Treaty interface	Military application: security, alliance implications

* OTEC (Ocean thermal energy conversion) has applications of military value, e.g., providing energy to military installations at sea. See "Military Applications and Implications of OTEC Systems," in Donald Walsh and Marjorie Cappellari, eds., *Energy and Sea Power: Challenge for the Decade* (Oxford: Pergamon, 1981), pp. 125–30.

Source: James Stavridis, "Naval Strategy and National Ocean Policy," *Proceedings of U.S. Naval Institute*, July 1984, p. 45.

TABLE 4.3.   Worldwide Ownership of Crude Oil Reserves (percentage)

	1963	1970	1975	1977	1979	1981
Seven majors	82	61	30	22	25	31
Other private firms	9	33	8	7	20	21
Producer governments	9	6	62	71	55	48

Crude Oil Sales by OPEC Governments and Private Firms (percentage)

	1970	1973	1974	1976	1978	1979
*Producers govts.**						
Direct sales	—	5.0	6.7	13.1	15.9	16.5
Commercial sales	—	2.9	5.6	11.4	17.6	25.7
Subtotal	1.0	7.9	12.3	24.5	33.5	42.2
Oil companies	99.0	92.1	87.7	75.4	66.5	57.8

* Direct sales are government-to-government supply contracts; commercial sales are contracts with small private traders, including sales on the spot market.

Source: Michael Renner, "Restructuring the World Energy Industry," *MERIP Reports,* No. 120 (January 1984), p. 13.

TABLE 4.4.   World: Primary Energy Consumption*

	1979	1982	1985	1986
By type				
Oil	3125	2815	2810	2881
Coal	1969	2046	2273	2309
Natural gas	1283	1330	1494	1507
Hydroelectric	417	458	511	519
Nuclear	153	221	348	373
World total	6047	6870	7435	7589
By area				
N. America	2140	1936	2026	2031
W. Europe	1328	1217	1245	1267
Australasia	86	90	92	100
Japan	370	340	371	372
Total OECD	3924	3583	3734	3770
Rest of free world	907	1032	1118	1150
Total free world	4831	4615	4852	4920
Communist bloc	2113	2220	2583	2669
World total	6947	6870	7435	7589

* Commercially traded fuels only.

Source: Petroleum Economist, August 1987, p. 291.

TABLE 4.5.   World Crude Oil Production (thousand barrels)

Year	World	OPEC	OPEC/World (%)	Gulf*	Gulf/World %
1973	21,209,000	11,315,925	53.35	7,524,179	35.47
1979	24,011,000	11,289,223	47.01	7,671,131	31,94
1980	23,059,000	9,838,245	42.66	6,534,309	28.33
1981	21,645,000	8,208,808	37.92	5,499,930	25.40
1982	20,645,000	6,936,656	33.59	4,486,489	21.73
1983	20,441,000	6,202,193	30.34	3,851,481	18.84
1984	20,744,000	5,983,077	28.84	3,619,778	17.44
1985	20,664,000	5,730,639	27.73	3,358,613	16.25
1986	21,863,000	6,691,615	30.6	4,277,440	19.56

* Saudi Arabia, Iran, Kuwait, Iraq, Abu Dhabi, Dubai, Sharjah, and Qatar.

Source: Petroleum Economist, June 1987, p. 252.

TABLE 4.6.   U.S., West European Dependence on
Oil Imports from the Persian Gulf
(as percentage of total imports)

	1977	1978	1979	1980	1983
U.S.	37.5	34.8	31.8	28.8	11.6
W. Europe	69.4	66.9	61.9	58,9	39.4
Japan	77.4	77.9	76.0	72.9	65.8

Sources: Figures up to 1981 are from *World Oil Trade*, June 1981, and figures for 1983 are from *Petroleum Economist*, July 1984, p. 258.

TABLE 4.7.   Gulf Oil Export (million barrels a day)

	1979	1980	1982	1983	1984	1985	1986
Saudi Arabia	9.2	9.6	6.3	4.35	4.2	9.2	4.6
Kuwait	2.5	1.6	0.8	1.0	1.1	0.95	1.3
Iran	2.6	1.1	1.8	1.75	1.45	1.5	1.2
Iraq	3.3	2.4	0.8	0.9	0.95	1.2	1.4
UAE	1.8	1.7	1.25	1.15	1.25	1.2	1.4
Quatar	0.5	0.5	0.35	0.3	0.4	0.3	0.35
Gulf total	19.9	16.9	11.30	9.45	9.35	8.05	10.25

Source: Petroleum Economist, July 1987, p. 256.

TABLE 4.8.   Value of Gulf Oil Exports (billions of U.S. dollars)

	1979	1980	1982	1983	1984	1985	1986
Saudi Arabia	57.5	102.0	78	45	46	27	20
Kuwait	16.7	17.9	9	10	11	9	6
Iran	19.1	13.5	19	20	13	14	5
Iraq	21.3	26.0	10	10	11	12	7
UAE	12.9	19.5	16	13	12	12	7
Quatar	3.6	5.4	4	3	4	3	1
Gulf total	131.1	184.3	136	101	97	77	46

Source: Petroleum Economist, July 1987, p. 256.

TABLE 4.9. Mine Production of Four Strategic Metals, 1950 and 1980 (thousands of tons)

	Cobalt				Copper				Manganese*				Nickel			
	1950		1980		1950		1980		1950		1980		1950		1980	
	Pro-duction	%	Pro-duction	%	Pro-duction	%	Pro-duction	%	Pro-duction	%	Pro-duction	%	Pro-duction	%	Pro-duction	%
Developing countries*	6.2	86	21.6	72	1063	42	3464	44	2504	33	7074	26	4	3	256	34
Developed market economy countries***	1.0	14	4.5	15	1224	48	2541	33	1164	15	7656	29	114	77	325	44
Socialist countries	—	—	3.8	13	238	10	1812	23	3954	52	11,967	45	30	20	167	22
Total	7.2	100	29.9	100	2525	100	7817	100	7622	100	26,697	100	148	100	748	100

* The figures for manganese are in actual weight. For others they are of metal content.
** Developing countries include New Caledonia, a French-occupied territory, and Cuba.
*** South Africa is in the developed market economy countries.

Source: Adapted from John E. Tilton, The Impact of Seabed Nodule Mining: A Quantitative Analysis, RR–83–33 (Laxenberg, Austria: IIASA, December 1983).

TABLE 4.10.   U.S. Direct Foreign Investment Position Abroad in
Mining and Smelting ($ millions)

	1966	1968	1970	1972	1974	1976	1978
All countries	3983	4837	5405	5667	5790	7058	7100
Developed countries	2328	2875	3286	3400	4007	4749	4800
	(58%)	(59.1%)	(61%)	(60%)	(67%)	(67%)	(68%)
Canada	1976	2370	2574	2480	2794	3200	—
Europe	19	26	36	46	37	34	—
Japan	0	0	0	0	0	0	—
Australia, New Zealand and South Africa	333	479	675	945	1175	1515	—
Developing countries	1655	1962	2119	2267	1784	2309	2300
	(42%)	(41%)	(39%)	(40%)	(31%)	(33%)	(32%)
Latin America	1066	1623	1712	1689	1131	1600	—
Africa	NA	317	340	406	439	534	—
Middle East	NA	NA	NA	3	3	8	—
Asia Pacific	NA	22	67	169	211	167	—

Sources: Amos A. Jordan and Robert A. Kilmarx, "Strategic Mineral Dependence: The Stockpile Dilemma," *Washington Papers,* No. 70 (London: Sage, 1979), p. 30; the figures for 1978 are from Michael Tanzer, *The Race for Resources* (London: Heinemann, 1980), p. 202.

TABLE 4.11. Net Import Reliance of the U.S. for Specified Strategic
Metals and Minerals, 1980–82 (as a percent of apparent consumption)

Metal/Material	1980	1981	1982	Major Foreign Sources (1987–81)*
Antimony	48	48	45	Bolivia, Canada, China, Mexico, Chile
Cadmium	55	64	69	Canada, *Australia*, Mexico, South Korea
Chromium	91	90	88	*South Africa, Zimbabwe*, Philippines, Yugoslavia, Brazil, U.S.S.R.
Cobalt	93	92	91	*Zaire, Zambia*, Belgium, Luxembourg, Finland
Columbium	100	100	100	Brazil, Canada, *Thailand*
Manganese	98	98	99	*South Africa, Australia*, Brazil, Gabon, France
Mercury	26	44	43	Spain, Japan, Italy, Algeria
Nickel	71	68	75	Canada, Norway, *Botswana, Australia*
Platinum group metals	88	83	85	*South Africa*, U.S.S.R., U.K.
Selenium	90	92	90	Canada, Brazil, *Thailand, Malaysia*
Tantalum**	—	—	—	Japan, China, U.S.S.R., U.K.
Tungsten	50	50	48	Canada, Bolivia, China, Thailand

* Indian Ocean littoral states are italicized.
** Figures withheld in 1983 by U.S. Bureau of Mines. But 1981 Bureau of Mines figures are 46 percent for 1975–78.

Source: "Mineral commodity summaries 1983," U.S. Bureau of Mines, reproduced in *Sea Power* 27, 5 (April 15, 1984), p. 186.

TABLE 4.12.   Offshore Crude Oil Production in the Indian Ocean
(thousand barrels/day)

	1970	1975	1979*	1980	1981	1982	1983
Abu Dhabi	269	462.7	596.8	1322	555.0	443.4	338.5
Divided Zone	—	315.7	395.2	403.0	268.0	158.0	216.0
Dubai	70	249.3	362.7	344.9	359.0	364.0	323.0
Iran	322	481.2	200.0	150.0	350.0	—	—
Qatar	172	—	275.7	192.7	167.5	129.2	—
Saudi Arabia	1251	1385.8	2828.0	2958.0	3000.0	2392.0	2100.0**
Sharjah	—	38.4	12.1	10.0	10.5	6.9	6.9
India	—	—	81.4	142.1	160.0	257.0	342.3
Brunei	146***	141.2	189.6	192.2	126.0	121.0	121.6
Indonesia	—	246.4	274.7	533.0	561.0	535.7	438.5
Malaysia	—	84.5	271.0	280.3	250.0	302.2	383.0
Australia	216	412.5	401.0	323.2	368.1	348.1	341.1
Total	2446	38.17.7	588.2	6851.2	6175.1	5057.5	4610.9

* 1979 figures are from Elizabeth Mann Borgese and Norton Ginsburg, eds., *Ocean Yearbook No. 4* (Chicago: University of Chicago Press, 1984), pp. 579–80.
** Estimate.
*** Brunei/Malaysia combined production.

Source: Elizabeth Mann Borgese and Norton Ginsburg, eds., *Ocean Yearbook No. 5* (Chicago: University of Chicago Press, 1985), pp. 493–94.

TABLE 4.13. Occupied Islands in the South China Sea

Standard Name	Chinese Name (Pinyin)	Vietnamese Name	Filipino Name	Claimed By	Presently Occupied By
Paracel Islands	Xisha Qundao	Quan Dao Hoang Sa		China, Vietnam	Beijing
Pratas Island	Dongsha Qundao			China	Taipei
Spratly Islands	Nansha Qundao	Quan Dao Truong Sa	Kalayaan	China, Malaysia, Philippines, Vietnam	
Amboyna Cay	Anbo Shazhou	Dao An Bang	Kalantiyaw	China, Malaysia, Philippines, Vietnam	Hanoi
Commodore Reef	Siling Jiao		Rizal Reef	China, Malaysia, Philippines, Vietnam	Manila
Flat Island	Antang Dao		Patag	China, Philippines, Vietnam	Manila
Itu Aba	Taiping Dao	Dao Thai Binh	Ligaw	China, Philippines, Vietnam	Taipei
Lankiam Cay	Yangxin Zhou		Panata	China, Philippines, Vietnam	Manila
Loaita	Nanyue Dao	Dao Loai Ta	Kuta	China, Philippines, Vietnam	Manila
Namyit	Hangxue Dao	Dao Nam Ai	Bingago	China, Philippines, Vietnam	Hanoi
Nanshan	Mahuan Dao		Lawak	China, Philippines, Vietnam	Manila
Northeast Cay	Beizi Jiao	Dao Song Tu Dong	Parola	China, Philippines, Vietnam	Manila
Pearson Reef	Bisheng Dao		Hizon	China, Philippines, Vietnam	Hanoi
Sand Cay	Bailan Jiao	Dao Son Ca		China, Philippines, Vietnam	Hanoi
Sin Cowe	Jinghong Cao	Dao Sin Tonh	Rurok	China, Philippines, Vietnam	Hanoi
Southwest Cay	Nanzi Jiao	Dao Song Tu Tay	Pugad	China, Philippines, Vietnam	Hanoi
Spratly Island	Nanwei Dao	Dao Truong Sa	Lagos	China, Vietnam	Hanoi
Swallow Reef	Danwan Jiao			China, Malaysia, Philippines, Vietanam	Kuala Lumpur
Thitu	Zhongye Dao	Dao Thi Tu	Pagasa	China, Philippines, Vietnam	Manila
West York	Xiyue Dao	Dao Ben Lac	Likas	China, Philippines, Vietnam	Manila

Source: Elizabeth Mann Borgese and Norton Ginsburg, eds., *Ocean Yearbook 5* (Chicago: University of Chicago Press, 1985), p. 260.

TABLE 4.14. Areas Covered
by Nodules in the Three Oceans
(million sq. km)

	Area Covered	Prime Areas
Pacific	32	5.20
Atlantic	8	0.85
Indian	15	0.50

Source: S. Z. Qasim, "A Technological Forecast of Ocean Research and Development in India," *Impact of Science on Society,* Nos. 3/4 (1983), p. 474.

TABLE 4.15. Metallic Content of the
Nodules in the Three Oceans
(in percentages)

	Pacific	Indian	Atlantic
Manganese	12.27	15.25	15.46
Iron	11.79	13.35	23.01
Nickel	0.846	0.534	0.308
Cobalt	0.290	0.241	0.234
Copper	0.706	0.292	0.141

Source: S. Z. Qasim, "Bonanza from the Sea," *Science Today* (Bombay), June 1981, p. 19.

TABLE 4.16.   The Pioneer Investors

Ocean Management Incorporated, members: INCO of Canada, AMR of West Germany, SEDCO of the U.S., Deep Ocean Mining of Japan.

Kennecott, members: Sohio of the U.S. (owned by BP of Britain), RTZ of Britain, BP of Britain, Mitsubishi of Japan.

Ocean Mining Associates, members: U.S. Steel, Union Seas of Belgium, Sun Ocean Ventures of the U.S., Samin Ocean of Italy.

Ocean Mineral Company, members: Amoco and Lockheed, both of the U.S.; Billiton and BKW, both of Netherlands.

Afernod, a state-owned French company.

Deep Ocean Minerals Association, a wholly Japanese consortium.

U.S.S.R.: State company.

China: State company.

India: Department of Ocean Development.

Source: "Law of the Sea Goes Down for the Third Time," *New Scientist,* September 13, 1984, p. 7.

TABLE 4.17.   World Marine Catch by Major Fishing Area

	1970	*1975***	*1980*	*1981*	*1982*
Atlantic	23.53	25.85	24.99	24.94	24.66
Indian	2.53	3.21	3.55	3.52	3.56
Pacific	34.71	30.42	35.56	37.81	39.31
World Totals*	61.40	59.29	64.70	66.82	68.20

* Exceeds the sum of the figures due to the inclusion of catches not included elsewhere.
** 1975 figures are from Elizabeth Mann Borgese and Norton Ginsburg, eds., *Ocean Yearbook No. 4* (Chicago: University of Chicago Press, 1984), p. 565.

Source: Elizabeth Mann Borgese and Norton Ginsburg, eds., *Ocean Yearbook No. 5* (Chicago: University of Chicago Press, 1985), p. 481.

TABLE 4.18.   Fishing Fleets of the Indian Ocean Littoral, 1983

	Trawlers and Fishing Vessels			Factory Ships and Carriers	
	grt.	no.	over 500 grt. %	grt.	no.
Southeast Asia					
Australia	37,026	213	0	1,053	3
Burma	4,916	25	0		
China	11,143	41	22.6	21,155	15
Indonesia	34,914	168	10.5	1,510	5
Malaysia	1,169	6	0		
Singapore	2,913	12	0		
Thailand	1,535	6	0		
South Asia					
Bangladesh	6,152	25	45.1	263	2
India	11,345	72	0		
Maldives	1,602	3	62.3		
Pakistan	398	2	0		
Sri Lanka	2,567	9	27.2		
Persian Gulf					
Bahrain	653	6	0		
Iran	5,395	24	37.8		
Iraq	24,711	20	91.6	10,413	2
Qatar	696	5	0		
Kuwait	10,708	71	0	788	1
Oman	604	2	0		
Saudi Arabia	1,606	7	0		
Horn & Red Sea					
Egypt	8,728	6	97.4		
Ethiopia	218	2	0		
Israel	2,010	2	100.0		
Somalia	5,188	14	79.0		
Yemen	6,533	22	42.6		
Southern Africa					
Kenya	1,144	5	0		
Mozambique	13,198	66	19.4		
South Africa	74,286	181	47.7	303	1
Island States					
Madagascar	3,216	22	0		
Mauritius	3,455	11	33.2		

Smaller vessels (less than 100 grt.) are excluded.

Source: Elizabeth Mann Borgese and Norton Ginsburg, eds., *Ocean Yearbook No. 5* (Chicago: University of Chicago Press, 1985), pp. 489–90.

5

Arms Limitation in the Indian Ocean: Retrospect and Prospect

K. SUBRAHMANYAM

All arms control measures adopted to date evoke a degree of cynicism. In three much-advertised cases—the Antarctic Treaty of 1959, the Outer Space Treaty of 1963, and the Seabed Treaty of 1971—countries agreed not to do something that, in any case, they were not thinking of doing at that stage. The Biological Convention was agreed upon because the great powers knew that it is not possible to control the spread of biological weapons or to use them in battlefield conditions. The Non-Proliferation Treaty was intended to license unlimited proliferation by a few nuclear "haves." The SALT I agreement did not stop proliferation or reduce nuclear weapons stockpiles but merely formalized certain limits which neither side considered it desirable to exceed. The Tlatelelco Treaty, defining a Latin American nuclear-free zone, was stillborn. The Anti-Ballistic Missile Treaty was once hailed as an authentic arms control achievement, but the growing controversy over its most crucial provisions and continuing efforts to develop a ballistic missile defense make it clear, in retrospect, that the treaty could be adopted only because a ballistic missile defense did not appear technologically feasible at the time.

Against this background, it is clear that the goal of an Indian Ocean Zone of Peace, often ridiculed as visionary, deserves to be taken no less seriously than other arms control proposals. However, as I shall seek to show, the widespread impression that the Zone of Peace proposal is India's baby is not correct. While supporting the declaration presented to the U.N. General Assembly on December 16, 1971, India has serious reservations about the subsequent interpretations of, additions to, distortions of, and overlays to

223

the original resolution. Extra-regional powers have been able to exploit differences among the littoral states to subvert the original proposal.

With the exception of the short-lived Indian Ocean arms control negotiations between the United States and the Soviet Union in 1977 and 1978, the 1971 resolution has had little impact. The militarization of the Indian Ocean is intensifying, and ever-advancing progress in military technology makes the prospects for meaningful arms control agreements in the region increasingly cloudy.

India and the Zone of Peace

The idea of the Indian Ocean as a Zone of Peace came about in the wake of a reference made to the developing situation in the area by the Prime Minister of Sri Lanka in the Cairo Non-Aligned Summit in October 1964. The Cairo summit declaration included the following statement:

> The conference considers that the declaration by African states regarding the denuclearization of Africa, the aspirations of the Latin American countries to denuclearize their continent and the various proposals pertaining to the denuclearization of areas in Europe and Asia are steps in the right direction because they assist in consolidating international peace and security and lessening international tensions.
>
> The conference recommends the establishment of denuclearized zones covering these and other areas and *the oceans of the world, particularly those which have hitherto been free from nuclear weapons,* in accordance with the desires expressed by the States and peoples concerned (italics added).
>
> The conference also requests the nuclear powers to respect these denuclearised zones.[1]

The origin of the concept of the Indian Ocean as a Zone of Peace should therefore be traced to various measures adopted and under consideration in pursuit of disarmament in the early 1960s. The Antarctic Treaty of 1959 had prohibited the establishment of military bases and fortifications and carrying out of military maneuvers and nuclear explosions in the Antarctic under full international control, including access at all times to the whole territory. The Soviet Union had submitted proposals to the United Nations in 1959 for the creation of a nuclear-free zone in Central Europe.[2] The U.N. General Assembly had passed a resolution (1884) (XVIII) in 1963 calling upon states to refrain from placing in orbit any objects carrying nuclear weapons or other weapons of mass destruction.[3] In 1963, the General Assembly, through its resolution 1911 (XVIII), approved the denuclearization of Latin America.[4] All these measures were aimed at excluding certain areas, ocean surfaces, and outer space from the deployment of nuclear weapons, which at that time could have been done only by the four nuclear powers. The Antarctic Treaty covered the Southern Ocean south of 60° south latitude. The Tlatelelco Treaty then under discussion also covered vast areas of the Atlantic and the Pacific oceans. The Sri Lanka Prime Minister appears to have been strongly influenced by the above contemporaneous developments in making her proposal.

The issue came up again at the Lusaka Non-Aligned Summit in September 1970. The summit urged adoption of a declaration "calling upon all states to consider and respect the India Ocean as a zone of peace from which Great Power rivalries and competition, as well as bases conceived in the context of such rivalries and competition, either army, navy or air force bases, are excluded. The area should also be free of nuclear weapons."[5]

One could see a subtle change in the formulation about the Indian Ocean between 1964 and 1970. While the earlier formulation focused entirely on the nuclear-free character of the proposed zone, the later formulation broadened the concept and laid more emphasis on great power rivalries and the elimination of bases. The reasons for the shift in emphasis are not difficult to discern. By this time the British Indian Ocean Territory had been formed and a communications facility was under construction in Diego Garcia. The Soviets had started sending their ships into the Indian Ocean and were building up the facility at Berbera. The concept of the Zone of Peace appears to have been derived from the South East Asian Plan for the Zone of Peace, Freedom and Neutrality then under discussion. Prime Minister Gandhi, in her speech at the Lusaka Non-Aligned Summit, referred to the possibility of the military bases of outside powers creating tension and great power rivalry.[6] Again the most fervent advocate of the concept at Lusaka was Prime Minister Sirimavo Bandaranaike of Sri Lanka.

In January 1971, at the Commonwealth summit, Mrs. Bandaranaike circulated a paper stating:

> Recent reports point to an increasing naval presence of the Soviet Union and naval fleets in the Indian Ocean. It would also appear that these fleets carrying nuclear capability are becoming part of the strategic system of the world powers. Another disturbing development is the militarization of the Indian Ocean. The same reports indicate that various islands and land based facilities are being utilized to facilitate the operation of these fleets.[7]

The ministerial meeting of the non-aligned countries in New York in September 1971 agreed that concrete steps should be taken at the 26th Session of the General Assembly to implement the decision relating to the Declaration of the Indian Ocean as a Zone of Peace contained in paragraph 8(b) of Resolution 12 of the Lusaka declaration. The same paragraph of the communiqué declared: "For the preservation of the peace, stability and security of South East Asia, the non-aligned countries urged the neutralization of the area so as to ensure that the region would be free of big power rivalries and interference and that its peace and security as well as the independence and territorial integrity of the states in the region would be fully safeguarded and guaranteed."[8] It was also in 1971 that the Seabed Treaty was concluded, prohibiting the emplacement of nuclear arms or weapons of mass destruction "on the seabed, the ocean floor and in the subsoil thereof."[9]

Underlying the proposal for the Indian Ocean Peace Zone were two major perceptions. First, reflecting the prolonged Vietnam war, was concern about great power intervention and a desire to shield the area from such intervention and rivalry. This concern was reflected in the Kuala Lumpur declaration of November 1971, as well as the Peace Zone move in the U.N. General Assembly in December. The second perception was that following the Antarctic Treaty, the Non-Proliferation Treaty, the Tlatelelco proposals, the Outer Space Treaty, the Seabed Treaty, and proposals for denuclearization of Central Europe, Africa, and the Middle East, it would be logical and possible to persuade the great powers not to deploy their nuclear weapons in the Indian Ocean and not to have forces and facilities in that waterspread.

In the speeches of the Sri Lankan Prime Minister and the Sri Lankan Permanent Representative to the United Nations, H. S. Amerasinghe, who was piloting the resolution in the U.N. General Assembly at that stage, one finds two parallel motivating themes underlying their approach: extending the doctrine of non-alignment from the littoral of the Indian Ocean into the waterspread and applying the concept of a nuclear-weapon-free zone to the Indian Ocean waterspread—an area where circumstances were favorable to adopt such a measure. Mrs. Bandaranaike claimed in her address to the U.N. General Assembly on October 12, 1971, that "the concept of a peace zone is inherent in the concept of non-alignment."[10] Previous approaches to disarmament, said Amerasinghe, had proved "totally inadequate, and some of the measures undertaken under that approach we consider to be blissfully irrelevant: blissfully because they create a false sense of security and lull the world into complacency; irrelevant for the reason that they call for the renunciation of what has already become obsolete or unnecessary, or import limitations or reductions that in no way reduce the arms race."[11] At the same time he emphasized that

> if there are regions of the world where the arms race has not yet assumed menacing proportions and where there is still even a remote possibility of preventing its intrusion, the countries in that region could best serve the cause of peace and their own interests by making a concerted effort to arrest and reverse such developments or forestall them in their region. There is one area of the world that is both historically conditioned to adopt such a policy and where actual circumstances are peculiarly favorable for the adoption of the policy—that is the Indian Ocean area.[12]

During this period India was totally preoccupied with the Bangladesh crisis. The Indian Prime Minister did not attend the Commonwealth conference in January 1971, since she was engaged in the Indian election campaign. The Indian delegation made only a brief intervention in support of the Sri Lanka delegation during the debate in the General Assembly. India did not initially join as a co-sponsor of the December 16 resolution.

The declaration was initially criticized by both Western and Eastern bloc nations. Only in the second half of the 1970s did the Soviet Union start to support the proposal. One of the two initial lines of criticism was that a group of states in a certain region could not establish a legal regime for the high seas in that region. The second line of criticism was that the extra-regional naval presence in the ocean area was required "in the interests of not only the security of the nations concerned but also of the states that rely on the stability created by a political and military balance."[13] Subsequently, in the wake of the oil embargo of 1973, came the justification that the oil lanes had to be protected and access to oil fields secured.

Very often, over-simplified and misleading issues are raised in connection with the Peace Zone issue—whether the advocates of the Peace Zone recognized that Western nations, and particularly the United States, had legitimate interests in the Indian Ocean. The answer has to be a resounding affirmative. All trading nations of the world have legitimate interests in all oceans of the world. There is no doubt that the Soviet Union has as much interest in the waters of the Atlantic and Pacific seaboards of the Western Hemisphere, from which it derives a significant portion of its food imports, as the United States and Western Nations have in the Indian Ocean, where the sources of their oil supply lie. That international shipping lanes should be available for unhindered maritime traffic and that the oil of West Asian oil fields should be accessible to the international community are not issues at all. That they are of universal international interest and, consequently, that there must be international regimes and responsibility for ensuring them are beyond doubt. What is at issue is the preferred method of achieving these objectives.

So far the only occasion when the oil supplies were disrupted was when the nations friendly to the West applied an embargo on Western nations in 1973. On three occasions the shipping lanes have been threatened: once when the Israeli military action closed the Suez Canal for nearly seven years; second, when arms supplied by the Western nations during ongoing hostilities have been used to attack tankers in the Persian Gulf; and thirdly, following the Nicaraguan precedent, when mines were dropped in the Red Sea by an unidentified party. Given these circumstances, it is more logical to ask the question whether all nations who raise objections to the Indian Ocean Peace Zone proposals on grounds of sea lane security and access to oil are really serious about them, or is their intention only to ask the question like jesting Pilate and not care about the answer.

The Antarctic Treaty calls for a regime on the high seas south of 60° south latitude which imposes certain restrictions on the deployment of nuclear-weapon-armed vessels. This Treaty was negotiated, and the legal regime established for the high seas, by a handful of countries including the state that objects to the Indian Ocean Peace Zone proposal as inhibiting nuclear deployments.

The Tlatelelco Treaty provides for a vast Zone of Application—stretching from a point located 35° north latitude, 75° west longitude directly southward to a point at 30° north latitude, 75° west longitude; from there directly eastward to a point at 30° north latitude, 50° west longitude; from there along a loxodromic line to a point at 5° north latitude, 20° west longitude; from there directly southward to a point at 60° south latitude, 20° west longitude; from there directly westward to a point at 60° south latitude, 115° west longitude; from there directly northward to a point of 0° latitude, 115° west longitude; from there along a loxodromic line to a point at 35° north latitude, 150° west longitude; and from there directly eastward to a point at 35° north latitude, 75° west longitude.[14] Perhaps the area of ocean surface included in this is as big at the Indian Ocean, if not bigger. Under Protocol II to the Treaty, the nuclear weapon powers should respect the statute of denuclearization and not introduce or deploy nuclear weapons in this zone. The United States and Great Britain are signatories to this protocol, and at that stage no objection seems to have been raised about a group of nations in a certain region establishing a legal regime for the high seas of that region. It is therefore obvious that this objection is not based on any principle and that the advocates of the Indian Ocean Peace Zone have sound precedents to go on.

The Seabed Treaty and the Outer Space Treaty are non-armament measures in which the nations concerned have agreed not to place nuclear weapons in outer space or on the seabed. The objective underlying the Indian Ocean Peace Zone proposal was to create another ocean, along with the oceans surrounding Latin America and Antarctica, that would be free of nuclear weapon deployment at a time when the introduction of nuclear weapons in the area was at an incipient stage, on the principle of non-armament measures. It would also appear that at that stage many nations naively took seriously the declarations of a desire for non-proliferation by the great powers and felt that an Indian Ocean Peace Zone excluding nuclear weapon deployment in the waterspread, among other things, would be a contribution to the objective of non-proliferation. It was a measure to halt the spatial proliferation of nuclear weapons. It is only in the course of the 1970s that the over-simplistic and naive signatories of the NPT (the bulk of whom are also advocates of the Indian Ocean Peace Zone proposal) realized that they had been persuaded to sign a treaty that violates the basic international norm that all nations of the world are equally entitled to the same categories of weapons of offense and defense, and that a group of states cannot establish a regime in international relations where some nations are entitled to a category of weapons and others are not.

India had a far more realistic view of the game of "non-proliferation" and therefore refused to accept a regime conceived by a few nations violating the basic international norms that all nations are entitled to the same category of weapons for their defense. Nor was India taken in by the concept of a "nuclear-weapon-free zone," which legitimized nuclear weapons in the hands of a few powers. For India, the Indian Ocean Peace Zone proposal was a test of good faith of those nations that loudly proclaimed their non-proliferation objectives day in and day out while proliferating nuclear weapons in absolute numbers, among more formations and platforms and over increasing areas of land and ocean space. India supported the non-proliferation objective and struggled hard to bring about a real commitment to non-proliferation on the part of the nuclear weapon powers. When she failed to achieve this objective, she refused to go along with the Non-proliferation Treaty. So also in the case of the Indian Ocean Peace Zone proposal, India supported the cause of halting the spatial proliferation of nuclear weapons into the Indian Ocean space without any naiveté or exaggerated expectations.

India is clearly opposed to all efforts to extend the proposal to cover any space beyond the oceanspread, or convert it into yet another attempt at disarming the unarmed—the first being the Non-proliferation Treaty. Here the Indian national perspectives may not necessarily be in total congruence with the non-aligned perspective projected in the United Nations and the non-aligned conferences where the procedure of consensus applies.

Many of the Western criticisms of the non-aligned approach to the Indian Ocean Peace Zone proposal are valid and justified. The extension of the Peace Zone proposal from the waterspread to littoral and hinterland countries lacks realism. The Indian concept of the proposal would not immediately disrupt alliance arrangements like ANZUS. If the proposal were to be extended to littoral and hinterland states, it would bring the territories of Australia and Israel within its purview. It is evident that such an approach would not constitute a step-by-step approach. It was one thing to ask the navies of extra-regional powers not to be deployed on the oceanspread on missions oriented toward the Indian Ocean area and to exclude nuclear weapons, and quite another to embark upon dismantling the existing alliance arrangements. The littoral nations that tried to extend the concept of the Peace Zone from the waterspread to the littoral and the hinterland states either did not comprehend the full consequences of the proposal or were doing so to sabotage the original proposal.

Similarly, the idea of the Indian Ocean denuclearization being extended to the littoral states was a non-starter. Australia, as a member of the ANZUS, was providing facilities to U.S. nuclear-armed vessels and had extensive facilities for command, control, communication, and intelligence relating to nuclear weapons. Israel had been a nuclear weapon power since 1968. The Indian proposal of restricting the Peace Zone to only the waterspread would have been implementable in spite of the status of Australia and Israel; but the overlay on the Peace Zone proposal introduced by Sri Lanka and Pakistan, that it should also extend to denuclearization of all littoral countries, made it unimplementable in view of the above.

Attempts have been made to prescribe conflict resolution mechanisms in the Indian Ocean littoral stipulating that the countries of the littoral and hinterland should also undertake arms control measures concerning their conventional, especially naval, armaments. Such efforts display an extreme degree of naiveté on the part of the advocates of such proposals. Their premise is that the new states of Asia and Africa, which have yet to achieve stability as nation-states, would be able to avoid the whole range of security problems during the period of their evolution that the European states could not avoid during three centuries of their evolution. This assumption ignores the basic fact that out of 120 instances of major inter- and intrastate violence during the period 1945–1975, only 16 were inter-state wars in the developing world. Most of the conflicts in the developing world arise out of the very process of evolution into modern nation-states. With the exception of the oil-rich countries of West Asia and relatively affluent developing nations, the bulk of the developing nations have had very modest defense expenditures not incommensurate with their actual needs. In addition, interventionism by various great powers adds to the security problems of developing countries. We are living in an age where great powers have created for themselves instrumentalities that are meant to give to the governments concerned vis-à-vis other nations options ranging from sending a protest note to landing the marines. Many of the littoral countries face problems of insurgency where very often there is external support to insurgents. The turbulence in one developing country spills across borders to the neighboring ones. With the jurisdiction of nation-states extended into the Exclusive Economic Zones (EEZ) under the Law of the Sea, the need to patrol and exercise control over those zones has become imperative, which in many cases calls for reinforcing a nation's naval capabilities. For these reasons, the prescriptions of conflict resolution mechanisms among the developing nations of the littoral and mutual force reductions at this stage have been far too simplistic.

While such criticisms against the attempts to add on to the Indian Ocean Peace Zone resolution are justified, the original resolution itself, restricted to the water surface, did not suffer from any of these infirmities and is therefore a worthwhile arms control measure. These very often well-meaning but impractical additions to the original concept provided adequate opportunities to the great powers to exploit the differences among the littoral nations and frustrate the proposal. Subsequently, in the wake of the 1973 oil crisis and oil price revisions, two developments arising out of them made it even more difficult to implement the Peace Zone proposal. The oil price hike made many developing nations of the littoral increasingly dependent on affluent Western nations for energy aid. Second, the oil-exporting nations of the Gulf, in light of their affluence, developed an acute sense of insecurity and a security dependence on great powers—especially the United States. Consequently, both categories of nations initiated a process of diluting the concept of the Indian Ocean as a Zone of Peace even while not giving it up formally.

Why the 1977–78 Negotiations Failed

The Peace Zone proposal was initiated at a time when détente was making progress, and perhaps the underlying hope of leaders like Mrs. Bandaranaike was that her proposal would extend détente to the Indian Ocean. It did not take very long for the non-aligned leaders to realize that a partial détente, limited to Europe alone, would not last long, and they did come out with a warning to this effect in the Algiers summit and in the Colombo summit.[15] The progress of détente was a necessary, if not sufficient, condition to realize the concept of the Indian Ocean as a Zone of Peace. A realist in the non-aligned world could easily see that as détente started eroding it was not going to be easy to implement the proposal of the Indian Ocean Peace Zone.

The high point of hope on the Peace Zone concept came when President Carter made his proposal for the demilitarization of the Indian Ocean in his news conference of March 9, 1977. Within 10 days, however, he had diluted his stand, and on March 19, 1977, he talked of hoping to establish with the Soviets "mutual military restraint in the Indian Ocean." On March 24, 1977, the Soviet President Kosygin responded to this offer during his tour of Africa, declaring that the Soviet Union was willing to discuss demilitarization of the Indian Ocean. On March 29, 1977, during Secretary of State Cyrus Vance's visit to Moscow, U.S.-Soviet working groups were set up to consider demilitarization of the Indian Ocean and curbs on arms sales to developing nations. Paul Warnke, the head of the U.S. Arms Control and Disarmament Agency, said at the end of his visit to Moscow on June 22–27 that both sides had been quite encouraged on the issue of demilitarization of the Indian Ocean.

At the second round of talks, in Washington in September 1977, the Soviets were reported to have proposed a ban on the deployment of ships and submarines armed with nuclear weapons in the Indian Ocean. According to a report in the *New York Times* of November 20, 1977, they appeared to have accepted a U.S. proposal to prohibit either country from significantly altering the size or character of its naval force currently in the ocean. On October 4, 1977, President Carter told the U.N. General Assembly that neither the United States nor the Soviet Union had a large military presence there, and that there was no rapidly mounting competition between the two nations. He added: "Restraint in the area may well begin with a mutual effort to stabilize our presence and to avoid an escalation in military competition. Then both sides can consider how our military activities in the Indian Ocean—the whole area—might be even further reduced." The third round of U.S.-Soviet talks on demilitarization took place in Berne, Switzerland, in December 1977. A joint communiqué was issued describing the talks as positive.

By February 1978, following the Soviet-aided Ethiopian counter-offensive against the Somali-backed guerrillas in Ogaden, Secretary of State Vance indicated that the United States was slowing down efforts to reach an agreement on demilitarizing the Indian Ocean, in retaliation for the Soviet presence in Ethiopia. On March 1, 1978, the U.S. National Security Adviser, Zbigniew Brzezinski, said the Soviet actions in Ethiopia could affect negotiations for a SALT agreement. Though he denied that the United States was deliberately tying the outcome of SALT to the Horn of Africa conflict, he pointed out that "linkages may be imposed by the unwarranted exploitation of local conflicts for larger international purposes." The next day, President Carter echoed Brzezinski's views in a news conference. *Pravda* called Brzezinski's remark crude blackmail impermissible in international relations. Vice President Mondale, addressing the U.N. Special Session on Disarmament on May 24, 1978, charged that in the Indian Ocean, naval presence there have hampered talks aimed at demilitarizing the area. On December 15, 1978, in Mexico City, the United States broke off talks on limiting sales of conventional arms since the United States was not willing to discuss U.S. arms sales in the Indian Ocean region. In June 1979, President Carter promised the Soviet side that talks on the Indian Ocean would be resumed in the near future.[16] But since SALT II, initialed in June 1979, was never ratified, there was no question of a resumption of the Indian Ocean talks. This is a brief account of publicly known facts on the U.S. initiative on developing an arms control arrangement in the Indian Ocean area in 1977–78.

There was no doubt that in the U.S. perception, any arms control arrangement in the Indian Ocean was to be related to U.S. global policy vis-à-vis the Soviet Union and was not to be a local regional arrangement. Brzezinski recalls

> the day sometime in 1978 when . . . I advocated that we send in a carrier task force in reaction to the Soviet deployment of the Cubans in Ethiopia. At that meeting not only was I opposed by Vance, but Harold Brown asked why, for what reason, without taking into account that it is a question that should perplex the Soviets rather than us. The President backed the others rather than me and we did not react. Subsequently, as the Soviets became more emboldened, we overreacted, particularly in the Cuban Soviet brigade fiasco. . . . That derailed SALT. The momentum of SALT was lost and the final nail in the coffin was the Soviet invasion of Afghanistan. In brief, underreaction then bred overreaction. That is why I have used occasionally the phrase *"SALT lies buried in the sands of the Ogaden."*[17]

Underlying the above was Brzezinski's worldview of the Soviet Union and the developing world. He felt that the Soviet strategic goal of détente was to deter the United States from responding effectively to the changing political balance and that the Soviets subtly combined elements of cooperation and competition, not to preserve the status quo but to transform it. Yet, according to Brzezinski:

> this Soviet thrust toward global preeminence was less likely to lead to a Pax Sovietica than to international chaos. The Soviet Union might hope to displace America from its leading role in the international system but it was too weak economically and too unappealing politically to itself assume that position. This was the ultimately self-defeating element in the Soviet policy. It could exploit global anarchy but was unlikely to be able to transform it to its own enduring advantage.[18]

In this view, a comprehensive and reciprocal détente required making it unmistakably clear that the Soviet Union must behave "responsibly" on fundamental issues of global order. Détente was incompatible with irresponsible behavior in Angola, the Middle East, and the United Nations (e.g., stimulation of extremist resolutions such as the one equating Zionism with racism).[19]

This harping on responsible behavior on the part of the Soviet Union with respect to developments in the Third World was not only Brzezinski's view. The linkage thesis, based on the same premise, was reiterated by Secretary of State George Shultz in June 1983.[20] This is in a sense a continuation of the bipolar worldview—wherever the United States was not acting in the Third World, the Soviet Union should be. It never occurred to Dr. Brzezinski and others who think like him to ask themselves how could Saudi Arabia and Egypt and other Arab states very close to the United States be stimulated by the Soviet Union to pass a resolution equating Zionism with racism. This lack of comprehension of the degree of autonomy of developing nations naturally leads to a view of the international system as a bipolar zero sum game. The United States was not prepared to discuss its arms supplies to the Indian Ocean nations (including deputing tens of thousands of advisers) with the Soviet Union but felt that Soviet support to Ethiopia in repelling Somali aggression (made possible partly by the Soviet supply of arms to that country) was not compatible with the spirit of the negotiations on Indian Ocean demilitarization.

It would appear that the U.S. intention in engaging the Soviet Union in the Indian Ocean talks was to freeze the status quo both in the ocean and on the littoral. Since the status quo was not likely to be frozen—not because of Soviet intervention, but due to the inevitable changes within the developing world—the negotiations based on such an unrealistic premise were foredoomed to failure.

The Soviet Union's approach to the Indian Ocean is largely influenced by the threat it perceives to its homeland and its borders from the activities of the United States. As far back at 1968, Moscow proposed that agreement may be reached for the cessation of patrols by submarines with nuclear missiles on board in areas where the borders of parties to the agreement are within range of such missiles. Mentioning this,[21] the SIPRI Yearbook 1972 says that it would perhaps be incorrect to draw the conclusion that this implied a proposal for the withdrawal of fleets, but it could imply an offer for a reciprocal limitation of military activity of the big powers in the oceans. In June 1971, the Secretary General of the Soviet Communist Party indicated Soviet preparedness to discuss the presence of the big powers' naval forces far from their own coasts and to solve this problem by making an equal bargain. He referred specifically to the Mediterranean Sea and the Indian Ocean.[22] A joint Indo-Soviet statement during the visit of the Indian Prime Minister to Moscow in September 1971 recorded the Soviet readiness to consider and settle the problem of peace in the Indian Ocean.[23] Similarly, the joint declaration issued in 1973 during Brezhnev's visit to India stressed the readiness of the two countries to work toward a favorable solution to the question of making the Indian Ocean a Zone of Peace.[24] Soviet Foreign Minister Andrei Gromyko said in the U.N. General Assembly in 1982 that if the question of foreign military bases in the Indian Ocean was solved, the Soviet Union was prepared to seek ways to reduce on a reciprocal basis the military activity of the non-littoral states in the Indian Ocean and the adjacent regions.[25] In 1977, in the U.N. General Assembly, the Soviet Union proposed to the nuclear powers to enter into negotiations to agree on the withdrawal of ships carrying nuclear weapons from some parts of the world ocean including the Indian Ocean.[26] The Soviet Union, in contrast to the U.S., supported the proposal to convene an international conference on the Indian Ocean.

On May 15, 1980, the Warsaw Treaty countries voiced their support of the proposal to turn the Indian Ocean into a Zone of Peace.[27] In December 1980, Brezhnev, during his visit to Delhi, proposed negotiations to assure the security of tanker traffic in the Persian Gulf.[28] This was subsequently elaborated to include a discussion on the international aspects of the Afghan problem. At the twenty-sixth meeting of the CPSU Congress in February 1981, the Soviet Union advanced the following proposals:[29]

> *not* to set up foreign bases in the Persian Gulf region and the adjacent islands; not to station nuclear or other mass destructive weapons there;
>
> *not* to use or threaten to use force against the countries in the Persian Gulf and not to interfere in their domestic affairs;
>
> *to* respect the non-aligned status chosen by states in the Gulf; not to involve them in military groupings with the participation of nuclear powers;
>
> *to* respect the sovereign right of the states in the region to their natural resources;
>
> *not* to create any obstacles or threats to normal trade exchanges or the use of marine communications linking the states in the region to other countries.

All this does not mean that the Soviet Union supports the Indian Ocean Peace Zone proposal as formulated by the littoral nations. The Soviet Union has frequently expressed its misgivings about freedom of navigation under the Peace Zone dispensation.[30] Second, the Soviet Union strongly resents the phrase "great power rivalry" used in the Peace Zone declaration.[31] Rivalry, according to the Soviets, is between two colonial powers. The socialist Soviet Union does not indulge in rivalry with the United States. Their actions in various littoral countries, such as arms transfers, they argue, help the concerned developing countries to stand up to pressures from the West. They have also been assisting national liberation movements in Angola, Mozambique, and Rhodesia. In terminological terms, they also maintain that they do not have "bases" in Dahlak or Aden. They attempt to explain their actions and policy in terms of ideology.

For most non-aligned nations—including those friendly toward the Soviet Union—the Soviet actions could be fitted into a framework of national interest defined in conventional terms, and therefore they tend to stick to the term "rivalry," much to the annoyance of the Soviets. While for reasons mentioned earlier, the Soviets would not mind denuclearization of the littoral states, India does not view the proposal with favor. The Soviets at the same time would agree to the Indian Ocean waterspread being freed of extra-regional nuclear-weapon carriers, since that would remove the U.S. threat from the Indian Ocean, and in this they have a mutuality of interests with India. The Soviet Union has significantly contributed to the strengthening of the Indian navy and does not go along with the views of those littoral nations that press for a freeze on the naval strengths of the littoral nations.

The style of approach of the two superpowers to the Peace Zone proposal is determined not only by their respective perceptions of their interests, but also by their self-images. The United States considers itself the manager of the present international order and the current system of international security. The Soviet Union considers itself as the manager of change, and as the weaker of the two superpowers it needs to have a united front with the developing nations wherever possible. The United States does not favor arms control proposals "not invented here." Hence, it approved of the Antarctic, Tlatelelco, and Seabed treaties, all of which developed regimes for parts or whole of the world oceans. In the case of the Indian Ocean Peace Zone proposal, the United States is not willing to forgo the current asymmetric strategic advantages conferred on it by the Indian Ocean providing a strategic deployment area vis-à-vis the Soviet Union. The asymmetry will be attenuated and there will be greater balance when Soviet aircraft carriers are able to operate in the ocean space south of the United States and the Soviet Union gets increased access facilities to ports in Latin America. This situation is not likely to come about before the mid-1990s.

The Prospects for Indian Ocean Arms Control

This is a retrospective analysis of arms control attempts relating to the Indian Ocean. Looking ahead, the prospects for progress toward the goal of the Indian Ocean Peace Zone do not appear to be bright in the near term.

First and foremost among the examples of growing militarization of the region is the establishment of the U.S. Central Command with its operational jurisdiction over 19 nations and its Joint Rapid Deployment Task Force. Brzezinski has disclosed that the Rapid Deployment Force was initiated by Presidential Directive 18, signed on August 24, 1977. This was a consequence of the emphasis given by the more influential section in the U.S. security establishment to the momentum and character of Soviet military programs, the vulnerability of the oil-rich Persian Gulf, and the growing Soviet projection of power in Africa and Asia. In other words, the Rapid Deployment Force was not a response to Soviet intervention in Afghanistan, but perhaps was being created in anticipation of Soviet actions. Brzezinski himself agrees that the Soviets took the RDF and the MX missile seriously.[32] In that event, one wonders whether the permanent stationing of a carrier task force in the Indian Ocean since January 1979, in the wake of the fall of the Shah of Iran; the creation of the RDF; the exclusion of the Soviet Union from the Arab-Israeli settlement; the indefinite postponement of the Indian Ocean and conventional arms transfer talks; the Brzezinski strategic overtures in China; and, finally, the Iranian hostage crisis with the expectation of U.S. intervention, all taken together, did not trigger off the panicky Soviet intervention in Afghanistan.

On the other side, it is also possible to argue that the Soviet switch of support to Ethiopia, the coup in South Yemen replacing Robbaya Ali, and the increasing Soviet arms flow into Iraq aroused U.S. alarm about pressure on Saudi Arabia and the Gulf oil fields. This may in turn be traced to the overtures of Sadat, the Shah, and the Saudis (all pro-West) in trying to wean Siad Barre, Robbaya Ali, and Sardar Daud away from their alignment with the Soviet Union. The likely Soviet reaction to the neocontainment policy of President Carter was predicted accurately by William Hyland in late 1979.[33]

So long as the U.S. perception of the international system is that it has to manage it all by itself, that the Soviet Union is out to exploit global anarchy in a self-defeating manner, and that the entire developing world is a mere object of competition between the two superpowers, a realistic arms control system in the Indian Ocean area will be difficult to achieve. As mentioned earlier, the arms control measures achieved so far are of two categories. The first category consists of non-armament measures undertaken before arms were introduced into an area. The Antarctic Treaty, the Outer Space Treaty, the Seabed Treaty, and even the Tlatelelco Treaty, which has not come into force, belong to this category. The Indian Ocean littoral nations tried to bring in the Peace Zone proposal under this categorization. Now it is no longer possible to do so, since the introduction of the permanent U.S. carrier task force in the Indian Ocean, the setting up of the U.S. Central Command, and the conversion of the Diego Garcia facility into a full-fledged base. If the United States is to dismantle all these, the Soviet Union has to match it with similar reductions in arms either in the Indian Ocean area or somewhere else where the United States has vital interests threatened by analogous Soviet actions. That is not likely for quite some time to come.

Second, certain new developments involving the southern oceans in global superpower strategy are also likely to come in the way of an arms control arrangement restricted only to the Indian Ocean. In the potential use of outer space for its global strategy, the United States has a vital need for the Indian Ocean. This is the case with respect to real-time reconnaissance; real-time navigation; command, control and communications; battlefield management; and strategic warfare, including the proposed ballistic missile defense. The U.S. Groundbased Electro-Optical Deep Space Surveillance (GEODSS) system will scan the globe with the ability to spot a one-foot-diameter object from an altitude of 25,000 miles. Of the five GEODSS systems planned by the United States, one is being established in Diego Garcia.[34]

Of late, the United States has been developing satellite interception systems based on the use of a miniature homing vehicle (MHV) fired from a F-15 aircraft. Soviet reconnaissance satellites are usually at much lower altitudes than U.S. satellites. They also have highly elliptical orbits, with their perigees over the Southern Hemisphere to permit longer dwell time over the Northern Hemisphere. Therefore, for maximum effectiveness, the U.S. interception of Soviet satellites has to take place over the Southern Hemisphere, when they will be at their lower altitudes. Defense Secretary Weinberger has stated in his FY 1985 Congressional Budget testimony that "F-15 aircraft, from which the MHV will be launched, could be based in the southern hemisphere for 'attempted intercepts' of satellites in highly elliptical orbits with perigees in the South."[35] If the militarization of outer space goes forward, there is a high probability that the United States will use the Indian Ocean and Diego Garcia for satellite interception. If this hypothesis is correct, then the chances of an arms control arrangement requiring dismantling of Diego Garcia facilities are bleak.[36]

Third, given the massive size of the forces allotted to the U.S. Central Command in the Indian Ocean, it is reasonable to expect that the Soviets will develop measures over a period of time to create uncertainties for the use of such massive forces in areas adjacent to its southern borders, which have been included in the operational jurisdiction of the Central Command. This may involve counter-deployment of Soviet carriers (of the type now under construction) and an increase in the number of Soviet submarines armed with surface skimmer missiles and cruise missiles in the Indian Ocean area. In turn, this may necessitate the Soviets securing further infrastructure support for such deployment beyond Aden and Dahlak.

Yet another complicating factor is the likelihood of the Chinese deploying their missile submarines in the second-strike mode against the Soviet Union in the Arabian Sea. This again is likely to lead to increased deployment of Soviet ASW forces, both in the Indian Ocean and the South China Sea.

If these developments take place, then there is likely to be a sizeable Soviet naval power deployment in the Indian Ocean, and Southwest and South Asia will find themselves trapped between the massive Soviet land power and a significant Soviet seapower. If the traditionalist perceptions regarding the impact of military power and its suasive potency were to be accepted, one would have to consider what the balance of influence will be in these regions of Asia under those circumstances, and whether U.S. naval power and the RDF would balance both Soviet land power and seapower deployed in the Indian Ocean.

This author does not accept the basic premise of the utility of military power in various circumstances as envisaged by the advocates of seapower and intervention. But those who pursue policies based on such perceptions will have to ponder emerging changes in the regional environment. One is reminded of the situation in 1972 when SALT I was signed. At that stage there was a distinct opportunity of banning the MIRVing of the missiles. But the United States passed that opportunity by because of its confidence that it would be able to maintain the technological lead vis-à-vis the Soviet Union in respect to MIRVs for many years. When the latter rapidly caught up with MIRV technology and started to put multiple warheads on its missiles, there was a great hue and cry about the throw weight of the Soviet missiles and the window of vulnerability of the U.S. land-based missiles.[37] One wonders, similarly, whether those who argue today in favor of balancing the Soviet military superiority on land with a naval presence in the Indian Ocean will not regret their stand when the Soviet Union begins to deploy aircraft carrier groups in the Indian Ocean.

It is often said that many of the littoral states, whatever they may say in public on the Zone of Peace proposal, do want to have a U.S. military presence—if not an adjacently visible one, at least one over the horizon. This is no doubt true, as judged by a near total lack of protest from the countries concerned over the establishment of the Central Command. But the central question is what is the nature of the threat faced by these countries and whether the measures adopted by the United States will serve the U.S. national interests and international interests. Or, alternatively, will they prove counterproductive, as happened in Iran?

Most U.S. writers as well as the leaders of the littoral states have said that a direct Soviet invasion is one of the least likely contingencies. Most of the insecurity arises out of fears about their own neighbors or domestic upheavals. In the case of domestic upheaval in a large and populous nation like Iran, it is evident that the United States cannot intervene without having to face an unacceptable level of casualties. This was the case even in much smaller Lebanon. No doubt, there are a number of small countries with very small populations where intervention against domestic upheaval is possible. But every time such an intervention takes place, it contributes to the rise of tension in the area and provides opportunities for the rival superpower to extend its influence in certain other small countries of the area. Activities in Oman result in rival activities in South Yemen. Securing influence and facilities in Somalia and Kenya lead to the rival extending its influence in Ethiopia. It would be useful to do a cost-benefit analysis of the policy of active interventionism vis-à-vis a policy of mutual restraint.

Similar considerations hold in regard to the sense of insecurity experienced by these developing countries vis-à-vis their neighbors. Wars in the developing world cannot be fought over a period of time without resupply operations from the industrialized countries. There are a few developing countries that can supply certain categories of arms and ammunition, but they are unlikely to do so if there are sufficient pressures from the major powers. It is also obvious from the experience of the Iran-Iraq war that when wars are fought with such extensive reliance on outside sources for material, it is not possible to have decisions on the battlefront. It only results in episodic engagements and casualties and the front does not move much.

The Iran-Iraq war has also demonstrated a number of other conclusions that are yet to have an impact on the political consciousness of the world. It proved that the sense of nationalism prevailed over religious and ethnic affinity. This happened when the Iraqis invaded Khuzistan and the Arab population of Khuzistan did not rise in revolt against the Khomeini regime and join them. Also, when the Iranians crossed the border in a counteroffensive, the Shia population of Iraq did not rise against the Baghdad regime.

Second, the war also demonstrated the limitations of powerful armadas of industrialized nations in securing the safety of maritime traffic. When a country imposes a blockade or declares a war zone and starts attacking vessels in that zone it is acting entirely within international law, and it becomes difficult to intervene without running the risk of having to participate in the hostilities. In other words, when the sea lanes are seriously threatened, it is not possible to intervene without extending the hostilities. However, the question does arise about the credibility of the stand of industrialized nations that talk of the safety of oil lanes and at the same time supply the missiles and aircraft to attack the ships.

Third, the fears regarding access to oil and other strategic minerals being denied appear to be unfounded. Presumably, these fears originate from the memories of the imperialist era, when a metropolitan power could prevent the export of vital minerals from the colonies without undue concern for the interests of the peoples of the colonies. Such denial of access to strategic minerals is no longer a valid proposition because most of the newly emerged nations depend upon such exports of oil and other raw materials to maintain their economies. Any such denial of access to vital minerals will result in adverse impact on their economies and the employment situation within these countries. Looking back on the oil crisis of 1973, it is quite obvious that it only had a demonstration effect and could not have been continued for long. In any case, today most of the oil producers are hostages to threats of sequestration, the precipitous fall in their living standards, and threats of very serious internal social disruption if they are to resort to any embargo.

In these circumstances, while granting the interests of the United States and the rest of the industrialized world in access to oil and the security of sea lanes to and from West Asia, the real issue is what is the best method of ensuring those interests. The excessive emphasis on military means appears to overlook the changes that have come about in a world that had had no historical precedent—totally decolonized, entirely covered by nation-states, and with a much higher level of political consciousness than ever before. The military-oriented approach appears to have underlying it the worldview of the early twentieth century, which is today totally obsolete. The U.S. perception about the developing world and the Soviet Union is distorted in three ways. First, there is a general trend to interpret the international transactions as a bipolar zero sum game between the United States and the Soviet Union, with not enough allowance made for the autonomy of the function and decision making of developing countries. Second, the degree of integration of the Soviet Union into the international system and economy has not been appreciated, and the view that the Soviet Union is out to exploit the anarchy in the international system is an extrapolation of the image of the Stalinist Kremlin, which talked of the collapse of the capitalist system and the socialist bloc emerging victorious. Third, while all the time the West talks of the Soviet Union not having anything to offer to the developing world other than weapons, the emphasis of the West itself has been on military competition with the Soviets and not in terms of competition in economic and technological development in the developing world. These are areas in which Moscow is not in a position to compete, and yet these areas have not been exploited adequately by the West.

Having been decolonized recently, the developing nations are sensitive about their autonomy in political and economic spheres. Most of them would like to be self-reliant in respect to their security and development. It is only the regimes with very narrow bases that would like to depend on extra-regional powers for their security. With regard to development, most of the developing countries have reservations in dealing with multinationals and private capital. After the recent experience of the debt crisis engulfing many developing countries, there will be greater awareness about the risks of launching on this path of development. For the countries of the developing world, the United States has the image of an inheritor of the mantle of the colonial powers. Hence, the countervailing power of the Soviet Union is looked upon as a major factor in sustaining the autonomy of the developing nations. This image is further reinforced by the respective attitudes adopted by the United States and the Soviet Union toward national liberation movements and apartheid.

There is nothing to substantiate the view that the Kremlin is out to exploit anarchy in the world. The days when the Soviet Union could claim to be the center of communism are gone and the history of the last four decades shows that national interests override ideological affinity. Yugoslavia, North Korea, China, and Albania highlight the fact that a Marxist government need not necessarily be a pro-Soviet government. As Dr. Brzezinski himself has said, Marxism today does not provide an attractive political or economic model for most of the countries of the world. For the Soviets to attempt to extend their influence by exploiting the mistakes of the United States is no more illegitimate than for Washington to do the same vis-à-vis the Soviet Union in Egypt, Sudan, or Somalia. The country that swears by competition should be able to understand the view of non-aligned nations that a world managed by two like-minded superpowers is not in their interest and that a certain amount of competition between the two superpowers is good for the autonomous functioning of the developing nations. Consequently, most of the developing nations are unable to subscribe to the idea of a world order managed by one superpower or jointly by two like-minded superpowers. The complaint about the Soviet Union in the developing world is that it is too much status-quo oriented and that the competition between the two superpowers is not based on ideology but on power considerations. Thus, on the Non-Proliferation Treaty, the two superpowers are in agreement. On the Law of the Sea, there was not much disagreement between them on many issues during the negotiating stage. On the North-South dialogue and global economic negotiations, the Soviets stay on the sidelines and controversy is between the Western industrial nations and the developing nations. So also on issues such as apartheid, Namibia, and Palestine, where the Soviet Union only supports the developing nations and is not a main contender. Therefore, the view that the Soviet Union is out to exploit anarchy in the world does not make sense.

There is a view that the developing nations are pliable client states liable to be manipulated by either of the two superpowers. But, on the contrary, the antagonism between the two superpowers and their predictable, mutually hostile behavior are often manipulated by developing nations for their own parochial purposes. That Israel calls the shots in the Middle East situation is the perception of most of the Arab states (including solidly pro-Western states like Saudi Arabia and Jordan). Siad Barre of Somalia felt that in a situation in which two superpowers countervailed each other and Ethiopia lost the support of the United States, the time was opportune to seize Ogaden. Saddam Hussein of Iraq thought that against the background of the superpowers countervailing each other and U.S.-Iran hostility, the opportunity was ripe to settle scores with Iran. South Africa plays a similar game vis-à-vis its black neighbors. That some of the local states and regimes rely on extra-regional powers for their security vis-à-vis their neighbors is only half the truth. The other half is that some of the local powers attempt to manipulate the predictable cold war behavior pattern of the superpowers to their advantage. It will not help to nurture the egos of the superpowers' strategic establishments to face this unpleasant reality. Therefore, the tendency is to cling to obsolete stereotypes.

Let us now analyze the proposition that the littoral nations depend on extra-regional powers for their security vis-à-vis their neighbors. Of the 43 littoral and hinterland states of the Indian Ocean, 19 have populations over 10 million; 6, between 5 and 10 million; 7, between 1 and 5 million; and 11 have populations of less than a million. Most of these countries have faced various kinds of security problems—conflicts with neighbors (India, Pakistan, Afghanistan, Thailand, Malaysia, Idonesia, Iran, Iraq, Jordan, Egypt, Somalia, Ethiopia, Mozambique, Lesotho, Botswana), insurgencies (Thailand, Malaysia, Indonesia, Burma, Bangladesh, India, Pakistan, Afghanistan, Sri Lanka, Iran, Iraq, Oman, Sudan, Ethiopia, Kenya, Uganda, Mozambique, Zimbabwe), attempted coups (the Maldives, the Seychelles, the Comoros, Kenya, Pakistan, Iran, Iraq, Saudi Arabia, Egypt, Sudan, Somalia), secessionist movements, religious strifes, tribal conflicts, border claims by neighbors. This is not an unnatural situation. The European and North American nations went through such conflicts over a period of well over three centuries when they were evolving into nation-statehood. It resulted in two world wars and there is a semblance of stability today among them only under the threat of nuclear annihilation. In spite of that, problems such as Quebec, Northern Ireland, Basque and Croatian secessionism, and Greek-Turkish conflict persist. It is nobody's contention that these conflicts would justify the Soviet navy patrolling off the coasts of Quebec, the Irish Sea, the Gulf of Valencia, and the Adriatic. The developing world is bound to be turbulent for decades to come, till the developing nations settle down as stable nation-states. All of them are bound to have a sense of insecurity during this period. The issue is whether the presence of the navies of extra-regional powers and their force deployments in the area will help to stabilize the situation or add to tension, and whether the interventionist use of or demonstration of force will be in the interest of the powers concerned and international peace and security. No amount of external naval presences and force availabilities will stabilize the situations in the developing nations any more than did their having been colonies for nearly two centuries. The colonial powers decolonized when they found that it was no longer cost-effective to continue colonial occupation, mainly because of the rising tide of political consciousness in the developing world. The same heightened political consciousness makes the use or demonstration of force by extra-regional powers in the developing world increasingly dysfunctional.

Much has been written in the West about Admiral Alfred Mahan and the power of suasion and flexibility of naval power. Mahan wrote about a world when a major portion of its population did not resist colonial occupation. That world no longer exists. Today the U.S.S. *New Jersey*'s one-ton shells have failed to persuade the Druzes in the Lebanese hills to fall in line with U.S. wishes. The mighty naval presence of U.S. and Allied navies in the Indian Ocean had no influence on the course of the Iran-Iraq war, nor did it prevent someone from dropping mines in the Red Sea. One could also ask whether the nearby presence of the U.S. navy had any influence on the developments in the Central American states. It is not the contention here that in all these cases the intervening power applied the full force of which it was capable, and it is difficult to predict what would have happened if more force had been applied. But it is no longer possible to argue that naval power can be readily applied to various situations to influence developments on land. This is not the simple and straightforward proposition it used to be when Britannia ruled the waves.

In present-day circumstances it is difficult to envisage a developing country marching into another and occupying large areas with large populations, except in exceptional circumstances (as happened in Bangladesh, Uganda, and Kampuchea, where the invading forces were hailed as liberators and genocidal tyrant rulers were replaced). In all other cases, keeping a population under occupation is very costly—costlier than the invasion itself. Therefore, in cases of countries with very small areas and populations, the occupation of foreign territories involving large populations is not a cost-effective proposition. This was the lesson of Vietnam, Afghanistan, and Lebanon. Even Israel would not be able to continue its occupation of the West Bank if it were to bear the costs all by itself.

Therefore, the real and more probable security threats the larger developing nations face among themselves are not outright invasion and occupation but mostly border incursion, support to insurgents, or a neighbor attempting to settle scores on limited objectives. No doubt mini- and micro-states, of which there are 15 in the Indian Ocean hinterland and littoral, are vulnerable to occupation à la Grenada. They are Bahrain, Bhutan, Botswana, the Comoros, Djibouti, Kuwait, Lesotho, the Maldives, Mauritius, Oman, Qatar, the Seychelles, Singapore, Swaziland, and the United Arab Emirates. Some of them are vulnerable to a takeover even by a few hundred men, as was attempted in the Comoros and the Seychelles. The risks they face are not different from that of 60–65 other mini- and micro-states of the international system. All these states depend upon the U.N. system and the international norms for their security, and not on the proximity of some powerful navies. The thesis that some countries of the region rely on the stability created by the political and military balance resulting from extra-regional naval power can be extended to the Western Hemisphere, Africa, and the South Pacific to justify the naval expansion of certain powers to countervail the current dominant naval presence of one power.

It is no doubt true that the limitations on the use of military power by one populous developing nation against another has not been adequately grasped. Most of the elites in the developing world do believe in the conventional wisdom of the possibility of an unconstrained use of force, including the naval force, against themselves. If the constraints are highlighted, some of them fall back upon the argument of hegemonism without explaining how such hegemonism could be exercised by a developing country. Most of these fears are due to the mechanical transposition of analogies of exercise of power by current superpowers and great powers in the colonial era.

However, though it has not been articulated explicitly, an increasing awareness is gaining currency that many of the problems of insecurity of the developing nations cannot be adequately tackled through security linkages with superpowers. Hence the ambivalence displayed by many of the developing nations that maintain security linkages with great powers while also subscribing to the doctrine of non-alignment.

There is bound to be a time lag between the reality of a development on the ground and the full understanding of its implications by military professionals, strategic thinkers, and political leaders. This happens to be the case with respect to the use of force in international relations. Such a lag in understanding with respect to the colonial situation led to costly colonial wars like the first and second Indochinese wars, the Algerian war, and wars in Mozambique, Angola, and Zimbabwe. Similarly, the political and military establishments of the major powers have yet to realize that in a world of nuclear weapons, with two mutually countervailing power centers, the developing nations have more maneuverability to frustrate the use of force against them by either of the two superpowers than was possible when Mahan wrote his thesis. Vietnam, Afghanistan, Central America, and Lebanon exemplify the application of conventional politico-military thought to a world where current political realities have made the conventional wisdom wholly irrelevant. The task before us today is to bridge this enormous gap between the realities and the policies pursued on the basis of assumptions wholly out of date. At the same time, so long as the major powers of the world act on such obsolete assumptions, the nations who are adversely affected by their policies have to take countermeasures to influence the perceptions of the intervening powers and attenuate the impact of their interventionism.

India and the United States have common interests in ensuring the freedom of the seas, access to the oil resources of West Asia, and safeguarding the sea lanes. Indeed, the entire world can be united in pursuit of these objectives, as in the case of environmental pollution, acid rain, and the warming of the atmosphere. It is a conflictual approach to international relations that leads to a perception that access to energy materials or safeguarding of sea lanes should be the concern of one set of nations to the exclusion of another set of nations. In turn, this appears to be based on a certain moralistic approach. The Indian view has been that these matters of common interest are capable of solution on the basis of the collective approach exemplified during the enactment of the Law of the Sea Treaty.

Notes

1. *Two Decades of Nonalignment* (New Delhi: The Ministry of External Affairs, 1983), p. 23.

2. *SIPRI Year Book, 1968/69, World Armaments and Disarmament* (Stockholm: International Peace Institute), pp. 298–99.

3. Ibid., p. 308.

4. Ibid., pp. 308–309.

5. *Two Decades of Nonalignment*, p. 56.

6. *Review of International Affairs* (Belgrade) no. 491 (September 1970), pp. 21–23.

7. *National Herald* (Lucknow), January 23, 1971.

8. *Two Decades of Nonalignment*, p. 65.

9. *The United Nations and Disarmament 1970–75* (New York: United Nations, 1976), chapter VI.

10. Quoted in K. P. Misra, *Quest for International Order in the Indian Ocean,* (New Delhi: Allied Publishers, Pvt. Ltd. 1977), p. 85.

11. UN Doc A/C 1/PV 1904, November 29, 1972, pp. 4–5.

12. UN Doc A/C 1/PV 1834, November 23, 1971, p. 77.

13. UN Doc A/C 1/PV 1849, December 10, 1971, pp. 16–17.

14. Article 4 of the Treaty for the Prohibition of Nuclear Weapons in Latin America, quoted in *SIPRI Year Book, 1969/70*, pp. 239–240.

15. Paragraph 16 of the Algiers Declaration, Edmund Jan Osmanczyk, *The Encyclopedia of the United Nations and International Agreements* (Philadelphia: Taylor and Francis, 1985), p. 558. The Colombo Declaration may be found in *Two decades of Nonalignment,* section on "Interference and intervention in the internal affairs of States," p. 427.

16. The entire account is based on "Facts on File" 1977 and 1978.

17. Zbigniew Brzezinski, *Power and Principle* (New York: Farrar, Straus, and Giroux, 1983), p. 189.

18. Ibid., p. 148.

19. Ibid., p. 150.

20. *Department of State Bulletin,* July 1983, p. 66. Secretary Shultz's statement before the Senate Foreign Relations Committee on June 15, 1983.

21. *SIPRI Year Book, 1972*, p. 554.

22. Ibid., p. 553.

23. I. Redco and N. Shaskolsky, *The Indian Ocean: A Sphere of Tensions or a Zone of Peace* (Moscow: Scientific Research Council on Peace and Disarmament, 1983), p. 47.

24. Ibid.

25. Ibid.

26. Ibid., p. 48.

27. Ibid., p. 51.

28. Ibid., p. 61.

29. Ibid., pp. 60–61.

30. UN Doc A/C V/PV 1841, Dec. 1, 1971, p. 47; *The United Nations Disarmament Year Book,* Vol. 4 (New York: United Nations, 1979), p. 304.

31. Redco and Shaskolsky, op. cit., pp. 53–54.

32. Brzezinski, op. cit., p. 515.

33. "The Sino-Soviet Conflict: A Search for New Security Strategies," *Strategic Review,* Fall 1979, p. 59. William Hyland wrote:

Surveying the new "quadruple entente," the Soviets could easily perceive that one of the gaps in the "encirclement" was the area that the British used to call "the northern tier," the string of Middle Eastern States running from Turkey to Afghanistan (more recently termed the "arc of crisis"). The Soviets seem to have made a strategic decision to exploit this gap. Their moves have included the remarkable new relationship with Afghanistan, the switch in support from Somalia to Ethiopia and the related intervention with Cuban troops, the signing of a friendship treaty with Turkey in June 1978, the Soviet-inspired coup in South Yemen in that same month, and some probing for an accommodation with Pakistan.

34. Robert C. Aldridge, "Ground-based Surveillance Systems," *First Strike* (London: Pluto Press, 1983), pp. 215–216; *Defense Electronics,* June 1984, p. 45.

35. "Secretary Weinberger on the MHU," *Aerospace Daily,* July 10, 1984, p. 5.

36. I am grateful to my colleague Air Commodore Jasjit Singh for the research work on this issue. Please see also editorial commentary in *Mainstream,* October 27, p. 1 and November 3, 1984, p. 3 issues.

37. This has been dealt with in Raymond Garthoff's article "SALT I: An Evaluation," in *World Politics,* October 1978, pp. 25–32.

6

India, the United States, and Superpower Rivalry in the Indian Ocean

SELIG S. HARRISON

In the climax of *The Fourth Round,* a much-discussed novel in India depicting a new Indo-Pakistan war, Baluch nationalists proclaim an independent republic and India comes to their aid by launching a combined land, sea, and air strike on the Pakistani port of Gwadar, a Baluch stronghold. The United States, alerted by an intelligence tip from an Indian major general, intervenes to block what it sees as a Soviet proxy bid for control of the northern reaches of the Indian Ocean. While 70 Indian ships are still heading across the Arabian Sea, a U.S. marine amphibious brigade is going ashore in Gwadar harbor. American supply ships are already shuttling back and forth between the landing site and the U.S. naval base at Diego Garcia. A U.S. carrier battle group stationed nearby in the Gulf of Oman arrives just in time to do battle with the advancing Indian armada. Indian missiles kill or injure nearly 100 American crew members on a U.S. guided-missile destroyer, American A-7 fighter planes retaliate by bombing an Indian corvette, and a U.S. submarine sinks the ship with Harpoon missiles, killing all 75 hands aboard. The American Embassy in New Delhi is gutted by a mob of some 100,000 people as Indo-American relations reach a new low.[1]

To many Americans, this scenario would seem absurdly improbable and melodramatic, even for fiction, but to most politically conscious Indians the prospect of some form of American intervention on Pakistan's side in the event of another conflict is not far-fetched. The nascent Indian tendency to perceive the United States as a possible military adversary can be partly explained by the fact that the United States has resumed sales of sophisticated military equipment to Pakistan in the aftermath of the Soviet occupation of

Afghanistan. Many Indians also recall the historical reality that President Nixon sent the *Enterprise* to the Bay of Bengal during the 1971 Indo-Pakistan war. But Indian apprehensions are magnified by another significant factor: the marked improvement in American capabilities for intervention in South Asia that has taken place as a by-product of the growing military confrontation between the United States and the Soviet Union in the Indian Ocean and its "natural extensions."[2]

Much of the increase in the superpower military presence in the Indian Ocean region since 1979 has been related to American and Soviet perceptions of security threats in the Persian Gulf and the Red Sea. Significantly, however, the American forces that would be used in any hypothetical crisis in the Gulf cannot be based there, given the political divisions within and between the Gulf states concerning the need for a direct American presence. The carrier battle groups that figure in Central Command scenarios for U.S. intervention in Iran must therefore be parked "over the horizon" in the Arabian Sea and the Gulf of Oman, at shifting locations that are generally closer to Karachi and New Delhi than to Abadan. Similarly, Diego Garcia, where the Joint Rapid Deployment Task Force bases 17 giant containerized supply ships for use in the Gulf, is just over 1000 miles from the southern tip of India and only slightly farther from the western Indian Ocean island states of the Seychelles, Mauritius, and Madagascar; but it is 2300 miles from the mouth of the Red Sea and nearly 3000 miles from the most critical Saudi Arabian oil fields. Indian fears that the U.S. forces in the Arabian Sea could be used in South Asia are not surprising, since the Central Command has formally designated Pakistan as one of the 19 countries within its purview.

The Indian reaction to the American buildup in the Indian Ocean is only one of the more striking manifestations of the powerful political impact of the superpower military presence evident throughout the region, especially among the smaller and more vulnerable western Indian Ocean island states. In addition to aggravating internecine rivalries between regional states (e.g., India and Pakistan or Ethiopia and Somalia), the superpower rivalry reinforces domestic political conflict within states, between the in-group receiving military aid and economic subsidies from one of the superpowers and the out-group seeking to win control. More important, it has generated a pervasive regional climate of anxiety. On a tour of six diverse western Indian Ocean states,[3] I found frequently articulated fears of embroilment in an American-Soviet military conflict, together with a strong desire to escape from the psychological pressures produced by the continuing American and Soviet search for overt and covert military and intelligence facilities. A study of public opinion in a variety of other littoral states shows a similar preoccupation with the danger of an escalating superpower presence.

It is the prospect of an increasingly unstable cycle of challenge and response between Washington and Moscow that accounts for the depth of the anxiety in the region. While the United States has achieved naval superiority in the Indian Ocean, the Soviet Union has increased its land-based deployments of ground and air forces in the Transcaucasus and is continuing to en-

hance its capabilities for power projection in Southwest Asia. Soviet reconnaissance aircraft based in Aden now carry on surveillance missions over the
northern Indian Ocean and the Arabian Sea, and the Pentagon predicts that
Soviet reconnaissance of Diego Garcia by TU-95 BEAR D planes is only a
matter of time.[4] As the Central Command becomes more of a reality, Moscow could well respond by deploying some of its projected Forrestal-class
aircraft carriers and amphibious landing craft in the Indian Ocean region.
Above all, the likelihood of increasing deployments of nuclear weapons in
the region arouses widespread uneasiness.[5] Imminent moves by both the
U.S. and Soviet navies to start deploying sea-launched conventional and
nuclear cruise missiles in their Indian Ocean forces have become a focus of
special concern. Yet at the same time, new opportunities for a reduction of
regional tensions are emerging as Soviet forces withdraw from Afghanistan,
the Iran-Iraq war ends, and the superpower arms control dialogue deepens.

Despite the size and diversity of the Indian Ocean region, there is, nonetheless, a striking similarity in public attitudes throughout the area concerning the threat of superpower military escalation, reflected in a growing convergence in official thinking. In place of the goal of a fully demilitarized Zone
of Peace to which all of the littoral states have been nominally committed,
most governments in the region are now pursuing the more modest objective
of stabilization or control of the American-Soviet military rivalry on the basis
of mutual reductions leading to various concepts of a balance. At the same
time, most of them want the Zone of Peace conference to be held soon, in order to push the superpowers to the bargaining table for arms control discussions. Most of the littoral states recognize that the global military rivalry of
the superpowers will require both of them to maintain some degree of military
deployments in the region for the indefinite future, and most of the Indian
Ocean states have aid, trade, and investment links with one or both of the
superpowers that dictate varying degrees of restraint in their opposition to
the superpower military presence. There is a widespread recognition that
some aspects of the military deployments of both superpowers in the region are not related solely to the American-Soviet rivalry. But the new mood
of realism in the region has not canceled out the Zone of Peace ideal. Rather,
it has produced a desire to implement the Zone of Peace concept by stages in
the form of workable American-Soviet regional arms control agreements.

With memories of the Soviet occupation of Afghanistan still fresh, it
might be assumed that the Indian Ocean states would view the Soviet Union
as the principal disturber of the peace. However, now that the U.S. naval
presence in the region is larger and more visible than the Soviet naval presence, the United States has also become a prime target for regional anxieties.
The Soviet presence in Afghanistan has been repugnant but distant to most
states of the region. The Joint Rapid Deployment Task Force advertises its
capabilities for intervention in littoral states, while the Soviet Union emphasizes its lack of such capabilities, contending that its naval forces are designed solely to counter American forces.

This study will begin by surveying the political impact of the superpower military rivalry in the Indian Ocean region, focusing on some of the salient cases in which pressures for new military and intelligence facilities are distorting domestic political life and intra-regional relationships. I will then analyze the similarities and differences in the attitudes of regional states toward the superpower military presence and the Zone of Peace issue. As the largest littoral state, India will receive special attention. The likelihood that New Delhi will seek to project its own military power in the western Indian Ocean during the decades ahead will be assessed in the perspective of Indian relations with the principal littoral states concerned. Finally, I will examine the interplay of American, Soviet, and Indian interests in the Indian Ocean as a pivotal factor likely to govern the larger pattern of superpower relations in the region. In this context I will discuss several of the more critical political issues that would have to be addressed by the superpowers in order to facilitate the trade-offs required for meaningful regional arms control agreements. In particular, I will consider the implications of the Soviet force withdrawal from Afghanistan and the desirability of American-Soviet mutual restraint agreements in Iran and Pakistan.

The Politics of Bases in the Indian Ocean

Seeking to justify the American military presence, some observers have emphasized the fact that superpower military deployments in the Indian Ocean region are not exclusively a function of the American-Soviet military rivalry per se.[6] For example, Walter K. Andersen points to cases in which Soviet naval deployments have reflected political rather than military objectives. He even goes so far as to argue that the "major reason" for the Soviet naval presence in the region has been the Soviet desire for political parity with the United States and for political influence in critical countries where "progressive" elements are seeking to win power or to defend it in the face of American pressures.[7] Viewed from the perspective of the littoral states, however, it is highly artificial to make a distinction between the military and political aspects of the superpower rivalry. In countries where Washington and Moscow want to retain or obtain military or intelligence facilities, they reflexively seek to create the political conditions that will help them get what they want. Even in cases where one of the superpowers is not particularly interested in military or intelligence facilities, its desire to keep its options open and to deny such facilities to the other superpower prompts overt and covert efforts to establish a congenial political environment.

The political impact of the superpower rivalry can be seen vividly in microcosm in the smallest of the Indian Ocean states, the Republic of the Seychelles. With its strategic location, midway between Mombasa and Diego Garcia, it attracts unusually intense American and Soviet interest; and with its fragile polity, it is peculiarly vulnerable to external intrusions into its domestic power struggles.

The population of the Seychelles is only 62,000. Yet it exemplifies in exaggerated degree the problems of political integration and mobilization common to economically less developed countries caught in the turmoil of rapid social change. The *Seychellois* are the descendants of French and British settlers, African slaves, and indentured Indian laborers. Intermarriages have dulled ethnic distinctions, but a strong undercurrent of color-consciousness complicates the emergence of a coherent national personality. Anthropologists and other observers, seeking to explain the indiscipline and the free-wheeling individualism characteristic of Seychelles society, point to the psychological legacy of colonialism and plantation slavery. At the same time, they underline the fact that the Seychelles, as an ethnic mélange, faces problems of integration different from those multi-ethnic states with clearly defined social blocs. The *Seychellois* are not securely anchored in either African, Asian, or European roots but have not yet established a unifying composite identity of their own.[8] "Those who are afflicted by this malady of un-belonging," wrote Shiva Naipaul after a visit to the Seychelles, "become, to a greater or lesser degree, unhinged."[9]

Compared with most other former domains of the Empire, the Seychelles had acquired little political experience prior to its gaining its independence from Britain in 1976. The *Seychellois* elite was unusually small and faction-ridden, even by Third World standards, and the departing colonial authorities handed over power to a wealthy, British-oriented segment of this elite that was sharply divorced from the impoverished majority of the Seychelles populace. James Mancham, the playboy Prime Minister who was deposed in a 1977 coup by the present President, France Albert Rene, matter-of-factly acknowledges in his memoirs that Rene enjoyed the greatest support "among the poorer section, where his seductive rich-versus-poor approach had the maximum impact," while he himself had the backing of "the better-educated part of the community and the women." Rene's use of an "emotional class" approach, he suggested, was simply not cricket.[10] Mancham's book, *Paradise Raped: Life, Love and Power in the Seychelles,* provides a classic study in the alienation of elites in economically less developed countries. It is replete with contemptuous comments about his own society and celebrates unabashedly his personal devotion to the use of power as a vehicle for the pursuit of jet-set night life. Now a British citizen, Mancham boasts that he consistently opposed independence and bemoans the fact that the British succumbed to the pressures of the freedom movement led by Rene. To the extent that he expresses a political philosophy, it is revealed when he refers to the "crowd of leftists" surrounding U.S. Senator Edward Kennedy.[11]

Given the ultra-conservative character of the local leadership patronized by the British, it is not surprising that a polarization of political forces occurred during the decade that preceded independence, that Rene's opposition movement espoused a Seychelles-style socialism, and that British and American intelligence agencies, seeing Red, subsidized Mancham and opposed Rene,[12] implanting a deep suspicion in Rene's mind toward London and Washington that has yet to be erased. Rene is a British-trained lawyer who studied political science at the London School of Economics. In a two-hour conversation with him in April 1984, I found him to be an earnest, intellectually acute political leader with a cosmopolitan outlook. He is frankly seeking to establish a centrally planned economy in the Seychelles but does not fit the crypto-Communist label applied to him by Mancham and often echoed by Western officials and the Western media. He won power with Tanzanian, not Communist, help. His People's Progressive Front is not organized like a Marxist-Leninist party[13] and does not question private property rights. It embodies an amalgam of ideas gleaned from the British Labor and French Socialist parties and from Catholic social action groups in the United States and Europe as well as from the Soviet Union, China, and North Korea. Some of the key figures in his regime are former Catholic priests who preach a purist brand of socialism reminiscent of that espoused on U.S. campuses in the late 1960s. Brother David Deniscourt, an American priest, supervises the educational program of the National Youth Service, one of the more controversial programs initiated by the Rene regime. All Seychelles children are required to spend two years away from their families in government-run Youth Service encampments. Critics say that the Youth Service is not only inefficient but could also become a vehicle for Communist indoctrination. Supporters, pointing to the widespread incidence of child labor and prostitution in the Seychelles, argue that it is socially healthy to get children away from their mercenary mothers. Rene himself defends the Youth Service as a necessary response to the endemic sense of rootlessness and indiscipline in the Seychelles and as the fastest way to create a body of socially conscious administrators.

Rene speaks in much the same language of non-alignment and distributive justice heard from most political leaders throughout the economically less developed countries. He describes the Front as an "avant-garde" movement in which "there is no Marxism but there's a lot of how to live together." "I have repeated time and time again that I am not a Communist and that we will never allow any great power from either East or West to install a military base on our territory," he declares. "But our problem is our strategic position. Both superpowers believe that the other will not permit us to be non-aligned and that we will not be firm enough to remain non-aligned."

The Rene regime continues to permit the United States to use a satellite tracking and telemetry facility set up in 1967 under an agreement with Britain. The United States pays $2.75 million in rent in addition to spending some $4 million annually in "invisibles" to maintain the station and related facilities for 104 Americans who run it. Since 1982, the United States has also given the Seychelles modest direct economic aid to cover diesel oil and other commodity imports. This aid reached $2.3 million in fiscal 1987 and $3 million in 1988. The Soviet Union, for its part, has provided substantial military aid, including armored personnel carriers, jeeps, patrol boats, a radar air defense system, several ground-to-ground rockets, and a small number of SAM-7 ground-to-air missiles. More important, 15 to 20 Soviet military advisers are attached to the 800-man Seychelles armed forces. Moscow has also given $4 million worth of fuel oil and cement and has helped to repair ten diesel oil storage tanks built during World War II by Britain on St. Anne's Island. Both the U.S. and Soviet navies have access to commercial oil refueling facilities in the Seychelles port of Victoria.

Moscow and Washington alike profess support for Rene and respect for the non-alignment of the Seychelles. Against the background of pre-independence British and American support for Mancham, however, Rene has continued to harbor suspicions that the United States would like to displace him. His suspicions were intensified when Mancham supporters, together with South African and British mercenaries allegedly recruited by Pretoria, staged an abortive coup in November 1981. According to Rene's advisers, one of the captured coup leaders, Martin Dolinchek, testified that the CIA, fearful of a leftist victory in the Mauritian elections, had asked South African intelligence officials to organize the coup. To Western readers, accounts of the 1981 coup and subsequent coup attempts in August 1982 and December 1983 have their comic opera aspects.[14] But the Seychelles regime takes a grimly serious view of what it regards as a persistent danger that the United States may decide at some point to help support Mancham or another rival to Rene.

As a key non-aligned diplomat in Victoria observed, "Grenada reinforced Rene's psychological dependence on the USSR." Moscow sent two destroyers to Victoria Harbor during the 1982 coup attempt by army mutineers and has informally signaled that it is prepared to intervene in Rene's defense if this should ever become necessary. Former American Ambassador David Fischer reaffirmed U.S. support for Rene following a post-Grenada appeal by Mancham for U.S. intervention, and did so once again after an anti-Rene demonstration in Victoria by supporters of the London-based, pro-Mancham "Mouvement Pour La Resistance" in 1984. But the atmosphere in Victoria continues to be one of Byzantine intrigue in which domestic power struggles within the regime take on a cold war coloration in the eyes of foreign observers. Thus, Jacques Houdoul, Development Minister and former Foreign Minister, and James Michel, Army Chief of Staff and Education Minister, are often depicted as more convinced Marxists than others in the ruling party and thus as Soviet favorites, while former Defense Minister Ogilvy Berlouis has been labeled as pro-American. In reality, such labels generally distort the nature of rivalries that are primarily local in character.

In the short run, Rene appears to be strong enough to preserve a non-aligned position. Looking ahead, however, if Rene begins to slip, a continuing escalation of the superpower presence in the Indian Ocean and a growing search for military and intelligence facilities could well prompt efforts by Washington or Moscow, or both, to manipulate the internal divisions within the fragile Seychelles body politic. The desirability of acquiring bases in the Seychelles to avoid over-dependence on Diego Garcia and to gain more space and operational flexibility was emphasized by the Chairman of the House Military Installations Subcommittee during congressional hearings on the Rapid Deployment Force.[15] At present, Moscow acquiesces in the tracking station but does not want to see it broadened into a National Security

Agency electronic monitoring facility or an anti-submarine listening post. The United States would be alarmed if Moscow should get bunkering facilities for the Soviet navy, landing rights for operational military aircraft, intelligence facilities, or covert access to oil refueling facilities. For example, in 1984, Western governments were concerned over the Soviet role in repairing the oil storage tanks on St. Anne's Island. A French military intelligence specialist told me that the ten tanks on the island collectively could hold up to 60,000 tons of oil and that access to three or four of them could "radically alter" Soviet naval capabilities in the southern Indian Ocean. However, most evidence indicates that no Soviet technicians have been on the island since 1986, and the Rene government says that the purpose of the repair program was to help the Seychelles navy.

A successful effort by the Russians to enlarge their military capabilities in the southern Indian Ocean by acquiring facilities in the Seychelles could well lead them to reduce their present efforts to acquire facilities in Madagascar. The size of the military and economic aid investments needed to pursue Soviet objectives in the Seychelles is relatively insignificant. By contrast, as its economic problems have multiplied in recent years, Madagascar has sought more and more foreign economic aid, and Moscow has been unable to compete with Washington and Paris in helping the Didier Ratsiraka regime. In military terms, however, Madagascar's port of Diego Suarez, the site of a former French naval base, is clearly the most desirable locale for a naval installation in the southern Indian Ocean. Despite categorical statements by Ratsiraka that no foreign power will be permitted to establish a base there, Moscow and Washington are engaged in their present competition for political influence in Antananarivo primarily because they foresee the possibility of a post-Ratsiraka political realignment in Madagascar that could lead to a change in this policy.

When Ratsiraka first came into the limelight as Foreign Minister in 1972, he initiated military aid and other links with the Soviet bloc that provoked U.S. efforts to destabilize his regime. In 1971, Madagasar expelled the U.S. Ambassador, and it was not until 1980 that Ratsiraka agreed to accept a new U.S. envoy. The rapprochement between Washington and Antananarivo was negotiated by Ambassador at Large Vernon Walters, who had known Ratsiraka when the Malagasy leader was a student in the French military academy and Walters was military attaché in the U.S. Embassy in Paris. The United States has subsequently accepted the non-aligned bona fides of the Ratsiraka government and has helped to ease its balance-of-payments problems. Madagascar soft-pedaled its anti-U.S. rhetoric on Puerto Rico and its pro-Soviet rhetoric on Afghanistan and has permitted U.S. oil companies to explore off the Madagascar coast. Above all, Ratsiraka has rebuffed continuing Soviet overtures for access to Diego Suarez and other facilities. However, behind-the-scenes tensions between the United States and Madagascar persist. Washington suspects that the substantial Soviet military aid advisory mission is overstepping its purported role. On a quiet visit to Antananarivo in April 1984, Walters gave Ratsiraka evidence suggesting that the Russians were using sensitive communications equipment, provided to Madagascar under the Soviet military aid program, for electronics eavesdropping on U.S. ships and submarines. Madagascar, for its part, blames the Reagan Administration for the stringent economic reform demands made by the International Monetary Fund as a condition for foreign exchange help.

Madagascar has begun to acquire increasing amounts of French weaponry. The United States also provided $4.5 million in military aid between 1985 and 1987 in addition to $75,000 per year in a military training program that was still continuing in 1988. However, the Ratsiraka regime remains overwhelmingly dependent on the Soviet Union for its military equipment, spare parts, and related technical support. The only fighter aircraft it has are 12 Mig-21s and 4 Mig-17s. Its army and gendarmerie rely exclusively on Moscow for artillery and armored personnel carriers. Soviet radar systems provide its air defense. More than 70 Soviet military advisers are attached to the Malagasy armed forces. Moscow also has 30 economic advisers and a strong presence in the cultural field. Some 2000 Malagasy students were enrolled in Soviet universities in 1984, and 50 Soviet professors were teaching in Madagascar, mostly in Antananarivo. However, French cultural influence in Madagascar continues to be much stronger than that of the Soviet Union, the United States, or other foreign countries. In 1984, France had more than 700 teachers and technical assistance experts scattered throughout the country, and some 10 percent of these were engaged or married to Malagasy men and women.

Alarmist scenarios, suggesting the possibility of a Soviet-sponsored coup, emphasize accumulating economic problems, the weakness of the political infrastructure built during Ratsiraka's personalized rule, and Soviet links with key sectors of the military leadership. For example, Professor Tovananahary Rabetsitonta of the University of Madagascar, a leader of Monima, a party critical of Ratsiraka, predicted that the failure of U.S. and IMF support to solve Madagascar's economic problems will open the way for a Soviet-instigated military coup or a defeat in the 1989 elections. In this view, even though Ratsiraka has strong army support, much of the gendarmerie would like to displace him, blaming him for the 1975 assassination of his popular predecessor, Colonel Richard Ratsimandrava.

As in many other countries, the IMF's economic liberalization policies, strongly backed by the United States, have meant higher food and commodity prices for already hard-pressed low-income groups in Madagascar, and it remains to be seen whether significant increases in productivity will result from these politically controversial policies. The IMF's free market doctrine ignores the powerful position occupied in Madagascar by middlemen, who are predictably holding down prices paid to the farmers for their produce while jacking up consumer food prices, thus discouraging the increased agricultural productivity envisaged by IMF economists.

As Madagascar's economic problems have burgeoned, Western economic aid has steadily increased. In 1986, the World Bank's aid consortium provided $332 million, while International Monetary Fund compensatory aid and standby credits totalled $46 million. In 1987, International Development Association and I.M.F. credits reached $113 million. Bilateral American aid went up from $8 million in 1987 to $27 million in 1988. In addition, the United States helped to arrange the rescheduling of $170 million in private bank debt in 1984. Except for $2 million in food aid, Moscow's help has been confined to a stretch-out of military aid payments. The extent of Madagascar's dependence on Washington, Paris, and other Western aid sources makes speculation concerning a Soviet coup appear far-fetched, at least with respect to the foreseeable future. Nevertheless, even a brief visit to Antananarivo underlines the degree to which Madagascar's tenuous political stability depends on Ratsiraka. Initially unified around him in the early years of independence, the major Malagasy political parties are increasingly polarized between the Soviet-oriented AKFM and Ratsiraka's military-based Arima at one extreme and the more conservative Monima and Vong parties at the other, with the moderate socialist MFM occupying a shifting position in between.

Both Moscow and Washington, eyeing this polarization, are intensifying their courtship of Madagascar's political and intellectual leaders. Since both of the superpowers now support Ratsiraka, the impact of their competition in Madagascar has not, so far, been destabilizing in the 1980s. American and Soviet aid has contributed to the stability of the Ratsiraka regime. However, should internecine conflicts within the military leadership or economic stresses lead to a sudden political upheaval, there is a danger that the superpower competition could once again prove to be destabilizing, as it was in the 1970s.

In geopolitical terms, Madagascar and its immediate island neighbors, the Comoros and Mayotte, derive special importance from their proximity to the Mozambique Channel, a critical choke point for southbound oil tanker traffic. An average of 12 tankers with more than 200,000 tons of oil pass through the Channel daily. Mayotte, a French territory whose residents enjoy French citizenship, has a four-mile-wide lagoon that has long been viewed as a possible site for a naval base. Paris has been keeping the option of a base open by resisting periodic demands from the Comoros for the reintegration of Mayotte with the Comoros. The United States has studied possible base sites in the Comoros and has found Comoros leaders ready to entertain U.S. proposals for an American base. The former American Ambassador to Madagascar, Robert Keating, a Reagan political appointee, who was concurrently accredited to the Comoros, established cordial U.S. relations with Comoros President Ahmed Abdallah. In September 1984, Keating accompanied Abdallah on a tour of the interior, the first time a foreign ambassador had been invited to do so. Keating told an audience at Mutsandu, with Abdallah beside him, that the United States "understood the importance to the free world of the Indian Ocean and the countries of this region." Keating is identified with the strategic views advanced by retired U.S. Admiral Robert J. Hanks, who believes that protection of the Cape Route requires additional air bases in the Mozambique Channel area to permit more intensive anti-submarine surveillance.[16] The United States has not made serious overtures to the Comoros for a base because to do so would provoke Madagascar, creating an opening for intensified Soviet efforts to obtain the use of Diego Suarez. However, the Reagan Administration launched a training program for Comoros military officers with a $50,000 grant in fiscal 1988.

Significantly, since France turned over Diego Suarez, Madagascar has kept 1500 trained port technicians and laborers on the payroll. Ratsiraka hopes to develop Diego Suarez as the leading commercial ship repair center in the southern Indian Ocean, but the presence of readily available specialized personnel would also facilitate its reconversion into a military base if shifting political circumstances should make this appear desirable to a successor regime.

In the Seychelles, Madagascar, and the Comoros, where Rene, Ratsiraka, and Abdallah have ruled with varying degrees of authoritarian control, stable political systems providing for the orderly transfer of power are not yet firmly rooted. It is the lack of solidly based political institutions that makes these countries vulnerable to potential superpower pressures for military bases. By contrast, non-alignment has relatively secure domestic political foundations in Mauritius, with a vigorous parliamentary tradition established during the British period and a largely literate, politically sensitized populace.

Mauritius faces formidable economic problems, notably widespread unemployment and underemployment, heavy foreign indebtedness, and a precarious dependence on preferential European Economic Community sugar prices and quotas. Its communal and ethnic conflicts could conceivably take an ugly turn as the assertiveness of newly dominant Hindu populist forces provokes a growing Moslem and Creole response. Despite some dire prophecies,[17] however, the possibility that domestic convulsions could open the way for a U.S. or Soviet base presence appears less likely in Mauritius than in other western Indian Ocean states. There are no significant Soviet-oriented political forces in Mauritius, and Moscow maintains a cautiously low profile. Soviet relations with Mauritius hit rock bottom in late 1983 when the Soviet Ambassador, angered by Prime Minister Aneerood Jugnauth's protracted delay in granting an audience, left in a huff, returning after a calculated six-month absence. The United States openly aided the late Prime Minister Seewoosagur Ramgoolam in his unsuccessful reelection campaign in 1982, fearing that Ramgoolam's challenger, Jugnauth, would be overly dependent on his alliance partner Paul Berenger, who was viewed by Washington as dangerously anti-American. As it happened, during his brief tenure as Finance Minister before his rupture with Jugnauth, Berenger made peace with the IMF and acquired a more moderate image. The United States now recognizes that the prospects for a Soviet-oriented government in Mauritius are negligible and has established a cordial relationship with the Jugnauth government.

The principal American objective in Mauritius is to soften the Mauritian demand for the return of Diego Garcia and Mauritian opposition to the steadily expanding U.S. base presence there. The United States also has a secondary interest in using Mauritius as a source of food supplies and other logistical support for Diego Garcia. Some elements in the Pentagon were talking informally in 1988 of seeking a base in Mauritius in the event that political changes in the Philippines should force the United States out of the Subic naval base or Clark Field. Even if such thinking were to gain adherents in Washington, however, it is unlikely that the idea of a U.S. base presence would receive much support in Port Louis. There is a broad base of intellectual and political support for non-alignment as the safest course for Mauritius. Moreover, Port Louis seeks to keep its foreign policy broadly attuned to that of India, the mother country of its largest ethnic group, and Mauritian leaders are keenly aware that New Delhi would regard a superpower military base in Mauritius as a direct challenge to its own ambitions for regional influence.

The Jugnauth government has adopted a pragmatic approach to relations with Washington designed to get an increased sugar quota, expanded World Bank, IMF, and U.S. economic aid, and increased U.S. private investment. As part of its public relations backup for this posture, Mauritius has offered to sell food to Diego Garcia and to permit Mauritian laborers to work there. The rationale for this policy reversal is that Mauritius cannot force the United States to vacate the base by refusing to provide logistics support and might as well get what immediate economic advantages it can by cooperating with Washington, while continuing to push for the return of Diego Garcia to Mauritian sovereignty.

Support for the Mauritian demand for the return of Diego Garcia cuts across all political groups. Among intellectuals and politically conscious elements, one hears expressions of concern that the continuing buildup of the base could involve Mauritius in some form of superpower conflict. As a mass political issue, the Diego Garcia demand gains added sensitivity from the feeling that Mauritian "lackeys" of the British colonial rulers sold out the Mauritian interest during the negotiations leading up to independence. Responding to popular uneasiness over the secrecy still surrounding many aspects of the 1965 agreement under which Mauritius gained its freedom in return for agreeing to the detachment of the Chagos Archipelago, of which Diego Garcia is a part, a bipartisan Select Committee of the Legislative Assembly conducted a year-long investigation culminating in an exhaustive report published on June 1, 1983. Signed by former Foreign Minister Anil Gayan, then a private citizen, the report cited the testimony of the late Governor General Ramgoolam and others to prove that the British had "blackmailed" Mauritius by making independence conditional on the excision of Diego Garcia.[18] The report points to the 1960 United Nations Declaration on the Granting of Independence to Colonial Peoples, which stated that the transfer of power to peoples living in trusts and non-self-governing territories should be effected "without conditions or reservations." In particular, the report underlined a passage in the U.N. Declaration stating that "any attempt aimed at the partial or total disruption of the national unity and the territorial integrity of a country is incompatible with the purposes and principles of the Charter of the United Nations."[19] "Notwithstanding the blackmail element," the report declared, "which strongly puts in question the legal validity of the excision, the Select Committee strongly denounces the flouting by the United Kingdom government, on these counts, of the Charter of the United Nations."[20] The report cites detailed evidence indicating popular anxieties in 1965 over news reports that Britain planned to lease Diego Garcia to the United States as a military base following its severance from Mauritius. Ridiculing testimony from Ramgoolam and others professing ignorance of Britain's intentions, the report recalled the "psychosis prevalent in the public mind" prior to the 1965 negotiations and expressed "regret that none of the parties forming the Mauritian delegation thought it fit to allay the fears of the population. The Select Committee strongly condemns the passive attitude of the political class represented . . . in the delegation. . . . Their silence, in the light of repeated warnings from responsible sections of public opinion, bordered on connivance."[21] Apart from the 1983 report, a study of the proceedings of the Legislative Assembly shows that the Diego Garcia issue has been a continuing focus of controversy.[22]

Reflecting on the 1965 negotiations in a conversation in April 1984, Ramgoolam, then 83, said that the British had told him they would use Diego Garcia as a communications station. "If I had known that it would become an American base," he declared, "I would have analyzed the situation more deeply and would have discussed arrangements to retain our control over its future. It is not good for Mauritius that it has become a nuclear base. It is not good for us or our neighbors that a nuclear war could take place in this vicinity. If the superpowers would leave us alone it would be much better for us. We would like to see the superpowers agree to freeze their armaments buildup in this region and then reduce it. Such an agreement, with mutual concessions, should make clear that Diego Garcia would not be used as a nuclear base."

Deputy Prime Minister Gaetan Duval has periodically suggested that Mauritius might lease Diego Garcia to the United States—for the right price—if it reverted to Mauritian sovereignty. Foreign Minister Gayan told me in 1984 that "we wouldn't rule that out if agreeing to lease it would get it back." However, it is doubtful that the continued use of Diego Garcia as a military base would be politically digestible in Mauritius for very long in the improbable event of a deal with the United States and the British providing for its return. Harish Boodhoo, then one of the key leaders of Jugnauth's governing Mauritian Socialist Movement, said flatly in 1984 that "if we get it back we would not allow any superpower to militarize it. At the present time, we are helpless, and so we are trying to live with it as a reality even though we don't like it. But if it were returned to Mauritius, we would not want to be responsible for a superpower presence there. We would like to see this madman's race in our area end, especially the nuclear race."

At the initiative of Mauritius, the 1983 Non-Aligned Summit in New Delhi elevated Diego Garcia from an Indian Ocean issue alone to an anticolonial issue, attacking the base not only as a threat to the peace but also as a residual imperialist presence perpetuated in contempt of the littoral states.

Since the NAM summit, however, Jugnauth has made his tactical shift on Diego Garcia by softening his position on food sales and labor for the base. India, too, motivated by its own economic objectives in Washington, has softened its demands for the return of Diego Garcia to Mauritius, placing the issue in the context of the need for a broader reduction in the presence of both superpowers in the Indian Ocean.[23]

Mauritius under Jugnauth articulates the Zone of Peace demand in relatively restrained terms that are similar to those enunciated throughout the littoral states. When the late Indira Gandhi visited Port Louis in 1982, Jugnauth urged that India and Mauritius work for a "mutual and balanced" reduction of the superpower military presence in the Indian Ocean "in the short term." "We want to be practical," he told me in March, 1984. "We know that we are powerless. But we hope to persuade the superpowers to start with a freeze and then negotiate further mutual and balanced reductions." Diego Garcia, he said, "is a very modern nuclear base which is definitely a threat to us." The United States, he added, "is responsible for obstructing the Zone of Peace conference, which could help us to bring about negotiations between the superpowers."

In similarly restrained terms, focusing on the need for a superpower dialogue, Malaysia has called for the "gradual" removal of foreign military bases in the region, together with "the prohibition of new bases,"[24] and Indonesia has urged the superpowers to "freeze their military presence with a view to its reduction and eventual elimination."[25] An authoritative Indonesian analyst, noting that "the American fleet clearly rules the waves of the Indian Ocean," concluded that a strong U.S. presence was necessary to forestall Soviet dominance, but that it is now "in the best interests of the Indian Ocean nations to have an equilibrium between the superpowers. . . . The American-Soviet rivalry must be maintained in reasonable balance at as low a level as possible."[26]

President Rene of the Seychelles told me that "while we are very disturbed by Diego Garcia, which is so close to us, we recognize that the Zone of Peace idea cannot be separated from the broader relationship between the superpowers. We want to see a resumption of bilateral arms control negotiations." Maxime Ferrari, who served as Foreign Minister of the Seychelles from 1979 until mid-1984, suggested that representatives of the Indian Ocean littoral states, perhaps selected by a Zone of Peace conference, should be present as observers in a resumed American-Soviet dialogue on Indian Ocean arms control. "We want de-escalation by stages," he said.

Australian Foreign Minister Bill Hayden, announcing a new Indian Ocean policy on January 17, 1984, emphasized the "goal of the resumption of the American-Soviet talks on arms limitation in the region." In a major address on June 20, 1984, he reaffirmed that "we have a particular responsibility to promote disarmament and reduce superpower tensions in the region," adding with deliberate ambiguity that "the asymmetry between the military capabilities of the superpowers in the region is intrinsically destablizing." The national conference of the Australian Labor Party soon thereafter pushed for a stronger government posture, demanding that "as an immediate goal, Australia should urge the USA and the USSR to refrain from establishing new bases, upgrading their existing facilities or expanding their navies in the Ocean. We should also urge negotiation between these two powers, and other powers with a naval presence, aimed at reducing forces to the lowest possible level."

The most militant position on the implementation of the Zone of Peace concept is taken by Madagascar, which is seeking to play host to a second conference after the initial conclave envisaged in Sri Lanka. "The Indian Ocean Zone of Peace idea means a balance of zero," said Guy Rajaonson, National Security Adviser to President Ratsiraka. "We will need another conference soon after the first one in Colombo, and the first business of both conferences will be to get rid of foreign bases."

For the most part, the littoral states want to see a Zone of Peace conference convened soon, if only to push the superpowers to the bargaining table. Pakistan and Bangladesh, eyeing Indian nuclear development, have frequently used the issue of a nuclear-free zone to throw cold water on the idea of a conference, arguing that a Zone of Peace would be meaningless in the absence of assurances that the littoral states themselves will not deploy nuclear weapons. However, this approach is not widely shared. For example, Indonesia has observed that "the security situation within the region will be a material factor for the success of the conference, but this should not constitute a prerequisite or a precondition for convening the conference itself."[27] Similarly, Malaysia, while stating that the establishment of a nuclear-free zone "could facilitate" progress toward a Zone of Peace, did not give this objective decisive priority.[28] Even Sri Lanka, which emphasizes the need for a nuclear-free zone, has long been pushing for the conference despite U.S. opposition, partly reflecting its pride as the originator of the idea and as potential host country. Foreign Ministry officials in Colombo were privately critical of the United States for opposing the conference. The Soviet occupation of Afghanistan could be discussed at the conference, these officials said in 1984, and most of the 42 potential participants would be critical of the Soviet presence. As an example of the independent attitude of regional states, Nihal Rodrigo, Director of the U.N. Division in the Sri Lankan Foreign Ministry, noted that Madagascar and the Seychelles, both of which receive Soviet military aid, voted against Moscow on two key 1983 votes in the U.N. Ad Hoc Committee on the Indian Ocean. Paul Berenger, a leader of the Mauritian Militant Movement and one of the more vigorous advocates of the Zone of Peace concept, often depicted as pro-Soviet, said in 1984 that he would have "no objection" if the United States raised the issue of the Soviet presence in Afghanistan and Kampuchea at a Zone of Peace conference. "We have no special love for them," he added. "We are not tilting toward the Soviet Union by challenging Diego Garcia."

The nominal American posture on the issue in the U.N. Ad Hoc Committee is that the United States would support the "establishment of a realistic zone of peace in the Indian Ocean." What such a redesigned Zone of

Peace concept would entail was spelled out in a proposal presented in May 1982 by Australia, the United States, and seven other committee members.[29] Instead of focusing only on the elimination of foreign naval forces and bases in the Indian Ocean and its littoral states, the proposal argued, the Zone of Peace concept should deal more comprehensively with a variety of factors affecting the peace and stability of the region. Among the 26 necessary criteria for a Zone of Peace were support for the nuclear non-proliferation treaty and for nuclear-free zones in the region as well as "the withdrawal of foreign occupying forces from the states of the region." Above all, the United States has emphasized that the concept should embrace hinterland states in order to take into account "the military occupation of a hinterland state by a superpower." The Soviet Union wants to retain the definition of the Zone of Peace specified in the original 1971 U.N. Declaration on the Indian Ocean, limiting the Zone to its water surface, islands, seabed, airspace, and coastal military installations. Praising this definition as "quite realistic," Moscow has warned that proposals to broaden the concept "might impede the achievement of possible agreements . . . playing into the hands of opponents of the peace zone." However, a Soviet spokesman, acknowledging the sincerity of those non-aligned states seeking a broader concept, has reaffirmed "the readiness of the Soviet Union to consider the alternative seriously."[30]

Since February 1982, the U.S. position in the Ad Hoc Committee has been that the United States would refuse to participate in a Zone of Peace conference unless the Soviet Union would first withdraw its forces from Afghanistan. "It would be a serious mistake," said the American delegate on one occasion, "and indeed a contradiction in terms, to attempt to implement a Zone of Peace while one of the states defined to be in the region, the hinterland state of Afghanistan, continues illegally to be occupied by foreign military forces."[31] The American posture has reflected indifference, at worst, or insensitivity, at best, to the climate of regional public opinion. As indicated above, even relatively moderate governments in the region, notably those of Sri Lanka and Mauritius, have viewed the U.S. attitude as the principal obstacle to the proposed conference. Ironically, the United States acquired an image of "rigidity," "haughtiness," and obstructionism, as against a Soviet image of flexibility in the pursuit of peace,[32] during the very period when 115,000 Soviet troops were occupying Afghanistan.

Assuming that Soviet forces withdraw by February 1989, as envisaged in the United Nations settlement concluded in April 1988, the American image would be further damaged if the United States should continue to oppose a conference favored by the majority of littoral states.

India, the Soviet Union, and the United States

In the evolving interplay of American and Soviet interests in the Indian Ocean, a critical and often underrated factor is likely to be an increasingly important Indian regional security role. India boldly asserted its readiness to project power in its immediate neighborhood by intervening in Sri Lanka in 1987. In Pakistan and Bangladesh, as in Sri Lanka, India frankly seeks to exclude superpower military aid and bases in order to achieve a balance of power reflecting India's preponderance in population and resources. It is also generally recognized that New Delhi's regional economic influence is expanding as Indian industrial technology grows more sophisticated. But the emergence of India as a major military power throughout much of the Indian Ocean has received little attention. In time, New Delhi's naval reach to the western Indian Ocean island states and to East Africa is likely to grow in effectiveness, and a divergence of United States and Indian interests in the Indian Ocean could well develop, especially if Washington continues to provide sophisticated military equipment to Pakistan.

An examination of the "Big Navy" debate in India reveals that the main thrust of Indian concern is likely to be westward. The Indian naval presence at Port Blair in the Andaman Islands is significant in military terms, but it is most often depicted by Indian writers as a defensive bastion against Chinese and other pressures from the east rather than as the cutting edge of Indian geopolitical expansion in Southeast Asia. The Andaman Sea, writes Maharaj K. Chopra, "may be described as a four power lake," and Indonesia, Burma, Thailand, and Malaysia, "should they so decide, could debar India from any presence in its waters."[33] It is to the south and west that New Delhi sees a greater opportunity for the relatively unimpeded development of enhanced military and political influence. The protection of the Indian-controlled Minicoy, Laccadive, and Amindivi islands, off the Karnataka and Kerala coasts, known collectively as Lakshadweep Territory, is invariably cited as a primary justification for a buildup of the Western Fleet. Another key Indian objective in the Indian Ocean relatively close to home is the continued neutralization of the Maldives as a military base for other powers. When Iran and the Soviet Union showed interest in obtaining the Gan airfield as a base following the departure of the British in 1976, New Delhi quickly scotched the idea, persuading the Maldives to convert Gan into a tourist resort. Pakistan has since made a series of overtures to the Moslem-majority populace there, but Maldives leaders have been careful not to offend New Delhi.

Pointing to the significant number of people of Indian origin not only in the Maldives but also in Mauritius and the Seychelles, P. K. S. Namboodiri writes that "they have strong cultural and emotional bonds with the subcontinent. They look toward India not only as a source of economic and technical assistance, but also for their security. The security of these islands is a legitimate concern for India."[34]

Mauritius, with a Hindu majority of 52 percent, coordinates its foreign policy closely with India, and its rare displays of independence, such as its votes with the U.N. majority against the Soviet presence in Afghanistan, have come only after informal consultation with New Delhi. India strongly supported Prime Minister Aneerood Jugnauth and his Hindu populist faction in consolidating political power in Mauritius during the 1982–84 period, and the former Indian High Commissioner in Port Louis, Prem Singh, has been attacked by non-Hindu elements for allegedly playing a proconsul-type role. The motivation for Indian involvement in Mauritian politics was a conviction that non-Hindu leaders, notably Paul Berenger, were favoring the Creole and Moslem ethnic minorities, and that this anti-Hindu posture would provoke ethnic tensions that could ultimately lead to a refugee exodus comparable to the flight of Indians from Uganda. But New Delhi also has an unmistakable long-term sense of identity with Mauritius as a natural outpost of Indian influence. Business and aid ties have been intensifying, and a retired Indian civil servant serves as Security Advisor to Jugnauth.

Significantly, Mauritian leaders were divided on ethnic lines when I asked whether India would be able to have naval facilities in Mauritius if it should ever want them. Harish Boodhoo, whose political base is in the dominant Hindu community, replied that "as a littoral country, everyone would wish India to become a power. History has shown that India has no paternal or hegemonistic attitude." Sir Satcam Boolel, former Deputy Prime Minister in the MSM government and leader of an anti-Jugnauth Hindu faction, said that "Indian naval facilities would definitely be accepted by Mauritius, and if they [other leaders] say otherwise, they are merely being diplomatic." Governor General Veeraswamy Ringadoo, former Finance Minister in the MSM government, said that India "would no doubt be able to get facilities here if it wanted them." Jugnauth, the incumbent MSM Prime Minister, was predictably more cautious, observing that "India is going to become bigger and more powerful in this region, no doubt, it's only a question of time, but it's hypothetical just now whether they would get special facilities here." By contrast, non-Hindu leaders expressed immediate reservations, notably former Foreign Minister Jean de L'Estrac, a leader of the Mauritian Militant Movement, backed largely by Creole and Moslem interests, who said that it would be "a difficult decision."

President Rene of the Seychelles spoke of India as "the awkward grandfather of the region," observing that "India would like to play a big role, but it has a complex, that people will say they're being imperialistic." While sidestepping a direct reply to a question about base facilities, Rene said that the Seychelles would welcome Indian intervention in the event of future coup attempts against his regime. "India should say, 'we're not going to stand by and let that sort of nonsense go on.' That would deter the adventurers. The Soviet Union says it. This is a role that India could play." Indian officials indicated that Rene had expressed this attitude directly to New Delhi after the unsuccessful 1981 coup attempt. During her August 1982 visit to Mauritius, the late Prime Minister Indira Gandhi was asked whether New Delhi would be prepared to intervene in the Seychelles in the event of further trouble. She replied that "we sympathize with the Seychelles, but we don't think it would be wise for us to get involved in military intervention." This prompted an Indian strategic analyst to write that "India's present naval capability is inadequate to convey help to these islands in case of trouble . . . but if Indian security planners give enough weight to the stability and security of the Indian Ocean islands as relevant to our own found to improve our security interaction with them by providing training, communication equipment and by exchanging information."[35]

In 1984, India gave the Seychelles two helicopters and initiated training programs for five helicopter pilots and two air force technicians. Indian economic aid totaled $2.5 million and was accompanied by another $5 million in commercial credits for the purchase of Indian goods. An Indian destroyer visited the Seychelles for the first time in June 1984, setting the stage for regular ship visits similar to those long established in Mauritius. Madagascar also had an Indian ship visit in 1984. Guy Rajaonson, President Ratsiraka's National Security Adviser, said that "we are not disturbed by the prospect of greater Indian influence. India is a littoral state and will certainly have a greater military presence in the region, and this issue should not be mixed up with the issue of the foreign military presence, as some Western countries like to do in opposing the zone of peace."

Kenya, where there is an Indian community of 70,000 with a strong role in industry, looks increasingly to India as a source of technology. Kenyan students find it cheaper to live and easier to adjust in India than in Britain or the United States. The Kenyan government views the Indian developmental experience as more relevant to Kenyan conditions than to Western experience, especially in the field of small-scale industry. There were 4000 Kenyan students in India in 1984, most of them financed by Kenya itself, in addition to 100 specialized students covered by Indian government scholarships. Kenya now sends more military trainees to India than to any other country. In 1984, 35 Kenyans were enrolled in three- to six-month officer training courses in the Indian army, air force, and navy. The Indian navy had two ship visits to Mombasa in 1981 and one in 1984.

An interesting augury of India's developing thrust toward the western Indian Ocean is the emergence of an Indian bloc in the politics of the French territory of La Réunion. At least 150,000 of the Réunion population of some 400,000 is of Indian origin, and the leader of the underground independence movement on the island, Georges Sinemale, said that the figure exceeds 200,000. Sinemale, whose parents came there in 1848 from Tamilnad as plantation laborers, told me that "France fears the 'Indian peril' because the Indians here are the most oppressed economically and are not assimilated culturally." Conversations with French officials on the island in March 1984 revealed suspicions that New Delhi is fomenting Tamil unrest, and in September sub-surface tensions erupted when the Tamil mayor of Sainte-Marie was arrested on embezzlement charges. "His incarceration," reported a French journal, "was regarded by a large proportion of the Indian community as an attempt by the authorities to crush what is the first real Tamil political experience on the island. The mayor personifies a trend that has been running through the Indian community for the past few years. More or less explicitly, he believes that power in La Réunion should one day fall into the hands of the Indians as it has done in Mauritius."[36] French suspicions were reinforced in early 1984 when India asked France for permission to open a Consulate-

General on the island. Paris responded icily that La Réunion is a part of metropolitan France.[37]

Even now, India has significant capabilities for protracted naval operations in the northern Arabian Sea and the northern Indian Ocean, and its reach to the western Indian Ocean is gradually expanding. The Indian navy has 2 British aircraft carriers; 3 Soviet missile destroyers; 9 Soviet submarines; 2 West German submarines; 24 frigates of mixed size and origin, including 2 made in India; and 2 maritime reconnaissance aircraft squadrons. Significantly, it also has 2 replenishment ships, 5 support tankers, and a repair ship, a support capability sufficient to sustain a small task force. Six more Soviet missile destroyers, 2 Soviet missile cruisers, 4 minesweepers, and 4 West German submarines are on order. New Delhi has so far stopped short of a visible power projection capability, such as a naval infantry force. A leading military spokesman explained that

> the question of acquiring the bigger surface vessels like troop landing ships and amphibious ships should not be immediately taken up because that would create apprehensions. Our expansion should focus more on submarines and maritime reconnaissance aircraft and fast patrol vessels and missile vessels . . . until such time as everybody around us reconciles himself to the fact that India has 40 submarines, that it is a major naval power, even though not a visible one; after that, when the idea has sunk in for a period, then the time will come for the rest.[38]

The possibility of a nuclear-armed Indian navy cannot be discounted. In 1980, India became the sixth country to launch a satellite on its own, and in 1983 it staged a second successful test, using a rocket that could be converted into an intermediate-range ballistic missile (IRBM) with a 3,300-mile range and an 880-pound warhead or, with greater difficulty, a comparable submarine-launched ballistic missile. Another, more ambitious test was scheduled for late 1988. Expert estimates suggest that it will take Indian scientists another 5–10 years to master some of the technology that would be needed to make IRBMs, including warhead miniaturization, heat shields for the nose cone, and gas velocity for thrust. But India already has the indigenous knowledge and skill necessary for inertial guidance systems and solid fuel propulsion as well as for anti-ship cruise missiles and other non-ballistic missiles.

The growth of Indian influence during the decades ahead in the Indian Ocean, including a naval presence supported by base facilities, need not conflict with the flexible deployment of a significant American naval presence in the region. While India is receiving substantial Soviet aid in building its navy, it does not give preferential treatment to Soviet naval vessels in its ports. In my view, if the United States were to show greater sensitivity to Indian security concerns relating to Pakistan, India would be prepared to reciprocate by giving a correspondingly greater recognition to the legitimacy of the U.S. naval presence in the Indian Ocean in the context of the global and regional superpower rivalry.

The climate of Indo-American relations remained troubled in 1988, primarily as a consequence of an American military aid relationship with Pakistan that reflected a myopic U.S. preoccupation with perceived U.S. interests in the Persian Gulf and Afghanistan. In Indian eyes, Islamabad wants to use the Afghan crisis as a means of bolstering its power position vis-à-vis New Delhi, just as it used the cold war for the same purpose when it entered into its earlier, ill-fated alliance with Washington in the 1950s. Moreover, India sees the specter of a new American-Pakistani alignment as a part of a larger challenge embracing China.

To some extent, it was possible for Indians to forgive and forget after the 1954 American military aid agreement with Pakistan. The United States was, after all, a newcomer on the Asian scene and had shown goodwill toward India through its economic help. President Eisenhower had given a formal undertaking to Prime Minister Nehru that American weapons were intended solely for use against Communist aggressors, pledging that the United States would not permit their use against India. When Pakistan did turn its F-104s and Patton tanks against India in 1965, the United States made good on its assurances, albeit tardily, by cutting off petroleum and spare parts to Islamabad and clamping an embargo on arms sales to South Asia.

This time, administration officials do not seek to justify American arms aid to Islamabad wholly in terms of the threat posed by Soviet forces in Afghanistan. On the contrary, they acknowledge that Pakistan wants American help primarily to strengthen itself vis-à-vis India, and they have pointedly declined to give either public or private promises to New Delhi that the United States would not permit its weaponry to be used in an India-Pakistan war. In his controversial October 1984 speech to the Council on Security Studies in Lahore, Deane Hinton, the U.S. Ambassador to Pakistan, did not rule out American support for Islamabad in a conflict with New Delhi. "If the contingency you're talking about is from the east," he said, "then we will not be neutral if there is an act, committed by anybody, of flagrant aggression. There's all kinds of things we can and would do. Whether they would be effective, arrive in time, is a very complex equation."

In the U.S. debate over the F-16 issue, many observers have asked why India should be afraid of its smaller neighbor, given New Delhi's inherently superior military potential and its growing defense production base. But fear of Pakistan does not explain the Indian reaction to the F-16s. Rather, India is outraged over what it regards as U.S. interference in the evolution of a natural balance of power in South Asia. Indian generals are confident of their ability to subdue Pakistan in any protracted conflict and do not believe that Islamabad would launch an all-out frontal attack. Their concern is that Pakistan, armed with a highly sophisticated aircraft such as the F-16, might engage in more limited military provocations, forcing New Delhi to pay an unacceptably high price to enforce its military superiority.

Pakistan, for its part, has its own ever-present fears of Indian intentions. These anxieties result not only from its military vulnerability as the smaller of the two countries, with one-eighth India's population, but also from the fact that it is a fragile multi-ethnic state torn by growing internal tensions.

India and Pakistan are inescapably enmeshed in a complicated love-hate relationship. They share many common elements of an overlapping cultural heritage and a nascent sense of South Asian regional identity that could conceivably draw them closer together in future decades. Viewed in a historical perspective, however, the process of adjustment between Hindus and Moslems that began with Partition is still in its early stages. New Delhi and Islamabad remain trapped in a vicious circle of enmity and distrust that is likely to continue for some time to come before there is an accommodation—or another explosion. For the United States, it would be the ultimate folly to become further caught up in this struggle, especially at a time when both countries are actively working to develop militarily applicable nuclear capabilities.

Instead of exacerbating Indo-Pakistani tensions and fostering a South Asian arms race, the United States should have encouraged the impulses for a concerted response to the Soviet challenge in Afghanistan that were beginning to stir in New Delhi and Islamabad during the latter part of 1980. It should be remembered that encouraging signs of a mutual desire for improved relations were beginning to surface in New Delhi and Islamabad even after the United States and Pakistan began to discuss expanded military assistance. Indian Foreign Minister Narasimha Rao made a significant visit to Pakistan as late as June 1981, in which he suggested that India and Pakistan should adopt a common posture toward the Soviet challenge in Afghanistan as part of a broader effort to forge more compatible foreign policies. India has "an abiding interest, even a vested interest in the stability of Pakistan," he declared, given "the geopolitical situation in which both of our countries find themselves . . . we should develop an individual and, if necessary, a joint capacity to resist a negative impact on us by external trends and external elements." Indian Foreign Secretary Ram Sathe also visited Islamabad during the spring of 1981 and was scheduled to make another visit until it became clear that the United States would be providing Pakistan with F-16s as part of its military aid package. India was reconciled in early 1981 to the prospect of U.S. military assistance to Pakistan addressed to the military problems posed for Pakistan by the Soviet occupation of Afghanistan. For example, though New Delhi would no doubt have made pro forma protests, Indian public opinion would have been able to digest American sales to Pakistan of F-20 (F-5G) interceptors, light tanks, anti-aircraft helicopters, and 105- and 120-millimeter howitzers, which would have a specific relevance to the mountainous Afghan frontier, as distinct from equipment intended primarily to improve Pakistan's balance of power with India, such as F-16s, M48 tanks, 155-millimeter howitzers, TOW missiles, tank recovery vehicles, and Huey Cobra assault helicopters designed for use against tanks. It was not the fact of a renewal of a U.S. military aid program for Pakistan, as such, but rather the character of the package that produced such a sharp impact in India, providing ammunition for the hawks in New Delhi and setting in motion a chain reaction of suspicion and recrimination that has not yet fully abated.

While India and Pakistan are cautiously probing once again to find the bases for a relaxation of tensions, progress in the Indo-Pakistan dialogue has so far been extremely limited. Neither India nor Pakistan has shown a readiness for significant compromise on the key issues relating to a projected friendship treaty or "no war" pact, or to the creation of a military subcommission that could consider proposals for disengagement in sensitive frontier areas where the armed forces of the two countries now confront each other. The relationship between India and Pakistan is still a volatile one, peculiarly sensitive to the slightest shifts in the American posture toward the subcontinent.

When the F-16 decision was announced in 1981, a long-simmering debate in India over whether and when to allocate scarce foreign exchange reserves to a new generation of fighter aircraft was soon resolved in favor of spending some $650 million on 40 Mirage 2000s. Similarly, the hawks in New Delhi were given a new lease on life when, in December 1982, just one month after President Zia Ul-Haq's visit to New Delhi, Zia induced President Reagan to upgrade the offensive capability of the F-16s by providing the ALR-69 radar system. Since then, demands have persisted for new Indian military procurement in the Soviet Union and elsewhere that would "put Pakistan in its place," and prospects for constructive evolution of the dialogue with Islamabad have become more tenuous than ever.

American policy toward South Asia should be based on a recognition that American and Pakistani interests are overlapping but not identical. The two countries have shared important interests during the period of the Soviet military occupation of Afghanistan and will continue to have a significant but reduced mutuality of interests so long as a Soviet client regime remains in Kabul. However, their interests diverge with respect to India. This means that future U.S. military assistance to Pakistan should be highly selective. If the Communist regime in Kabul survives, American aid should be designed to make a contribution to Pakistan's Afghan-focused defenses while avoiding items that would serve primarily to bolster Islamabad's military capability vis-à-vis New Delhi. Thus, the United States could provide large-scale concessional credits and grants for the construction of a sophisticated radar defense system covering the long Pakistan-Afghan frontier, as well as for a variety of infrastructural and other economic needs related directly or indirectly to the defense of border areas of the Northwest Frontier Province and Baluchistan (e.g., roads and airfields). Some infrastructure aid has already been planned but has been obstructed or delayed by competing outlays for F-16s and other costly hardware items. The United States could also sell certain items of weaponry, such as helicopters, mountain artillery, light tanks, and 105- or 120-millimeter howitzers. But it would not continue the sale of F-16s or other attack aircraft. American interests would be best served by encouraging Pakistan to deal with its India-related military needs, aircraft included, through commercial purchases from France, Sweden, Britain, and other Western suppliers.

The United States should also redefine its commitments to Pakistan under its 1959 mutual security agreement with Islamabad. This agreement, invoking the 1957 Eisenhower Doctrine, requires Washington to "take such appropriate action, including the use of armed forces, as may be mutually agreed upon" in the event of armed aggression against Pakistan by "any country controlled by international Communism." Pakistan contends that India and the Soviet Union are undeclared military allies. Islamabad argues that the 1959 agreement covers contingencies on the India-Pakistan border and that Pakistani forces can properly use their American weaponry on both frontiers. Previous U.S. administrations rejected this interpretation, but, as noted earlier, the Reagan Administration has pursued a policy of calculated ambiguity. The agreement as revised would relate solely to aggression by Soviet or Afghan communist forces. It would permit American support for Pakistan in such contingencies in the event of concurrent Indo-Pakistani hostilities. In a conflict limited to Indian and Pakistani forces alone, however, Washington would have no obligations to Islamabad.

Administration officials often explain their tilt toward Pakistan by arguing that India, with its extensive military reliance on Moscow, has already become a virtual Soviet ally and that the United States has nothing more to lose. But this is a dangerous over-simplification. India turned to the Soviets for arms in the 1960s only after the United States had started its military aid to Pakistan and only after New Delhi had made an unsuccessful bid for large-scale U.S. military aid. Moreover, New Delhi has consistently attempted to offset its dependence on Moscow. As one example, key components of the Indian-style Mig-21 aircraft made in India under a Soviet license are imported from the West. In recent years, New Delhi has been gradually increasing military procurement in Western Europe. More important, India has rebuffed Soviet efforts to obtain special military facilities in Indian ports.

India's non-aligned foreign policy is, by its nature, flexible in the pursuit of national self-interest. It is not designed to achieve equidistance between the superpowers, but rather to make use of the superpowers in order to promote Indian interests, even if this means temporarily leaning in one direction or the other. For more than three decades, the Soviet Union has identified itself with Indian regional aspirations, while the United States has generally sided with Pakistan and China. India has adapted to this situation by frequently tilting toward the Soviet Union. Conversely, if the United States were to give greater recognition to Indian regional primacy, New Delhi would gradually modify its posture during the decades ahead, though it would take time for Washington to undo the mistakes of past decades.

So far, New Delhi has carefully stopped short of de facto military collaboration with Moscow, but it would be unwise to assume that such restraint will continue to govern Indian policy regardless of the nature of U.S. policies toward Pakistan. As observed earlier, many politically conscious Indians were willing to forgive, though hardly to forget, American military aid to

Pakistan in the 1950s as the product of U.S. inexperience on the world stage. However, coming as it does after the 1965 and 1971 Indo-Pakistan wars, in which Pakistan used its U.S. weaponry against India, the Reagan Administration's resumption of military aid to Islamabad is viewed more darkly. At best, it is regarded as evidence of a growing divergence of geopolitical and strategic interests between Washington and New Delhi; at worst, it is seen as revealing deliberate malevolence. An atmosphere of xenophobic resentment is now building up among many key military and political figures who could have a major voice in shaping New Delhi's regional military role in the decades ahead. Given continuing provocations in the form of multiplying American weapons aid to Islamabad, this atmosphere could lead over time to a variety of punitive, anti-American moves in the Indian Ocean designed to limit the American military presence or to constrain and harass American forces in their use of existing facilities, including Diego Garcia. So far, Indian diplomatic and political support for Mauritius in its claim to Diego Garcia has been pro forma, but New Delhi could easily convert this issue into a growing embarrassment for the United States.

Situated closer to India than to any other country, the U.S. naval base complex on Diego Garcia is a constant affront to Indian regional ambitions. The fact that it was built on a British colonial territory over the protests of most Indian Ocean littoral states is likely to make it a continuing target of regional criticism. If the United States had a detached posture toward the Indo-Pakistani military rivalry, however, Diego Garcia would no longer impinge directly on Indian security concerns. New Delhi should then be prepared to make a tacit, pragmatic accommodation with U.S. use of the base for purposes relating to U.S. global military communications and to the deployment of U.S. forces in the Persian Gulf and Southwest Asia, except for contingencies involving India and Pakistan alone.[39]

Even if the United States were to taper off its military sales to Islamabad, New Delhi would no doubt continue to make significant military purchases from the Soviet Union. But this would not, in itself, be adverse to American interests in the context of a detached American posture toward the subcontinent in which a compatible Indo-American relationship would be developing side by side with continuing Indo-Soviet links. What makes the growing Indo-Soviet military relationship worrisome is not the resulting degree of Indian dependence on Moscow. As already observed, India has retained its freedom of action, offsetting its Soviet dependence with increasing arms purchases from Western countries. Close Indo-Soviet ties would become menacing to the United States only if Washington continued to array itself against Indian regional ambitions, prompting an Indian desire to retaliate in its own perceived interests.

The Reagan Administration has attempted to improve U.S. relations with India and to reduce Indian dependence on the Soviet Union by liberalizing exports of computers, electronic equipment, and other dual-use high technology with defense applications. In 1987, licenses were issued for potential exports totaling $1.143 billion. But high-technology alone is not likely to bring major geopolitical payoffs in India unless the United States ends the pro-Pakistan tilt in its military aid policy.

Western images of Indian life have been dominated for so long by snake charmers, naked fakirs, and starving peasants that it is difficult for many Americans to grasp the extent of progress achieved by India since independence. Despite continuing poverty in the countryside and sporadic domestic political upheavals, India has built the ninth largest industrial economy in the world. It makes most of its own consumer goods as well as its own industrial machinery. It exports a wide range of industrial items from machine tools to power-generating equipment and builds steel mills, oil refineries, and fertilizer plants in other Third World countries. In addition to its demonstrated nuclear capability, India has become the sixth country to launch a space satellite with its own launch vehicle. With its growing military-industrial complex and the world's third largest pool of scientists and engineers, India is certain to play an increasingly significant regional military role, and an American policy that ignores this emerging reality would be dangerously shortsighted and self-defeating.

Afghanistan: After the Soviet Withdrawal

An American shift to a more detached military aid posture in South Asia has become a realistic policy objective in the context of the 1988 U.N. agreement on a Soviet combat force withdrawal from Afghanistan. At the same time, it should be recognized that Soviet—and American—involvement in the Afghan civil war has not ended. The conflict between rival Afghan factions that set the stage for the occupation is likely to continue with foreign encouragement in a new and more virulent form.

On one side, the Soviet-subsidized Republic of Afghanistan is entrenched in its city-state in Kabul and surrounding areas, supported not only by Soviet money and advisers but also by its own elaborate Afghan military, paramilitary, and secret police apparatus. On the other, scattered groups of resistance fighters, while better coordinated militarily than in the past, continue to lack the political infrastructure that would be necessary to follow up their military successes by establishing secure liberated areas in the countryside.

The prevailing Western image of the Afghan struggle has been grossly oversimplified. In this imagery, there is a sharp dichotomy between an illegitimate Kabul regime, unable to establish its writ beyond the capital, and an alternative focus of legitimacy collectively provided by the resistance fighters, who are seen as controlling most of the country's land area. It is true that the Kabul regime does not have a firm grip on much of the countryside, but neither does the resistance. In reality, most of Afghanistan, now as in past decades and centuries, is governed by free-wheeling local tribal and ethnic warlords.

Until its destruction in 1973, the monarchy had provided the sole focus of political legitimacy and authority in Afghanistan for more than three centuries. The Afghan state was just barely a state. It was loosely superimposed atop a decentralized polity in which separate ethnic and tribal communities paid obeisance to Kabul only so long as it accorded them substantial autonomy. The number of politicized Afghans who wanted to create a centralized state was minuscule in relation to the total population. This politicized elite consisted of three distinct groups: Western-oriented intellectuals, who made up the largest segment; Soviet-oriented Communist factions; and Islamic fundamentalist elements with Moslem Brotherhoood links in the Persian Gulf and the Middle East. None of these groups had substantial independent organizational networks in the countryside. They were all equally dependent on alliances with the local tribal and ethnic leaders, who held the real power then and who continue to hold the real power in Afghanistan today.

The concept of legitimacy has little meaning against the backdrop of recent Afghan political history. The destruction of the monarchy left a political vacuum in which no consensus existed concerning the future of the Afghan polity, and no one group could make a clear-cut claim to greater legitimacy than another. Neither the Communists nor the Islamic fundamentalists claimed more than a few thousand members each in 1973. But even a few thousand disciplined, highly motivated members loomed large in what was such a limited political universe.

In addition to posing ideological challenges to the Western-oriented elite, the Communist and fundamentalist movements were vehicles of social protest by disadvantaged elements of the Afghan populace. The Parcham (Flag) Communist faction represented many of those in the detribalized Kabul intelligentsia and bureaucracy who felt shut out of power by the narrow dynastic in-group that dominated both the monarchy and the republic set up by Zahir Shah's jealous cousin, the late Mohammed Daud. The rival Khalq (Masses) faction had more of a tribal base, drawing largely on out-groups within the Pushtuns, Afghanistan's largest ethnic bloc. As the American anthropologist Jon Anderson has observed, the Khalqi leaders consisted largely of politicized "second sons and younger brothers" from the weaker tribes in the Ghilzai branch of the Pushtuns, searching for channels of social ascent in the face of the monopoly on military, bureaucratic, and professional jobs enjoyed by the Durrani Pushtuns centered in the royal family.[40] By contrast, the strongest fundamentalist cadres were organized in ethnic minority areas, such as the predominantly Tajik Pansjer Valley. The much-publicized resistance hero, Ahmad Shah Massoud, and his mentor, Jamaat Islami leader Burhanuddin Rabbani, built their organizational base in the Pansjer long before the Soviet occupation, preaching not only the Jamaat brand of fundamentalism but also the cause of Tajik liberation from Pushtun exploitation.

The intractability of the political stalemate in Afghanistan today can only be understoood if one recognizes that the present conflict began as a civil war. To be sure, many Afghans who welcomed the Communist takeover in 1978 were alienated by the brutality and over-zealous reforms of the late Hafizullah Amin, and most Afghans today feel that the Communist leaders who succeeded Amin have sullied their patriotic credentials as a result of their collaboration with the Russians. At the same time, it has been a mistake to think of the Afghan struggle in black-and-white terms as one between the Russians on one side and all Afghans on the other. The essence of the Afghan dilemma has been that a small but well-organized minority of Afghans has either supported or tolerated the Communist regime.

On a visit to Kabul in March 1984, I was reminded forcibly that dedication and a patriotic self-image are not a monopoly of the resistance fighters. The Afghan Communists see themselves as carrying forward the abortive modernization effort launched by King Amanullah in the 1920s. The Communist organization is clearly much stronger now than it was in 1978, even if one assumes that many of the new party recruits are mere job-seekers. Communist sources claim that the party membership rose from its 1978 level of some 5000 to 150,000 in 1986. A U.S. government intelligence analyst contends that 75,000 would be a more accurate number but acknowledges, in any case, that the party "is unmistakably growing. Expansion of membership among peasants and soldiers has meant a smaller pool of capable, committed activists for the resistance to draw on."[41]

Based on my 1984 visit and subsequent research, my own estimate is that the party had between 25,000 and 35,000 hard-core activists in 1988, allowing for the fact that many new recruits are ideologically unreliable job-seekers. Moreover, the number of Communist true believers is continually enlarged by the return of at least 20,000 Afghan youths who have been sent to the Soviet Union for training. The number of Afghans on the Soviet-subsidized payroll of the Kabul regime appears to be some 350,000, including about 60,000 in the army, another 75,000 in various paramilitary forces, and at least 25,000 in the secret police. Communist activists have been installed in key positions throughout the government structure, with 64 percent of the party membership concentrated in military and paramilitary command posts.[42]

The Afghan Communists have rationalized their collaboration with the Russians as the only way available to consolidate their revolution in the face of foreign "interference." As German journalist Andreas Kohlschutter of *Die Zeit* reported after a visit to Kabul, the commitment of the Communists to rapid modernization enables them to win a grudging tolerance from many members of the "modern-minded middle class, who feel trapped between two fires: the Russians and fanatic Muslims opposed to social reforms."[43] Confronted with a choice between the Communists and the Islamic fundamentalist leaders of the major resistance groups, such Afghans simply sit on the sidelines. In Kabul I found a widespread ambivalence toward the post-1980 Communist leaders as "moderates" who are trying to live down Amin's extremist mistakes.

Amin had sought to centralize the country overnight, riding roughshod over the autonomy traditionally enjoyed by both the Pushtun tribes and by non-tribal ethnic minorities. His attempts to replace established local power structures with a Communist administrative network aroused an armed resistance that helped to set the stage for the Soviet occupation. Amin also alienated businessmen, merchants, and small and middle landowners with his doctrinaire land reform and economic policies. Most important, he directly challenged the power and prerogatives of Islamic dignitaries, provoking the active intervention of Islamic fundamentalist groups throughout the Persian Gulf and the Middle East in support of the nascent anti-Communist insurgency.

In contrast to the excesses of the Amin period, post-1980 Communist leaders have pursued soft-line policies designed to undercut the insurgency. In particular, Kabul has now adopted a system of local government consciously structured to avoid a collision with grass-roots tribal and ethnic elites. On paper, at least, the tribes as such have representation in local government machinery in accordance with their numerical strength. The Communist Party promises not to run candidates for local bodies below the level of the *woleswali,* or district (roughly equivalent to several counties in the United States), which will give the tribes de facto autonomy if the promise is kept.

Apart from its offers of local autonomy, Kabul has also sought to moderate the image of monolithic Communist rule at the national level associated with Amin by emphasizing its character as a "national democratic revolution" in which non-Communist Afghans can share power. On December 22, 1985, *Pravda* signaled this new emphasis on power-sharing, conceding that "far from all people in Afghanistan, even among working sections of the population, accepted the Revolution."[44] This foreshadowed subsequent pronouncements acknowledging more explicitly the limitations of the Afghan Communists, especially one in *Literaturnaya Gazeta* on February 17, 1988, attacking the "false belief" that a countrywide Communist regime could be established in Afghanistan's "medieval broth" of tribal and ethnic conflict.

As Moscow's pressure for power-sharing has increased, non-Communists have been appointed to highly visible but relatively powerless government positions as deputy prime minister and as deputy ministers and advisers in various government ministries. A non-Communist businessman has replaced a top Communist leader as president of the National Front, the regime's major organizational link with cooperative non-Communists. In a move heralded as paving the way for new political parties, the governing Revolutionary Council announced in 1986 that non-Communist "organizations and socio-political groups" could be formed, provided they were ready to cooperate with the National Front.[45] The new Constitution promulgated in 1987 went further, authorizing a "multi-party system," and several small parties nominally competed with the Communists in elections for a bicameral parliament in April 1988. But the government acknowledged the difficulties of conducting an election under wartime conditions, reporting a turnout of 1.5 million voters. Similarly, when local elections were held in 1985, Kabul conceded that voting had been completed in only 8 out of 29 provinces.[46]

To counter the accusation by resistance groups that it is anti-Islamic, the regime emphasizes that it has spent $25 million since 1980 to revitalize Islamic worship. The lion's share of this sum has been used to rebuild 1118 mosques and to construct 118 new ones. But a significant share has also gone to provide new houses and other emoluments to the *imams,* or presiding dignitaries, of the mosques, as well as stipends to 11,570 other functionaries of mosques and religious schools.[47] Land owned by religious dignitaries and their institutions is exempt from land reforms.

Significantly, *imams* and *mullahs* are given power of review over the textbooks used in teaching 21,000 women said to be enrolled in literacy courses.[48] A special effort has been made to recruit women in mass literacy programs in order to capitalize on the resentment engendered among many younger urban women by orthodox Islamic resistance to women's education.

In place of Amin's harsh land redistribution measures, Kabul now permits peasants to own up to 45 acres, focusing its agricultural policy on price subsidies and services for farmers, such as motor and tractor pools, agricultural banks, and the distribution of fertilizer. Similarly, in an effort to win over businessmen and merchants, the Communist regime issued decrees in 1980 guaranteeing private property rights and granting tax holidays up to six years for new investments, together with customer-free imports of machinery.

Far from offering an alternative focus of legitimacy to Kabul, the resistance groups are themselves divided along ethnic, tribal, and sectarian lines. Repeatedly during the past five years, they have failed to establish a collective identity despite intense pressure from Washington and Arab capitals. Morover, since they are organized primarily to conduct military operations, most of them do not have disciplined political cadres capable of building an underground political and administrative infrastructure at the local level. The Pansjer Valley, Kandahar and Herat cities, and parts of Ghazni district are conspicuous exceptions to this generalization. In these areas, one or more resistance groups have relatively solid political foundations that could conceivably become the basis for liberated zones similar to those established in China, Vietnam, Guinea-Bissau, and other Third World countries where guerrilla armies have been successful. Kabul is likely to face significant resistance in the Pansjer indefinitely despite the relentless onslaught of the Soviet military juggernaut in offensive after offensive. But the fact that the Pansjer is an ethnic minority Tajik area, and a stronghold of the fundamentalist groups, limits its potential as a rallying point for the resistance in the Pushtun areas and other parts of the country where the fundamentalist appeal is weak.

Islamic fundamentalism is not as strong in Afghanistan as it is often assumed. It is arrayed against the entire traditional Islamic leadership as well as against Western-oriented and Communist modernizers alike. More important, with their pan-Islamic ideology, the fundamentalist groups have alienated the powerful tribal hierarchy in the Pushtun areas by calling for the abolition of tribalism as incompatible with their conception of a centralized Islamic state.

Except in the Pansjer Valley and several urban areas, the fundamentalist groups have never had significant locally based organizations, but the advent of a Communist Afghanistan in 1978 gave their exiled leaders a golden opportunity to build cadres among the Afghan refugees in Pakistan. Since 1978 they have received substantial support from fundamentalist elements in the Middle East and the Gulf. Most of the $2.1 billion in American and American-orchestrated aid to the resistance channeled through Pakistani authorities has also gone to the fundamentalists rather than to tribally based Pushtun elements of the resistance. One reason for this is that the Zia Ul-Haq regime in Islamabad depended on political support from the Pakistani fundamentalist groups. Another is the legacy of Pushtun irredentism. The Pushtuns in Afghanistan have periodically demanded the return of Pushtun areas annexed by the British Raj a century ago and later bequeathed to Pakistan when it was created in 1947. Pakistani leaders fear that Pushtun refugees from Afghanistan might now combine with Pakistani Pushtuns to demand the creation of a separate "Pushtunistan" in the Pakistani-Afghan borderlands. Thus, Islamabad consciously sought to prevent Pushtun groups from using the conflict to coalesce politically and to strengthen themselves militarily.

The United States accepted the Pakistani rationale that military effectiveness should be the only criterion for aid allocations. This gave Islamabad carte blanche to channel aid to the relatively cohesive fundamentalist paramilitary cadres, based in Pakistan, rather than to the more loosely organized but locally prestigious Pushtun tribal guerrillas operating in the Afghan countryside. As a result, in the continuing civil war likely to follow the Soviet departure, the fundamentalists will be better organized and better armed than ever before.

The United States was cool to the United Nations negotiations on a Soviet force withdrawal from the inception of the U.N. effort in 1982 until the first Reagan-Gorbachev summit in November 1985. Soon after the summit, however, the United States announced its qualified support of the U.N. withdrawal agreement that was then beginning to crystallize. The accord was nominally between Islamabad and Kabul but provided for guarantees by both Moscow and Washington. Formally pledging to serve as a guarantor, the Reagan Administration conditioned its acceptance of the U.N. accord on the resolution of one, and only one, outstanding issue: the duration, stages and "irreversibility" of the Soviet withdrawal process. The Administration did not seek to alter the essential character of the bargain embodied in the accord. A Soviet commitment to a complete withdrawal was to be exchanged for the termination of U.S. weapons aid to the Afghan resistance.

This change in American policy set the stage for progress in the U.N. negotiations that was accelerated as Mikhail Gorbachev moved to reshape Soviet foreign policy. Gorbachev's desire to remove the increasingly costly Afghan conflict as an impediment to improved superpower relations was reflected in a series of significant Soviet concessions in the U.N. dialogue during the next two years. By the second Reagan-Gorbachev summit in December 1987, agreement had been reached on all aspects of the agreement except the duration of the withdrawal. Thus, in the expectation of a settlement, Moscow played its trump card on February 8, 1988, announcing its readiness for a nine-month disengagement, with half of its forces to be removed in the first three months. Two weeks later, however, under pressure from Congressional critics, the Administration added a major new condition: the termination or suspension of Soviet military aid to the Kabul Communist regime.

The demand for "symmetry" directly collided with the underlying *real-politik* approach of the withdrawal agreement. The U.N. formula had carefully avoided placing Moscow in the position of conceding defeat by abandoning its Afghan clients. Distinguishing between military aid to a U.N.-accredited government and aid to insurgents, it did not address the issue of Soviet weapons aid to Kabul. It did not require the replacement of the Kabul regime as a precondition for the withdrawal. At first, when Washington made its demand, a collapse of the negotiations appeared likely. In a last-minute triumph of diplomatic legerdemain, however, Moscow and Washington negotiated a secret side-agreement that permitted the withdrawal to go forward within the framework of the U.N. accord.

Both superpowers would give their clients enough arms beforehand to last for the nine-month withdrawal period or longer. Both would then suspend aid for an unspecified period. This meant that the U.S. would be in compliance with the ban on its aid in the agreement when the withdrawal started. Moscow would not have to concede publicly that it had suspended aid. But the Reagan Administration, anxious to placate conservative critics of the agreement, would be free to state that it reserved the right to violate the ban on its aid when, and if, Moscow should resupply weaponry to Kabul. During the withdrawal, the United Nations would seek to promote a non-aligned coalition government in which the armed forces would no longer be under Communist control. The issue of Soviet military aid would then be neutralized and both sides would give economic and military aid to the new regime.

Given the fragility of this compromise, the likelihood of continued civil war with covert foreign support was taken for granted by most foreign observers in mid-1988. Among Afghans, however, significant support existed for a non-aligned coalition government that would reduce the level of violence in the country and thus attract the international support necessary for a major reconstruction effort.

Most Pushtuns, including Pushtun resistance commanders and the majority of the returning refugees,[49] looked to former King Zahir Shah as a key figure in such a regime. The former monarch has long advocated a "national unity" government in which the Communists would be reduced to a junior partner's role, with the armed forces, the police and the intelligence services in non-Communist hands. This has been resisted by the Communists, who have unsuccessfully appealed to Zahir Shah for power-sharing within the framework of the Communist regime. A coalition regime has also been rejected by the fundamentalists, who have demanded a government under their aegis with no Communist participation.

What appeared to be emerging in mid-1988 was a complex struggle in which tribal and fundamentalist factions would fight each other as well as the Kabul regime. Moscow, for its part, indicated its readiness for a coalition regime, but appeared confident that the Communists would, in any case, survive as a political force. While the Kabul regime might not prevail over much of the country, Soviet analysts suggested, the Communists would remain strong enough to prevent a fundamentalist takeover.[50]

The U.N. agreement provides only for the withdrawal of Soviet combat forces, pointedly omitting any reference to Soviet advisers.[51] Thus, so long as Moscow continues to have a client regime in Afghanistan, however limited in authority, Soviet military advisers can remain there, maintaining airfields, military communications and other military facilities in a state of readiness. Moscow will be in a position to reintroduce its forces on short notice. Nevertheless, in the event of a future military crisis involving the movement of Soviet forces through Afghanistan, the United States and its allies would have much more warning time than at present. A Soviet combat force withdrawal clearly serves Western security interests in the Gulf and Southwest Asia by relieving the immediate military pressure resulting from ongoing Soviet force deployments and from the ongoing operational use of Soviet bases. With respect to Soviet advisers, it should be kept in mind that Moscow had some 6000 military advisers in Afghanistan when the non-Communist Mohammed Daud regime was unseated by the Communists in 1978.

American security interests would be served by a non-aligned coalition government because such a regime would be likely to limit the Soviet advisory presence and seek to renegotiate or abrogate the 1978 Soviet-Afghan treaty concluded by the Communist regime. Article IV of the 1978 treaty provides that "the High Contracting Parties shall consult with each other and shall, by agreement, take the necessary steps to safeguard the security, independence and territorial integrity of the two countries." This has been compared to the 1948 Soviet-Finnish treaty, which provides for the possible return of Soviet troops "by mutual agreement" in the event that "Finland, or the Soviet Union through the territory of Finland, becomes the object of military aggression."

Should a coalition government emerge, the United States should press for restrictions that would confine Soviet military advisers to Kabul. In a non-aligned Afghanistan, there should be no Soviet military bases, and the presence of Soviet advisers at military installations around the country would signify a covert Soviet base presence in violation of the U.N. accord.

Avenues to Détente in the Indian Ocean and the Persian Gulf

Apart from the specific modalities of the 1988 United Nations' force withdrawal agreement, an enduring Afghan settlement would have to be accompanied by parallel understandings between the United States and the Soviet Union designed to neutralize Iran and Pakistan as arenas of great-power conflict. In particular, Washington and Moscow would have to make appropriate diplomatic efforts to reassure each other that neither would introduce combat forces or mutually threatening bases or facilities into the two countries. Such mutual restraint agreements in Iran and Pakistan, accompanied by a winding down of the conflict in Afghanistan, would enhance opportunities, in turn, for a larger Soviet-American arms control dialogue during the decades ahead addressed to the Indian Ocean region as a whole.

Former Secretary of State Cyrus Vance wanted to propose a mutual restraint agreement to Moscow covering both Pakistan and Iran following the Soviet occupation of Afghanistan in 1979 but was prevented from doing so by then National Security Adviser Zbigniew Brzezinski. Recalling this episode in his memoirs, Brzezinski explained that he "failed to see what U.S. interest would be served by making the Soviet Union in effect the co-guarantor of neutrality in the Persian Gulf region."[52] In the immediate aftermath of the Soviet occupation, Brzezinski's view had resonance, but the Vance approach would serve U.S. interests in the context of the Soviet combat force withdrawal.

As a practical matter, the opportunity for a formal or informal mutual restraint agreement in the immediate future would be greater in Iran than in Pakistan. Washington is already deeply involved with Islamabad, while both superpowers feel excluded from preferential access to Tehran. Nonetheless, Moscow continually says that it fears a new U.S. effort to gain military access to Iran in the period after the Ayatollah Ruhollah Khomeini, and Washington points to the threat of a Soviet invasion of Iran as the principal justification for its Central Command buildup.

In the case of Pakistan, both the United States and the Soviet Union have understandable reasons for their mutual suspicion. Many in Washington fear that Moscow may seek to break up Pakistan, if necessary, in order to establish naval bases at Karachi and Gwadar. This anxiety is rekindled periodically by Soviet threats to punish Islamabad for its pro-Washington stance by arming Baluch insurgents. Moscow has its own suspicions that the Pentagon wants military bases on the Pakistani coast. Pakistani officials privately say that Islamabad has agreed to permit American P-3C anti-submarine and reconnaissance aircraft to refuel in Pakistani airfields. These stopovers are of marginal importance to the United States but are perceived by the Soviet Union as the cutting edge of what might become an expanding American base presence.

The danger of a U.S.-Soviet collision in Pakistan could become acute if the United States should seek to install electronic intelligence facilities there. In the 1950s and 1960s, Pakistan permitted the United States to base U-2 spy planes on its territory and operate electronic monitoring stations in return for U.S. military hardware. Washington obtained valuable intelligence relating partly to arms control. But the United States paid a heavy political price for these benefits because it was the American military buildup of Pakistan during this period that opened the way for Soviet military aid to India and Soviet penetration of the Afghan armed forces. Since the loss of U.S. facilities in Iran, the National Security Agency has been eyeing Pakistan once again, this time as a possible location for monitoring the lift-off stage of Soviet anti-satellite missile and intercontinental ballistic missile tests in central Asia as well as for early warning in the event that Soviet anti-satellite missiles are fired at U.S. satellites from central Asian sites.

The Pakistani bureaucracy, as well as Pakistani public opinion, is deeply divided over the American connection. Former Foreign Minister Agha Shahi was eased out in 1982 partly because he felt that the Zia regime was moving too far and too fast into the American camp. Shahi reflected what became the dominant trend of public opinion when he stressed the urgent need for the United States to "change from a policy of raising the costs of the Soviet occupation [of Afghanistan] or excluding that superpower from the [Middle East] peace-making process to one of enlisting its cooperation in arriving at peaceful settlements."[53]

At one point during the U.N. negotiations over Afghanistan, Moscow went beyond the concept of mutual restraint agreements, signaling its possible interest in a more far-reaching approach suggestive of a condominium. The initial U.N. draft text of the proposed guarantee of the Afghan settlement by the superpowers envisaged separate but identical Soviet and American statements. But in its revised draft, submitted at the August 1984 round of negotiations, Moscow proposed a joint U.S.-Soviet statement. The United States and the Soviet Union, in this document, not only were to pledge their own "non-intervention" in Pakistan and Afghanistan but were also to promise to join in resisting intervention by third parties.

The United States clearly should avoid any hint of a condominum while pursuing more limited agreements designed to prevent a U.S.-Soviet military confrontation. Moscow and Washington are engaged in a serious political and economic competition in the Indian Ocean/Persian Gulf area. The recent Soviet normalization of relations with Oman and the United Arab Emirates indicates that this competition is likely to intensify. Precisely for this reason, however, the superpowers should search for ways to make their rivalry less dangerous and less costly. For example, the Indo-American Task Force on the Indian Ocean has recommended that "the United States, the USSR and other concerned countries . . . explore the possibility of agreements ensuring unimpeded oil tanker traffic through the Strait of Hormuz and other 'choke points.'" Former State Department official Christopher Van Hollen made similar proposals in the Summer 1981 issue of *Foreign Affairs*.

Against the background of a relaxation of tensions in Afghanistan, Iran, and Pakistan, the United States and the Soviet Union could begin to confront the overarching long-term challenge of regional arms control. Indeed, the Soviet withdrawal could be used to open the way for a larger arms control dialogue, with a formal agreement barring Soviet bases in Afghanistan linked to a U.S. quid pro quo concerning one or more of the U.S. bases in the Persian Gulf and the Indian Ocean.

The superpower arms race in the Indian Ocean and the Persian Gulf could prove to be not only more dangerous than is generally realized but also more expensive. A Congressional Budget Office projection suggested that the Central Command would entail cumulative defense budget increases surpassing $45 billion in 1988.[54] Although the United States has achieved naval superiority in the Indian Ocean, Soviet capabilities for competing with the United States are growing. As observed earlier, Moscow could well seek to deploy some of its projected Forrestal-class aircraft carriers and amphibious landing craft in the Indian Ocean region.

In devising new approaches to regional arms control, it is helpful to recall the principal elements of the draft treaty that was under discussion between the United States and the Soviet Union in 1977 and 1978.

The agreement would have prohibited both sides from altering "significantly . . . past patterns and levels of military deployments" in the region, from acquiring new bases, and from expanding then existing facilities. A considerable area of agreement emerged in four rounds of negotiations concerning the precise character of the actual past patterns and levels of deployments of the two sides. Thus it was envisaged that the Soviet Union could continue to deploy 18 to 20 surface vessels, up to one-half of them combatants. The United States could continue to station its three-ship force at Bahrain and to send three task forces per year into the Indian Ocean. At least one of those could include a carrier battle group, provided that only one task force would be deployed in the area at any one time and that it would not remain for more than 65 days. Similarly, since neither side had previously deployed strategic bombers carrying offensive weapons in the region, neither could introduce such systems.

The sensitive issue of submarine operations was handled with calculated ambiguity. As explained by U.S. participants in the talks, given the U.S. policy of neither confirming nor denying the existence of nuclear weapons in a particular military environment, the negotiations could not address the nature of "past patterns and levels of deployment" of submarines in the region frontally and explicitly, as in the case of surface vessels. Nevertheless, in seeking to counter past Soviet charges of U.S. nuclear saber rattling, the United States had informally assured some of the major littoral states that it did not operate routine patrols of nuclear-missile-firing submarines in the Indian Ocean and that the transit of such submarines there, if it had in fact occurred, had been at a "low level." The Soviet Union, these sources note, was aware of this American posture, so U.S. readiness to agree to the "past patterns and levels" concept had a significant diplomatic and political meaning in Soviet eyes.

The draft agreement took cognizance of the fact that neither side had previously established in the Indian Ocean facilities dedicated to supporting forward-deployed submarines and contained an explicit pledge that neither would introduce such facilities in the future. However, the agreement did not cover operations by submarines relying on bases or support facilities located outside the Indian Ocean. One of the unresolved issues in the negotiations was how to define the geographic boundaries of the Indian Ocean so as to permit the United States to use its bases in western Australia to support naval units, including submarines, and to upgrade and expand these bases as desired.

Moscow had one frequently stated, overriding objective in the 1977–78 negotiations: to remove or reduce the threat of U.S. nuclear weapons aimed at the Soviet Union from submarines or other launching facilities located in the Indian Ocean. Washington sought primarily to place limits on the Soviet building of conventional forces in the region. The negotiations had reached a promising stage when the United States broke them off, nominally in protest over the Soviet move into Ethiopia.

In Soviet eyes, the most important unresolved issue was the U.S. refusal to bar carrier-based aircraft capable of reaching Soviet targets. But agreed-to limits on numbers of ships and the amount of time during which they could be stationed in the Indian Ocean would have meant a reduction of the strategic threat to the Soviet Union and its local forces from U.S. forces there.

The Soviet Union retains an undiminished interest in limiting U.S. strategic deployments in the Indian Ocean. The United States, for its part, has a greater interest than ever in limiting the Soviet conventional buildup, given the continuing growth in Soviet capabilities. Moreover, as noted earlier, anxieties are growing in many of the Indian Ocean littoral states as a result of the uncontrolled escalation of the superpower military presence. Since the United States now has a larger presence than the Soviet Union, Washington is incurring increasingly heavy political and diplomatic costs in some countries.

The United States has greater bargaining flexibility as a result of the new Trident submarine-launched ballistic missile. Its predecessors had ranges of only 2500 nautical miles, and it was often argued that the proximity of the Arabian Sea to major Soviet targets would make it desirable for U.S. missile-firing submarines to patrol regularly there. Given the 6000-plus-mile range of the Trident II (D-5) missile, the proximity argument is less compelling.

The United States was unwilling in 1978 to accept limits on its carrier-based aircraft in the absence of adequate reciprocal restrictions on Soviet land-based strike aircraft, including aircraft based at facilities inside Soviet territory adjacent to Southwest Asia. Washington argued that it needs to offset the advantage enjoyed by the Soviets because of their proximity to the Persian Gulf, where America has vital interests. Moscow countered that the immediate security of the Soviet homeland itself is threatened by U.S. nuclear weapons deployed so close to its borders. This issue has been complicated by the subsequent acquisition of new bases by both powers. At this stage, however, the development of the new bases has not, in most cases, passed the point of no return, and the opportunity still exists for regional trade-offs encompassing land- and sea-based forces alike.

The major American objectives in such trade-offs should be to preclude the Soviet use of military facilities in Afghanistan as operating bases, together with other limitations on Soviet forces based outside Soviet territory, notably at Aden in South Yemen and at Dahlak Kebir Island off Ethiopia. Moscow no doubt would emphasize the threat it perceives from Diego Garcia, as well as from nuclear-capable aricraft based on U.S. carriers in the region. If land-sea trade-offs prove possible, an agreement on time limits for ship deployments could again be explored. Although the United States should not foreclose its option of deploying nuclear-missile submarines in times of crisis, it should go as far as possible in limiting its nuclear presence in the Indian Ocean.

Like the problem of mutual force reductions in central Europe, arms control issues relating to the Indian Ocean/Persian Gulf region are closely interwoven with larger arms control issues and can only be confronted effectively through direct discussion between the superpowers. At the same time, both Washington and Moscow should be prepared to acknowledge in some form the legitimate interest of the littoral states in the nature and level of military deployments in the region. For example, a Zone of Peace conference or, in its absence, the existing U.N. Ad Hoc Committee could create an arms control working group that could be given a consultative role in any Soviet-American arms control dialogue. As indicated earlier, most of the littoral states now view a Zone of Peace conference as a symbolic exercise that would help to push the superpowers to the bargaining table. In place of the goal of a fully demilitarized zone originally envisaged, the littoral states are now seeking to stabilize the Soviet-American military rivalry through mutual force reductions. The United States should no longer stand in the way of the proposed conference now that Moscow is withdrawing its forces from Afghanistan.

Both superpowers are politically and psychologically alienated from public opinion throughout the littoral states and would profit from a relaxation of tensions. Such a relaxation would require parallel negotiating processes linking observance of the U.N. agreement on Afghanistan with mutual restraint agreements in Iran and Pakistan as well as a broader arms control dialogue. For the Soviet Union, the end of the eight-year Afghan occupation offers an opportunity to erase damage to its image that has been especially severe in the Gulf and the Arab world. For the United States, the Soviet withdrawal is likely to mean a reappraisal of relations with Pakistan, which will no longer be a "front-line" state and will encounter growing skepticism when it demands the most advanced weaponry in American arsenals. As suggested earlier, if the Communist regime in Kabul survives, limited military assistance to Islamabad would be desirable. But a continuation of sophisticated military aid at the levels that have prevailed since 1980 would place the United States on a collision course with India—a course that would become increasingly damaging to American security interests as New Delhi achieves growing regional power and importance in the decades ahead.

Notes

1. Ravi Rikhye, *The Fourth Round: Indo-Pak War 1984* (New Delhi: ABC Publishing House, 1982), esp. pp. 203 and 216–241.

2. As "natural extensions," the Persian Gulf and the Red Sea have been specifically included within the scope of the projected American-Soviet arms control

agreement discussed in 1977 and 1978 and in the Zone of Peace discussions in the U.N. Ad Hoc Committee on the Indian Ocean.

3. In addition to a representative spectrum of officials, political leaders, journalists, scholars, and businessmen, I was able to meet the following ranking leaders in the six countries visited: the late Prime Minister Indira Gandhi of India; President Junius Jayewardena of Sri Lanka; President France Albert Rene of the Seychelles; Prime Minister Aneerood Jugnauth of Mauritius; Guy Rajaonson, National Security Adviser to President Didier Ratsiraka of Madagascar; and Deputy Foreign Minister Philip Leakey of Kenya. In La Réunion, a territory of France, I met Capitaine de Vaisseau Michel Karle, Commander of French naval forces in the southern Indian Ocean and French military intelligence specialists in southern Indian Ocean affairs who requested anonymity.

4. *Soviet Military Power* (Washington, D.C.: U.S. Department of Defense, 1984), p. 125.

5. Selig S. Harrison, "The United States and South Asia," a paper prepared for a conference on "Defense Planning for the 1990's and the Changing International Environment," sponsored by the National Defense University, Washington, October 7–8, 1983. See also William Arkin, "Limiting Nuclear Navies," *International Herald Tribune,* July 9, 1988, p. 5.

6. "Emerging Issues in the Indian Ocean: The Military Dimension," a paper prepared for the Indo-American Task Force on the Indian Ocean, co-sponsored by the Carnegie Endowment for International Peace and the Indian Committee on Cultural Relations, November 25–December 2, 1984, pp. 72–73.

7. "The Soviet Union in the Indian Ocean: Much Ado About Something, But What?," *Asian Survey,* September 1984, p. 914.

8. See Marion and Burton Benedict, *Men, Women and Money in the Seychelles* (Berkeley: University of California Press, 1982), esp. pp. 103–149.

9. Shiva Naipaul, "A Seychellois Identity," *The Spectator,* November 19, 1983, p. 12.

10. *Paradise Raped* (London: Methuen, 1980), p. 118.

11. Ibid., p. 147.

12. Ibid., esp. pp. 116–117, 152, 193.

13. See *The Constitution of the Seychelles People's Progressive Front* (Victoria, Mahe: Government Press, September 1978).

14. For example, see "Private Eye Foils Seychelles Coup," *The Sunday Times* (London), December 4, 1983.

15. *Hearings on Military Posture and HR 2614,* Committee on Armed Services, U.S. House of Representatives, 97th Congress, 1st Session, p. 280.

16. Robert J. Hanks, *The Cape Route: Imperiled Western Lifeline* (Cambridge, Mass.: Institute for Foreign Policy Analysis, February 1981).

17. For example, see "The Indian Ocean: A New Caribbean?," *AfricAsia* (Paris), February 1984, pp. 35–36.

18. *Report of the Select Committee on the Excision of the Chagos Archipelago* (Port Louis, Mauritius: Mauritius Legislative Assembly, Government Printer, June 1983), pp. 14, 36.

19. Ibid., p. 37.

20. Ibid.

21. Ibid., pp. 32–33.

22. For example, see April 18, 1973, esp. p. 608; April 3, 1979, esp. p. 113;

April 10, 1979, esp. pp. 302–306; April 16, 1981, esp. pp. 486–494; and July 27, 1982, pp. 1248–1250.

23. See the late Prime Minister Indira Gandhi's press conference in Port Louis on August 24, 1982, and her Washington press conference on July 30, 1982.

24. *Views Expressed by Member States of the Ad Hoc Committee on the Indian Ocean,* Background Paper, United Nations, General Assembly, New York, Document A/AC/159/L55, July 5, 1983, p. 25.

25. Ibid., p. 19.

26. Kirdi Kipoyudo, "Important Developments in the Indian Ocean Area," *Indonesian Quarterly* 10, 2 (1983).

27. *Views Expressed by Member States of the Ad Hoc Committee on the Indian Ocean,* op. cit., p. 74.

28. Ibid., p. 36.

29. *Proposal for a Set of Principles on the Indian Ocean as a Zone of Peace,* United Nations, General Assembly, Ad Hoc Committee on the Indian Ocean, Document A/AC. 159/L44, May 21, 1982.

30. B. Tuzmakhamedov, "Space Limits of Peace Zone in the Indian Ocean," *Soviet Review,* No. 50 (December 12, 1983), pp. 28–29.

31. *Views Expressed by Member States of the Ad Hoc Committee on the Indian Ocean,* op. cit., p. 30.

32. Dieter Braun, *The Indian Ocean: Region of Conflict or 'Peace Zone'?* (London: C. Hurst and Co., 1983), pp. 184–185.

33. *India and the Indian Ocean: New Horizons* (New Delhi: Sterling Publishers, 1983), p. 119.

34. P. K. S. Namboodiri, with J. P. Anand and Sreedhar, *Intervention in the Indian Ocean* (New Delhi: ABC Publishing House, 1982), p. 234.

35. P. K. S. Namboodiri, "India and the Security of the Indian Ocean Islands," *Strategic Analysis Quarterly* (New Delhi: Institute of Defense Studies and Analyses, 1982), p. 385.

36. "La Réunion: The Tamil Question," *La Letter De L'Océan Indien* (Paris), September 8, 1984, p. 1.

37. "French Permission Sought to Open Consulate in Reunion Island," *The Hindu* (Madras), March 17, 1984, p. 3.

38. *India, the United States and the Indian Ocean,* report of the Indo-American Task Force on the Indian Ocean (Washington, D.C.: Carnegie Endowment for International Peace, 1985), p. 60.

To encourage candid discussion, the Task Force agreed that individual participants would not be quoted by name in the report.

39. Ibid., chapter three, presents a revealing dialogue between Indian and American specialists concerning possible Indian concessions in Indian Ocean policy in return for U.S. policy changes relating to Indian security concerns.

40. Jon Anderson, "Afghan Analogies, Afghan Realities" (unpublished ms.).

41. Craig M. Karp, "The War in Afghanistan," *Foreign Affairs,* Summer 1986, p. 1038.

42. Bakhtar News Agency, Kabul, May 14, 1986; cited in *Daily Report: South Asia,* Foreign Broadcast Information Service, May 15, 1986, p. C1.

43. "Wir Warten Auf Unser Schicksal" (We Are Waiting for Our Fate), *Die Zeit,* Dec. 28, 1984, p. 3.

44. *Pravda,* December 22, 1985, First Edition, p. 5; cited in *Daily Report: USSR International Affairs,* Dec. 24, 1985, p. D1.

45. Declaration of the Revolutionary Council, Bakhtar News Agency, Nov. 14, 1985, published by the Permanent Representative of the Democratic Republic of Afghanistan to the United Nations, Nov. 29, 1985.

46. Kabul Domestic Service in Pashto, April 5, 1988, cited in FBIS South Asia Report, April 6, 1988, p. 41; April 15, 1988, cited in FBIS South Asia Report, April 18, 1988, p. 56. See also Bakhtar News Agency, Kabul, May 10, 1986, published by the Permanent Representative of the Democratic Republic of Afghanistan to the United Nations, June 1, 1986.

47. Bakhtar News Agency, Kabul, March 8, 1986, published by the Permanent Representative of the Democratic Republic of Afghanistan to the United Nations, April 1, 1986.

48. Ibid.

49. A 1987 random sample poll conducted by the Afghan Information Center in Peshawar of 2287 Afghan refugees in 106 out of 249 camps in Pakistan showed that 71.65 percent of those polled wanted Zahir Shah to lead a postwar Afghan government. See Selig S. Harrison, "Pacifying Afghanistan," *The New York Times,* Dec. 4, 1987, p. A31.

50. Alexander Prokhanov, "Report from Kabul," *Liternaturnaya Gazeta,* February 17, 1988.

51. For an elaboration of the terms of the projected U.N. agreement, see my article "A Breakthrough in Afghanistan?," in *Foreign Policy* (Summer 1983); my essay "The Soviet Union in Afghanistan: Retrospect and Prospect," in Hafeez Malik, ed., *International Security in Southwest Asia* (New York: Praeger, 1984); "South Asia: Avoiding Disaster," *Foreign Policy,* Spring 1986, pp. 134–40; and "Toward Afghanistan Peace, *New York Times,* March 17, 1986, p. A22.

52. Zbigniew Brzezinski, *Power and Principle* (New York: Farrar, Straus, Giroux, 1983), pp. 435–437.

53. Agha Shahi, address at Villanova University, Dec. 7, 1984.

54. *Rapid Deployment Forces: Policy and Budgetary Implications,* prepared for the Senate Subcommittee on Sea Power and Force Projection by John D. Mayer, Jr. (Washington, D.C.: U.S. Congress, Congressional Budget Office, 1983), p. 11.

Appendix

Conclusion and Recommendations of the
Indo-American Task Force on the Indian Ocean

The task force examined the military, political, and economic environment in the Indian Ocean and its natural extensions, principally the Persian Gulf, the Red Sea, the Gulf of Aden, and the Gulf of Oman, focusing on the danger of a military confrontation between American and Soviet forces involving littoral and hinterland states. In particular, the group considered the potential impact of emerging issues throughout the region on Indo-American relations.

Reviewing the escalation in superpower military deployments in the region since 1977, the task force noted with satisfaction that American and Soviet ship deployments, after reaching a peak in 1981, had declined perceptibly since 1983. While still at higher levels than in 1977, the blue-water naval forces of the two sides have not escalated for nearly two years. At the same time, Indian members expressed anxieties concerning the qualitative change in American deployments reflected in the regular stationing of a carrier battle group in the Arabian Sea. They also called attention to the continuing growth in American and Soviet infrastructural support facilities, especially the prepositioning of equipment and weaponry in military container vessels at Diego Garcia for use by U.S. rapid deployment forces. American members emphasized that Soviet land-based air capabilities in and adjacent to the region had increased since 1977 and that the development of Soviet strategic air bases in Afghanistan would significantly affect the military balance.

With respect to the deployment of strategic nuclear weapons, the task force agreed that the Indian Ocean has so far remained substantially free of nuclear weapons deployment. There was evidence in the 1960s and 1970s suggesting that the United States might have intended to deploy nuclear-missile-firing submarines in the Indian Ocean. In practice, however, regular patrols of such submarines did not materialize. Although the United States retains the option of submarine-launched nuclear missile deployments in the region, utilizing its facilities in western Australia, and of B-52 deployments from Diego Garcia, the Indian Ocean currently remains the only major ocean that has not been the site of the deployment of strategic nuclear weapons systems.

Looking ahead to emerging changes in military technology, the task force concluded that a failure of global arms control efforts, especially the collapse of the ABM Treaty, could open the way for various forms of new and destabilizing military activity in the Indian Ocean by both superpowers, including possible nuclear deployments. Cruise missile deployments will pose verification problems that are likely to aggravate nuclear anxieties in the Indian Ocean region as well as in other parts of the world. Given its location, the northern Arabian Sea could acquire special sensitivity in the context of U.S. anti-satellite and other interception systems related to the Strategic Defense Initiative and Soviet counter-measures. The group warned that the present relative stability in superpower conventional naval deployments could abruptly change in a climate of increasing tension at the global and regional level.

The task force underlined its concern that continuing instability in the region, arising from interacting regional and extra-regional factors, could draw the superpowers into a direct confrontation. Among the more explosive focal points of instability singled out by the members were the war in Afghanistan and the concomitant conflict developing in the Afghanistan-Pakistan borderlands; Indo-Pakistan tensions; the Iran-Iraq war; and uncertainty surrounding the political future of Iran.

The group agreed that the United States and India have a common stake in preserving the sovereignty and territorial integrity of the states of the region on the basis of existing borders. While disagreeing on some aspects of the Afghan issue, notably the factors that led to the Soviet intervention, American and Indian members shared similar apprehensions that the security of Pakistan could be adversely affected by the protracted continuation and possible expansion of the Afghan conflict and a further influx of Afghan refugees. Pointing to Iran as a critical nexus of superpower distrust, the task force observed that the Soviet Union remains fearful of the reestablishment of American military influence there, while the United States, for its part, maintains the present level of its Indian Ocean naval presence primarily in preparation for the "worst case" scenario of a Soviet invasion of northern Iran. Despite this vicious circle of distrust, however, it is noteworthy that neither the United States nor the Soviet Union have, in fact, intervened with combat forces during a series of crises in recent years. The record since the withdrawal of Soviet forces in 1946 suggests a mutual awareness of the dangerous potential of a military confrontation there and the emergence of a tacit understanding concerning the need for mutual restraint.

Against the background of continuing Indo-Pakistan tensions and the provision of advanced American military technology to Pakistan, the American members expressed their understanding of the Indian perception that the presence of a U.S. carrier battle group in the Arabian Sea, together with the U.S. base at Diego Garcia, could lead to intelligence sharing with Pakistan in the event of an India-Pakistan war and possibly to more direct forms of American intervention on Pakistan's side. India is also concerned that Saudi Arabia, China, and other third parties may transfer U.S. military technology and equipment to Pakistan and that American military sales to China could affect the India-China military balance, especially in the Indian Ocean. The Indian members, in turn, indicated their understanding of the American perception that India could help to improve relations with its smaller neighbors by demonstrating greater sensitivity to their concerns, including their perceived security concerns, thus making it easier for the United States to avoid embroilment in intra-regional tensions. They acknowledged the existence of widespread suspicions and misperceptions in the United States concerning the integrity of Indian non-alignment, especially in relation to Soviet military aid. The group recognized that the major reasons for India's arms procurement in the Soviet Union lay in differences with the United States over aspects of its arms sales and technological transfer policies and in liberal Soviet financial terms. The task force agreed that sustained confidence-building measures by both sides would be necessary to manage the tensions resulting from the American naval presence in the Indian Ocean, the U.S. security relationship with Pakistan, and the fears expressed by some littoral states concerning the anticipated development of the Indian navy.

While recognizing the gravity of the problems troubling Indo-American relations and the need for more sustained efforts to accommodate differences, the task force emphasized the strong foundations of the relationship, anchored in common values as open societies with representative political systems, growing economic and cultural linkages, and a shared commitment to the maintenance of freedom of navigation and other international legal regimes. A more mature relationship is developing as India becomes increasingly strong and self-confident in its role as a major self-reliant power with acknowledged maritime capabilities in the Indian Ocean region and a leading force in the Non-Aligned Movement. Citing Indian moves to liberalize its economy, the group felt that recent Indo-American understandings designed to facilitate U.S. dual-use high-technology exports to India reflected a welcome new flexibility on both sides that could lead over time to a significant expansion of economic interdependencies with sophisticated technological content.

The task force reviewed the unsuccessful efforts of littoral and hinterland states since 1971 to advance the concept of the Indian Ocean as a Zone of Peace. The discussion highlighted Indian support for proposals to convene a Zone of Peace conference on the basis of the 1971 United Nations Zone of Peace Declaration, as distinct from the subsequent variations of the proposal, and an American emphasis on global and regional arms control negotiations as a more promising means of pursuing the objectives of the 1971 declaration. The Indian members and some American members felt that a conference would be a desirable first step in arms control initiatives. Despite differences on the issue of a conference, however, the group found considerable common ground with respect to the desirability of arms control efforts and concluded that the issue of a conference need not be a major irritant in bilateral relations.

The group agreed that the Law of the Sea Treaty constituted a landmark in the development of an international legal regime in the seas and considered it significant that most of its key provisions had been universally accepted as customary law. The American decision not to sign the treaty, based on objections to the seabed mining provisions, after earlier support for these provisions, had created complications, but the United States itself had benefited from many aspects of the treaty, including freedom of passage through straits. The task force expressed its support for the "Common Heritage of Mankind" principle underlying the treaty and its hope that India and the United States could find mutually acceptable ways to apply this principle in developing the resources of the seabed and Antarctica, consistent with India's commitment to the treaty in its present form and U.S. policies favoring the involvement of private enterprise.

The task force recognized that the roots of political instability and military conflict often lie in economic factors that are largely beyond the control of littoral and hinterland states. Pointing to the debt burden of many states in the region, the danger of recession in the West and Japan, growing global protectionism, population pressures, and natural disasters such as the drought in Africa, the group envisaged a regional environment marked by turbulent economic, political, and social change. In such an environment, the task force concluded, the superpowers should exercise great restraint to avoid embroilment in internecine conflicts that do not relate directly to their vital interests but could all too easily lead to dangerous confrontations.

Recommendations

The task force warned that the risks of a Soviet-American confrontation in the Indian Ocean region continue to be dangerous. The group concluded that the principal security concerns of the littoral and hinterland states, the United States, and the Soviet Union are rooted in a vicious circle of distrust and cannot be effectively addressed in isolation from each other. Thus, the task force urged parallel negotiating processes to reduce tensions in the region:

Iran and the Superpowers. Iran is a focal point of Soviet-American distrust. The United States bases its Central Command force planning on the "worst case" scenario of a Soviet seizure of the Abadan oil fields. The Soviet Union fears that the United States may seek to make Iran once again a military ally. The United States and the Soviet Union should continue to exercise the mutual restraint that they have demonstrated in recent years in Iran and should make appropriate diplomatic efforts to reassure each other that neither will introduce combat forces or mutually threatening bases or facilities there.

An Afghanistan Settlement. The growing tension on the Afghanistan-Pakistan border makes a negotiated settlement of the Afghanistan conflict increasingly urgent. The U.N. mediation effort has produced acceptance of the principle that a Soviet combat force withdrawal within a defined time period and a cessation of foreign support for Afghan resistance groups should be orchestrated in a coordinated set of agreements. The United Nations should be fully supported by the powers directly concerned and by littoral and hinterland states as it seeks to build on the progress so far made.

A Zone of Peace and Neutrality. It is apparent that an enduring Afghan settlement would require parallel Soviet-American dialogues relating to Pakistan as well as to Iran. At this stage, it is difficult to envisage the emergence of a Zone of Peace and Neutrality, as has been proposed, in which the military presence of the superpowers would be excluded from Iran, Afghanistan, and Pakistan. Nevertheless, the United States and the Soviet Union should begin to explore understandings concerning the need for mutual restraint in all three of these countries. This region adjoins three of the world's most populous nations, and many countries, including the United States and India, have an interest in access to the adjacent oil-bearing areas. The possible development of nuclear weapons by regional powers underlines the importance of prudence and restraint by both superpowers in dealing with this area.

Arms Control and the Indian Ocean. Changes in military technology, notably the advent of cruise missiles, anti-satellite weaponry, and space-based and operated anti-missile systems, could make the Indian Ocean waterspread and the littoral and hinterland states a theater of growing tension between the superpowers, marked by an expanding competitive search for facilities in the region. The impact of these changes cannot be meaningfully discussed in regional arms control negotiations limited to the Indian Ocean, such as those on naval limitations conducted by the United States and the Soviet Union in 1977–78. It would be desirable for the superpowers to give attention in some form to issues of specific concern to the Indian Ocean region as part of their global arms control dialogue. At the same time, when and if it is appropriate in the global context, the superpowers should resume a separate dialogue on regionally defined issues with an eye to the possibility of a freeze and subsequent reductions of military deployments and facilities in the region.

Soviet-American Trade-offs. Any regionally defined arms control negotiations between the superpowers deemed to be appropriate in the global context should proceed from a recognition that the environment for such negotiations has changed since the 1977–78 dialogue. The United States perceives a Soviet security threat to the region primarily centered in the land-based military potential of the Soviet Union, the Soviet Union perceives a U.S. security threat primarily centered in U.S. naval power, and regional powers perceive threats arising from both regional and extra-regional sources. Thus, renewed negotiations could no longer be limited to naval limitations alone but would have to reflect larger trade-offs. Among many examples that could be cited, the United States perceives a potential threat from Soviet strategic aircraft, or tactical aircraft posing an offensive threat to neighboring states, based in Afghanistan; the Soviet Union fears the deployment of dual-capable aircraft based on U.S. carriers in the Arabian Sea, and various littoral states voice concern that Diego Garcia might become a base for nuclear forces, or that both superpowers might deploy cruise missiles with nuclear warheads in the region. The problem of trade-offs is complicated by the fact that while both sides feel that their vital interests are involved, the direct security of its national territory is involved in the perceptions of the Soviet Union.

The Security of Choke Points. The security of oil tanker traffic in the Indian Ocean region is a common concern of the littoral and hinterland states and the superpowers alike. To supplement the international recognition of this common stake embodied in the Law of the Sea Treaty, the United States, the Soviet Union, and other concerned countries, including India, should explore the possibility of agreements ensuring unimpeded oil tanker traffic through the Strait of Hormuz and other "choke points."

The task force recommends the following measures by the United States and India to build mutual confidence and to promote closer relations:

Clarifying the U.S. Commitment to Pakistan. The United States should clarify, and if necessary redefine, its obligations to Pakistan under the 1959 mutual security agreement between the two countries to rule out U.S. involvement in any conflict limited to Indian and Pakistani forces alone. In this connection, the United States should make clear that the inclusion of Pakistan as one of the 19 countries covered by the Central Command does not relate to contingencies involving Indian and Pakistani forces alone. Similarly, the United States should make clear that the mission of its carrier battle group in the northern Arabian Sea relates to perceived security threats in the Gulf region and not to any conflict in South Asia limited to India and Pakistan alone. There should be greater exchange of views and perceptions at appropriate governmental levels to reassure India that U.S.-Pakistan security relationships would not involve intelligence sharing adverse to Indian security interests.

Indian Confidence-Building Initiatives. India should take steps to help remove suspicions and misperceptions in the United States concerning the nature of its military aid relationships with the Soviet Union, possible intelligence sharing, the leakage of high technology, and policies governing ship visits by Soviet and U.S. naval forces. As part of a broader increase in exchanges of military personnel between the two countries, the Task Force recommends visits by members of the U.S. Congress, journalists, and U.S. officials to all major Indian military and naval establishments based on principles of reciprocity and due deference to considerations of security.

Ocean Resource Development. India and the United States should give special attention to cooperation in ocean resource development within the framework of the new Indo-U.S. agreements governing high-technology imports. India's new Department of Ocean Sciences could utilize expanded imports of American electronics equipment and computers needed for hydrospace data processing, and efforts should be made to facilitate this form of technological cooperation. Where feasible and available, the United States should share with India marine resource and other Indian Ocean data relevant to India's exploitation of its 200-mile Exclusive Economic Zone.

Asymmetry in Informational Exchange. There is great asymmetry between the United States and India with respect to the availability of literature on each country's perceptions and policies relating to the other. While the entire range of U.S. literature and official documentation relating to international relations is readily available to Indians and is studied in India, Indian periodicals and books and official pronouncements are not widely disseminated and studied in the United States. This situation needs to be rectified and a much greater effort is called for on both sides to improve mutual understanding, including more intensive informational exchange programs on the part of India.

Selig S. Harrison	K. Subrahmanyam
Convenor, American Delegation	Convenor, Indian Delegation
Walter K. Andersen	Vice-Admiral (Ret.) M. P. Awati
Joel Larus	V. S. Mani
George W. Shepherd, Jr.	C. Raja Mohan
Gary Sick	K. R. Singh
W. Howard Wriggins	M. A. Vellodi

Index

Walters, Vernon, 253
Warnke, Paul, 231
Watt, James, 189
Weinberger, Caspar, 5, 33, 35, 111, 183,
    236–37
West Germany, 109
    and Antarctic Treaty, 201
    arms exports by, 129–30(*tab.*)
    Indian research vessel from, 199
    LOSC rejected by, 199
    and Persian Gulf operations, 37
    and seabed mining, 149, 152
Weston, Rae, 190
Wilson, Harold, 15
World Bank
    and Madagascar, 254
    and Mauritius, 257

Yemen
    fishing fleet of, 222(*tab.*)
    U.S. arms/aid to, 77(*tab.*), 80(*tab.*),
        82(*tab.*)

Yemen, North. *See* North Yemen
Yemen, South. *See* South Yemen
Young, P. Lewis, 173–74

Zahir Shah, 272, 277
Zaire
    and U.S. cobalt, 191–92
    Western intervention in, 186
Zambia
    arms imports to, 129(*tab.*)
    IBRD loan to, 187
    and U.S. cobalt, 191–92
Zia Ul-Haq, 268, 276, 280
Zimbabwe
    arms imports to, 129(*tab.*)
    costly colonial war in, 243
    and U.S. chromium, 192
Zone of Peace conference, as arms control
    forum, 283
Zone of Peace, Indian Ocean. *See* Indian
    Ocean Zone of Peace
Zumwalt, Elmo, 95, 118, 176